31472400242446

D0392545

DATE DUE

RFK JR.

ALSO BY JERRY OPPENHEIMER

*Crazy Rich: Power, Scandal, and Tragedy Inside
the Johnson & Johnson Dynasty*

*The Other Mrs. Kennedy: Ethel Skakel Kennedy,
an American Drama of Power, Privilege, and Politics*

*State of a Union:
Inside the Complex Marriage of Bill and Hillary Clinton*

*Just Desserts:
Martha Stewart—The Unauthorized Biography*

*Front Row: Anna Wintour—
The Cool Life and Hot Times of* Vogue's *Editor in Chief*

*House of Hilton: From Conrad to Paris, a Drama of Wealth,
Power, and Privilege*

Toy Monster: The Big, Bad World of Mattel

Madoff with the Money

Seinfeld: The Making of an American Icon

Barbara Walters: An Unauthorized Biography

Idol: Rock Hudson—The True Story of an American Film Hero
(with Jack Vitek)

RFK JR.

Robert F. Kennedy Jr.
and the Dark Side of the Dream

Jerry Oppenheimer

St. Martin's Press
New York

www.stmartins.com

Library of Congress Cataloging-in-Publication Data

Oppenheimer, Jerry.
    RFK Jr. : Robert F. Kennedy Jr. and the dark side of the dream /
Jerry Oppenheimer.—First edition.
        pages cm
    ISBN 978-1-250-03295-9 (hardcover)
    ISBN 978-1-250-03296-6 (e-book)
    1. Kennedy, Robert Francis, 1954–   2. Environmental lawyers—United States—
Biography.   3. Environmentalists—United States—Biography.   4. Kennedy,
Robert F., 1925–1968—Family.   5. Kennedy family.   I. Title.
    CT275.K4585253o67 2015
    973.922092—dc23
[B]
                                                                        2015017975

Our books may be purchased in bulk for promotional, educational, or business use. Please contact your local bookseller or the Macmillan Corporate and Premium Sales Department at (800) 221-7945, extension 5442, or by e-mail at MacmillanSpecial Markets@macmillan.com.

First Edition: September 2015

10   9   8   7   6   5   4   3   2   1

*For Caroline, Trix, Mr. R. Toby and Jesse, Louise,
Julien and Max, and in memory of Cukes*

CONTENTS

RFK JR.

PROLOGUE

This is the story of the scion of one of the most famous, most powerful, most privileged contemporary political dynasties the free world has ever known, an heir to an immense fortune who had every advantage, yet was plagued, as will be documented, by horrific addictions and paralyzing insecurities. Still, he was considered the undisputed leader of the third generation of Kennedys—and one of the most polarizing. Once believed to be the standard-bearer, the future hope of the dynasty, Bobby Kennedy Jr. was seriously considered to be the clan's second coming—the next Kennedy to command the Oval Office.

In the beginning, the Kennedys had high hopes for Bobby, that he would be their new symbol after the assassinations of his father and uncle, that he would invigorate the Camelot myth, that he would be the so-called royal family's shining representative.

It never happened.

As his story shows, he became the end, rather than the fulfillment, of the dream.

While he had teased the media through the years about throwing his hat into the political arena like his father and uncles before him—a

public service career was practically guaranteed of RFK's namesake—
he always feared that the skeletons in his closet, and there were many,
would be unleashed. Instead, he would curiously fall back on family
values and fathering his six children from what would be two of three
marriages as his reasons for not running for political office.

Instead, he made a name for himself in the less controversial but increasingly popular and sometimes glamorous environmental movement.

He had been named one of *Time* magazine's "Heroes for the Planet,"
heralded as one of *Rolling Stone*'s "100 Agents of Change," dubbed by
People magazine "America's Toxin Avenger," and called "a self-made
nemesis of big-time polluters . . . carrying on his father's tradition of cru-
sading against the powerful." He was a professor of governmental law at
Pace University School of Law, the co-director of the school's Environmental Litigation Clinic, president of Waterkeeper Alliance, and a senior
attorney for the Natural Resources Defense Council.

Unlike the other iconic Kennedy namesake, his far more handsome
first cousin and pop culture icon, John F. Kennedy Jr.—"John-John"
to an older generation—Bobby was far more complex, driven, and
reckless, a monument to scandal, controversy, and excess, a life that
paralleled the decline in the power, prestige, and politics of America's
royal family. As the *Time* columnist Margaret Carlson cogently once observed, "When you look at the third generation of Kennedy men, much
of what remains of a once powerful dynasty is good teeth, good hair and
the best public relations a trust fund can buy."

All that Bobby and his cousin John shared was the Kennedy blood
and the tragic assassinations of their fathers. While John, after his father's
death, was brought up by a controlling and domineering mother, but
one who obsessively looked out for his care and well-being, Bobby,
after his father's death, was essentially given up by his angry, widowed
mother.

With his father gone, Bobby's uncle Ted was thought to be the acting
patriarch. But he had his own serious personal problems with which to
contend. As a result, Bobby's sole male role model during his troubled
adolescence through his even more unsettled young adulthood was a
closeted and ill-at-ease homosexual—a decades-long Kennedy family
acolyte by the name of Kirk LeMoyne "Lem" Billings, who had trans-

ferred his obsessive, intimate love from the late president, beginning when they were at boarding school together, to Bobby himself.

The first time the gay bachelor spent time with young Bobby, he came away enthusiastically declaring, "I've just met the smartest little boy! He's just like Jack!" Later he would use drugs with Bobby while at the same time convincing him that he could be president one day.

As another of Bobby's first cousins, Christopher Kennedy Lawford, who early on idolized Bobby, and who like Bobby was long addicted to drugs, candidly observed: "The loss of Robert Kennedy was the loss of one of the most consequential figures of that time. Bobby Jr. existentially got an enormous amount of star power carrying those initials. He also got a lot of magnetism from Lem's fixation. Lem had decided that Bobby was the next bearer of Kennedy greatness—and none of us were about to argue."

President Kennedy, Bobby's uncle, considered biography his favorite literary form. The reason? It attempted to answer the question: What was he really like?

In an effort to answer that question, this, then, is Robert Francis Kennedy Jr.'s story.

ONE

Parochial Schooling

Ethel Skakel Kennedy gave birth to her husband's namesake, Bobby Jr., on January 17, 1954, at Georgetown University Hospital, in Washington, D.C. He was the third of her and Robert Francis Kennedy's children, coming after Kathleen and Joe II in what would one day be a brood of eleven. As it happened, Bobby came into the world at an ironic moment in the Kennedy clan's chronology—just a few days after the Hollywood sexpot Marilyn Monroe married her second husband, the Yankee slugger Joe DiMaggio. In the Kennedy family drama, Marilyn would famously play a starring role as the reputed mistress of both Bobby's father and Bobby's uncle, the president, during the era known as Camelot.

Eight more siblings would follow on Bobby Jr.'s heels, as his young, athletic, and zealously Catholic twenty-six-year-old mother was determined to have a bigger family than that of her revered mother-in-law, the Kennedy family matriarch, Rose Fitzgerald Kennedy, who had given birth to only nine.

But young Bobby was the special one of Ethel's children, for he was named after the idolized U.S. Senator from New York, the assassinated presidential hopeful who, during JFK's ill-fated administration, had served as his brother's Attorney General of the United States, the nation's highest law enforcement officer.

RFK, at twenty-nine, had been out of work during a portion of the time Ethel was carrying Bobby. He had quit the job his father, Joseph Patrick Kennedy—onetime reputed Prohibition-era bootlegger, ex–Hollywood mogul, Wall Street speculator, former U.S. ambassador to Great Britain under FDR, and notorious philanderer—had secured for him through his friend Joseph McCarthy.

An Irish Catholic, an alcoholic, considered evil incarnate by many, the Republican senator from Wisconsin was chairman of the powerful Permanent Subcommittee on Investigations of the Senate Government Operations Committee, better known as the McCarthy Committee.

RFK had a law degree from the University of Virginia in Charlottesville and a diploma from Harvard when he was hired as an assistant to the McCarthy Committee's general counsel. He shared his father's and McCarthy's determination to search out and destroy suspected Communists in the U.S. Army, in federal government agencies, and just about anywhere else, many of whom were innocent and whose lives were ruined. He also went along with a parallel McCarthy persecution of homosexuals in government that became known as the "Lavender Scare."

Fortunately, RFK, an heir to the fortune his father had made, and his wife, Ethel, an heiress in her own right, didn't have to support their fast-growing family on his paycheck. His starting salary was $95.24 a week. He received a couple of raises along the way, eventually earning $7,334.57 annually.

But after just seven months he quit his job. He blamed his decision on McCarthy's right-hand man, Roy Marcus Cohn, who was two years younger than RFK but had earned a national reputation as the tough prosecutor who had controversially helped send the convicted Soviet spies Julius and Ethel Rosenberg to the electric chair. RFK despised Cohn because it was Cohn's job that RFK had once coveted but didn't get. Moreover, he intensely disliked him because of his sexual preference; Cohn was a closeted homosexual, and RFK had a thing about those kinds of people.

Looking to his father again for another job, the patriarch secured his third son—born after Jack and before Ted—a position as an assistant on what was known as the Hoover Commission, then headed by former president Herbert Hoover, who had just turned eighty. Ambitious, restless for action, and hungry for power, RFK found the job, which had to do with the stuffy reorganization of the Executive Branch, tedious and boring, and he began feeling depressed.

But the birth of Bobby Jr., his namesake, lifted him out of the doldrums. Once again after his father made a call on his behalf, RFK was named counsel for the Democratic minority of Joe McCarthy's subcommittee. The appointment came just in time for the beginning of the infamous, history-making, nationally televised Army-McCarthy hearings that began four months after Bobby Jr.'s birth at the height of the nation's red scare and at a dark moment in the Cold War.

Bobby was an easy birth for Ethel, who had at her side throughout the Kennedy family's longtime nurse Luella Hennessey-Donovan. Years later, Lulu, as she was known, recalled that Ethel had only one burning concern: how her first two, Kathleen and Joe, would respond to having a new brother who would garner much attention. After a week in the hospital, Ethel took Bobby home; she had prearranged for his siblings to be waiting outside to greet him.

"Ethel would say, 'Look at what the new baby brought home to you.' They'd each get a basket with a gift and then they'd each kiss the baby and say thank you," said the dutiful nurse who idolized the Kennedys. "It was quite a good idea."

She stayed with Ethel and the infant Bobby for another few days, but would return eighteen months later when Ethel had her third son, number four in the lineup—David Anthony Kennedy, born June 15, 1955. The closest in terms of bonding with Bobby, he'd also be the first, but not the last of her brood, to predecease her, succumbing in his case to a drug addiction that both brothers would share.

ANIMALS AND BIRDS SEEMINGLY were always part of Bobby's life even, he once claimed, when he was still in a crib. His mother had told him that when he was a baby he was fascinated with the bugs he saw crawling around in the garden of the Kennedy estate, Hickory Hill, in McLean,

Virginia, where the family had moved when he was three months old. The spectacular mansion had once belonged to Bobby's uncle Jack and his aunt Jackie and had been a gift to both couples by the Kennedy patriarch.

At nine, Bobby had a veritable menagerie at the family's fabled northern Virginia homestead, which included a variety of small pests, the scourge of most homeowners, ranging from raccoons to rats to snakes. He claimed he once bought a couple thousand ear-shattering crickets to feed to his lizards. He also had his own mini–poultry farm, in addition to a horse, a calf, and a variety of other animals.

The 2008 thriller *Snakes on a Plane* could have been based on an experience Bobby had as a kid when he took a sack of his pet reptiles aboard a flight from Washington National to LaGuardia in New York and all of the slithery, scary things accidentally got loose in mid-flight. As female passengers screamed and may have jumped onto their seats, Bobby crawled around and gathered them all up.

One of the stories he liked to tell about his childhood was about a visit he made to the Oval Office when his father was attorney general of the United States and young Bobby presented his uncle the president with a small spotted salamander that he had recently caught on Hickory Hill's almost six acres.

His mother had dressed him in short pants for the visit, and Bobby always kept a photograph of himself seated near Uncle Jack as the president gently poked the seven-inch amphibian with one of those presidential pens he used to sign bills into law. Uncle and nephew then gave it a new home in the White House fountain. There were those other visits to the weekend White House at Camp David, in Maryland. While his father and uncle held private meetings at the presidential lodge, Bobby, with Secret Service agents close by, tried to scope out the fierce wolverines that inhabited the surrounding woods.

In 1963 when JFK was murdered, Bobby had been taken on a safari in Kenya and participated in the capture of a huge leopard tortoise. Because he was a scion of Camelot, he was permitted to bring it home in a suitcase, unquestioned, as if he were a diplomat. It helped that his escort was his aunt Eunice's husband, Sargent Shriver, who then headed the JFK-established Peace Corps. Many years later the turtle, stuffed, was on display, along with a multitude of other Kennedy memorabilia, in the den of Bobby's own Hickory Hill–like estate in the fashionable New York City suburb of Mount Kisco, home to a number of celebrities.

At eleven, Bobby decided to become a falconer when his father, soon to be elected to the United States Senate from New York—his stepping-stone, he believed, to a second Kennedy presidency—gave him a red-tailed hawk, which Bobby named Morgan LeFay, after the sorceress in the King Arthur legend, which he had read about in T. H. White's book *The Once and Future King.*

Through the years Bobby's stories often conflicted, or were contradictory, or were outright inventions, even about something as mundane as who had interested and trained him in falconry. In his co-authored 1997 book, *The Riverkeepers*, about how he and a colleague battled Hudson River polluters, he said an engineer at the Pentagon had taught him the sport, which involved training falcons, which are birds of prey, to hunt for quarry.

Later, however, in a blog at PetPlace.com, an online source of pet information, headlined "Robert F. Kennedy Jr.—The Bird Rehabilitator," he was quoted as saying that an obscure Arab friend of his father's, one Alva Mai Nye, supposedly a State Department operative, had "piqued" his interest in falconry.

Also at the age of eleven Bobby had read a book called *My Side of the Mountain,* written by the naturalist and children's book author Jean Craighead George, which tells the story of a boy who runs away from home to the Catskill Mountains of New York State, where he lives in a hollowed-out tree with a falcon and a weasel.

In 1999, in writing about the book and how it also influenced his interest in falconry, Bobby observed, "I thought the Craigheads might be the only family in America that was having more fun than the Kennedys. Obsessed with falcons as I was from birth, I read [the book] in 1964. . . . My years as a falconer helped drive my own career choice as an environmental lawyer and advocate."

AN ABUSER OF DRUGS for at least some fifteen years of his life, and a reputed sex addict for many more, according to his own diary entries and other accounts, Bobby once noted that the "central tenet" of his mother's life was her "devotion" to Catholicism, and that his father's "devotion" had even "rivaled" hers—and that all of it had carried over to him.

In his book *The Riverkeepers,* coincidentally published the same year his brother Michael was embroiled in a sex scandal involving his family's teenage babysitter, and his congressman brother Joe's wife wrote a tell-all critical of him seeking an annulment because he wanted a Catholic church wedding with his secretary girlfriend, Bobby waxed nostalgic about how religion was a major part of his family's home life when he was growing up.

For instance, he noted that his rosary-carrying mother always led the family in prayer as they knelt, and that the family attended daily Mass with her on holidays and in the summer. He recalled that they had "fainted from hunger" during high Mass; that Sundays were a day of fasting; that prayers were said before and after meals; that on Fridays fish was served, and they read about and "prayed with particular fervor" to various saints.

His parents, he stated, "frequently" quoted St. Paul's mantra, "To whom much is given, much is expected," and he said he and his siblings strived to "give them our best."

Bobby noted that he and his brothers and sisters had received parochial school educations, but that wasn't always the case.

His first school, with just eight classrooms, was on the fringe of Georgetown—Our Lady of Victory, founded by a Father Yingling. As it turned out, Bobby's matriculation there suddenly caused a problem for his uncle Jack's administration when it was revealed that Our Lady of Victory was all-white at a time when the Kennedy administration was advocating school integration, and the nation's first civil rights bill would soon be passed.

For Republicans and especially Southern politicians, the revelation by the school's Mother Superior that "We have no Negroes here. . . . Apparently, there are no Negroes in our Parish" sparked a furor—the "Benghazi" of its time for the democrats of Camelot—and put the Kennedys on the spot. RFK wanted to immediately have Bobby transferred to the nonsectarian Landon School, in Bethesda, Maryland, but Ethel fought against the move, desiring that the namesake get a full Catholic education, just as she had gotten.

Ethel Skakel had inherited her religious fervor from her mother, the former Ann Brannack, a simple office worker from a blue-collar Irish Catholic South Side Chicago family who had struck it rich when she wed Ethel's father, George Skakel, a shrewd businessman, who wasn't Catholic and who couldn't countenance his wife's fanatical adherence. Rather than fight it, though, he had looked the other way when she raised Ethel (and her siblings) in her own religious image.

As a Catholic childhood friend recalled, "If we missed a day of church it wasn't a sin, but for Ethel it was. She was very devoutly religious, extremely so. She used to tell me she'd only marry a Catholic."

Her room in her family's mansion in wealthy Greenwich, Connecticut, had a large cross over the bed along with hanging rosary beads, and her night table was stacked with books on Catholicism. She once seriously teased a male cousin into crying by telling him he was going to hell rather than heaven because he wasn't raised as a Catholic.

At Manhattanville College of the Sacred Heart in New York City's Harlem, Ethel took Communion every day, meditated afterward for an hour, and said her rosary. Like her future mother-in-law, Rose Kennedy, Ethel was an active member of Children of Mary, an organization for zealous young Catholics, and led three-day class retreats that consisted of prayer and silence.

As a nun who knew her, Mother Elizabeth Farley, recalled, "Ethel had a lot of faith, and inherited a lot of faith, and influenced others with her faith."

Nevertheless, the political heat on the Kennedy administration far outweighed her desire for Bobby to have a Catholic (and presumably all-white) education. To end the embarrassing scandal, the fifth-grader was quietly transferred from the all-white Our Lady of Victory to the exclusive but integrated Sidwell Friends, of the Quaker persuasion, whose political alumni over the years included Nancy Reagan, Julie Nixon, and Chelsea Clinton.

The transfer, however, did not go over well with Our Lady of Victory's principal. She asserted that racism was not the issue, and claimed that

Bobby and his sixth-grade brother Joe often missed school with the excuse that they had colds and that the transfer to Sidwell was because the fancy private school had a tutoring program for kids like the Kennedy brothers who got poor grades and had repeated absences.

Bobby completed elementary school, sixth grade, at Sidwell, temporarily leaving behind his mother's desired Catholic education for him.

As he noted in *The Riverkeepers,* his parents had "supplemented our parochial school instruction in the Catholic creed by emphasizing the life of saints and particularly the joys of martyrdom, secular or religious."

AS HE PREPARED TO BEGIN his junior high school years, a world of change was happening for young Bobby.

His mother had become pregnant with her ninth, which would tie the record set by the Kennedy matriarch, Rose. Despite Kennedy spin to the contrary, the kids' parents rarely were around, leaving their eight children behind with nannies and other volunteer help—Ethel and RFK, always obsessed with his political future, traveled to West Berlin, Greece, and Rome, where they met with Pope Paul, and everywhere spread the Kennedy gospel.

At thirty-eight, RFK, already looking ahead to a presidential run, announced at the end of August 1964 that he had decided to seek election to the U.S. Senate from New York. During the campaign, Bobby's spirited mother would be on the road day and night tirelessly campaigning for RFK, shaking as many as eight hundred hands at one of her highly publicized, exuberant campaign coffee klatches; women of all political persuasions came out in droves just to be in the presence of a Kennedy wife. With RFK running, the Camelot myth was alive and well.

The candidate and his wife used cute and lively young Bobby and his photogenic siblings, too, whenever they could to promote RFK's election. For instance, during the shooting of a campaign commercial directed by the famous agent and producer Leland Hayward, Ethel had gathered together her brood and dryly told a reporter, "Well, here we are, just an average American family."

In order to establish the required residency in New York State, the multimillionaire candidate leased a twenty-five-room mansion,

Marymeade, in chic Glen Cove on Long Island. They also had an elegant suite with three bedrooms at the Carlyle Hotel in Manhattan. Nevertheless, RFK was termed a carpetbagger by some of the media and by his political opponents, since he still retained Hickory Hill and was registered to vote in Massachusetts, not in New York, where, before he announced his candidacy, he had very little political connection.

After a rigorous nine-week campaign, RFK won the election, beating the republican incumbent, sixty-four-year-old Kenneth B. Keating. And six days after RFK was sworn in, Ethel gave birth on January 10, 1965, to her sixth son—number nine in the Team Kennedy lineup—who was named Matthew Maxwell Taylor Kennedy in honor of the U.S. ambassador to South Vietnam, a close friend of the clan's.

Ethel told reporters she expected to have more. Always good for a fun quote back in her young, kicky days as a popular Washington party-giver and fashionista, she exclaimed, "Children are cheaper by the dozen."

Because Hickory Hill was overrun with Ethel's brood and Bobby's menagerie of animals, something had to be done to bring about some peace and quiet.

Eleven-year-old Bobby, already becoming something of a behavior problem to his mother, who now had nine rambunctious children—six boys, three girls, and counting—was sent away (along with his brother Joe) to the exclusive Georgetown Preparatory School, in Bethesda, a half hour or so from home. There, at the oldest all-boys Jesuit private school in the United States, he began boarding in September 1965 as a seventh-grader.

If he had stayed there and succeeded academically, he would have been in the Georgetown Prep Class of June 1971. But it didn't turn out that way.

FOR MOST OF BOBBY KENNEDY JR.'S adult life, he was said by those who knew him intimately, to have had an inferiority complex in regard to the level of his intelligence; he never thought he was very smart, according to one of those close observers. He never believed that he had, for instance, the brainpower of his father, or his uncle Jack, or even his uncle Ted. He had always considered himself something of a dimwit, which was far from the reality, but that's what he believed. So, in his late fifties, around 2011, he decided to have his intelligence evaluated by voluntarily submitting to take an IQ test.

Subsequently, he confided to a longtime friend, the journalist Peter Kaplan, that his score had shocked him; it was, he boasted, off the charts, placing him, he claimed, in the brilliant range, although he was said to have kept the actual score to himself.

Despite his claimed high IQ, however, Bobby was never much of a student, and academics were usually never a high priority, which was the case, too, with his forebears Jack, Ted, and RFK. And certainly it was never high on the achievements of his mother's family, the Skakels. There were no outstanding students on either side.

Bobby's history teacher at Georgetown Prep—G Prep as it was known to students and faculty—was a learned man and a bit of an eccentric. During class, if something struck Dr. Paul Locher as interesting he would hold up his index finger, signaling a pause in the lesson, take out a little notebook that he kept in his tweed jacket pocket, and write down whatever it was he thought was important at that moment.

One such instance occurred when he asked Bobby to name the queen of England. Tim Ruane, who shared classes with Bobby, sat near him in homeroom and had a locker next to his in gym, recalled that moment years later. Bobby had hemmed and hawed and finally told Dr. Locher that he didn't know the answer.

"This stunned Dr. Locher, and he pulled out his little pad and wrote down, presumably, that Bobby Kennedy didn't know the answer to a simple question," said Ruane, who later went on to become for a decade the chief copy editor at *The Washington Post*, and once edited a convincing, well-thought-out op-ed piece by Bobby about an environmental controversy involving the Potomac River.

"I remember Locher looking at Kennedy in shock," said Ruane. It was incredible to the teacher that the son of the famous junior senator from New York, the nephew of the late president, and even the grandson of the former ambassador to Great Britain had no idea who the queen of England was. He had come to the conclusion that Kennedy was a dummy.

"As a student," recalled Ruane, "Bobby was haphazard."

When Bobby arrived for seventh grade, his famous family name and his father's fame had preceded him, but as another classmate, Maurice Nee, observed, "Bobby didn't act like a big shot because he was a Kennedy. Kids like us that age didn't let anybody act like a big shot. You tell each other how much their shit stinks."

Nee, who went into the family's furniture business, noted, "Sure, we had a Kennedy in our class, but we thought, 'Yeah, so what.' That's how I felt and I think that's the way it was for most people."

Still, Bobby stood out for his feats of daring and what his classmates considered his exotic and offbeat hobby.

The seventh-graders, about twenty in all, held their classes in one of the chapel's stuffy basement storerooms that had been converted into a makeshift classroom. The back wall of the chapel itself was made of brick, and that's where Bobby showed off his Kennedy steel.

"He could climb straight up the wall, like ten feet, and we would just be standing there watching in awe," Nee had never forgotten. "He was always real skinny and lanky and he could get a really good grip on the bricks and he had absolutely no fear. He climbed up that wall like he was Spider-Man."

Every so often Bobby brought his pet falcon to school for a show and tell—some of his classmates were impressed, others thought he was a weirdo because he loved birds and had a menagerie at Hickory Hill.

"Our school was on ninety acres bordered by woods and Bobby would bring his falcon on campus and he would take it out to the field with his leather glove on his hand, and it was pretty cool to watch," said Robert Katzen.

Nee noted that everyone else in the class used the woods merely as a shortcut to get to a nearby shopping center, "but Bobby's mind went into different things. Nobody else was into falconry or conservation."

Ruane, who had been admitted on a partial athletic scholarship—he was a star in football, basketball, and baseball—noted that football was "the thing" at Prep and either one was a player or a member of the Pep Club or "you were considered out of it," and that's where Bobby stood. "He wasn't involved in any of that. The idea of him having a zoo at home or flirting around with birds was *way* out there for us. We were all supposed to be football tough guys, but Bobby was a quiet, unassuming, off-the-radar kind of guy who was never a part of the in-crowd, and the in-crowd thing stemmed from football. Georgetown Prep was known for religion and football and I don't think religion was even a close second. Bobby was not an athlete, period, and was not physically gifted by any means."

To see her son play football at Georgetown Prep, however, was one of the reasons Ethel Kennedy had sent him there, along with the Catholic education it offered, taught by stern Jesuit priests and younger liberal Jesuits in training, called scholastics. The first day of class, Bobby attended Mass in the chapel and was given a Bible that was a primary text in his early Catholic studies.

Ethel also sent Bobby to G Prep because of the stern discipline it offered, and for him that discipline was in effect twenty-four hours a day, five days a week as a boarder. On weekends, however, one of the Kennedys' many helpers, or Ethel Kennedy herself, usually with two dogs in her convertible, would arrive to pick up Bobby and his brother Joe, and then someone would return them on Sunday evening. She had once invited Bobby's entire class and some of his teachers for a field day at Hickory Hill, where they swam in the pool, toured Bobby's menagerie of animals, and watched the surfer film *The Endless Summer* in the pool cabana.

As one class member who made the tour recalled, "It was a circus out there."

In class, Bobby was required to wear a pressed white shirt, tie, and blue blazer and have his shoes shined, but he had difficulty abiding by the rules. Georgetown Prep was a big change for him in that there had been little if no discipline in effect at Hickory Hill.

His homeroom teacher one year was a layman with what a classmate described as a "Napoleonic complex, a real tyrant," who for weeks endlessly picked on Bobby and gave him a hard time. "I was always sitting there thinking, my God, I hope this man doesn't choose me next." Bobby later told the classmate that he was just going to ignore the harassment because his mother was aware of what was going on, and called the teacher "a pompous ass."

Algebra I was taught by a scholastic in his twenties who suddenly realized that his students were trampling all over him. He decided to make an example of Kennedy. One day Bobby sleepily shuffled into class in his bedroom slippers and the young first-year teacher went ballistic. He kicked Bobby out, and the rest of the class immediately realized that if a Kennedy was being firmly punished, they had also better shape up.

It wasn't the first or last time Bobby had gotten caught and punished for being sloppy. His nemesis—everyone's nemesis at G Prep—was the Jesuit Father Thomas J. Dugan, the Prefect of Discipline. "He was an ex–Golden Gloves boxer, an Irishman, and he would clobber you and just go nuts on you, and if you were out of line you got cuffed," recalled Nee. "There was always somebody walking the track, which was one of his famous penalties. Sometimes the person would be carrying a chair while walking the track, just to make it a bit harder. If two guys got into a fight they would be walking the track in opposite directions."

As Robert Katzen observed, "Father Dugan ruled with an iron fist, and we feared him. When it came to discipline you did not want to be on the other end of the stick. In the lunchroom we had epic food fights and he once singled out two or three guys and made them fill a cup with catsup and mustard and drink it. He would not be adverse to popping you on the back of the head and meting out corporal punishment, and I'm sure Bobby was on the receiving end."

Knowing the price he would have to pay if Dugan caught him looking unkempt, Bobby tried to spruce up his appearance, but when Dugan, who seemed to have superhuman vision, spotted him with his shirttails outside his trousers, he bopped him hard on the head while barking, "Tuck in your skirt, sweetheart!" like a Marine Corps drill instructor.

In 2005, Mark Judge, a journalist who had graduated from Georgetown Prep in the 1980s, wrote a book about his time there, entitled *God and Man at Georgetown Prep.* It caused quite a storm, especially among the alumni and administration going back decades, because Judge, a conservative Catholic, had alleged that "alcoholism was rampant" among the "left-wing Jesuits" and claimed the school had been a hotbed of "rampant homosexuality." Half of the faculty, he asserted, "was gay."

Beginning in the mid-sixties, Bobby's time at Georgetown Prep, it was commonly known that the Jesuit scholastics who were studying to be priests, but also taught, were heavy drinkers. "We had a joke," recalled a classmate of Bobby's, "that every Friday afternoon a beer truck stopped at the cloisters where the priests lived. We as students didn't consider it a problem, but we knew the Jesuits drank a lot."

If there were blatant instances of homosexuality involving faculty members and students, it was kept quiet by the administration. But students in Bobby's class, for instance, had their suspicions. As one noted, "Wrestling in phys ed was kind of a big thing. One of the scholastics in his late twenties was very fond of a classmate of mine and he was always asking him to wrestle. The undercurrent was that the scholastic was gay, and I would have guessed that he was. Whether there was any more contact other than that I never heard, and I never knew of any guys in our class who said Father So-and-so did this to me, but over time more and more of this kind of stuff became known."

In mid-July 2014, Pope Francis labeled the church sex abuse scandal "a leprosy in our house," and claimed that one in fifty Catholic clerics were pedophiles—"about two percent."

BOBBY'S DARING—DEMONSTRATED WHEN HE climbed up the brick wall in seventh grade—had almost resulted in another fatal Kennedy tragedy during the summer vacation of 1966, when he was between seventh and eighth grade.

Hanging out at the Kennedy compound, he jumped off the roof of one of the family's garages, crashed through a window, and was almost killed. He had severed a tendon, and required one hundred stitches to close the critical lacerations on his leg.

When the fall semester began in September 1966, he returned to Georgetown Prep wearing a cast and on crutches. "He had this huge book bag, like a lawyer's tan briefcase, because we had a million books that we had to carry all the time," recalled Maurice Nee. "He had that bag and the crutches and his cast, and his desk was all the way on the other side of the classroom, farthest from the door, and closest to the window, which was detrimental to his attention span, and every day he had to hobble and hop to get there. He felt miserable, I'm sure."

Bobby's daredevil and reckless antics, however, would continue for years and, curiously, he sometimes used his various scars—accompanied by dramatic accounts of how he suffered them—as part of his seduction technique with sympathetic young women. But that was still to come; he wasn't chasing girls, nor were girls chasing him. Yet.

Back in school Bobby had bonded with an eighth-grade newcomer whose family happened to be friends of his parents and whose father was a prominent Washingtonian who would have a major role a few years hence in the resignation of President Richard Milhous Nixon.

Like Bobby, his new best friend also was the namesake of a famous father. John Sirica Jr. was the son of the federal judge John Joseph Sirica, who gained fame beginning in 1972 as the jurist who presided over the case of the Nixon operatives who had broken into the office of the Democratic National Committee headquarters in the Watergate complex on June 17, 1972. Their trial in Sirica's courtroom signaled the beginning of the end of Richard Nixon's presidency. Facing impeachment, he resigned in what became known as the Watergate scandal.

While Judge Sirica, a Republican, known as "Maximum John," meted out stiff sentences, he also was known as a man who was amiable, a bit shy, and unassuming, and that's how his son, known as Jack, was viewed by Bobby and other classmates at Georgetown Prep. The two namesakes had quickly bonded, with young Sirica becoming the first in his class to discover the popular late-sixties rock band Creedence Clearwater Revival. In 2014, as the political editor of the Long Island newspaper *Newsday*, he was still rocking to the group's music.

"Bobby and I certainly were friends, and good friends at Georgetown Prep," recalled Sirica, who was invited to Hickory Hill for sleepovers a number of times, a claim none of Bobby's other classmates could make. "One time the kids, as sort of a joke at dinner, had me sit at the head of the table, knowing full well that their father always sat there. But he was great about it, a nice warm guy."

As for life at Hickory Hill, Sirica remembered it as "a big crowd of people."

Life there would once again change dramatically.

TWO

Daddy's Dead

During the late winter of Bobby's first semester of ninth grade at Georgetown Prep, the winter of 1967 when he was about to turn fourteen, his father began to seriously consider throwing his hat in the ring for the presidency of the United States; the election was just a year away. It was little more than four years since his brother John had been assassinated, and the New York senator's close advisers, such as Ted Sorensen and Arthur Schlesinger Jr., were fearful it could happen again. RFK was being warned to stay out of the race, and leading that refrain was his even more fearful brother Ted, who had lost one brother to bullets and didn't want to lose another.

As Bobby's close cousin Christopher Kennedy Lawford, then thirteen, a year younger than Bobby, observed years later, RFK's decision to run "invoked a level of fear in the family, especially in my mother [Patricia Kennedy], who was closest to him in age and experience . . . I could feel it and see it in her face. Whenever the campaign came up, she would get this tightness around her, like she was trying to ward something off."

On the other side, though, was Ethel Kennedy, then the mother of ten. Ethel was convinced RFK could win, and was cheerleading the push for him to announce. "Without any question," RFK's political adviser Fred Dutton told the *Chicago Tribune*, "Ethel was a major factor." Her brother Jim Skakel, a staunch Republican who, like the rest of the Skakels, disliked the Kennedys intensely, agreed, observing years later, "The crowds, the press, the hyper state. It was as bad as cocaine. Ethel liked the fast lane. You could not debate with her. There was no two-way street."

Two historic events happened on Saturday, March 16, 1968. In Vietnam, where the war was raging, a young army officer by the name of William L. Calley Jr., a lieutenant in Charlie Company, 11th Brigade, American Division, entered the village of My Lai with orders to let the civilians go free and kill the Vietcong soldiers of the 48th Battalion and their sympathizers. Instead, some five hundred civilians—unarmed men, women, and children—were murdered. The My Lai Massacre, as it came to be known, would be exposed by the journalist Seymour Hersh. But on that same Saturday when RFK announced for the presidency, he and the rest of the world were still unaware of the slaughter. The war, however, was a major factor in his decision to run.

Also unknown to the rest of the world was a secret Ethel and RFK were closely guarding: She had just learned that she was pregnant with her eleventh child.

For dramatic effect, RFK had chosen to announce his great plan, which was televised nationally, from the same podium in the U.S. Capitol where his brother had announced his own candidacy.

He told the world: "I run because I am convinced that this country is on a perilous course and because I have strong feelings about what must be done . . . to end the bloodshed in Vietnam and in our cities . . . to close the gaps between black and white, rich and poor, young and old, in this country and around the world . . ."

He was, he declared, "in it to win."

His campaign would last eighty-five days.

BUSY RACING AROUND THE COUNTRY with the candidate and rarely around to supervise her children, Ethel Kennedy had hired a twenty-one-year-old former Boy Scout and college dropout by the name of Bob

Galland and paid him $67.60 a week to help oversee her young tribe. It was an impossible task.

He found them to be spoiled, arrogant, undisciplined know-it-alls. "You're talking to young Bobby and he's just gotten back from Africa with Lem Billings and I'm going, 'Jesus Christ, what am I going to teach this kid about? Racoons?' None of my experience made any impression. They'd already done it all."

While Ethel often proclaimed she wanted to be with her many children, she was rarely ever home; others said that she was often absent, involved with political campaigns or other activities. Bobby and his brother David were usually without any familial adult supervision, virtually left to their own devices. Bobby still had about three more months remaining before finishing his freshman year, ninth grade, at Georgetown Prep. There, virtually overnight, he had the distinction of being the only student whose father might soon be the next commander in chief, but his classmates still weren't impressed.

At Hickory Hill, recalled Galland, who was overseeing the older Kennedy children, "It was incredible. There wasn't anybody to say, 'Don't do that.' It was hard to control them."

An elderly neighbor whose modest home backed on Hickory Hill had come face-to-face with their out-of-control behavior.

He suddenly found that his property was being vandalized: Firecrackers had been placed in his mailbox—one even had been taped to a living room window and exploded—debris had been left on his steps, a signpost had been knocked down. The neighbor had become so upset that he once fired a shotgun into the ground to scare off the young Kennedy intruders.

"Mrs. Kennedy ought to come on home and watch her children. . . . There is no upbringing over there. No one is controlling those kids," seventy-one-year-old Jack Kopson said at the time.

But the pregnant Ethel was adamant about campaigning, seeing RFK win, and becoming First Lady.

However, she still played up her role of doting mother when she told the press boys on the campaign bus: "I plan to remain active in my husband's campaign [but] I want to spend at least three or four days a week at home with my children . . . I try to keep our family life happy and easygoing so [RFK] doesn't have to worry. It's important for him to know the children are well. . . . We miss our children when we're away from home. Of course, I miss Robert when I'm home and not with him. It seems I'm caught in the middle."

One of the few times Bobby was seriously disciplined—by his father, not his mother—was when he was twelve years old. He, along with his brother David, were angry that a new highway was being built near their home, thinking it would end their country-like, free-for-all paradise at sprawling Hickory Hill.

"In protest," Bobby recalled in *The Riverkeepers,* "we dislodged some stacked highway culvert pipes and smashed them down an embankment, a crime for which we were soon caught."

As punishment, RFK made his namesake and his brother sweep boardwalks at Cape Cod that summer, far from being the worst kind of penance.

Still, many years later, Bobby made it clear in his book that he still considered his father's punishment unfair.

BY THE TIME BOBBY was in his high school freshman year, with his father running for the nation's highest office, the wild and crazy culture of the late sixties had begun to penetrate the hallowed halls of George-town Prep. The hippie counterculture—free love, psychedelic drugs—was abroad in the land, and Bobby would become a part of it all.

The first LSD and marijuana Be-In event had been held in San Francisco in January 1967, heralding the "Summer of Love." The druggie-psycho-hippie Charles Manson Family was in the California desert planning the "Helter-Skelter" murders of the actress Sharon Tate and others. The first documentary devoted to a rock festival—*Monterey Pop,* starring Jimi Hendrix and Janis Joplin, who would die of drug and alcohol abuse—made it to the screen. The first issues of *Rolling Stone* rolled off the presses, with major reporting of the emerging hippie movement and the counterculture.

And the New Journalism guru Tom Wolfe published *The Electric*

Kool-Aid Acid Test, documenting the world of a band of "Merry Pranksters" and their use of psychedelic drugs. One of their stops on a cross-country, Kerouac–like, acid-fueled road trip was the rented estate in Millbrook, New York, where the father of LSD, Timothy Leary, had set up headquarters. And Millbrook, where Bobby would next go to school, was where his drug experiences would begin.

At Georgetown Prep in suburban Bethesda, meanwhile, Bobby and his Jesuit-trained classmates had only to hitchhike twenty minutes or so down Rockville Pike to be in the center of the hippie action in the nation's capital—the neighborhoods of Georgetown and Dupont Circle, where the sweet smell of marijuana was in the air, where head shops and tie-dye boutiques were springing up everywhere, where dealers were selling loose joints, and where battalions of barefoot girls with daisies in their hair hung out looking to get high and get laid.

At G Prep itself the disciplinarian Father Dugan and the other Jesuits saw the onslaught and did their best to bar the door.

"Among us freshmen, drugs didn't come on the scene at school, but Bobby disappeared a lot, so who knows what was going on with him," recalled Tim Ruane. "But soon a good portion of us—almost all of us—were smoking marijuana and a good portion were doing LSD and mescaline. In our freshman year we were drinking. I would say we were pretty much binge drinkers."

ON THE ROAD, RFK, with Ethel at his side, was exuberant if exhausted, winning one primary after another: Indiana, Nebraska, Colorado—but then came Oregon, a state with minuscule black, Catholic, and poor populations, his main constituency. The Beaver State, however, had lots of hunters who railed against gun control, one of the candidate's themes, especially since Dallas. Moreover, his opponent, Senator Eugene McCarthy of Minnesota, running on an anti–Vietnam War platform, was demanding a debate with RFK in Oregon, but he refused. The Kennedy juggernaut had hit a roadblock.

RFK became the first Kennedy ever to lose an election; McCarthy won the Oregon primary by about six percentage points.

A day later, RFK and his team arrived in Los Angeles. It was

Wednesday, May 29, 1968. Six days remained before Primary Day, Tuesday, June 4.

The journalist Jack Newfield saw how the grueling campaign had aged RFK. "His face looked like an old man's; there were lines I had never noticed before. The eyes were puffy and red and pushed back into their sockets. His hands shook . . . He was so tired . . ."

Ethel Kennedy had contacted her friend Nicole Salinger, wife of the longtime Kennedy aide Pierre Salinger, with instructions to have Bob Galland bring six of his Kennedy charges—David, Michael, Kerry, Courtney, Christopher, and Max—to the City of Angels posthaste so they could be part of the California campaign, where victory was key and, within the Kennedy camp, at least, seemed certain.

Galland and the children flew out the next day, were met at LAX by Ethel, and put up at the Beverly Hills Hotel; on the eve of the primary, Monday, June 3, they all would move temporarily to a beach house in Malibu owned by the director John Frankenheimer. David was knocked down by a big wave in the rough Pacific surf, and nearly drowned. His father saved him, but wound up with a bruise on his right eyebrow from the gritty sand.

Back at the house, RFK told his children he had a plan, recalled the campaign journalist Theodore H. White: "Mummy's so tired that she's going to rest next week and I'm going to take care of you myself. How do you like that?"

According to Galland, "The kids were constantly badgered by the press. Cameras in their faces, microphones in their faces. The photographers would be walking backward taking pictures and the kids would run ahead and get down on hands and knees so a guy walking backward would stumble and fall over them. Ethel got a kick out of it."

Finishing his freshman year at G Prep, Bobby was not part of any of it. He was permitted to remain in school. But when classes ended, his mother's plan called for him to join the remaining days of the campaign with the rest of the family, leading up to RFK's expected nomination at the Democratic National Convention in Chicago in late August. After California, the New York primary was next, on June 18, and the plans called for Bobby to be there for that one.

The crucial California campaign ended on Tuesday, June 4, at eight P.M.

when the polls closed—eleven o'clock on the East Coast, where the population either continued watching the political hullabaloo on TV or had gotten ready for bed. Years later, many would recall exactly what they were doing late on June 4, 1968, just as many had on November 23, 1963.

In the Royal Suite on the fifth floor of the Ambassador Hotel, the tribe had gathered to watch the results: In the entourage were RFK's siblings Teddy, Jean Kennedy Smith, and Patricia Kennedy Lawford, who all along had feared something bad might happen to her brother. But that night she was feeling upbeat and positive. Drinking and watching the TV were such friends and supporters as the journalists Jimmy Breslin and Pete Hamill, and key advisers Ted Sorensen and Richard Goodwin. On instructions from Ethel, Bob Galland had taken the children back to the three-bedroom bungalow at the Beverly Hills Hotel.

Around eleven-thirty, knowing he had won the very important primary—that day he had also swept the vote in South Dakota—RFK gathered Ethel, wearing an orange-and-white minidress and high heels, and headed down to the pandemonium of the Ambassador's Embassy Ballroom to address the celebratory throng. He had declined the usual police security detail. But he had several bodyguards with him—a former FBI agent, Bill Barry, and the black athletes Rosey Grier and Rafer Johnson. His lack of protection did not go over well with law enforcement. As Los Angeles Police Chief Thomas Reddin would later observe, "I got the impression that he wished to appear to be antipolice and antiestablishment, and not to need our help because politically it was the smart thing to do at the time."

With Ethel on the podium with him waving jubilantly to the crowd, RFK thanked his supporters: "I hope that we have as much good fortune in our campaign. . . . My thanks to all of you, and it's on to Chicago, and let's win there!"

At the Beverly Hills Hotel, twelve-year-old David, along with Bob Galland, watched on the TV as his father pressed his way into the crowd after flashing the V-for-victory sign.

In his dorm room in Bethesda, Bobby Jr. already was asleep.

Those who stayed up around the country to watch the finale on TV were eyewitnesses to the most horrific scene since Dallas. Sirhan Bishara Sirhan, a twenty-four-year-old Palestinian fanatic, screamed, "Kennedy, you son of a bitch!" and emptied the chamber of eight bullets from his .22-caliber Iver-Johnson Cadet revolver. People in the ballroom screamed. Newscasters were in shock. The cameras showed RFK on the gray concrete floor, mortally wounded. He had been shot in the head. Sirhan, an immigrant from Jerusalem, was hauled off to jail, yelling, "I did it for my country."

The popular CBS newsman Roger Mudd, long a friend of the Kennedys', who had actually made his journalistic bones covering the JFK assassination, later recalled: "It was like Hades—this screaming that was going on. It was absolutely unworldly. The ring of people around RFK's body got heavier and thicker and there was this screaming and guys just slamming at each other trying to wrestle Sirhan to the ground . . . Ethel just grabbed on to my arm. She was just shaking and I sort of shouldered my way through, just sort of forcing, forcing, forcing and pulling her with me and yelling, 'Let Ethel through, let Mrs. Kennedy through!' And finally the crowd opened up enough for her to go through and she went through."

RFK was rushed a mile away to Central Receiving Hospital, where, in Emergency Room No. 2, his wife watched as he was placed on a heart-lung resuscitator. Then he was transferred to Good Samaritan Hospital. Shortly after three in the morning, a team of surgeons began an almost four-hour effort to save his life. He had been struck at close range by three bullets—one had hit the mastoid bone and lodged in the midline of his brain, another had to be removed from the back of his neck, and a third had grazed his forehead. The surgeons had removed all but one bullet fragment from RFK's brain, but he was breathing on his own. Ethel, fearing the worst-case scenario, decided that St. Patrick's Cathedral would be the setting for funeral services, with burial at Arlington National Cemetery, next to JFK.

BOBBY KENNEDY JR. WAS two months away from turning ten when his uncle Jack was shot to death, an event he had not seen on TV as had so many millions of others. This time he had been sleeping in his dorm room at Georgetown Prep when his father was gunned down.

"I was fourteen years old when my father was killed," he wrote years later in *The Riverkeepers*.

"Father Dugan woke me up at 6:00 a.m. and told me there was a car waiting outside to take me to Hickory Hill . . . At home someone told me Daddy had been shot."

Despite the horror unfolding in Los Angeles, the big house didn't seem filled with gloom. Friends of the wounded candidate and his devastated wife had arrived. TVs, radios, and newspapers with headlines blaring the assassination were turned off or torn up. Still, Bobby and Joe, not expecting the worst, had rounded up a game of touch football, while their sister Kathleen had gone out with friends and returned with ice cream.

Bobby recalled that he and his older siblings, Joe and Kathleen, who also had been away at boarding schools, were flown to California on Air Force Two, the jet used by Vice President Hubert Humphrey. (Credible press reports at the time, however, stated that Bobby and the older siblings were flown aboard the Jet Star, part of the presidential fleet, and were accompanied by Lem Billings, about to begin playing the role of surrogate father to Bobby.)

It was the first time young Bobby had seen his father since he had gone on the western swing of his ill-fated campaign. It was not a pleasant scene.

"My father's head was bandaged and his eyes were black," he wrote. "His face was bruised, especially around his eyes. My mother was beside him, holding his hand, where she stayed all night. Each of us spent time with him that night, holding his hand, praying, saying good-bye, listening to the pumps that kept him breathing.

"In the morning," Bobby continued, "my brother Joe came into the ward where all the children were sleeping and told us, 'He's gone.' We all cried."

Unbeknownst to the public, a decision had been made to allow RFK, who was brain dead, to die. This had occurred after midnight on June 6. In attendance were Ethel and RFK's siblings Jean, Pat, and Ted, along with JFK's widow, Jackie, and Ethel's obstetrician, Dr. Blake Watson.

As I revealed in my 1994 book, *The Other Mrs. Kennedy*, Watson disclosed, "We were in intensive care while Bobby was on the table. Ethel was there beside him and I was behind her. The doctors were talking to the family about what to do, because all along there had never been any sign of brain waves. They all talked for a while and then all agreed to pull the plug. Ethel was very staunch and very self-controlled. . . . It was only a few minutes after they took the apparatus off that he didn't breathe anymore."

The official announcement of RFK's death was made at 1:44 A.M. on Thursday, June 6, 1968, by his devastated press secretary, Frank Mankiewicz.

In his book, Bobby recalled "standing vigil" near his father's casket during the wake at St. Patrick's Cathedral as a crowd "in the hundred thousands" filed past. He noted that in Washington, as the funeral procession passed by the Mall, "thousands of homeless men organized by the late Martin Luther King Jr.'s poor people's campaign . . . stood there quietly, heads bowed and holding their hats against their chests.

"We buried my father near his brother, beneath a simple black slab engraved with his name and the years he lived."

BOBBY KENNEDY JR. NEVER RETURNED to Georgetown Prep. His classmates, and friends like Jack Sirica, who had graduated in what would have been Bobby's Class of 1971, never understood why.

The next time the son of the Watergate judge and the son of the slain presumptive presidential candidate came face-to-face was in 1993 when the country was memorializing the twenty-fifth anniversary of RFK's assassination. Sirica was a reporter in the Washington, D.C., bureau of *Newsday*, and had requested and was granted an interview with his one-time classmate and friend. Bobby was just then ending his first marriage and about to marry his second wife, with whom he had been carrying on an affair. Bobby, driving a minivan, picked up Sirica at LaGuardia Airport in New York and drove him to the Manhattan offices of his Natural Resources Defense Council, where they chatted.

"He was," said Sirica, "grown up, personable, and down to earth."

Bobby told Sirica that after the funeral in New York and burial at Arlington, a reception was held at Hickory Hill. While the guests were drinking and eating, Bobby went upstairs to his father's room and lay down on his father's bed.

"He had pictures on his wall," he recalled, "of my aunt Kick [Kathleen] in her nurse's uniform during the war, and pictures of my uncle Joe and Jack."

Like RFK, all three died young.

Bobby told Sirica, "I remember sitting there thinking they all looked so young and they were all dead. And I lay there and wept for probably an hour or more, and then my father's best friend, Dave Hackett, came in and sat with me. He just sat there silently for I don't know how long. . . . Then he said to me, 'He was the best man I ever knew.'

"That's the only thing that I remember. I don't remember after that."

THREE

Surrogate Father

Sometime in August of that tragic summer of 1968, George Clifford Buell, headmaster of Millbrook School, a British-style boys' boarding academy in the bucolic Hudson Valley of New York State, was vacationing with his family in Newport, Rhode Island, when he received an urgent call.

The newly widowed Ethel Kennedy and her son, young Bobby, Buell was told, were eager to visit Millbrook. Ethel planned to enroll him for the next semester, beginning that September, just a few weeks away, and the headmaster was required to meet with them as soon as possible.

As Peter Cole, a Millbrook English teacher who got to know Bobby during his troubled matriculation, noted years later: "Millbrook was known as a place where the rich and famous would tuck their children away, starting with the Buckleys."

William F. Buckley Jr., the caustic conservative editor and writer, first learned to pen an essay at Millbrook. His brother, James Buckley, then a future Republican U.S. Senator from New York, also attended Millbrook. When James came to speak at the school during Bobby's tenuous enrollment, the two would have a memorable confrontation.

Like Bobby, so many of the boys at Millbrook came from troubled wealthy families. Divorced parents or parents in the throes of divorce had sent their sons there to keep them out of the way. Bobby's case was an exception as he was the only newcomer whose father, a political hero seeking the nation's highest office, had just been murdered.

Besides a Kennedy, Bobby's Millbrook class would also include a descendant of Theodore "T.R." Roosevelt Jr., the Republican twenty-sixth president of the United States. In fact, Robin Roosevelt and the nephew of the slain Democratic thirty-fifth president would have a difficult, short-lived relationship as roommates that had nothing whatsoever to do with any family political differences.

As it turned out, it was not the best of times, nor was Millbrook the best of schools, for a troubled boy like Bobby, who already was earning a reputation for bad behavior. Despite the enrollment of boys from famous families, Millbrook was going through a turbulent time that reflected the tumultuous late-1960s era, the horrendous year 1968 in particular.

Prior to RFK's assassination, a rabid racist had murdered the civil rights leader Rev. Dr. Martin Luther King, igniting riots by African Americans in four major cities. The war in Vietnam, which had divided Americans, accelerated with the surprise Tet Offensive. President Johnson, who succeeded JFK as commander in chief and had supported the war, stunned an already shocked nation when he announced: "I shall not seek and will not accept the nomination of my party as your president." In Chicago, the police had bludgeoned, beaten, and Maced antiwar demonstrators outside the Democratic National Convention. That year the electorate voted Republicans into the White House—the politically doomed Richard Nixon and the corrupt former Maryland governor Spiro Agnew. And in San Francisco, an area called Haight-Ashbury had become a hippie haven, serving up sex, drugs, and rock 'n' roll.

It seemed as if the whole country was going up in flames. And, at Millbrook School, up in smoke, like the title of Cheech and Chong's pot comedy. Drugs and their dangers—from marijuana to psychedelics and more—had entered the school like a flood. Beyond that, there were at least four headmasters in five years. The old masters, the kind who had held the school together, who had been there for decades, were leaving or retiring, being replaced by new blood.

"It was like a staffing earthquake as far as Millbrook was concerned," observed a teacher from that time.

A classmate of Bobby's recalled their time as "Millbrook at its darkest, with inept leadership at the top. We were there during a pretty difficult time and there's no way anyone could call Millbrook posh or exclusive who visited at that time. Millbrook was kind of a third- or fourth-tier school then. It just wasn't that remarkable to be going there with people from famous families like Kennedy and Roosevelt."

Moreover, the headmaster, though he had not even reached middle age when Bobby matriculated, was having serious physical problems, along with a serious addiction that would not be revealed until years after he left the school. He was an alcoholic.

THE ASSASSINATION HAD DEVASTATED forty-year-old Ethel Kennedy. Pregnant with her eleventh child, concerned about her youngest—ages five, three, and one—she needed some space and time to gather her thoughts and try to recover from the terrible trauma she had just suffered.

Angry and frustrated, she took out her rage on Bobby, who was an easy and available target. For instance, a week after his father's funeral, at his brother David's thirteenth birthday party at a grim Hickory Hill, Bobby had spiked everyone's milk with a laxative.

Infuriated, his mother demanded, "Just leave home. Get out of my life!"

Ethel thought a getaway was necessary, so sixteen days after RFK was buried, she moved her children, including the dogs Brumus and Freckles—RFK's beloved springer spaniel, who had been on the campaign trail with the candidate—from the Virginia suburbs of the capital to Edgartown on Martha's Vineyard, where she joined her bereaved sisters-in-law—Jean, Pat, Joan, and Jackie—and all of their children.

Soon after, aboard the chartered sixty-foot yawl *Mira*, sailing across twenty miles of Nantucket Sound to Hyannis Port, "haggard, tired" Ethel was ready for some calm. Her moods could swing drastically. Suddenly she became angry at Bobby, ordered him below deck, literally beat him with a hairbrush, and once again ordered him to get out of her life.

Since she considered him the most difficult and troublesome of her seven sons and three daughters (with another child due at any moment), she quickly decided to hand him off to a longtime Kennedy family friend and insider.

KIRK LEMOYNE "LEM" BILLINGS was a New York advertising agency executive who Ethel also knew was a closeted homosexual; she'd even given her sixth-born, Michael, the middle name LeMoyne in honor of Billings.

Bobby later acknowledged that Billings "became a surrogate father to me." But there was much more to their close relationship.

To those who had been close to Ethel from the time she was young, the choice of a homosexual to oversee her rebellious son wasn't a big surprise. When she was growing up, Ethel's family, the wealthy and unruly Skakels of Greenwich, Connecticut, had its own Lem Billings. Good-looking, patrician, erudite Martin Boswell McKneally, just twenty-one and in prelaw at Holy Cross, had been hired by Ethel's mother as a tutor and sometime father figure to her seven children, but especially for her three badly behaved and academically underachieving sons. Like Billings with the Kennedys, McKneally, nephew of a Catholic nun at the school where seven-year-old Ethel was a student, soon became a close Skakel family confidant and insider.

"From the beginning," he once revealed, "I was highly attracted to the boys, who were extraordinarily handsome and could have been in pictures . . . we became great friends." Later, though, he caused a breach with some of the Skakels when he began attending family events "with his live-in," recalled Ethel's brother Rushton Skakel. "And the live-in, who was older, was the male member and Martin was the female. Oh, wow, what a shocker."

Of the Skakel sisters, McKneally considered Bobby's mother, Ethel, the most interesting. He described her when she was young as "hyper-kinetic . . . flighty . . . lost . . . never very bright." Some would describe Bobby that way, too, in his younger years.

For an obsessively devoted wife like Ethel Skakel Kennedy, who worshipped her husband's every word, thought, and act—except for his womanizing, which she refused to believe, or tried to ignore—her choice of the gay Billings as young Bobby's close guardian was considered strange by those who weren't aware of the Skakel-McKneally history. What made it even more bizarre was that one of RFK's little-known prejudices, of which Ethel was well aware, was his utter loathing of homosexuals.

His disdain had quietly surfaced in the early 1950s when he went to work as a young lawyer on the staff of the Senate Permanent Subcommittee on Investigations under its chairman, the demagogue Joe McCarthy. McCarthy was close to the Kennedy family—he was godfather to RFK and Ethel's firstborn, Kathleen, and he had dated Pat Kennedy and Eunice Kennedy.

While RFK supported the Wisconsin lawmaker's red-baiting, he detested McCarthy's chief henchman and the committee's chief counsel, the swarthy and secretive Roy Cohn, mainly because he was gay. While Evan Thomas, one of RFK's respected biographers, noted that "there was much fault in Cohn . . . Kennedy's loathing may have been more personal. He would from time to time display deep homophobia, and Cohn's homosexuality was unacknowledged but obvious."

Cohn, who would later die from AIDS, was aware of RFK's feelings about him, so gave him little committee responsibility, and referred to Kennedy as "a rich bitch."

McCarthy, an alcoholic, and Cohn, a self-loathing and closeted Jewish homosexual, had, in fact, actually shared Bobby's homophobia; they had embarked on a gay witch hunt—the so-called "Lavender Scare"—in the pursuit and firing of real or suspected homosexuals working in government.

Later, when RFK served as attorney general of the United States in his brother's administration, his homophobia once again surfaced, this time in regard to the black novelist and playwright James Baldwin.

"To some aides," according to Thomas, "Kennedy said unpleasant things about Baldwin, slurring the writer for his homosexuality."

Less than three months before JFK's assassination, Martin Luther King Jr. was the main speaker in the nation's capital at the historic March on Washington, which brought thousands to hear him make his famous

"I have a dream" speech. RFK, however, was not a great supporter of the black civil rights leader. As attorney general, he had ordered King's telephones wiretapped, doing so at the request of the FBI director, J. Edgar Hoover, who personally despised King *and* the powerful Kennedy brothers.

On one of the taped conversations prior to the march, King was overheard telling an adviser that one of the March organizers, Bayard Ruston, might drink too much at the event and, because he was homosexual, "grab one little brother." The homophobic RFK thought it was important enough to pass the scurrilous intelligence from Hoover, a rumored homosexual himself, on to his brother in the Oval Office.

The evening prior to the March, RFK was chatting with the socialite Marietta Tree, the U.S. delegate to the United Nations, at a dinner party in Georgetown when, in reference to King (who wasn't gay), he shocked her by stating: "So you're down here for that old black fairy's anti-Kennedy demonstration." He then went on to tell her, "If the country knew what we know about King's goings on [his sexual habits], he'd be finished." (The same, of course, would have been true about the philandering, hypocritical Kennedy brothers themselves.)

Even stranger than Ethel's choice of Lem Billings to essentially oversee young Bobby's life was the timing of the decision. Just months before RFK was murdered, in additional to campaigning for the presidency, he had been finishing what would be his last book, *To Seek a Newer World.*

The Georgetown University law professor Peter Edelman, a close associate of RFK's, recalled that one of the key people in the production of the book was gay and that RFK "absolutely could not deal with a homosexual copy editor." Ethel must have been aware of the situation and had been wholeheartedly supportive, so it became even more of a mystery as to why she had handed her son over to the kind of man whose sexual lifestyle her husband found repugnant.

Moreover, RFK never had the kind of relationship that his brother Jack had had with Billings. RFK, much younger, remained only distantly friendly with Billings, mainly to appease the Kennedy family. As a confirmed homophobe, he would never have put his young namesake (or any of his sons, for that matter) in Billings's custody.

. . .

NOT LONG BEFORE HE WAS gunned down, RFK had talked about the possibility of an African safari; he and his family were known for their exotic and adventurous travels. A year earlier, RFK and Ethel had themselves visited Africa, a trip he believed would help with his presidential campaign by winning black voters. Billings avidly volunteered to fulfill RFK's promise and accompany the boy on a six-week trip through East Africa beginning a month after the assassination, into the Serengeti Plain of northern Tanzania, with visits to the Lake Manyara and Ngorongoro national parks and a side trip to Egypt.

Suddenly fatherless and grief-stricken, fourteen-year-old Bobby, who had been taught the clan mantra set in stone by his grandfather Joe that "Kennedys don't cry" and "Kennedys don't complain," had found himself looking for wild animals in the bush on a photographic safari with a fifty-two-year-old family friend who was clearly slowly falling in love with him, as, years earlier, he had fallen in love with the boy's uncle, the late president.

With professional 35mm cameras, Bobby and Billings documented their African adventure, which also included a rafting trip in Egypt's Valley of the Kings, and, oddly, a VIP visit to a nightclub to watch the gyrations of a bevy of belly dancers, hosted by members of the Egyptian Supreme Court, an evening of salacious interest more to the hormonal adolescent than to his gay, middle-age chaperone.

The safari photos became quite lucrative because at that time, in the wake of the latest Kennedy tragedy, anything a Camelot heir did became front-page media fodder. Aware of the demand, Billings brokered a deal with *Life* magazine for an interview about their adventure and for the photos. The questionable story put out was that young Bobby wanted to use the money to build a memorial to his father in the Serengeti National Park.

But as the New York *Daily News* noted later: "The young Kennedy had not been averse to trying to make [his] trips pay for themselves. He sold his 1968 African pictures to *Life* magazine for what K. LeMoyne Billings, his traveling companion, called 'a small fortune.'"

Like dialogue from a clichéd buddy movie, the glib Bobby told

Life that he had to take care of Billings because he was afraid of animals, and Billings, often teased by Bobby, noted that he had to "endure him." It made for a cute narrative. Bobby also reported that he enjoyed the baboons showing off; described photographing elephants from a tree; learned that giraffes weren't the smartest animals, and that the two of them, Billings and Bobby, feasted on wildebeest.

Back at the Kennedy compound before summer's end, away from Billings for the time being, he continued his bad behavior, feeding LSD to his parakeet, and forcing his brother David to trip on the psychedelic mescaline. Hallucinating, looking wide-eyed at his brother, he imagined the worst, screaming, "You're dying just like Daddy!"

According to the Kennedy matriarch, Rose, in conversations with Robert Coughlan, the ghostwriter of her hagiographic 1975 memoir, *Times to Remember*, next to Jack Kennedy, Billings was convinced that Bobby Jr. was "the best of them all, very much like his uncle, with the brains and spirit and a hell of a personality."

The first time Billings was introduced to Bobby Jr., the two had spent several hours alone in the boy's room at Hickory Hill. The enthusiastic preadolescent regaled the gay bachelor with stories about his pet collection.

"I've just met the smartest little boy! He's just like Jack!" he enthused to RFK and Ethel in his high-pitched, effeminate voice, which RFK made fun of behind his back.

JACK KENNEDY AND LEM BILLINGS had gotten to know each other in their sophomore year while working together on the Choate school yearbook. For Billings, a year older than Kennedy, it was love at first sight, and from the instant they met he was sexually attracted to the handsome scion of America's royal family.

He eventually worked up the courage to express his feelings via a bizarre, relatively secret method of communication that had long existed at Choate, one supposedly passed along through the ages from the elite British private schools where homosexual experimentation was more common. If a boy was interested in having a sexual liaison with a classmate, he could write his desire on a piece of toilet paper, easily disposable to avoid incrimination. And that's precisely what Billings had done, hoping against hope that Kennedy would be amenable.

He wasn't.

In a letter to Billings, Kennedy angrily insisted, "Please don't write to me on toilet paper anymore. I'm not that kind of boy."

However, an intimate of Billings, Lawrence J. Quirk, claimed that Billings, whom he met in 1946 when both worked in Jack Kennedy's first congressional campaign, had confided to him that their relationship did, in fact, involve sex acts—"a friendship that included oral sex, with Jack always on the receiving end."

Quirk, who acknowledged his own bisexuality, asserted that Billings "believed that this arrangement enabled Jack to sustain his self-delusion that straight men who received oral sex from other males were really only straights looking for sexual release."

As he further observed, "Jack was in love with Lem being in love with him and considered him the ideal follower-adorer."

Billings was a strapping, bespectacled, "grizzly-bearish" fellow with big feet and a large head topped by curly, dirty blond hair, who always seemed to be smiling. He possessed a "high, screechy laugh" and a "high, nasal whine of a voice" that, according to Quirk, "instantly tabbed him as gay." Standing next to Jack, or lying close beside him in a lawn chaise at the Kennedys' oceanfront estate in Palm Beach, as one old photograph showed, Billings appeared to dwarf his chum.

All the Kennedys were very much aware of Billings's sexual preference, or suspected it, accepted it, and welcomed him into their exclusive inner circle—practically adopted him—and he became a part of the family, although the patriarch found him annoying at times.

When Kennedy and Billings were at Choate and later, when they were seemingly joined at the hip at Princeton for a time before Kennedy transferred to Harvard at his father's behest, Billings always accompanied him home on vacations. Irked, Joe Kennedy would sneeringly ask his wife, "Do we have to have that queer around all summer?"

Rose Kennedy, however, had a different, more positive take on Billings. In her memoir, published eleven years after the first Kennedy assassination, she wrote that Billings had "remained Jack's lifelong close friend, confidant, sharer in old memories and new experiences . . . He has really been part of 'our family' since that first time he showed up at our house as one of 'Jack's surprises.' "

While Billings was accepted by the Kennedys—mainly because of his puppy-like devotion and love for Jack—he was aware that he had, for a man, embarrassing feminine mannerisms. "People think I'm a joke," he once acknowledged. "They make fun of my voice. But I'm stuck with the Kennedys emotionally, and I will be to the end of my life."

About the odd Kennedy–Billings relationship, Eunice Kennedy Shriver, one of Jack Kennedy's five sisters, once remarked: "It's hard to describe it as just friendship; it was a complete liberation of the spirit. President Kennedy was a completely liberated man when he was with Lem."

Billings was the president's frequent overnight guest at the White House. His constant presence had caused consternation for Kennedy's advisers, who feared blackmail or other political repercussions, but Kennedy didn't seem to care. The close White House relationship sparked Gore Vidal to disparagingly call Billings the "chief faggot at Camelot." According to Vidal, Kennedy "felt quite comfortable in the company of homosexuals as long as they were smart enough to hold his interest."

When Kennedy was killed, the historian Sally Bedell Smith, in a biography, referred to Billings as "probably the saddest of the Kennedy widows."

BY HANDING OVER YOUNG BOBBY to Lem Billings, Ethel Kennedy apparently didn't mind his sexual persuasion. The rigidly Catholic Kennedy wife who once considered becoming a nun before she married RFK might have changed her mind, however, had she been aware that Billings had gotten into a number of scrapes involving what he delicately described as "men's room monkey business." But he was able to avoid scandal, he claimed, through Kennedy intercession and influence—the quid pro quo for his steadfast loyalty.

But the Skakel family, unlike Ethel, wasn't as accepting of Billings.

George Terrien, Ethel's alcoholic brother-in-law who had married her pill-popping and alcoholic sister, Georgeann, had gotten to know Billings and disliked him, mainly because of his homosexuality.

"Everyone knew Lem was queer—the Kennedys, the Skakels, everyone," he once said.

Terrien had been RFK's roommate at Harvard and later at the University of Virginia Law School, and he was particularly upset about what he saw clearly as Billings's growing infatuation with young Bobby.

"I never could figure out why Ethel would let Lem have such an intimate relationship," he said. "She always remained blind to what he really was."

FOUR

"Unrequited Love"

With the fall 1968 semester soon to begin at Millbrook School, the headmaster, George Buell, met with fourteen-year-old Bobby and his mother. Ethel was six months pregnant and due around Christmas. Accompanying them was the omnipresent Lem Billings, now playing a major parenting and mentoring role. It was immediately decided that the boy would begin classes forthwith.

The only demand that Ethel made of Buell was that Bobby—as thin as a rail, pale, and, as a classmate recalled, wired like "a radio on scan"— be given a slot on the football team, since his father had played the game avidly when he was at Harvard. The headmaster said it would be done.

Then Ethel toured the school library and, according to one account, exploded when she couldn't find a copy on the shelves of *The Enemy Within*, her husband's book about Jimmy Hoffa and corrupt labor unions, based on his time in the 1950s as chief counsel of a Senate investigating committee.

"Where's my husband's book! Where's my husband's book!" she demanded of the librarian, Ann Grove.

Ethel, however, mentioned nothing to Buell about young Bobby's emotional state due to the loss of his father, and nothing about his progressively bad behavior and growing use of drugs. According to several former faculty members who were briefed by the headmaster, it was not clear that she was even aware of his drug use.

"We never saw Ethel on the campus again. She never visited Bobby," said James Hejduk, who had arrived to teach music at the same time that Bobby began his Millbrook matriculation.

"But Lem," he clearly recalled, "was around a lot, and we as faculty were told who he was and that he was Bobby's caretaker, as it were, in a *loco parentis* kind of role. He was coming up and he was taking Bobby out to dinner and things like that. His appearances were unusual in that you never knew when he was going to show up. Of course, that gave most of us the thought—does this guy have a job other than caring for Bobby? He was a man that seemed to obviously be of independent means and have a lot of time on his hands, like a supporting-cast kind of person, one of those people who traded on the Kennedy name and reputation."

While completing his masters degree program in music at Indiana University in Bloomington, Hejduk had been working in support of RFK's ill-fated presidential run—"trying to do my bit, handing out brochures, and just trying to wave the flag for the cause," he recalled nostalgically. Naturally, then, he was joyfully surprised when he arrived at Millbrook for his first teaching job to find the namesake of his political hero beginning classes there, too.

He also immediately perceived that the relationship between Bobby and Billings "was probably one of those unrequited-love kind of things."

Mark Bontecou, a scion of the wealthy Bontecou family of Millbrook, which had once owned a good part of the land on which Millbrook School resided, also recalled how Billings was a constant companion of Bobby's during the school year. Even when Bobby was invited to weekend lunches at the Bontecou estate, it was Billings who accompanied him.

"He seemed a very pleasant fellow," Bontecou, a classmate of Bobby's, said. "But the one thing that struck me even at that tender age was that I felt Lem was just *obsessed* with Bobby—the way he watched over him, the way he was hugely protective of him. I got the impression he felt an obligation that somebody had to care for Bobby because Mrs. Kennedy was not a hands-on mother at all. I don't know whether she wrote to Bobby, but she certainly didn't telephone or visit him."

Another classmate, Brian Carroll, remembered "this odd character" Billings, who was always on campus fawning over Bobby: " 'Bobby, are you eating? Bobby, do you have clothes?' And Bobby was sort of always unkempt."

While Mark Bontecou was unaware of any contact by Bobby's mother, another classmate, Scott Riviere, who had had some hellish visits to Hickory Hill, recalled that she "used to almost threaten me to tell her what Bobby was doing because of the pot and other things."

Recalling those Millbrook School days and his contacts with Ethel Kennedy, Riviere said Bobby's mother had "tried" to get him to "spy" on her son. "But I wasn't going to go there. Bobby was dealing with whatever he was dealing with, and I just felt that she was a control freak, but I also didn't feel like her heart was in it. It seemed like she was just trying to get something on him."

Riviere said he considered telling Bobby about his mother's clandestine contacts with him, but ruled it out. "One time I kind of alluded to something with him, but I just felt it wasn't going to serve any purpose except to get him crazy, so I decided not to."

Only Lem Billings was in Bobby's corner. Bobby appeared to have been virtually given up by his own flesh and blood.

Of the Kennedys, only his uncle Ted had shown up at Millbrook to see how his nephew was doing. He attended one of the parents' weekends, but was never seen on campus again.

In his memoir published after his death, the senator said he tried his best to act as the patriarch, especially for his newly deceased brother's children, among them the teenage Bobby. But it wasn't an easy task.

"In the months and years after Bobby's death, I tried to stay ahead of the darkness," he stated. "I drove my car at high speeds . . . I sometimes drove my capacity for liquor to the limit."

And, he admitted, he had "invented" sundry unnamed "excesses" to "anesthetize myself."

In one sorry episode, he was returning home from a trip to Alaska, having taken over the senate's Indian Education subcommittee, of which RFK had been chairman. On the plane he had gotten drunk, became rowdy, and was quoted as bellowing, "They're going to shoot my ass off the way they shot off Bobby's."

Beyond the senator, young Bobby's aunt Jackie had inquired about his welfare but never visited.

"We had a couple of calls from Jackie—'How's my nephew doing?' That kind of thing," recalled the headmaster's widow years later. "Sometimes I answered the phone and I would hear her wispy voice, and then I would get George to talk to her." After the calls, her husband joked and reminded her that he had danced and socialized with Jackie years earlier when he was invited to debutante coming-out parties in Newport.

On October 20, 1968, little more than a month after Bobby began classes at Millbrook, Jackie shocked the Kennedy family, and America, by marrying one of the world's richest men, Aristotle Onassis, whom she had been seeing for several years following the murder of her husband.

THE ONLY OTHER ADULT who was practically a member of the Kennedy family and who was concerned enough about Bobby's welfare to check in on him with Headmaster Buell was the Kennedy family nurse, Luella Hennessey-Donovan, nicknamed Lulu. She contacted Buell on several occasions to ask about the boy's well-being. "We would get a telephone call from that funny old nurse, who sounded like an old-time nanny, and she would say, 'It's President Kennedy's birthday and Bobby needs to go to Mass and observe that,' and George would have to take him," recalled the headmaster's widow. "But we never saw Ethel. She never visited."

Hennessey-Donovan had cared for three generations of Kennedys, beginning in the 1930s. Her charges had included Jack, Ted, and RFK, whom she always believed would become a priest. As confidante and caregiver, Hennessey-Donovan was at Ethel's side after she gave birth to most of her brood of eleven. At the White House, she rocked John-John to sleep.

Her involvement with Ethel began when Ethel was twenty-three and suffered from postpartum depression after the July 4, 1951, difficult and painful birth of her first child, Kathleen.

One of Ethel's big fears through all of her pregnancies, Hennessey-Donovan recalled, was that she would have a mentally handicapped child.

There were two such children, one on the Skakel side, one on the Kennedy side, the best known being Rosemary Kennedy, one of RFK's sisters, who was put away and famously forced by the patriarch to have a prefrontal lobotomy when she was twenty-three. Rose Kennedy later revealed she would never forgive her husband for that "awful operation." Hennessey-Donovan, who helped care for Rosemary for a time, later founded the Kennedy-Donovan Center for people like Rosemary.

Ethel's sister Georgeann Skakel Dowdle had gotten rubella during her first pregnancy. The baby, a daughter, who was named Alexandra, was born blind, deaf, stunted, and retarded in June 1952. As the long-time Skakel family confidant Martin McKnealy later revealed, "The Skakels now had their own Rosemary, but only the inner circle knew about it." Ethel, pregnant at the time with her second child—her first son, Joe—and involved in Jack Kennedy's first senatorial campaign, practically fell apart, thinking that it could be her baby who would be born with defects. Hennessey-Donovan helped her through the pregnancy and normal birth at a Boston hospital.

It was only with the birth of Ethel's sixth child, Michael, in 1956, that a physical defect in one of her children became apparent, leaving her unnerved. For a woman who believed all Kennedys were perfect, physically and emotionally, unlike her own troubled Skakel siblings, it came as a shock that her fourth son had a strange physical flaw, one common to frogs and ducks rather than humans, which was a closely held secret for years. But Bobby revealed it at an extremely curious moment—in church, during his eulogy for Michael, who died in a bizarre 1997 skiing accident.

Pointing out that Michael was "the greatest athlete of our generation . . . who would spend so much of his life in the water," he disclosed that his brother "was born with webbed feet. He always regretted that our mother had his toes surgically corrected. He felt the webbing might have propelled him to the level of an Olympic swimmer."

Bobby, too, suffered from a genetic condition, neurological in nature, which didn't surface until he was forty-three. Known as spasmodic dysphobia, it caused his speaking voice to become strained and stilted, and he sounded as if he were choking up. It was a rare disorder that affected only his voice box, and was never considered life-threatening; he was just one of an estimated .02 percent of the population so affected.

Before the syndrome struck, Bobby had a strong speaking voice, and could engage a large room without using a microphone. But as it worsened, he reached a point where, he once acknowledged, he couldn't bear to listen to himself speak, especially on a nationally syndicated radio talk show he co-hosted called *Ring of Fire*, which aired on the mostly liberal, financially troubled Air America network; the show began broadcasting in 2004 and went belly-up in 2010. Later, his program was picked up by another broadcasting entity. But Bobby's voice problem never stopped him from being one of the most outspoken and controversial of his generation of Kennedys.

More serious, however, was his other issue—an addictive personality. For some years he was hooked on drugs, but he eventually kicked the habit. Still later, his addiction to sex would spark scandal and destroy relationships.

DURING THE FALL AND WINTER of 1968, with Bobby and most of his seven older siblings away at schools, and with the three youngest—eighteen-month-old Douglas Harriman Kennedy, who had been born prematurely, three-year-old Matthew, and five-year-old Chris—at home at Hickory Hill, being looked after by a slew of volunteers and friends, the very pregnant Ethel Kennedy resumed life, but faced the frightening reality of childbirth for the first time without the man she loved and worshipped.

A battalion of reporters was staking out Georgetown Hospital on December 11—the imminent birth of her post-assassination child was international news—when she arrived with an entourage that included Hennessey-Donovan; Ethel's brother-in-law Ted, the senator; RFK's campaign manager, Fred Dutton, and longtime Kennedy friend Rafer Johnson, the 1960 Olympic gold medalist in the decathlon.

In typical Ethel fashion, the doyenne of Hickory Hill arrived like a Hollywood diva with five suitcases, plus her own sheets and pillowcases—Porthault, naturally—with strict instructions that her bedding be laundered separately from the hospital's steerage linens. All that was missing for her arrival was a red carpet. Even her exclusive sixty-dollar-a-day (considered expensive in 1968) private room in the maternity ward had gotten special attention: a new coat of her favorite color, pink, and a bouquet setting of pink and blue flowers. Across the hall, Hennessey-Donovan had her own private room. And there were special duty nurses to attend to Ethel around the clock.

The next morning a cesarean was scheduled, and at eight A.M. she was wheeled into the delivery room, with Ted and Luella Hennessey-Donovan on either side of the stretcher. Shortly before nine, she gave birth to her fourth daughter, eight-pound, four-ounce Rory Elizabeth Katherine Kennedy, a name that had meaning.

Ethel had ruled out the name Roberta in honor of her late husband, the baby's father, but she wanted a name close to the sound of Bobby, so she chose Rory. Elizabeth was in honor of her close friend Elizabeth "Liz" Stevens, wife of the TV producer George Stevens, and Katherine was for her chum Katherine "Kay" Evans, wife of the influential syndicated columnist Roland Evans. They were among a group of trendy, prominent, energetic women who orbited around Ethel, jealously guarding their territory and riding shotgun for her.

Ethel had gone through the birth of her eleventh "like a soldier," Hennessey-Donovan reported. "I thought it would be very upsetting because the baby would never see its father. It was kind of a traumatic few minutes, but then everything was fine."

A week later, six days before Christmas 1968, Ted Kennedy was driving Ethel home to Hickory Hill with her newborn when she suddenly asked him to make a detour: Arlington National Cemetery.

With the infant Rory swaddled all in pink in her mother's arms, they stood quietly over RFK's grave.

FIVE

Practically Naked

Millbrook's teaching staff had been advised at a special faculty meeting called by Headmaster George Buell that Bobby Kennedy Jr. "was coming to town and we were gently told how not to behave with respect to him," remembered Peter Cole, who taught English. Cole got to know Bobby better when the boy joined the Millbrook ski team, which Cole coached. "We were instructed not to go blabbing around to everybody that, 'Oh, we have Bobby Kennedy Jr. on our campus.' 'Be discreet' was the message. And we learned at that meeting that Lem Billings would often be seen on campus with Bobby."

But there was a leak and the press had gotten wind of Bobby's isolated new school in the woods and hills on the edge of the town of Millbrook. They identified it, and pretty soon the school's mailroom was being deluged with letters and gifts for the slain presidential hopeful's namesake. Soon groupies had begun sneaking onto campus in hopes of meeting and romancing a Kennedy scion.

"He would receive boxes and just piles of mail from people he never even knew," recalled classmate Brian Carroll, "and all these ridiculous teenage girls started to show up. I thought it was really horrible, actually, because the guy was a total train wreck."

Before classes formally began, and before Bobby actually arrived on campus, Buell also called a student meeting held in the school's white-steepled, New England village-green-style Flagler Memorial Chapel and announced that the son of the recently slain presidential hopeful would be joining them.

"He gave us a quick background thing just so people would kind of know that this was the son of RFK and he was to be treated like any other classmate," recalled Class of 1972 member Tom Kellogg, who noted that no other student had ever received such a coming attraction. "It wasn't that Bobby or his dad were famous. It's that this was an unusual circumstance, that this was a new student whose dad had just been killed. It wasn't viewed as this is a celebrity kid."

On his arrival at Millbrook, Bobby's first exposure to school tradition was an embarrassing one. He had to stand practically naked in his underwear, forced to participate in an odd custom known as "heights and weights," in which he and other boys had to strip down and pass through a gauntlet of male teachers in the athletic department.

"The first actual physical contact, as it were, that I had with Bobby Kennedy was the first day of school when all of us faculty were assigned to check the new boys' vital statistics for the director of athletics, Fred Knutson, a Latin teacher, who was supposedly keeping track of the kids' growth, or something like that," said James Hejduk, the new music teacher, who thought it all very strange. "I just remember standing there and a bunch of boys in their underwear were passing in front of me, Bobby Kennedy being among them—a skinny and wan little kid. I probably was reading too much into it, but it was soon after his dad's assassination and he looked kind of beat up."

Lem Billings had a close friend at Millbrook, Jack Bower, rumored to be gay or bisexual, who was an assistant headmaster and chairman of the English department, and who was excited to have young Bobby Kennedy as one of the incoming sophomores.

"Knowing Jack, he was impressed with the star power of the Kennedys, the glamour and glitz of Camelot," observed Peter Cole, who taught under Bower. Before becoming a teacher, Bower had worked for Metro-

Goldwyn-Mayer and had often boasted to his students and faculty colleagues about his friendships in Hollywood with such glamorous stars as Elizabeth Taylor. But during his fourteen years at Millbrook there had been suspicions and rumors that Bower, who died in 2002 of a stroke at seventy-seven, had gone beyond acceptable teacher-student behavior.

He was known to have spent "a fair amount of time entertaining boys" at his secluded bachelor's cottage, according to one former Millbrook teacher, and another recalled how a boy who became a close classmate of Bobby's "was kind of taken under the wing" by Bower. "I'm not sure Jack's intentions were fully honorable as far as [the student] was concerned," said the former teacher. "I think Jack probably tried to get him into bed."

Bower knew something about psychology, and how to handle young minds; he had studied with the existential psychologist Rollo May, the author of *Love and Will*, and Bower was said to have written a book called *Dictionary of Pastoral Psychology*. As one of his students noted, "He knew enough about psychology to be kind of twisted about it in some ways, and manipulative." At one point, Bower ran a live-in summer program at Millbrook for boys from New York's City's mean streets, some of whom were gang leaders. While he was popular with some of his regular students, many were "uncomfortable" with him, suspecting he was a sexual predator. Moreover, he was considered a strict disciplinarian who once described himself with Hollywood panache as a "loving heavy."

Like Bower, most of the faculty, especially the younger teachers, seemed "starstruck" that the Kennedy boy was now part of the student body.

"It was a pretty excited faculty and [they] felt the Kennedys were the royal family. I was personally kind of excited about us getting this kid," said Cole, who later became an attorney. "It was pretty amazing to look out the window and see Uncle Teddy Kennedy, who we saw just once on campus, there to visit Bobby, and I got the impression he seemed somehow involved in the boy's care, along with Lem Billings."

In his early days, Bobby also had to undergo another Millbrook tradition: the initiation.

New students were called Bennys with a special day, Benny Day, reserved for them. At night a film was shown in the Barn, Millbrook's main auditorium. But when the movie ended and the lights came up, only the Bennys were left. All the others—Millbrook had a small enrollment of fewer than two hundred—were in wait outside.

"They were lurking in the dark to rough us up on the way back to the dorm," said Nick Forster, who later would get into some trouble with Bobby. "It was pretty barbaric, actually, and pretty frightening."

Martin Lynn, looking back to that time when he was a member of Bobby's class, observed, "There was a lot of *Lord of the Flies* tough stuff—hazing, all that stuff that was a fact of life back then."

Another classmate, Peter Kisting, son of a Broadway stage company manager, remembered the freshman hazing he received—being dunked and held down in a full barrel of apple cider until he felt like he was drowning, and the push-ups he was forced to do whenever accosted by a sadistic, demanding senior, a sixth-former.

But Bobby, Kisting remembered, was "treated with deference. I wouldn't call it overall respect for him, but they had respect for his name. People were careful not to step on his toes. Some of us used to wonder if he would be one of the upcoming presidents from the Kennedys. He had the Kennedy genes."

While Bobby would play football for one season, he didn't make Millbrook's varsity squad as Ethel Kennedy had wished. Instead, he was a scrawny wide receiver on Millbrook's losing third-string team, known as Third Football, described by one classmate as "undersized and generally decimated."

He had two other interests, however: One was working in the school's Trevor Zoo—Millbrook actually had a genuine zoo—as part of the school's required community service program, where he pursued the sport of falconry; his other interest was getting high, an extracurricular activity that would last for years, and one in which Lem Billings eventually actively participated.

At Millbrook, Bobby had started playing a dangerous game with substance abuse, starting with marijuana and psychedelics, and his drug use would only grow worse.

GEORGE BUELL HAD BEEN HEADMASTER of Millbrook since the retirement in 1965 of the school's founder, Edward Pulling, known as "The

Boss," an Englishman who had degrees from Princeton and Cambridge. He had started the school on farmland in Millbrook with twenty-one boys in 1931, and with the gracious assistance of his wife, Lucy Leffingwell Pulling, whose father was a major figure at J. P. Morgan and Company.

Although Buell, a good-looking man, was only in his late thirties when Bobby arrived, he suffered from a serious physical ailment, and an addiction, alcoholism, that he had kept well hidden. Physically, he had painful arthritis and would require several hip replacements, then still a relatively new procedure; the first such surgery would cause him to take a permanent leave of absence from Millbrook near what would be the dramatic end of Bobby's stay at the school; the final surgery would end Buell's life.

Beyond his health issues and drinking problem, Buell had another headache with which to contend: overseeing the education of a very troubled and rebellious Kennedy adolescent, whom Buell would soon learn had a serious addictive personality himself.

Drugs had become part of the scene at Millbrook, and Bobby would become a major player. As he acknowledged some years later: "Soon after my father's death I made a series of choices involving drugs that started me down a road from which I had to struggle to return." It would not be a pleasant situation, especially in that late-sixties era when, as Bob Dylan sang, "The times they are a changin'."

Buell, a father of four, died at fifty-nine in Boston's New England Baptist Hospital, known for orthopedic surgery, shortly before the Thanksgiving holiday in 1989 from postoperative complications involving his third hip replacement. But his widow, who had remarried, clearly recalled many years later that Bobby's matriculation at Millbrook caused much consternation for her husband, who had tried his best to deal with him.

"It was obviously a credit to the school and to us that the Kennedys chose Millbrook, and, of course, we wanted to do everything we could to help Bobby," she asserted in her late seventies, looking back to that time. "We were thrilled to be helping and participating. I had a feeling of great compassion and sadness that this child had to cope with his terrible tragedy.

"Bobby," she remembered, "was very cute, small and thin and kind of wispy, not a strapping boy, and he just prompted feelings of needing care, although he remained very arm's length with people who tried to approach him. I know George could never get him to talk about his experience with his father. I don't think Bobby knew how. So, part of it was really almost how do we handle this, and do it right. We didn't want to mess up, so there was a lot of that, too—our concern about being tactful. I don't know if my husband was walking a tightrope, but the situation with Bobby was very delicate.

"At the same time, there were so many shifts going on in the culture in those days, and marijuana had come to the campus. How do you deal with this? We had never even heard of marijuana before," she continued. "Then the boys started growing their hair long, and what do you do about that? It was all very puzzling and confusing. George had to make some very unpopular decisions."

Those decisions included establishing stern restrictions on student life: no cigarette smoking (not obeyed), mandatory haircuts (not obeyed), and the most major—ejecting boys caught, or even suspected, of dealing or using drugs, which would eventually result in Bobby's downfall at Millbrook.

As Bobby's classmate Mark Bontecou recalled: "Drugs were the flavor of the month, and the masters, some of them left over from my father's day at Millbrook, hadn't a clue. Drugs were pretty readily available. There was a lot of pot, psychedelics like LSD, and there might have been cocaine."

All of them and more would be smoked, snorted, ingested, and injected by Bobby, classmates asserted.

Since most, if not all, of the Millbrook teaching staff had had no experience with marijuana, Buell had come up with a curious way for them to identify its odor and apprehend the miscreant toker. At a faculty meeting, the headmaster passed around what he called "awareness wafers."

"It was during Bobby's first year and my first year at Millbrook, and we were given these things by Buell and told to smell them, which was supposed to give us an acquaintance then with the smell of marijuana should we ever encounter it in the dorms, and so at least we'd know what marijuana smelled like," said James Hejduk, the music teacher. "They looked like large Communion wafers and they had the aroma of marijuana, evidently. I was a conservative straight guy, so even as a musician at Indiana I simply wasn't involved in drugs. I didn't even smoke, for God's sake. That whole drug culture thing was new to me. I was just like clueless."

HEADMASTER BUELL BELIEVED THAT BOBBY should be put together with a proper first roommate, someone who hopefully would look out for him and make sure he didn't get into trouble. The New York City boy Marc Giattini was chosen. He came to Millbrook from the exclusive and private all-boys Allen-Stevenson School, founded in 1883, and located on Manhattan's Upper East Side, a school that required him to wear a preppy uniform of blue blazers and gray flannel pants. Notable alumni had included Michael Douglas, Michael Eisner, Peter Benchley, and James MacArthur—who played Danno Williams on TV's *Hawaii Five-O.*

"I graduated and was bound for Millbrook and sometime over the summer got a letter from the then-headmaster, Buell, who said that given what had happened, they thought I was the best candidate for being Bobby's roommate, and this was literally weeks after the assassination, and the world was falling apart," recalled Giattini, who, like Bobby, came in as a sophomore, known as the fourth form.

"Marc was pretty carefully selected because he was absolutely straight, up front, and smart," Peter Cole observed. "Obviously, Buell didn't want to throw Bobby in with just anybody. Marc, a very streetwise New York kid, but very well mannered, very mature, very smooth and polished, was viewed as a big brother type for Bobby, and Bobby, who was somewhat withdrawn, needed that desperately. His dad was dead. He didn't seem to have a relationship with his brothers and sisters. His mother, who might have been on campus once in her life, was never around.

"You could see it in his clothes and in his posture and his personal grooming habits," Cole noted, looking back to that time.

"He was a rumpled, skinny kid who always gave me the impression that his teeth needed brushing. His hair was a mess. His clothes were generally in need of a bath and so was he. I can picture him with his black tie undone at the throat and half of his shirttail in and half out. That was how he looked ninety percent of his waking hours. This was a pretty lonely kid with a family who, I guessed at the time, were just kind of shoving him aside. I saw Bobby as lost."

The black tie—part of Bobby's bedraggled signature look at Millbrook—was the same one he had worn three months before at his father's funeral. He would wear it in memory every school day, in every class, in the cafeteria, everywhere. Even when it became stained with food and other detritus, he never had it cleaned.

Besides the tie, the small room—two small desks, bunk bed, bookshelves—he shared with Giattini on the second floor in what was known as the Dining Hall Dorm had become a veritable shrine to Bobby's father. The walls were covered with black sheets with framed photographs of his dead father attached to them. Small lights and possibly candles, which were generally banned for safety reasons, lit the space.

"We had a very interesting year together," Giattini recalled. "Bobby was a birder and a falconer and he had this great animal interest. I would go to sleep, and sitting about a foot away from me on a desk chair was Bobby's hooded falcon."

But Giattini lasted with Bobby only through the first academic year. As Peter Cole observed, "Marc had struck me as the ideal guy to be a big brother to Bobby, but it was too big of a job for him. Obviously, Marc was not particularly impressed with the fact that he had a star next to him. And Marc was as grown-up as Bobby was infantile, which may explain why they didn't get together [as roommates] after the first year."

After Giattini, Bobby would have at least two other roommates, underscoring his chaotic time at Millbrook, and his difficulty in getting along with most of his classmates.

By his second academic year, Bobby had seemingly all but given up the shrine to his father, whom he never talked about to anyone during his matriculation.

He was then rooming with another classmate, Jamie Fanning, one of several Millbrook boys with whom he had started getting high. Bobby's room, in the sophomore West Dorm, now had just a few framed photos, and a small bronze bust of his father that he kept on a bookshelf, virtually hidden high above the desk in their small room. On the walls, black-light hippie posters had replaced the funereal black sheets. The small

bust of RFK was believed to be a model of one of two that had been commissioned by Ethel Kennedy in the wake of the assassination.

Against school rules, Bobby also kept a sparrowhawk, about the size
of a pigeon, which flew around loose in the small dorm room.

"Bob always seemed dirty, like personal cleanliness dirty. He was sort
of always grungy, a terrible mess, and he almost was proud of it," said
Fanning, having never forgotten their time together. "The room was
filthy, and Bob let the bird, which perched on the bust, shit all over the
place, including all down that bust of his dead father. I thought, anything
goes with this guy. Bobby was Machiavellian. He was kind of sinister.
You didn't want to get too close to him."

—————

SIX

"Rumpled Kid"

In Bobby Kennedy Jr.'s co-authored book, *The Riverkeepers*, he told the story of how he and an environmentalist colleague, John Cronin, had battled "powerful corporate and governmental polluters" in order to clean up the Hudson River.

Rarely autobiographical in his various public writings over the years, Bobby included an atypical, eponymous chapter about his claimed happy childhood, about his early interest in insects and animals, about his mother's family, the Skakels—and he painted a glowing picture of his boarding school time at Millbrook.

His selective memory, however, was far different from the reality.

Written off and glossed over in just five paragraphs in the book's 304 pages was his abbreviated, very troubled and turbulent matriculation. There was nothing about his often-bizarre behavior, or his drug use and other misdeeds. He left readers with the false impression that he went from Millbrook and, as he wrote, "followed my father's path through Harvard and the University of Virginia Law School."

Bill Adler, whose *The Kennedy Children: Triumphs and Tragedies* was published in 1980, clearly but erroneously stated: "He graduated from

Millbrook School in 1972, and applied to Harvard for undergraduate work." In 2013, Millbrook School's profile in Wikipedia stated that Bobby was among the school's "active alumni body." Among the included "notables" was "Robert F. Kennedy, Jr. 1972—Environmental law attorney."

The fact is, Bobby did not graduate from Millbrook in 1972 or any other year. He actually was expelled, and was forced to go to two other boarding schools where he was considered a problem student before he finally was able to get a high school diploma.

In *The Riverkeepers*, he mentioned nothing about the fact that his mother wanted to be rid of him following his father's assassination, and he made only one brief mention of the role that Lem Billings played in his life at the time.

However, he wrote that Millbrook's "chief attractions" for him were the school's zoo and its natural history and ornithology programs. And he mentioned that he had joined the "informal falconry program."

Bobby painted an idealized portrait of his life at Millbrook and his pursuit of his falconry hobby. "In the autumn we captured and trained kestrels, red-tails and immature 'passage' hawks on their first migration. . . . I've caught upwards of fifty hawks a day," he boasted, "squatting atop a ridge line on Schunemunk Mountain in the Hudson Valley in autumn. . . . We flew wild red-tails, falcons, and goshawks and pioneered many of the game-hawking techniques still used by American falconers. . . . We talked about hawks every spare moment, at meals, between classes, and after chapel. . . . At Millbrook I learned taxidermy and basic veterinary skills. . . ."

He made his time at Millbrook sound so pastoral and humane. But those who knew him well back then, such as Richard O. "Rob" Bierregaard Jr., a veteran falconer and expert on birds of prey, saw an entirely different persona.

Bierregaard, who was a couple of years ahead of Bobby at Millbrook, was one of a small group who spent much time at the school's Trevor Zoo as part of the school's required community service. For Bierregaard, who loved the outdoors and always wanted to be a scientist, that involved caring for a barred owl, a chinchilla, and a skunk, and later "Empress," a golden eagle, then the zoo's premier animal.

Millbrook's motto was *Non Sibi Sed Cunctis*, Latin for "Not for one's self, but for all." Everyone had to participate in required community service, whether it be working in the school post office, washing dishes, performing grounds maintenance, or handling the zoo's inhabitants.

Bobby had chosen the latter, but the way he described his falcon and birding interest in his book was not the way Bierregaard, who later went on to teach ornithology at the University of North Carolina, remembered.

To Bierregaard, who was one of the leaders of the falconry group at Millbrook, Bobby's pursuit of the sport was more like a scene out of a horror movie.

"Myself and a couple of others had our hawks and we'd go out in the countryside hunting rabbits and squirrels," Bierregaard said, looking back years later. "But one of the reasons why I didn't spend much time with Bobby was his idea of falconry. Next to the school there was a cow pit where the local dairy farmers threw their dead cows, and it was full of rats. Bobby would take his hawk and go hunting rats in the midst of the rotting cow carcasses—and he sort of reveled in how off-the-wall that was.

"It was disgusting and it wasn't my idea of having a good, healthy time with my hawks, so I let him do his falconry in the dead cow pit, and I went and chased rabbits in the woods," continued Bierregaard, still revolted years later by the memory. "It's pretty sick hunting rats in the midst of rotting cow carcasses. It was a turnoff and it was gross. Bobby and I were together at the zoo flying hawks, but I really didn't want to interact with him. There wasn't great chemistry. He was wild, that was obvious."

Another classmate of Bobby's and a falconer, Sumner Pingree III, was aware of what he termed "Bobby's rat scene up at Bel Aire Farm" and, like Bierregaard, thought it was sickening. "It was contrary to the situation that we otherwise engaged in with our birds, which was simply walking in the woods and catching squirrels and occasional rabbits and so forth. What Bobby was doing wasn't the bird hunting in its natural habitat, per se."

Jamie Fanning, son of a conservative Republican thoroughbred horse trainer "who didn't think much of the Kennedys," roomed with Bobby his last academic year at Millbrook, and did a variety of drugs with him. Fanning had accompanied Bobby to the fetid, foul-smelling pit located on Bel Aire Farm—dubbed "Smell Air" by Millbrook faculty and students because of the revolting odors that occasionally wafted over to the school.

Fanning, a self-described wild child at the time, recalled Bobby's visits to the pit, which he had witnessed, as "grotesque."

"I still to this day see him standing there in his black necktie that he wore every day over a blue oxford Brooks Brothers shirt and a beat-up tweed jacket, and wearing the wildest bell-bottoms that were purple with Day-Glo green stripes like he was some soul band guy, and in his funky boots—and there he was hunting rats out of that pile of dead sheep and cow carcasses.

"Bobby was an edgy, *edgy* guy. I know he had all that baggage with his father, but being in that pit—that was the kind of thing he would do. He almost did things to shock you on purpose. He was such an edgy kid that that thing, as bizarre as it was to be over there hunting these rats out of this pile of dead carcasses, was almost normal for him. It was a pretty dark, grim time; he was miserable and he was angry. It only got worse with the drugs."

Many years later Wayne Hall, a journalist friend of Bobby's, heard about the rat-pit story and asserted, "That's kind of a template for Bobby's life. Here he is a rich kid who could just go out with the rest of the falconers and do the normal thing. But Bobby's a rebel and instead he's out there in the middle of the rats trying to knock off bad things."

One of Bobby's Millbrook classmates was Ned Rousmaniere (pronounced roo-man-EER), whose father had a long and storied history with the Kennedy family: James Ayer "Jimmy" Rousmaniere was John F. Kennedy's roommate at Harvard, and as such was as much a Kennedy insider as Lem Billings, only Rousmaniere was heterosexual; his son Ned was one of eight children, seven boys and a girl. And the senior Rousmaniere thought little of Billings, whom he considered "just a clown" who never really matured. As for his close pal Kennedy, he was a "fun-loving, girl-crazed fool."

Ned Rousmaniere became a psychotherapist and had a take on what he termed Bobby's "morbid interest enjoying watching his hawk go after rats." Noting that Bobby's pursuit was "during the hippie time when love was in the air"—1968–69—"his displaying a morbid interest in seeing a hawk go after rats was countercultural."

Further, he suspected that Bobby had such a morbid interest long before his father died, and that the cow-pit bizarreness was unrelated,
as one might have assumed, to a twisted emotional response to the
assassination. As Rousmaniere observed, "Bobby was a kid from my
understanding who was pretty unregulated, pretty unsupervised. There
are a lot of kids who do that kind of thing whose dads are alive, who don't
go through a tragedy."

There was a major side benefit of being a member of what some called
the "rogue" falconry group. They were permitted to wander around in the
woods without teacher supervision, which allowed those like Bobby to
light up a doobie and not get caught. As Pingree, who acknowledged
smoking "the occasional joint," noted, "Anybody else wandering around
in the woods was immediately suspect. But we were walking around in
the woods with these birds, and even the birds sometimes were high,
literally and figuratively."

At one point, Bobby, possibly stoned, lost one of the birds in his care,
and a massive search was started. As a member of the falconry group
pointed out decades later, "If you were conscientious and you were
thoughtful and you took the rules of the road seriously, the chances of
losing a bird were relatively minimal. But Bobby was reckless."

When some injuries were discovered at the school's Trevor Zoo,
Bobby came under suspicion, despite the fact that he was known to
love the wildlife in his care. "It kind of followed him around," said the
music teacher James Hejduk. "There were some injuries to some of the
animals, to some birds, and some people had fingered Bobby on that—
that perhaps he had a hand in actually abusing animals. Everything in
those days got to the headmaster, Buell, because it was such a small
community. But I don't think anything ever came of it."

NOT LONG AFTER BOBBY ARRIVED at Millbrook, he brought with him
his newest pet, a lion cub named Mtoto Mbaya (meaning "Bad Boy" in
Swahili), to be housed and cared for in the Trevor Zoo. But Toto's Millbrook stay, like his owner's, didn't last as long as had been expected, especially after the fast-growing little fellow growled, then attacked and

took a bite out of the backside of the newly appointed science department chairman and zookeeper, Seward Trainer Highley.

Toto's playful attack on Highley—luckily, his bite wasn't major—was not unexpected, as he grew older and bigger by the day. "When Toto was just a little kitten, we'd go out in the fields and take him chipmunk hunting on occasion, but he never caught any chipmunks. As he got bigger, he became more difficult," Peter Cole recalled. "If you walked into the zoo, Toto would charge down the lane and land on your chest and you'd end up on your back with a big tongue in your face."

Toto was thought to have had a famous pedigree of sorts. He was first believed to have been one of three cubs from a litter born to Elsa, the lioness star of the 1966 British drama *Born Free*. The popular film was based on the true story of Joy and George Adamson, a game warden, who had raised Elsa, an orphan cub, to adulthood, eventually releasing her into the Kenyan wilds.

The playful and powerful ten-week-old Toto, still unweaned, had been a gift to Bobby from the close Kennedy family friend Jack Paar, a popular late-night TV talk show host, who had brought Toto and two other cubs back from Africa the previous summer. Paar, who was fascinated by lions, also gave one to his daughter, Randy, a student at Radcliffe College, and he kept the third in his suburban New York City home in preparation for an hour-long fall 1969 TV special *Jack Paar and His Lions*. When he procured the three cubs, he had the mistaken impression that they were from the famed Elsa's brood, an error that he acknowledged on the program.

Along with Lem Billings, Paar was one of Bobby's most frequent adult visitors at Millbrook, showing concern for the boy's well-being and also looking in to see how Toto was doing. A liberal Democrat who supported both Jack's and RFK's presidential runs, Paar also had close social ties to the Kennedys. Paar, his wife, Miriam, and Randy often were dinner guests of RFK and Ethel, and Paar would lecture his daughter on her table manners before arriving at Hickory Hill. At the table she once turned to RFK, when he was running the Justice Department, and said, "Mr. Attorney General, would you like one of my shrimp?" It was a story Paar liked to tell.

Paar's allegiance to the Kennedys was generously reciprocated in

March 1964, four months after JFK's assassination, when RFK was a guest on Paar's popular program—his first public appearance since the tragedy in Dallas. The heavily promoted, exclusive interview got huge ratings for Paar and mesmerized viewers across the country still traumatized by the assassination.

RFK, appearing at peace after mourning his brother, garnered a few laughs and much applause from the respectful studio audience. He revealed that his just-widowed sister-in-law, Jackie, was doing "fine, making an adjustment, and doing it well," that his brother Ted and family friend Dave Powers were spending time with little John Jr. and his sister, Caroline, "so they could see some men" in their saddened lives, and he declared that his late brother's major achievement as president was, in part, making "Americans feel young again."

Meanwhile, at Millbrook, Bobby was viewed by some fellow students as egotistical and irresponsible for strutting around the campus and on the sidelines at home football games with a potentially dangerous young lion on a leash.

Rob Bierregaard, one of the respected student leaders at the Trevor Zoo, recalls being particularly incensed at Bobby. "He used to walk the lion, which was of reasonable size, through the zoo complex, and all of a sudden it saw a deer and decided it wanted to go after it and started dragging Bobby on the leash. Somehow he avoided it catching the deer. The way he was handling the lion was dumb, and it seemed a bit arrogant. When the lion started trying to catch and eat other animals in the zoo the school decided that maybe it wasn't a good fit."

By late 1968, the end of Bobby's first semester, it was decided by Headmaster Buell and the still smarting zookeeper, Seward Highley, that seven-month-old Toto had become too big, weighing in at close to 130 pounds, and too dangerous. He had to go. His new home? Lion Country Safari in West Palm Beach, Florida. Randy Paar's cub and the one her father had been keeping at his home—he had named it Jack—had also been sent there.

In January 1969, Paar was filming his TV special on lions at Lion Country when Jack attacked, knocked Paar off his feet, and bit him on the right wrist, puncturing his skin. Several game wardens had to pull him off.

SEVEN

Breaking Bad

At fourteen and fifteen, Bobby Kennedy Jr., at Millbrook School, was proving his bad-boy bona fides with Jesse Pinkman zeal. While he didn't have a chemistry teacher like Walter White, aka "Heisenberg" of TV's *Breaking Bad*, the Camelot scion was doing everything he could to get high on whatever drugs he could get his hands on.

On one occasion, when Bobby was visiting the dorm room of a classmate, Nick Forster, with whom he played on the school's third-string football team, Forster happened to spot a pill of unknown origin on the floor near the radiator. It wasn't his, he claimed years later, and he thought it might have belonged to his roommate, or a former occupant.

"It was a fairly healthy-size pill with an omega symbol on it," he recalled, "and I showed it to Bobby and he's like, 'Oh, great!' He looked at it for a second, didn't know what it was, but popped it in his mouth and swallowed. Not that he was cavalier, but I think his goal was just to sort of get stoned at any cost, or to let me know that he was a little reckless. In my experience, he was interested in acting out for shock value."

Bobby's pill-popping, however, was no surprise to his roommate, Jamie Fanning.

"We'd have these conversations in our room at night, lying there before we'd fall asleep [Bobby on the top bunk, Fanning on the lower], and he told me that when you go to somebody's house 'always ask to use the bathroom and check in their medicine cabinet because they always have good pills that you can steal.'

"I thought, that's the kind of shit heavy drug users pull. But for this kid to say that to me at that time was pretty deep and dark. But that's the kind of kid he was, deep into bad stuff. I had smoked some pot for the first time with some older guys in June of my freshman year before I knew Bobby. It was so new to me. I was president of my freshman class, I was kind of a leader, and then I went astray.

"But Bobby was like somebody who had been around this stuff, and experienced it at too early an age. I turned sixteen that fall that he was my roommate, and he'd had all this shit going on in his life, and I thought, What the hell? We were just children. But he'd do anything to get high."

Fanning had concluded much later that Bobby back then was getting deeper into drugs because "he was really furious, really frustrated, and totally sad about his dad, but didn't talk about it. He was alone. His mom never came; there was no sign of her. His uncle Teddy came once in his limousine, and that was it."

His only interests were falconry, getting stoned, and his involvement with, and acting as ringleader of, a summertime gang known as the Hyannis Port Terrors, whose nefarious activities had started in the summer of 1967, a full year before his father's murder.

"Bobby said the Hyannis Port Terrors were the coolest thing ever, and he boasted about how they ran around and stole alcohol and did whatever they wanted to do," recalled Fanning.

The HPTs consisted mainly of Bobby, his troubled younger brother David, who would later die of a drug overdose, and two cousins. They were Bobby Shriver, one of the five children of Eunice Kennedy Shriver, the fifth of Rose Kennedy's brood of nine, and Christopher Kennedy Lawford, who also became ravaged by drugs, prior to finally getting clean. He was one of the four children of the hard-drinking, drug-abusing, and philandering British actor Peter Lawford and Patricia Kennedy Lawford, also an alcoholic, the sixth of Rose Kennedy's children.

Years later, Chris Lawford, after much therapy and drug rehab, diplomatically described the HPTs as "our pathetic homage to gang activity. Our purpose was to do some mischief and make a public statement demonstrating our incorrigibility brought on by raging hormones and a surge in testosterone."

Led by Bobby, their rampage that first summer was relatively innocent. They threw firecrackers at passing cars; untied docked boats; filled bags with dog feces, set them on fire, and left the messes on the porches of Hyannis Port residents. Another stunt was a bit more serious—shoving a potato in the muffler of a police car, causing it to backfire. The local cops rounded up the offenders, and showed up at RFK and Ethel Kennedy's house to report the incident. The gang members, expecting extreme punishment, instead heard "a roar of laughter led by Uncle Bobby," Lawford recalled in his memoir, aptly entitled *Symptoms of Withdrawal*.

By the summer of 1969, following Bobby's first troubled year at Millbrook, the HPTs' sophomoric stunts grew darker and more frightening, most if not all of them the brainchild of RFK's namesake, who, like some teenage terrorist, wore all black and often had a vicious-looking predatory falcon on his gloved hand.

One of the strangest escapades carried out by the HPTs involved a sick play on the many past Kennedy tragedies, the most recent being the assassination of RFK just a year earlier. Young Bobby would order one of his cohorts to hit the fender of a passing car, and when the driver braked in a panic, another of the gang fell near the front wheels, pretending to be dead. That was the signal for Bobby to scream, "You've killed a Kennedy! You've killed a Kennedy!"

As frightened pedestrians and motorists gathered, the HPT on the ground would jump up and jauntily walk away, with Bobby laughing maniacally. The motorist, who probably almost had a heart attack, and the shocked bystanders naturally were furious at the sick game.

But Bobby's only response when someone advised him to stop upsetting and antagonizing the townspeople of Hyannis Port was "Fuck them!"

When a local policeman nabbed Bobby Shriver for one of their twisted exploits, Bobby Jr. arrogantly took charge of the situation. He confronted the cop, hiding his hawk inside his jacket. When the officer demanded to know what he was concealing, fearing a weapon of some sort, Bobby responded, "I have a hawk and he's trained to kill cops." He then shoved its beak in the cop's face. Stunned, the officer jumped back, his hand on his Smith & Wesson, but luckily restrained himself, thus avoiding another real Kennedy tragedy by gunfire.

Taking drugs also was part of the gang's life, which included smoking marijuana, ingesting the psychedelic drugs LSD and mescaline, and popping amphetamines.

At Millbrook, Bobby arrogantly bragged about his stunts. His chum Jamie Fanning listened and thought it all sounded so cool, but much later came to the conclusion, "Bobby was self-destructive. I really think he was suicidal. He wasn't sure he wanted to be alive or not. He was pissed off at the world, but kept it bottled up."

BOBBY HAD READ IN *The Village Voice*, one of the country's first alternative weekly newspapers, which in the 1960s reported extensively on the beatnik and hippie scenes, that one could get high ingesting morning glory seeds, of all things. He immediately proposed the idea to Fanning and they got their hands on some, soaked them in water overnight to get rid of the poison that was usually sprayed on them to kill rodents, and the next morning blithely swallowed them. "I don't remember that we went on any great trips," recalled Fanning. "We only felt sick."

Bobby came up with another idea that he proposed to Fanning and a few others as a way to get "a rush," as he called it: hyperventilating, which was similar to autoerotic asphyxiation but without the sex.

But Bobby's version could be just as dangerous, as Fanning would soon learn.

Their classmate Peter Kisting, who sacrificed his gerbils and hamsters as a lure to help get Bobby's falcon down from trees, witnessed him hanging over the side of his bed with his head on the floor "until all the blood rushed to his brain, and then he would quickly sit up. He told me he got the feeling of being high. Some of us thought it was funny, but apparently it worked for him."

Remembering back to that time, Kisting believed Bobby used drugs, and boasted of his use of drugs, as a way to ingratiate himself with some of the other students who were either wary of him and kept their distance or thought he was snobbish. "I would say to Bobby, 'Do you have any pot?' And he would say, 'Yes, but not much because I have to divide it up for others' and he would give me something," Kisting said. "He made little baggies, and he would be one to give it away, not sell it."

However, other students, such as Tom Kellogg, who played soccer and ran track and didn't partake of drugs, viewed Bobby as haughty and superior. "I didn't find him to be pleasant," he recalled. "He ignored most of us. He wouldn't say hi, or strike up a conversation."

Their classmate Brian Carroll thought the same: "You could look Bobby in the eye and unless you were really, really close to him, you meant nothing to him. He'd just look right through you. My impression as a kid was that he was a severely wounded young person. My lasting memory is of Bobby with a gray broken or damaged tooth, dirty bell-bottoms, and a thick leather falconer's glove ready to head for the woods."

The music teacher James Hejduk had a problem back then characterizing Bobby as standoffish, but felt that he just "didn't try to draw attention to himself. There wasn't any of that 'I'm Bobby Kennedy.' I think it was the hangers-on that brought more attention to him, like Lem Billings, unwanted or wanted."

At one point, Bobby was standing in a school line, ignoring everyone around him, when an upperclassman angrily confronted him about his aloofness and in the course of the verbal attack invoked the name of his father's assassin. Bobby's friend Nick Forster was standing nearby when it happened. "I was horrified," he recalled. "This guy was saying, 'Fuck off, shape up, stop being such a pussy. Do you think we're all Sirhan Sirhan?' But Bobby respected and was drawn to that kid as a result of that criticism. It was something like, okay, here's a guy who's holding me to task and sort of calling [me on] my bullshit, and is not afraid to mention the unmentionable. Bobby seemed actually appreciative."

With Fanning, Bobby's other method of getting turned on by hyperventilating required a bit of a team effort. One was to breathe quickly and strenuously in and out and then hold his breath while the second squeezed his chest until he passed out. "I did black out," said Fanning, "but it wasn't like any kind of turn-on thing. It was more like—oh, cool, I fainted."

But for Fanning it was more serious. As he passed out, he hit and cut his head on the edge of the metal frame of the bunk bed in their dorm room. With a big, bloody, scary lump, Fanning had to be rushed by Bobby to the infirmary for emergency first aid.

The nurse's office was the last place any of the boys wanted to go, because the aged, silver-haired nurse in charge began any examination—whether it be for a sore throat or a stomachache—by having students drop their pants and cough while she held their testicles. The speculation was that she was either getting a thrill or, more likely, dissuading malingerers from coming to her office.

When Bobby and Fanning arrived, his head bleeding, she demanded to know how it happened. "We were really good liars," said Fanning. Bobby convincingly explained that his roommate had slipped on their dorm room's newly waxed linoleum tile floor; no further questions were asked, no trousers were dropped, and Fanning was given first aid.

With his HPT partners in crime, Bobby had been doing mescaline, which sent him on a ten-to-twelve-hour trip. A component of the cactus peyote, mescaline is one of the world's oldest psychedelics. A girl from another prep school had sent some in the form of what resembled a "big brown pill" to Fanning with a warning: "Don't do it by yourself. Share it with somebody."

Knowing that Bobby was one of the few people at Millbrook who did psychedelics such as LSD and mescaline, Fanning showed it to him and asked if he wanted to try it. Bobby's enthusiastic response was "Yeah, yeah, yeah! Let's do it Saturday night!"

That Saturday afternoon, Fanning played football, an away game, on Millbrook's varsity team. When he got back to his room, rather than wait for Bobby, he split the pill in half and "impatiently" took it. "Half an hour later," Fanning recalls, "I wasn't feeling anything, so I ate the other half. Then Bobby shows up and says, 'You still got that mesc?' I told him I didn't feel anything so I ate the whole thing. He goes, 'You asshole!'"

When the drug kicked in, Bobby was at his side to talk Fanning through his "crazy" first psychedelic experience. In the evening, Bobby escorted Fanning to the Saturday-night weekly movie shown on campus.

"People told me to shut up because I was being inappropriately loud, acting like a fool. I was up all night, but Bobby did a good job in keeping me in rein and not letting me make a total fool of myself. I had a good trip, if you could call it such a thing."

Psychedelic drugs were as readily available on the Millbrook School campus as candy bars were in the school's Milk Bar. Since the mid-sixties, the town of Millbrook, a weekend getaway for a number of wealthy New Yorkers, had been the world headquarters of the high priest of the psychedelic movement, Dr. Timothy Leary. Near the school was the former Harvard professor's rented estate, which he called the Castalia Institute, part of his League of Spiritual Discovery, its acronym LSD. Leary's legendary slogan was "Turn On. Tune In. Drop Out."

President Nixon had called Leary "the most dangerous man in America," and the illustrious Millbrook graduate William Buckley, in a *Times* essay, had noted, "Timothy Leary ran a kind of anti–Millbrook School for drug users."

The headmaster of Millbrook had warned students to stay away from Leary's place or face expulsion.

Along with the drugs, there was lots of free love on the grounds of Leary's Xanadu, attracting liberated young women and stoners of all sorts. Leary's place and the wild goings-on in the placid village caught the attention of the national newsmedia. For example, a lengthy piece in *The New York Times*, in a column entitled "The Talk of Millbrook," was headlined "Leary Drug Cult Stirs Millbrook. Uneasy Village Fears Influx of Addicts."

Local authorities were keeping a close watch on Leary's operation, and school officials believed that one in particular, the former FBI agent G. Gordon Liddy, assistant district attorney in Dutchess County, which encompassed Millbrook, was determined to nail him. When Bobby arrived at Millbrook School in 1968, Leary had just published a collection of his speeches, essays, and interviews entitled *The Politics of Ecstasy.*

It was believed by a number of Millbrook School faculty members that the conservative, Kennedy-hating prosecutor might target Bobby along with Leary.

"On the faculty, we believed that G. Gordon had a hair up his ass for Bobby and was going to bust him, and that could have been something

George Buell brought up in a faculty meeting," recalled Peter Cole. "A few of the members of the faculty that I was close to and I considered that threat to be something fairly serious. Our thought was, if you're a Republican politician and wanting to make a name for yourself, what better arrest could you make than a Kennedy."

Liddy later gained infamy as one of President Nixon's clandestine operatives who oversaw the 1972 break-in of the Democratic National Headquarters in the Watergate office building—the beginning of Nixon's fall from power.

While Bobby was never busted for drugs by law enforcement authorities while at Millbrook, that would happen later, for marijuana and still later for heroin. But Liddy did orchestrate a raid on Leary's estate. In his 1996 autobiography, *Will*, Liddy noted: "Local boys and girls had been seen entering and leaving the estate. Fleeting glimpses were reported of persons strolling the grounds in the nude. To fears of drug-induced dementia were added pot-induced pregnancy. The word was that at Leary's lair the panties were dropping as fast as the acid."

More than four decades after Bobby left Millbrook, he still clearly had it in for Liddy. In a 2013 *Huffington Post* blog post entitled "Obama and Nixon: A Historical Perspective," he called Liddy "a murderous former Dutchess County, New York, prosecutor and Adolf Hitler admirer."

He also wrote that Liddy was part of a group that had allegedly once planned to murder the Nixon critic Jack Anderson, a syndicated columnist. Citing a biography of Anderson, Bobby wrote that the means of death was to involve the use of a "massive dose of LSD," ironically one of Bobby's own favorite psychedelics along with mescaline back in the day.

EIGHT

Millbrook Triumvirate

In his second year at Millbrook, Bobby began boasting that he was doing certain drugs intravenously—shooting up, like any street junkie. One of those he told was his roommate Jamie Fanning. "I can't say that I saw him put a needle in his arm," he stated, "but he talked like he was and he bragged about it. He'd say, 'When you're shooting speed it's such a good rush.' It was that kind of talk, more bragging, but I believed him. I'd known him then for a few months and knew he'd do anything. It was pretty clear he had some intravenous drug use back then, and he was the only person we knew who did."

Cocaine rumors flew, too. There was campus talk that Bobby had reported to the nurse's office with a bloody nose, which sparked whispers that he had suffered some sort of drug-related nose injury. "From what I heard, Bobby had been taking a fair amount of cocaine and had a deviated septum [of the area separating the nostrils, sometimes caused by snorting cocaine] or something like that. It was the first time I had ever heard the term 'deviated septum' used and it related to Bobby and cocaine," recalled Bruce Whitcomb, a talented music student whose father headed the European advertising department for Time-Life and whose stepfather, a TV executive, gave local stations the green light to air *I Love Lucy.*

By the time the talk of cocaine and intravenous substances was in the air, there was campus chatter that Bobby Kennedy had become part of a Millbrook School "triumvirate" suspected by some classmates of leaving campus and sneaking into New York City to score methamphetamine and even heroin. But, recalled a classmate, "Bobby was fairly closed-mouthed about what he was doing there."

Bobby's confederates were Michael Parkinson, a promising artist from a well-to-do, politically connected Manhattan family, and a Philadelphia boy, Michael Amory Rivinus, who sported the longest hair in Bobby's class, and whose father was a corporate drug executive.

Parkinson—described as "pretty crazy, artistic, hippie, and rich" by Jamie Fanning—was one of Bobby's close bonds formed in what would be the first of his troubled, barely two academic years at Millbrook, during which he was required, it was said, to repeat his sophomore year because of poor grades and unacceptable behavior.

Like Bobby, Parkinson was skinny, glib, and frenetic. Both were increasingly reckless, had hyperactive and addictive personalities, and their friendship would endure into their dark adult years, a curious alliance that was tragically bound by drugs.

Moreover, Parkinson had the beginnings of a debilitating mental illness that was still undiscovered, or well hidden, when he was at Millbrook.

"Bobby and Michael became very close," says Peter Parkinson, the youngest of the Parkinson siblings, who idolized his older brother. "They were both interested in animals. Bobby had his falcon and Michael had wooly monkeys at home and at school.

"Bobby and my brother had a lot of camaraderie. Their bond was their pets, their intelligence, and their charisma, and Michael was a very, very talented artist, and Bobby liked art." During their time at Millbrook, Parkinson, who did striking caricatures of faculty and students for the Tamarack yearbook, had done a portrait of Bobby.

But Bobby and Parkinson also shared an interest in drugs, which Peter Parkinson noted was "not the highlight" of their friendship.

Parkinson, his brother said, became a close family friend to the

Kennedys and got to know Bobby's uncle Teddy and his aunt Jackie. Bobby's mother, Ethel, adored him.

BECAUSE OF MICHAEL'S CLOSE KENNEDY ties, his brother, Peter, was enlisted by Ethel to work at the Kennedy compound in Hyannis Port to help with some of the youngest of her eleven children. Parkinson was one of many young people who had usually worked for free and often were treated rudely and shabbily by Bobby's mom.

Over the years many such helpers had witnessed her bad behavior. Noelle Fell, one of a long string of secretaries who had gotten fed up and left because of Mrs. Kennedy's mistreatment, recalled how the mistress of Hickory Hill once slapped a foreign maid because she misunderstood an order. The woman ran out of the room crying, and when Fell attempted to calm her, she said, "I'm never going to work here again . . . no one has ever slapped me."

According to Bobby's classmate and friend Scott Riviere, the incident was typical of Ethel's bizarre behavior. He was among the very few at Millbrook whom Bobby had invited home to Hickory Hill, known to those harshly treated by the RFK matriarch as "Horror Hill."

Riviere had platinum Washington political and society credentials—his mother, Marilynn Himes Riviere, daughter of a onetime Republican U.S. congressman, had become a close friend of Jacqueline Lee Bouvier's when she first arrived in Washington.

While Bobby hadn't known Riviere before they met at Millbrook, his mother—a noted equestrian and one of America's first female helicopter pilots—and his stockbroker father had socialized at Washington parties with RFK and Ethel. "When they saw them at parties," Riviere recalled, "my father said they drove him crazy, particularly RFK, because he said all he did was sit and talk about himself, and my father thought they were *complete* bores."

The Kennedy family scenes Riviere said he witnessed during his visits with Bobby to Hickory Hill when they both were at Millbrook were still deeply disturbing to him many years later.

"Bobby then was very mixed up," Riviere observed. "He'd been through a lot with his father's death, and his mother wasn't easy. She was pretty tough, so he was in a really tough spot. Bobby never seemed to completely relax. It was as if he had attention deficit disorder. He had this nervous energy. He was just a very lost, damaged person at a time when we were all figuring out who we were and what we were about."

There were times at Hickory Hill when Riviere couldn't believe what was going on. As he later asserted, "Ethel Kennedy was not the image America had of her."

He had been helping Bobby build a hawk house in the Hickory Hill stables, he recalled. "There were some really bad Ethel scenes. Bobby had that hyperactivity and Ethel had that, too, and she couldn't control him and that drove her crazy. She would make these threats that she was going to take all his birds away from him and close down his project. Bobby was really angry at her, and my role was to try to keep things as balanced as possible."

One mother-son battle occurred just before a reporter and photographer from a major magazine—it might have been *Life*—were coming to do a feature on the late RFK's family's post-assassination life at Hickory Hill.

"There was no way Bobby was going to sit still for it," Riviere said, "and she was making all kinds of threats, and she was yelling at *all* her kids, and saying she didn't want any of them around her, but then the people from the magazine arrived and all of a sudden it was all sweetness and light."

Some of the saddest scenes Riviere said he witnessed at Hickory Hill involved several of Bobby's youngest siblings—Courtney, Max, and Rory, the girl born after the assassination.

"Rory was just a baby and Ethel had a volunteer taking care of her, and little Courtney and Max were like two lost children," he noted. "They would just follow me around all the time because they wanted attention from anyone, and they were just so sweet.

"It just killed me to go over there. I wanted to do something for them. The kids were just like a lot of abandoned souls wandering around—all those kids were so damaged. I saw the dysfunction at Hickory Hill and whenever I was there I just felt an overwhelming sense of sadness because there was just no one there with the kids. It was not anything like what the outside world thought. It was like everybody on the inside knew what was going on, but it wasn't public. When I was there I saw Bobby's family environment and how disconnected everything was—just completely disconnected.

"There was dog poop all over the house, and the volunteers were running around frantically, and everybody jumped when Ethel said jump, and everybody was nervous and afraid, including the kids. And then if somebody walked in whom Ethel thought was important she'd put on a big show.

"Ethel had volunteers doing *everything*, and she didn't want to have anything to do with any of her kids. It was hard watching that.

"My time spent at Hickory Hill—all that did was give me insight and more compassion for Bobby."

One school of thought was that it had all been different when RFK was alive and had control of the home situation. But Riviere was aware from his friend Bobby and others connected to the iconic Hickory Hill family that RFK was "never home," or rarely. His life revolved around his career as attorney general, as a senator, as a presidential candidate— and as a womanizer. As Riviere noted, "Ethel was still on her own when RFK was alive. They never saw him."

In October 2012, HBO aired an hour-long documentary called *Ethel*, which was filmed and directed by RFK and Ethel's last-born, Rory Elizabeth Katherine Kennedy, married and the mother of three. It painted a loving portrait of "Mummy," as some of her surviving children, among them Bobby, called their mother. Filmed in 2011 at the compound in Hyannis Port when Ethel Skakel Kennedy was eighty-four, it featured Bobby speaking lovingly of the happy marriage his parents had, and viewers were shown cute home movies that focused on Mrs. Kennedy's fun side. But none of the unpleasant reality as witnessed by Scott Riviere and many others who had spent time at Hickory Hill was depicted.

The TV critic for *The New York Times*, Alessandra Stanley, who reviewed the film under the headline "Cheerfulness Amid Calamity," seemed to have a sense of what really went on at Hickory Hill. She described *Ethel* as "maddeningly incomplete. Watching it," she observed, "is a little like reading a classified report redacted by Dick Cheney—so much material is blacked out that it's almost impossible to follow."

The film, for instance, showed Mrs. Kennedy at RFK's side at political events—"her husband's indefatigable helpmate . . . often with several children in tow . . . There is," noted Stanley, "obviously a talent for compartmentalizing in this family, which may explain how the children of Robert Kennedy can talk blithely of periods that are imprinted in the public memory as times of calamity and also disgrace."

When Scott Riviere heard about the film, he made certain to watch it because, he said, "I was curious about Ethel." His view? "It was well staged—here we all are, just one big *happy* family."

After the assassination, Ethel was under pressure from the Kennedy family, particularly her brother-in-law Steve Smith, the clan's icy, Machiavellian controller of the exchequer, to cut back on her wild spending and downgrade her lifestyle, so she began shopping for clothing, wearing the articles, and then returning them.

On one of his visits to Hickory Hill, Riviere heard angry complaints from the unpaid volunteers who were forced to participate in Mrs. Kennedy's shop-return scheme, and he once was even drafted to participate.

"She would send people who worked for her to McLean to pick up a dress for her for trial to buy and then she'd wear it to a party and then she'd return it. The shop owners would just get crazy, and didn't want to have anything to do with her. I was the new person, the kid, and one of her volunteers hands me a dress and tells me to take it in and return it to the dress shop because none of the others were going to go through that humiliation again, and then, of course, I got humiliated. The first time I was at Hickory Hill, her help couldn't wait to hand me a dress and tell me where to return it. She treated the volunteers terribly.

"If you came to Hickory Hill, it didn't matter if you were Andy Williams [to whom Ethel had been romantically linked back then] or if you were me, a teenager—when you walked into the house she put you to work."

The shops in McLean, Virginia, where Hickory Hill was located, weren't the only targets of Ethel Skakel Kennedy's shopping scheme. She also pulled, or tried to pull, her scam, all well-documented, in such upscale Washington, D.C., stores as Bloomingdale's and Saks Fifth Avenue.

One of the most blatant incidents occurred at a fancy dress shop called Saks West-End, in the tony D.C. suburb of Chevy Chase, Maryland. Ethel had picked out a $750 Oleg Cassini number, and opened a house account instead of paying cash up front. A week later the sales-woman, Jane Abraham, spotted Ethel in a newspaper photograph wear-ing the dress. Not long after, one of Ethel's embarrassed helpers arrived at the shop with the dress, asking to return it and seeking credit for her mistress. It was on a hanger, in a plastic bag, with a dry cleaner's tag attached.

Abraham refused to take it back and sent a note to Hickory Hill that read: "Dear Mrs. Kennedy, I'm terribly sorry but the dress has been altered, the dress has been cleaned, and we are not a secondhand store. If you don't care for the dress after wearing it, why don't you try selling it to the secondhand stores. . . ."

To the note and the dress, Abraham had attached the hard evidence—the newspaper photo of Ethel actually wearing the garment. She never again heard from Mrs. Kennedy.

BOBBY HAPPENED TO BE HOME from Millbrook on a break when his mother decided to pack up everyone and head to the Kennedy com-pound in Hyannis Port. As the station wagon was being loaded, and the younger Kennedy kids were about to be transported to the airport for a private plane flight to the Cape, Bobby's prized hawk took off and landed in a treetop on a neighboring property.

Needing help to retrieve the bird, Bobby telephoned Riviere, who was staying with his mother at the chic Georgetown Inn across the Potomac in Washington. Driven to Hickory Hill by his mother's chauffeur in her Rolls-Royce, Riviere was met with what he recalled was a typical chaotic scene.

"Ethel had people running around getting her ready for the trip, and Bobby was upset. He said, 'You have to help me [get the falcon], I don't know what to do!' But Ethel started throwing stuff at me to put in the car, and she had everyone working, and she wouldn't let Bobby get his bird down. When they left, I put on climbing spurs and climbed up to the top of the tree and got the bird."

Ethel's secretary at the time—she reportedly went through a num-ber of them—"was in tears" that day, Riviere recalled. He said he had to follow Ethel and the others to the airport and said, "The secretary was crying and she almost went off the road, and I'm thinking, 'God, we're going to be in a wreck.'

"Then Ethel realizes that this person is going to be house-sitting alone for her and be doing everything for free, and the woman is heaving and hyperventilating, and Ethel put her arms around her and said, 'You know, I couldn't do without you,' and then she walked up the steps and onto the plane, and now the woman is beaming because Ethel Kennedy had patted her on the head. I always had the feeling that people could put a lot of work into something for her and then she would roar in five minutes later and just take everything apart.

"I'd never heard such [blue] language from Ethel as I did during that incident when they were going to Hyannis Port. It was that thing she had, that sense of entitlement."

Besides her use of profanity at times, Ethel Skakel Kennedy also possessed a streak of brutality. Bobby had been the brunt of it when she punished him with a hairbrush, and his cousin Christopher Kennedy Lawford had also been a victim of her abuse.

Lawford didn't much care for "the Big E," as she was called behind her back, and thought of her as "volatile" and a "very big presence" in the clan—"way bigger than her five feet and four inches." He might have felt negatively toward her because of her treatment of him when he was just a kid, often kicking him out of the Hyannis Port house for "not standing up" when she came into the room, behavior that he noted didn't happen when his uncle RFK was alive, but "became endemic after he died. The punishment for egregious crimes could be worse."

That was underscored for Lawford after he once told a childish naughty joke and she came toward him, "tackling me and pummeling me." The most severe incident, however, was when she caught him having a physical altercation with her son David.

As Lawford told it, "She grabbed my hand with such force that she broke my thumb with a snap."

NINE

Friends Die

Michael Rivinus, the other member of Bobby's druggy Millbrook triumvirate along with Michael Parkinson, was described as "an edgy kid" who fought against school rules, such as the long line he was forced to stand in at breakfast while attendance was checked. His protest was to not eat, but rather to stand there and drink a can of Coca-Cola.

Rivinus actually grew his own marijuana near his home in Philadelphia's exclusive Chestnut Hill section, oddly enough with the consent of his father, Francis Markoe Rivinus, who ran one of the world's largest drug companies at the time, Smith, Kline & French Laboratories (later GlaxoSmithKline Corp.). The senior Rivinus gave classes on conservation, and was something of an eccentric who, wearing old clothes, was often spotted cleaning graffiti from buildings and litter from streets.

"My father felt that he would rather Michael grow marijuana than buy it, so he used to grow it between the rows of my father's corn patch in Chestnut Hill," says Mark Rivinus, one of the six siblings of Michael, who was the youngest. "It was almost like he smoked pot because he grew pot. It was almost like he had to harvest his crop. Michael was one of

these kind of people who, if he took something on like smoking marijuana, then he had to grow his own, so he was a farmer who smoked pot."

Along with Bobby and Parkinson, Rivinus had arrived at Millbrook
in the fall of 1968 as a sophomore, and his brother believes that "it's certainly possible" that Rivinus smuggled his harvested pot into the school,
where he divvied it up with Bobby, Parkinson, and other tokers.

High most of the time, Rivinus hated Millbrook and stayed for just a
year before returning home. But during that time he and Parkinson were
among the very few in Bobby's small, magic circle who were invited to
the Kennedy compound in Hyannis Port, where they would party and
get stoned.

"Michael became such a close friend of Robert's that he'd go to the
Kennedy compound, where he had a wonderful time and kind of regaled us with stories of the Kennedy elders," recounted Mark Rivinus
decades later. "Most of the senior members of the Kennedy family were
there one Thanksgiving, or Christmas, and for Michael to be in contact
with these people and welcomed into the clan was just kind of fun, being around this family that had such an incredible impact on American
life. Here he was, just a young kid who happened to go to a school where
one of their offspring happened to be, and all of a sudden he was mixing with them and shaking hands with Teddy Kennedy."

Michael would return home to Chestnut Hill happily boasting to everyone about his close Kennedy ties, telling neighbors of the Rivinus
family, "Oh, you have the same exact dishwasher the Kennedys have."
They were duly impressed.

In reality, young Rivinus did not enjoy such a warm and cozy relationship with America's royal family.

"It's clear that there were drugs related to Michael's relationship with
Robert Jr. At one point, Bobby and my brother actually got thrown off
the compound for smoking marijuana," reveals Mark Rivinus. "We don't
know who threw them out, but it probably was Bobby's mother, which
makes sense."

But Rivinus denied that his brother did harder drugs with Bobby
at Millbrook.

"Michael may have liked and been part of Bobby's pot-smoking
group, but he definitely wasn't into anything heavier than that. Thinking

of Michael and drugs is not like thinking of Robert Kennedy Jr. and heavy drugs. It just was not the same relationship."

After one year at Millbrook, Rivinus returned to Philadelphia and attended the private Miquan School, and was accepted at Harvard. But before starting college, he had planned a trip to Paris to study French. "Michael felt it was absolutely critical that he be a cultured person, and that French was the lingo of the educated class," says his brother.

The summer before classes began in Cambridge, Rivinus, just short of his nineteenth birthday, was on his Honda motorcycle en route to a piano lesson, possibly stoned, when he slammed into the rear of a Cadillac that, his brother says, had cut in front of him. He went over the top of the car, broke his neck, and died.

Michael Rivinus would be one of the first, but not the last, of Bobby's druggie friends and relatives who had harrowing, untimely deaths.

THE OTHER MEMBER OF BOBBY'S ill-fated triumvirate, Michael Parkinson, also eventually had a violent end because of drugs, and emotional issues. But as an artist he had gained some fame, helped by the Kennedys.

Like Michael Rivinus, Michael Parkinson also left Millbrook, in his case due to a behavior problem and drug use. He finally graduated from a New York City public high school, but his drug experimentation continued along with Bobby's.

In mid-July 1972, for example, there was a brief Associated Press report from the town of Villavicencio, in Colombia, South America, that Bobby had paid a thirteen-dollar fine for Parkinson, "who got in Dutch for playing rock music on a cathedral pipe organ," according to the news service, quoting local police.

"The boy [Parkinson, then seventeen] had the alternative of a thirty-day arrest" or the fine. The AP story, with a New York dateline, went on to report that Parkinson and Bobby, then eighteen, had arrived in Colombia two weeks earlier on what was described as a South American tour. "Witnesses reported Parkinson went into the local cathedral during Mass and without authorization started to play rock music on the pipe organ."

According to the short news account, seemingly based on sketchy information, "Young Kennedy was not with him [Parkinson] at the time."

But there was more to the incident than was fleetingly reported in some newspapers, according to Parkinson's brother, Peter.

"They were both, Bobby and Michael, on a drug trip when that happened in Colombia, and Michael almost died from the drugs," he revealed in 2013. At the time, Peter was working in Mississippi for Shell Oil, where the Parkinson brothers' father was an executive. When the psychedelic drug overdose happened, Peter was summoned to return home to New York to help deal with his brother's dire situation. It was believed that Bobby and Parkinson had traveled to Colombia with Lem Billings as their escort.

"We brought Michael back and he was sick for almost a month and almost died," Peter Parkinson said. "My parents were upset, as one can imagine." He said it was his understanding that the drug they had taken was some form of psychedelic magic mushroom, and that his brother "may have gone into the cathedral for some solace from a bad trip."

After Parkinson got well, he told a family friend that he and Bobby "were tripping on acid in the church."

In Bobby's *The Riverkeepers*, there was no mention of getting stoned and nearly arrested with his friend in Colombia, where the illegal drug trade—heroin and cocaine—was a way of life. Instead, he painted a sylvan picture of his many visits to the country—working manual labor one summer at a ranch managed by Lem Billings's nephew, or acting as a guide for his brother Michael's whitewater rafting business, or just sailing the Meta River in a canoe.

Three years after the near-fatal Colombian psychedelic overdose episode, Michael Parkinson graduated in 1975 from Pratt Institute in Brooklyn with a Bachelor of Fine Arts degree in painting and, in 1977, with a Master of Fine Arts in sculpture.

As a friend, Andrew Humes, observed, "Michael was a brilliant artist." One of the friend's prized pieces of art was Parkinson's Millbrook School portrait of Bobby.

"Bobby was kind enough, along with our father, to steer Michael in the right direction and have him take commissions for artwork, and so he would do painting, and so forth, and then he went into making little ceramic houses," said Peter Parkinson. "He was really talented with that."

In April 1980, Parkinson was featured in *People* magazine under a headline that teased, "Master Builder Michael Parkinson's Houses Aren't Homes, but It Takes a Kennedy to Afford Them."

While there was no mention of the Colombian psychedelic trip imbroglio with Bobby, or Parkinson's history of addiction and increasingly erratic behavior—facts the celebrity weekly probably was unaware of—the article instead presented him, at twenty-six, as a glib, urbane artist who was designing miniature ceramic homes for the rich and famous. And he was quoted as making a curiously bizarre comment about the taste of at least one of his close Kennedy clients, Bobby's aunt Jean Kennedy Smith. He told the magazine that she had "stuck a mirror" over a mantel, marring the ceramic model of her mansion that he had obsessively spent hours constructing.

"A typical case of Kennedy tackiness," he was quoted as muttering.

The article noted that the Kennedys "are used to his biting comments," and pointed out, "Ethel Kennedy has known Michael since he was a schoolboy palling around with young David and Bobby Jr. It was Bobby who commissioned Parkinson to do two of his earliest works, and other members of the family were soon weighing in with orders."

Besides the Kennedys, Parkinson's other clients for his miniature houses—each sold for as much as four thousand dollars—included Hugh Hefner, who commissioned a model of the Playboy Mansion in Chicago; William F. Buckley (a Millbrook alumnus); Peter Duchin; Lem Billings (his Manhattan town house, which Bobby would inherit after Billings's death); and a number of others.

As Andrew Humes, who had one of Parkinson's miniature English taverns, noted, "Michael loved society people. If you had some connection with somebody, he would wriggle himself into various social situations. He liked hanging out with important people, he was good at that, and he was an amazingly charming man. He loved flirting and he was the funniest guy."

He also loved to party, and he and Bobby regularly showed up together in the late 1970s and early 1980s at trendy Manhattan discos—Xenon, Studio 54—where cocaine, pot, and heroin were an integral part of the frenzied scene.

Besides making art, Parkinson was musical and played the bagpipes, often to the annoyance of others. But for the annual New York City Columbus Day Parade he and Bobby marched and played their bagpipes together, Peter Parkinson remembered.

Because of his emotional instability, Parkinson spent money wildly. Some sixty thousand dollars, part of his inheritance from his father, was used to buy a commercial on a New York City TV station. The theme was "Give Peace a Chance," according to Humes. "That was a nutty thing for Michael to do, because he didn't have a lot of money."

He once purchased an expensive, beautiful 1927 yacht, the 85-foot *Ranterra*, as an investment, sold it for half of what he paid, repurchased it for more than he had sold it for, and then sold it again for less. "He bought and sold the boat three times and with the fourth owner the boat finally sank," his brother said.

By the early nineties, his emotional problems and drug addiction had gotten worse. Attempts by Bobby, other Kennedys, and the Parkinson family to help him were to no avail. "He decided that he didn't want to get help," said his brother. According to Humes, Parkinson "was a bit of a crazy guy—I don't know if you'd call it exactly schizophrenia. He was on and off meds for a good part of the later period of his life. For most of the last four or five years of his life he was supposed to be on something, and when he wasn't he tended to go off the handle."

In those last years, Parkinson was living in what was described as "a crummy little apartment" at 177 East Third Street on Manhattan's Lower East Side—just a couple of blocks from the clubhouse of the Hell's Angels, at 77 East Third Street.

"It was a rather rough neighborhood," Peter Parkinson recalled. "I used to go down there and, frankly, I didn't want to get out of the car." According to his brother, Parkinson had gotten in "with sort of a street crowd. Michael was having tirades, and Michael had some altercations" with members of the legendary motorcycle organization. "He'd go down to the Hell's Angels and yell 'fuck you,' that type of thing, and I just know that they were rough."

Michael was found dead in the bathtub of his apartment in 1994. People who knew him speculated that because of his emotional problems he had committed suicide. Humes recalled that Parkinson was "doing drugs pretty heavily" at the time. But Parkinson's brother denied that suicide was the cause. "I think he was drugged, and probably murdered, that's my guess."

But there was never a police investigation.

There also was no obituary because, as Humes observed, "The circumstances of his death were embarrassing, and so his family didn't want to draw any attention to it at all. It was very sad."

In New York, there was a church memorial service for Parkinson. His close friend Bobby didn't attend, but sent his wife, Mary Richardson Kennedy, who also was a friend of Parkinson's. "My brother was a great artist and a very talented guy," Peter Parkinson said, looking back years later. "And if it hadn't been for drugs in his life, just like if it hadn't been for drugs in Bobby's life, Bobby might be doing something different today, and my brother might still be alive."

TEN

Chappaquiddick Summer

Bobby was on his summer break before starting his second year at Millbrook when, on July 18, 1969, two teenagers walking across a narrow wooden bridge near Edgartown on Chappaquiddick Island saw the outline of a submerged car.

Edgartown's police chief, Dominick Arena, arrived at the scene, dove in, and spotted a 1967 black Oldsmobile in the murky water. A diver from the fire department went down and surfaced with the license plate number: L78 207. Arena ran the plate. The owner's name and address was a shocker: Edward M. Kennedy, Room 2400, JFK Building, Government Center, Boston, Massachusetts.

His immediate thought was that Teddy Kennedy had drowned, yet another tragedy on the heels of his brother RFK's murder, thirteen months earlier.

But inside the sunken sedan was the body of a lone young woman, Mary Jo Kopechne, a pretty, petite blonde whose twenty-ninth birthday was just a week away. Her body was in a state of rigor mortis, and it was clear from her position that she had made a desperate attempt to escape before she drowned.

Arena's instant reaction: "Thank God it isn't one of the clan."

Kopechne had been close to RFK and Ethel for some five years. In 1964 she had been hired as a secretary in Bobby's father's Senate office, had spent time at Hickory Hill, and particularly liked young Bobby. At the Virginia homestead, she had typed RFK's anti–Vietnam War speech, had even helped phrase his presidential announcement, and during the campaign she was one of the "Boiler Room Girls," a small group of trusted staffers who compiled voter data.

And now she was dead after attending a reunion-like party in Edgartown of the Boiler Room Girls and other RFK campaign workers.

Less known was that she was there at the invitation of Bobby's uncle Ted, married, the father of three, a presidential contender in the hearts and minds of many, who had invited her to see the forty-sixth annual Edgartown Yacht Club Regatta.

The day the scandal broke, Bobby's mother, Ethel, had made an appearance at the opening of the first Connecticut Special Olympics, the family's favorite charity. Back at the compound, where the clan and top advisers had gathered to deal with the scandal, Ethel "couldn't process any of it," a family friend recalled. "Here was a woman who was still in a state of shock over the death of her husband, who had lost control of her children. And now the man who she was relying on to keep her on steady ground—the only shoulder she had to lean on—seemed to be self-destructing before her eyes."

Meanwhile, the widow, always the most loyal of the Kennedy women next to Rose, was called into action, telephoning high-powered Washington friends to get involved in what many soon came to believe was a cover-up involving Senator Kennedy's questionable actions in the death of Mary Jo Kopechne. Ethel also was ordered to call the Kopechnes to tell them that she and her brother-in-law would be at Mary Jo's funeral.

"She talked about faith, how it could help," the dead girl's father recalled.

At the funeral, a woman carried a red, white, and blue sign: KENNEDY FOR PRESIDENT, 1972.

Three days later, the last Kennedy brother of his generation pleaded guilty to leaving the scene of an accident, received a two-month suspended sentence, and was placed on a year's probation. It was a virtual slap on the wrist. If his name wasn't Kennedy, he would have faced more serious charges, many in the media and the public believed.

That night he went on national television, called his conduct "indefensible," and asked Massachusetts voters to decide whether he should resign. He would be reelected in November 1970, but the scandal would rage on, impacting any higher political aspirations, especially his later hopes of running for the presidency.

Many thought Kennedy was lying. He'd been caught lying before, but that situation was quite different. As an undergrad at Harvard, from where his brothers JFK, RFK, and Joe Jr. had graduated, Ted was caught cheating on an exam, which like Chappaquiddick had become part of the dark side of his curriculum vitae.

Fearing that a poor grade in Spanish would impact his goal to make the university's varsity football team as his brothers RFK and JFK had, he asked a dorm mate, Bill Frate, to take the final exam for him. They were caught and each received a one-year suspension. Years later, in his 2009 memoir, Kennedy devoted a chapter to the scandal. It was aptly entitled "The Harvard Screw-up."

Chappaquiddick was devastating for Bobby's mother, too. While publicly she was vocally supportive of her brother-in-law—now the family patriarch—privately she felt abandoned by him, revealed George Terrien, her brother-in-law on the Skakel side. "She had a lot of anger—anger toward Ted, anger toward Bobby for dying, and anger toward her sons."

In Bobby's case, his family role model had failed him miserably. When he returned to Millbrook for his second turbulent year, a classmate recalled him muttering, "My uncle is a major asshole, getting caught like he did."

AS THAT HELLISH CHAPPAQUIDDICK summer turned to fall, Bobby began his second—and what would be his most tumultuous—year at Millbrook.

The school often had guest speakers, and one of them during Bobby's matriculation was a famous graduate, James Lane Buckley, Class of 1940, brother of William F. Buckley Jr., Class of 1943, editor of the conservative *National Review*. Jim Buckley had come to speak when he was successfully campaigning for the U.S. Senate seat from New York as a member of the state's Conservative Party. One of his opponents was the Republican incumbent, Charles Goodell, appointed by Governor Nelson Rockefeller following RFK's assassination.

Before the assembled Millbrook students, with Bobby Jr. in the audience, Buckley exuberantly praised the use of no-knock warrants, issued by a judge or a magistrate, that permitted law enforcement officers to enter a home without giving any warning in order to avoid the destruction of evidence, often drugs. No-knock warrants had become controversial; there were many liberals who considered them to be unconstitutional and a violation of privacy.

While most of the Millbrook boys in the audience were bored with Buckley's speech, Bobby wasn't, and he surprised everyone by standing up and confronting the conservative politician—surprised them because he usually stayed under the radar and was considered by many who weren't in his small circle to be a quiet loner.

"But Bobby got up and made a big deal about how no-knock shouldn't be permitted," recalled his classmate Bruce Whitcomb. "I didn't know what he was talking about then and I don't think anybody else did. Bobby thought it was a civil rights violation. Everyone was surprised because here was this guy who was usually very quiet and suddenly in an auditorium in front of the whole school he got into this whole thing about civil liberties being breached if premises are searched."

There were those who thought about Bobby's intense reaction and concluded that it was a personal rather than a political issue with him—that he was against no-knock because of his use of drugs and probable fear that a search of his belongings without his permission might result in the discovery of contraband.

"I was there and I thought, well, okay, it's funny that he would pick something [to debate] that's related to the drug trade," recalled Brian Carroll, one of Bobby's dorm mates.

In *The Riverkeepers,* Bobby made the claim that immediately after his father's death he gave up a childhood dream to become a veterinarian and began to take a "greater interest" in RFK's political issues—"to pick up the flag where he dropped it"—citing civil rights and the war in Vietnam.

But the only political statement he had ever actually made during his time at Millbrook, classmates recalled, was taking credit for making a big peace sign in the snow with his snowshoes in the middle of the quadrangle near the West Dorm.

Along with drug use, Bobby was getting into all kinds of other trouble, ranging from petty behavior such as being late to classes, to pushing the envelope on the school dress code, to schoolboy vandalism.

Just before Millbrook let out for a long school holiday, possibly Christmas, Bobby, his friend Nick Forster, and a couple of others had gotten hold of some alcohol, became inebriated, and were caught. "We were not allowed to go home for the holiday on the day when everybody else in the class went home," Forster recalled years later. But Bobby and his crew had done something else under the influence that apparently went unnoticed at the time.

They had proceeded to deface the bulletin board in the main hall of the West Dorm. "We were acting up," recalled Foster. "And on the board somebody wrote, 'The Bear Sucks!' "

It was a reference to Rene Clark, Millbrook's "authoritarian" French teacher, dubbed "The Bear," who was master of Bobby and Forster's dorm, and who "took no guff from Bobby, who made his own rules."

When they returned from the holiday there was, according to Forster, "this sort of solemn gathering of all the dormitories, and Rene Clark asked for volunteers to confess to defacing the calendar, which none of us did confess."

On another occasion, wanting to be out on their own on the campus after midnight, they had invented a ruse, a fake celestial event that, as Forster recalled, "could only occur at one o'clock in the morning and that would allow us permission to go to the observatory, trudge through the woods, and just be out on our own."

In addition to the Trevor Zoo, Millbrook also had an actual observatory. "So we conjured up an astronomical oddity. Bobby," Forster asserted, "was singled out just by virtue of whom he was."

But not always—such as when he desecrated the sanctity of the white-steepled Millbrook chapel by inviting girls there, supposedly for sexual purposes. Early on, in the tradition of his Kennedy male elders, Bobby, only a sophomore at Millbrook, was already earning a reputation as a Casanova of sorts.

WHILE MILLBROOK WAS AN ALL-BOYS school back then, girls were sneaking on campus to meet the cute Kennedy scion as if he were a rock star, and there were girls bussed in from fancy finishing schools for school dances who were drawn to him because of his famous name and seeming celebrity status. And Bobby, a full-fledged Kennedy, took advantage of the situation.

As his classmate Brian Carroll observed years later, "Bobby preyed on visiting girls like a hawk on mice."

His roommate Jamie Fanning said, "I didn't think of Bobby as physically attractive, but he had that bad-boy twinkle in his eye that a lot of girls like. He talked about girls in twisted, sick ways, discussing oral sex—him on them—that none of us had ever tried, or even conceived of at the time."

Christopher West, Brian Carroll's roommate, asserted that when Millbrook had dances, "Bobby had women hanging all over him—the girls literally jumped all over him. And he used to take the girls over to the chapel, and it was very quiet over there, let's put it that way."

Along with being a quiet place to have a liaison with a liberated sixties coed on the night of a weekend dance, the chapel had an added perk: Well hidden inside one of the organ pipes was a stash of primo marijuana.

During his clandestine explorations of the chapel, presumably for various nefarious purposes, Bobby had discovered a set of stairs behind the altar that offered access to a very private attic-like space above the vaulted ceiling, a perfect place to bring a girl, or to smoke, or to do both. He had once brought his roommate, Fanning, up there, and while walking around Bobby had put his foot through the chapel's ceiling plaster; the damage was visible for months from the pews below. "At church on Sunday I can remember looking up and thinking, there's that freaking hole. Bobby was a little klutzy, always leaping before he looked, always charging into trouble. [But] the chapel was a good hiding spot to take girls."

The dances at Millbrook were held in the Barn, the school's big common area, and during one of the socials Bobby was so swarmed by Kennedy groupies that he didn't, for once, take advantage of the situation. Ned Rousmaniere, whose father had been JFK's roommate at Harvard, was nearby watching as "this gaggle of girls were just kind of hanging around Bobby, and I could tell he was really obviously uncomfortable and he wanted to get away."

Bobby was standing on the landing of the stairwell between the Barn's first and second floors, trapped by the girls. In order to escape from the adoring vixens, he opened the landing window, climbed out on the sill, and jumped in the dark eight to ten feet to the ground below.

It's rare for a Kennedy man, even a troubled, druggie prep school sophomore, to be caught actually running away from eager young women. But Rousmaniere, who went into the psychotherapy field, observed years later that based on his experiences with Kennedy men, "they were fine as long as they were in control. But this was not a situation that was in Bobby's control. I just think that whole thing of girls pursuing him and him being objectified just didn't sit right with him."

The fact, though, that Bobby could get any girl he wanted, if and when he wanted, had inspired one of his close classmates to actually impersonate him on the evening when the Millbrook boys were having a dance with girls bussed in from the Emma Willard School in Troy, New York— Jane Fonda's alma mater.

The boys and girls were matched by height, which usually resulted in "snickers, or guffaws, or howls of amazement when some dumpy guy got a gorgeous girl," recalled Nick Forster. "But at that dance some guy managed to convince several girls that he was Bobby Kennedy Jr., because all the girls were like, 'Oh, Bobby Kennedy Jr. goes here!' So that was a big deal. They were hoping to get him as their date for the evening. So this guy managed to convince his date that he was Bobby Kennedy Jr. and he fared very well."

Like Bobby, Forster came from a prominent political family, and like Bobby, he hated being at Millbrook. Like Bobby, whose newly widowed mother had turned him over to Lem Billings and Millbrook, Forster was there mainly because his parents were in the process of getting divorced. His father, a Millbrook graduate who had gone to Harvard at sixteen, was Bayard Stuyvesant Forster, a committed conservative Republican who had been a member of Nelson Rockefeller's cabinet, serving as New York State's commissioner of transportation. Young Forster's mother, a descendant of the wealthy Astors, was Clare Chanler, daughter of Lewis Stuyvesant Chanler, who had served as a lieutenant governor of New York in the early twentieth century.

Forster's parents also had ties to the Kennedy family. During their divorce, they had rented their palatial home in Garrison, New York—with a view of West Point across the Hudson River—to Bobby's aunt Patricia Kennedy Lawford, and Lem Billings was a mutual friend. During Billings's many Millbrook visits, he had taken Bobby and Forster to lunch, regaling them with stories about buying, renovating, and decorating houses in New York City, subjects they cared little about.

"Lem felt very strongly about wanting to be there as a presence in Bobby's worlds," observed Forster.

Forster was certain that he had gotten high with Bobby on occasion, and recalled being introduced to marijuana at Millbrook when he was just thirteen. "I was an early adopter," he said. "I was smoking pot on campus discreetly, not with passion and vigor," and was first turned on, he believed, by one of Bobby's roommates, Robin Roosevelt, a descendant of the "Rough Rider," President Teddy Roosevelt.

Short-time roommates Bobby and Robin were complete opposites. Unlike Bobby, Roosevelt was a brilliant student with no interest in sports or falconry, and certainly not heavy drugs, a boy who favored Beethoven over the Beatles, and spent all of his time reading and studying. Their only similarity was that Roosevelt cared little about his personal appearance and hygiene.

"Robin was a kind of geeky guy who always wore beat-up clothes, was often unkempt, and didn't shower," recalled their classmate Dudley "Dusty" Bahlman, who became a journalist. "The story goes that somebody in the dorm complained bitterly about Roosevelt's feet, which stunk to high heaven."

The tough dorm master, Rene Clark, confronted Roosevelt very publicly in the hallway outside his room and, with everyone on the floor watching, declared, "Roosevelt, you've got to do something about your feet. They stink!"

Clark then forced him to bathe.

In any case, one of them complained about the other and asked to separate. Bobby stayed in their room and Roosevelt was transferred to another. Bobby then began rooming with Jamie Fanning, who became a companion in drug use. Aside from Roosevelt's poor personal grooming habits, he also was gay, which may have played a role in the roommates' decision to part ways. Before his death at forty-five in 1999 from AIDS, the lifelong bachelor was working as an information officer for the United Nations' Palestine programs.

BY THE MIDDLE OF BOBBY'S second year at Millbrook, around January 1970, he was placed on a secret short list of students considered too difficult to remain enrolled. His behavior, particularly his drug use, had the administration concerned that if something happened to the young Kennedy, such as an overdose or worse, all hell would come down on the school and tarnish its reputation.

Peter Cole, who taught English and had gotten to know Bobby, said it was "generalized knowledge among the faculty" that a number of the students were using drugs, and that Bobby had later been identified as one of them.

"We as faculty members all seemed to have this awareness of Bobby's behavior and were totally unable to do anything about it," Cole asserted years later. "We did catch him finally and he was going to get tossed, but I felt sorry for the kid who I knew back then. I tended not to blame him as maybe I should have for his drug misdeeds. I just think he had a need for close companionship and maybe the people supplying the drugs or buying the drugs provided it."

George Buell, Millbrook's headmaster when Bobby first arrived, had left because of illness, and two others had followed. The new headmaster was Henry Callard, who had come from a prep school in Baltimore, and stayed at Millbrook for just a year. He was followed by an interim headmaster, Neil Howard, described as a "thoughtful, gentle, humble, scholarly guy," who had served for a time as coach of the school's ski team, of which Bobby had been a member.

Near the end of Howard's term in the spring of 1970, as the school was going through more administrative changes at the top, Bobby was asked to leave just weeks before the semester's end in June. The headmaster-elect was an educator named Donn Wright, who had been headmaster at the Hoosac School, a boarding academy about eighty miles north of Millbrook.

While Wright was still at Hoosac, but preparing to begin his regime at Millbrook, Neil Howard contacted him, expressing his concerns about Bobby's behavior and drugs.

"Neil asked me what my opinion was about retaining Bobby Kennedy, and I said, in my opinion, I think you ought to let him go," recalled Wright years later. "Neil told me that he was considering expelling Bobby because he had been using and providing drugs. I don't recall what kind of drugs it was, but Neil had quite a list of problems involving Bobby, and felt that Bobby had a reputation for breaking rules. It seemed to be the feeling that Bobby as a Kennedy felt he was above the law, that he was arrogant, and could do whatever he wanted and get away with it."

With Wright's support, Howard decided to quietly expel Bobby, and contacted Bobby's surrogate father, Lem Billings, to inform him of the decision. Wright also had a meeting with Billings.

"Bobby's departure was already a fait accompli when I met Billings, and he didn't try to change anybody's minds. He accepted it." Wright said he never heard from Bobby's mother after the decision was made to boot her son.

Peter Cole recalled that before that decision was finally made, Millbrook's administration was "bending over backwards to protect Bobby and keep him in. I don't think they felt any joy in showing him the door. We didn't dwell on it after he left, and the administration quite rightly didn't publicize it."

The decision to expel Bobby from Millbrook—the school from which he later indicated in *The Riverkeepers* he had graduated—was kept "very hush-hush," recalled the music teacher James Hejduk. "There was never any kind of disciplinary hearing or anything like that. He was here and gone.

"There was no gnashing of teeth and sobbing in the context of his leaving. It didn't come as a big surprise. Among the faculty there may have been a collective sigh of relief given the culture of those times, because things with Bobby would have only escalated, and the attitude was, okay, he's now the next school's problem."

One would have thought Bobby's embarrassing expulsion would have spelled the end of his relationship with Millbrook School. But, curiously, he was invited back as the honored commencement speaker for the Class of 1998, and he was even billed as a Millbrook alumnus, Class of '72. It was not pointed out that he had never actually graduated. While on campus for his much-ballyhooed commencement speech, he visited with his goddaughter, Zoe Haydock, who was in the Class of 2000.

In 2010, Millbrook School avidly promoted a speaking engagement Bobby had at the Cary Institute of Ecosystem Studies, a not-for-profit environmental organization in Millbrook. The school's pitch for getting people to come hear him praised the once-banished druggie as a "resolute defender of the environment," and noted that *Time* magazine had named him one of the "Heroes for the Planet."

Millbrook teachers and students who knew Bobby back in the day, when he was getting stoned and chasing rats with his falcon among a pile of cow carcasses, got a chuckle out of the fact that their alma mater kept the Kennedy scion's expulsion a secret and welcomed him back into the fold.

In James Hejduk's view, "Having a Kennedy speak was just a way to burnish Millbrook's image. It's salesmanship."

ELEVEN

Pot Bust

On August 9, 1970, *The New York Times* published an op-ed piece in which it questioned the "disproportionate" number of young people who were being arrested in marijuana-related cases. It noted that teenagers, "like blacks and Puerto Ricans of any age," had fewer civil rights, especially if they had shaggy, long hair and dressed like hippies, and asserted that law enforcement officers were wont to "roust" and "harass" them.

Written by Tom Buckley, a top *Times* man, citing "some observers," the piece claimed that cops were zealous in pursuing otherwise law-abiding pot smokers because of their "dislike of the life-style it exemplifies, which is often associated with antiwar and civil rights protests, loud rock music, sexual freedom and what is described as a disrespect for law and order, rather than to the seriousness of the act itself."

Further, Buckley noted that there were as many as forty million pot smokers in America at the turn of the new decade, the seventies, and that weed was probably safe because, before the enactment of the 1937 federal law banning marijuana, it had been prescribed by doctors to help cure migraines, asthma, and delirium tremens.

In publishing the pro-marijuana, anti-law-enforcement story, the liberal *Times* clearly had an agenda and a news peg. Just days before the story ran in the Gray Lady, two cousins named Bobby—Bobby Kennedy Jr. and Bobby Sargent Shriver III, Eunice Kennedy Shriver's son, both of them sixteen—had been hauled into Juvenile Court in the town of Barnstable on the Cape on charges of marijuana possession.

Bobby's arrest, his first but not his last for drugs, came less than two months after he was quietly expelled from Millbrook because of his drug involvement, but that humiliation clearly hadn't given him second thoughts, nor apparently did it cause the Kennedy family, especially his mother, to get him any professional help. Perhaps like so many of the Kennedys, he and she felt above the law.

The events leading to the bust were linked to Bobby's gang, the Hyannis Port Terrors, and a member of that troublemaking crew, a cabdriver in his early twenties who sported a beard and went by the name of Andy Moes. A decade or so later, Shriver, recalling what happened, claimed that on July 10, 1970, Moes had asked him and Bobby for marijuana so he and his girlfriend could get high and have sex, and offered to pay them ten dollars for a single joint. Shriver and Bobby, although both heirs to the Kennedy fortune, jumped at the money.

Ethel and her children were having dinner with the Shrivers on the Cape on August 5 when the police showed up with warrants and told the Kennedy widow and her brother-in-law Sargent Shriver, the former U.S. Ambassador to France under JFK, that Moes was actually a cop working undercover narcotics as part of a local and state police probe into drug violations, and the boys were being charged with possession, with a scheduled court hearing the next day.

Furious, Bobby's mother chased him out of the Shriver home, pushed him into some bushes, and ranted, "You've dragged your family's name through the mud," both cousins later claimed. At the time, Bobby's right wrist was in a cast. He had fallen and injured it a few months earlier when he tried to rescue his falcon, which had flown into a tree.

On August 6, the arrest hit the front pages of newspapers worldwide. "Robert Kennedy Jr. and Cousin, Shriver Son, in Marijuana Case," declared the page-one *New York Times* story in a two-column spread.

Anything the Kennedys did—especially of a scandalous nature—was media fodder; the arrest of RFK's teenage namesake involving drugs, coming so soon after the assassination, Ted Kennedy's Chappaquiddick affair, and Jackie's shocking marriage to Onassis, had triggered yet another media circus.

Bobby's uncle Ted had flown in from his Senate office in Washington to give his troubled nephew moral support, but he refused to comment to reporters who had met him at the airport in Warwick, Rhode Island, en route to the Kennedy compound. There was speculation at the time that the arrest of his nephews was timed to embarrass him as he prepared for reelection.

Sargent Shriver, campaigning for Democratic candidates, told reporters that Bobby, his son, "has never been involved in any such situation before, and we trust he never will be again. We are deeply distressed to learn that [he] has been charged with the possession of marijuana last month in Hyannis. . . . If he has done anything wrong, we are sure he will make reparations in a manly and courageous manner. We love him, and for all his sixteen years he has been a joy and pride to us. We will help him in every way to reestablish his sense of responsibility for himself and for others, his dedication to high ideals, his personal self-confidence and dignity.

"Young people today are being subjected to the most profound temptations and stresses. . . . We ask for human understanding of our son's plight, and we pray that God will help him. . . ."

Apparently his famous father was unaware of the fact that Bobby Shriver had previously smoked marijuana at his fancy boarding school, Exeter, as he tried to keep up with his Kennedy cousins, Ethel's kid in particular.

She issued the requisite concerned-parent statement through a family spokesman, and presumably drafted by one of the family's lawyers. "This is, of course, a matter for the authorities to decide," she stated. "But Bobby is a fine boy, and we have always been proud of him. I will stand by him." (She had already decided, however, that once the legal matter was resolved she was going to kick Bobby out on his ear, again.)

The press, which knew nothing about Bobby's recent expulsion from school because of drugs, or chose not to report it, was out in force with some one hundred reporters and more than a dozen TV crews when the grim-faced parents and the juvenile defendants—both looking suddenly clean-cut in jackets and ties and trimmed hair—arrived at the Barnstable District Court, with sixty-three-year-old Juvenile Court Judge Henry L. Murphy presiding.

When the judge asked them about the charges during the private hearing, which lasted less than a half hour, they both denied they had been in possession of marijuana. Because it was Kennedy's and Shriver's first offense, Murphy placed them on a year's probation.

In the op-ed piece that ran in the *Times* a few days later under the headline "It's the Young Who Get 'Busted' for Using Marijuana," the writer, Tom Buckley, referring to the Kennedy-Shriver case, noted how the families followed what he called a "script" that had become "dismally familiar. . . . The youngster gets a haircut, changes to his only suit of square clothes, looking as frail and naive as young Shriver for example, and he and his parents then face the television cameras to ask for understanding and to promise to try 'to do something' about the drug menace."

Back at her home in the compound, Ethel Kennedy told Bobby, "I'm throwing you out of the family!" She also called for help from Dr. Robert Coles, a Harvard psychiatrist and longtime friend of the Kennedy family, RFK in particular, to work with Bobby. Coles had once traveled with RFK through poor Mississippi, and he had devoted a couple of chapters of one of his books to Bobby's father. While Bobby and Coles would eventually have a long relationship, Bobby decided to skip therapy, raided his savings account for six hundred dollars, bought a used Ford Falcon, and drove across country with two friends, one of whom had been a prep school classmate and later became a New York attorney.

In Fresno, Bobby sold the car at a two-hundred-dollar loss, and like Depression-era hoboes, he and his friend snuck rides on freight trains, snacking on sausage and skid row wine, winding up in Texas. "I thought we were going to die of thirst," he later claimed. "We were completely black by the time we got off the train because we'd been riding on the piggyback cars that were exposed to the air."

On the road, having run out of money, Bobby and his chum panhandled or tried their hand at odd jobs. He later revealed that the only person he touched base with during his travels was Lem Billings.

"I was riding around with bums," he boasted some years later. "It was good. I could be one of them and not be a Kennedy."

During the final leg of his odyssey he wound up in Berkeley, where he bought drugs with money he had panhandled.

The matriarch Rose Kennedy considered Bobby's arrest an "inconvenient family matter," according to one of her biographers, Barbara Perry, who had gone through Mrs. Kennedy's diaries and letters, and quoted her as observing that marijuana was a "dreadful, dreadful curse for young people." She went on to say, "I had hoped that Bobby Shriver as one of the oldest boys amongst the Kennedy grandchildren would assume leadership against the drug." Mrs. Kennedy had actually gone as far as to send letters to Bobby Jr. and his cousins requesting that they form a "big Kennedy movement against the drugs and give it enough prestige and enough excitement so that a lot would join that group, the anti-drug users, instead of being one of the users. But my hopes of that have been more or less dashed."

TWELVE

Pomfret Blacks

I t's not easy to get into a private boarding school having already been expelled from one for using drugs and being a behavior problem, and then being placed on probation for marijuana possession, but the Kennedy name was of major weight. Thus, Robert F. Kennedy Jr.'s next stop on what was becoming a rocky road to a high school diploma was the Pomfret School, which was as troubled as he.

"When Bobby and I were there, Pomfret was in a state of constant upheaval, the economic situation wasn't very stable, there was too much freedom, not enough boundaries, not enough structure, and the curriculum was screwed up—it wasn't traditional anymore," said Lindsey Cole Miesmer, a member of the Class of '72, who later spent a decade as one of the school's trustees. She was a member of the first class of Pomfret women and a self-described "faculty brat" whose father, Charles Dodd Cole, had been head of the Connecticut boarding school's art department.

Beyond those issues, according to Joseph K. "Jay" Milnor, the headmaster when Bobby began his matriculation—it would turn out to be as disastrous as his time at Millbrook—the school was riddled with drugs and racial problems, and the male-dominated academy had difficulty in accepting women as fellow students.

A small group of mostly poor inner-city blacks, some of them militants, had been admitted to the school, and they ignited tensions with the rich, white preppies. As Milnor put it, "We had a war going on." And with the emerging feminist movement and a need to generate more income, Pomfret had opened its doors to coeds for the first time since its founding in 1894, but the young women felt they weren't being treated as equals. And, worse, it seemed that practically everyone was doing some form of recreational drug, mostly marijuana.

Isolated in the far reaches of Connecticut, and with all of the school's issues, it was the last place Bobby—with all of his issues—should have been sent, but it was the only boarding school that Lem Billings could find that would admit him. As Miesmer noted, "There was no school with any structure that Bobby could go to because Bobby was in trouble emotionally. Only a very liberal school [like Pomfret] that needed money would take him. Groton would never have taken him, or St. Paul, or Exeter-Andover, because to them he didn't have his act together. He would have given the trustees pause."

In his nineties and residing in an assisted-living facility in the spring of 2013, but still vibrant and active, Jay Milnor had never forgotten the first meeting he had with Billings and the new student's mother, Ethel Kennedy—"one *long* session," he called it. It was, he said, the first and last time she showed her face on the campus, but she made a lasting impression on the headmaster, who was still chuckling about it more than four decades later.

In a repeat of the request she had made when she and Billings first brought Bobby to Millbrook, Ethel Kennedy "was adamant that she wanted her boy to play football, and LeMoyne Billings seemed to be nothing but supportive of her demanding ways," recalled Milnor. "I would have hoped that Robert Kennedy Sr. would have been a little more flexible than his wife because Bobby wasn't cut out to be a football player in temperament, in size, and in inclination. He was skinny, he had a strange way of walking—it wasn't a strut, just a particular gait that was distinctive. But football's what she wanted for him.

"Bobby wasn't there when we spoke, and my feeling was that if he had been given a choice without his mother's interference or pressure or bias he might have selected not even being in athletics in the fall term. My thinking at the time was, he may not be cut out for it," continued Milnor. "I felt that Mrs. Kennedy had succumbed, or was sucked into the Kennedy mystique of athletic competition—touch football, that whole business. But she was a jock and more Kennedy than most Kennedys. Young Robert was not like his mother. And I have a keen memory of him struggling to play football. I just prayed that Bobby Kennedy wouldn't get killed."

One would have expected that the more important subject to be discussed during the all-important first meeting with the headmaster was a game plan to deal with Bobby's real problems—the drug use and bad behavior that had resulted in his expulsion from Millbrook. But, according to Milnor, the subject was never mentioned by Bobby's mother, or by Billings, whom Ethel dominated and had under her thumb.

Even more curious, Milnor says he wasn't even aware of why Bobby had left Millbrook or even why Pomfret was his next choice.

"I was never told why he was coming from Millbrook," maintained Milnor. "We just knew he had difficulty in fitting in, adhering, staying focused. It was a difficult time for him, and I guess in hindsight it was a mistake to admit him. But my hope had been that Bobby Kennedy would fit in and flourish. We were blind to the fact that he had a checkered past, and we would never have admitted him if he had been a complete washout elsewhere. But it was clear that he had problems. There was absolutely no incentive for the school to take him, and I had no knowledge of how and why they showed up at our doorstep, so to speak. It was just simply assumed that he could pass muster and had potential. The Kennedy name and money didn't enter into the discussion at all."

From his meeting with Ethel Kennedy, Milnor said he came away thinking she was a bit strange because of her adamant attitude toward athletics, and he recalled thinking, " 'I will hope for the best. If Bobby applies himself and abides by the rules and regulations as the overwhelming majority of other kids, he can cut the mustard.' But he was not fated to do that."

With classes about to start, the headmaster advised the faculty without "much to-do or fuss or bother" that he had enrolled the son of the slain presidential hopeful, his namesake, and he expressed the hope that things would go well and Bobby would succeed.

The troubled Kennedy had brought with him his falcon and his drug habit. The bird, which was kept in the biology lab, sparked jealousy and resentment in some of his classmates because pets weren't normally permitted, but the Kennedy scion had been given special dispensation. "The kids were all aflutter about it," recalled one of Bobby's teachers. On one occasion the bird escaped, Bobby freaked out and was visibly upset, and the whole school was recruited as a search party.

As for the drugs, his classmate John Seibel, who became an attorney, recalled, "Everybody was at least smoking pot—*everybody*—and a lot of people were doing LSD and other recreational stuff. But Bobby was doing a little more than some of the rest of us—a little more and maybe harder stuff than the rest of us. That kid could have gone down the tubes. He was really at a precarious place when he was at Pomfret . . . going off and having drug- and alcohol-fueled weekends at the Cape. I would go to Boston and smoke pot. They would go to Hyannis Port and do whatever they did." That very small group, described as Bobby's Pomfret "inner circle," was said to have included a future Oscar-winning documentary filmmaker and a future powerful labor relations lawyer in New York.

Bobby and Seibel shared some classes and Seibel was stunned that with all the drugs Bobby was inhaling and ingesting he still showed himself to be "an extremely bright and articulate guy. He had a distinctive sort of pause as he thought about what he was going to say, and had a very distinctive manner of speech. In Mr. Woodruff's English class we would discuss a book, and I just remember being really impressed with his insights. It was sort of an odd juxtaposition that he was this really articulate guy who was doing lots of drugs, and was pretty much into the substances."

When Bobby first arrived at Pomfret, he roomed with another new student, also a junior, who suffered from emotional problems. Bobby soon moved to a single in a dorm designated Lower Four. Of Pomfret's four dorm buildings, Lower Four was the most remote and the least accessible. Moreover, on his floor he was the only white boy. Considered a loner by many of his white classmates, he had bonded with the blacks who lived there—members of what was known as the Afro-Latin Society. While there was much hostility directed by the small group of black students toward the privileged white kids who dominated at Pomfret, Bobby was welcomed into their world.

As Milton Butts, an African American who had won a full scholarship to Pomfret awarded by *The Pittsburgh Press*, for which he had been a carrier, noted years later, "The blacks and whites hung separately."

Bobby and Butts had become friends on the lackluster Pomfret football team, whose mascot was a griffin, a mythological creature part lion, part eagle, a species Bobby could relate to since he'd once owned a lion cub at Millbrook, and raised big predatory birds. On the team, he played wide receiver and Butts was a lineman. Despite Headmaster Milnor's fears about Bobby playing football, he actually did relatively well for himself. "He was just very thin with long hair over his face," recalled Butts, "but he had no fear about coming out and hitting someone, or tackling someone."

In the Pomfret student community of some two hundred and fifty, "Bobby tended to associate more with the students who were not as privileged as the other students, and that included the black students," said Butts. "When we were going to a football game, Bobby tended to sit in the back of the bus with the African Americans, and he socialized in that way."

At Pomfret's little Tuck Shop, where students could buy snacks and watch television in the evening after study hall, Bobby ignored his few white friends from well-to-do families and hung out with the big-city, mean-streets blacks. In all, there were only about twenty African Americans in the entire school. Butts, the oldest of six, the son of a barber who worked three jobs to support his family, asserted years later, "That's the kind of person Bobby was then. He wasn't making a big political statement, but I think he just felt comfortable in getting into discussions that we, the black students, were getting involved in, everyday things but with a perspective given our background."

Bobby and Butts had taken an English class together with a popular young teacher by the name of Don Hinman, who featured books by and about black radicals. One such book that excited Bobby and provoked his interest was a recent bestseller, *Soledad Brother: The Prison Letters of*

George Jackson. Jackson, who reportedly had been involved in armed rob-
beries, was shot to death at the age of twenty-nine by a guard during an
escape from San Quentin. A member of the violent Black Panther Party
and co-founder of the Black Guerilla Family in prison, he previously had
been charged along with two others with murdering a corrections officer.

"Bobby," recalled Butts, "was one of the insightful and articulate folks
in Hinman's class and was active in talking about the book. He was just
very comfortable hanging out with 'the brothers,' and he didn't care what
other folks thought about that, and he always spoke his mind. Bobby had
every opportunity to identify with the students of privilege, but he chose
to hang with us. It was an opportunity to be himself, kick back and just
talk."

Butts, who went on to get an Ivy League education and became a
sociologist, believed that one of the reasons Bobby was accepted was
because of his Kennedy name and his liberal family's "focus on social
justice, and that seemed to be very much a part of Bobby regardless of
all the other parts of the tag that was placed on him."

The art department head's daughter, Lindsey Cole Miesmer, liked
Bobby and had noted his close interaction with the blacks, and years later
thought their relationship shed some light on Bobby's persona at the time.
"It was clear to me," she said, "that Bobby felt like an outsider, so he felt
way more comfortable with the black kids than he did with the other
white kids. He'd just lost his father, and his father was a champion of
helping blacks, so this kid who has just lost his father goes to a school
where there's a presence of black kids and he felt more comfortable with
them."

Relations were tense between the small group of blacks and the
preponderance of white students, and anger and sometimes violence
erupted. John Seibel, who had grown up in the all-white, affluent Washington, D.C., suburb of Bethesda, Maryland, recalled that there was "quite
a bit of hostility directed by the Afro-Latin Society to the privileged
white kids." Early on, Seibel and a couple of blacks had become friends,
but they soon distanced themselves from him. "I had my issues, I had my
problems," he said. "There was some really nasty stuff that went on. The
animosity was more of a wagon-circling by the black students. They felt
sort of removed from their element and under siege. I was actually

threatened by a couple of people, so I was impressed that Bobby was embraced by the Afro-Latin Society. He wasn't just tolerated. He was *embraced*."

Regarding Bobby's friend Milton Butts, Seibel noted that Butts had once roomed with a white classmate, but was soon "made to feel that it was unacceptable to associate with us anymore because we were white devils." Seibel and some other whites had begun mockingly calling him "Militant" Butts, not Milton Butts, because "he became a militant kind of guy."

Don Hinman, in whose class Bobby was turned on to the writings and literature of late-sixties black radicals, was a relatively junior member of the faculty when young Kennedy was scheduled into his class. "It was a wonderful time to teach," he noted years later, "but that was a very tough time for Bobby. There was lots of energy and ideas in the classroom, but drugs unfortunately had hit."

He recalled that Bobby spent a lot of time with the black students and that the school at that time was very involved in civil rights teachings and issues, but he also remembered that Bobby had a privileged white kid's view of the world. "People were talking about inexpensive places to go skiing and Bobby chimed in that the really cheapest places to ski were in Chile, where he had vacationed. He also didn't understand why the black kids were upset that he had in his dorm room closet three or four expensive suits. He said, 'It's not what you have, but how well you take care of what you have that's important.' My wife, who happened to be present, almost whacked him."

Hinman was aware that Bobby had problems and was a problem himself, so he kept close tabs on him. Bobby also happened to be a resident in the dorm that Hinman had the responsibility of overseeing as a dorm master and a member of the discipline committee. As such he routinely did a bed check around eleven P.M., and on one particular night not long after the fall term had started, all seemed accounted for and asleep.

But around midnight he got a call from the assistant headmaster, who seemed suspicious and asked him to double-check Bobby's room. Hinman considered the request a bother because he had already opened Bobby's door, peeked in, and "saw this body in the bed and didn't want to wake him up. So I went down to check again and I was surprised to find that he wasn't there—he had actually stuffed his bed with a pillow and blankets to make it look like he was present and accounted for. We found out he had left campus and was in Boston. The school's notion was 'If he's taking off on us, he really doesn't want to be here.'"

At the time, Bobby had a crush on a cute blonde, a fifteen-year-old bartender's daughter named Kim Kelley, who lived on the Cape near the Kennedy compound, and there was campus chatter that Bobby was sneaking out to see her, or even smuggling her into the school itself.

In the compound, he had gotten together with her in the home that had once been JFK's and was known within the clan as the "President's House." When his mother angrily discovered the surreptitious get-togethers there, Bobby and Kelley found another place in the compound to hook up and party, a child's playhouse that had a bed in it. His mother, who had already practically disowned Bobby and couldn't countenance the Kelley girl, banned her from the compound and booted Bobby out of her home there. Desperate to be with the Kelley girl, Bobby was said to have once scaled a tree and climbed into her second-floor bedroom at home.

But that was nothing compared with the trouble that lay ahead for the two teen lovers.

Like Kim Kelley, most girls swooned over Bobby.

His classmate Lindsey Miesmer, looking back many years later, thought he was "a cute guy who had great Kennedy eyes and was tall and skinny. But his manner was also very sweet. I never went out with him, but I sometimes ate meals with him and I remember him pulling out my chair for me and being a polite guy, and back in the late sixties, early seventies, everybody was pretty rude, but he was one of the few guys who was more of a gentleman to me. I didn't expect any kind of special treatment. It was just very subtle with Bobby. It was just a vibe that I picked up that he was very sensitive."

Continued Miesner, who became a family therapist: "I felt it was hard for him to be a Kennedy at Pomfret, and I just felt like I wanted to give him space. I also felt he needed friends. I think he was treated differently because he was a Kennedy, and I knew he was very troubled. He was just doing lots of drugs, and the poor kid was just really screwed up. I have to say I was worried about him. He just seemed lost to me and that made me sad. I wanted to reach out to him, but I was shy."

Like all Pomfret students, Bobby had been assigned an adviser to help him deal with any school or academic issues. But Warren Geissinger, looking back to that time in 2013 at the age of ninety, recalled, "I didn't do much advising with Bobby because we didn't have that kind of a relationship. He was really a loner and was at the school at a time when he was really not himself, and very troubled—within himself, mixed up, didn't want to talk much. We never had a real conversation. The only thing is—I thought he was one of the brightest kids on the block."

Geissinger, who along with his wife, Barbara, taught music at Pomfret from the mid-fifties to the mid-seventies, had been present when Ethel Kennedy and Lem Billings met with Headmaster Milnor on the day Bobby arrived to begin classes, and he thought the arrangement was odd and not favorable to Bobby's emotional health.

"Ethel only came once, never had any other contact about her son, and all she wanted to do when she was here that one day was to just go down and watch football practice, and demand he play. But everything involving Bobby had to go through Billings—*everything*, all the correspondence, any and all communication about Bobby. I was told by Billings, 'Nothing ever goes directly to Ethel.' And I think Billings had a way of editing things—painting the picture of Bobby's performance smoother than it really was. I had written a report on Bobby, and Billings answered it and didn't agree with me, and that's when I thought, 'Uh-oh, he's in charge here. He's taken over.'"

Because of Bobby's problems, Pomfret's physician Dr. David Bates, a school trustee, described as an old-fashioned country doctor, was said to have spent some time counseling him. At the same time, Billings, following Ethel's lead, had gotten in touch with Harvard's Dr. Robert Coles to help Bobby with his problems. More than three decades after RFK was murdered, Coles wrote a book entitled *Lives of Moral Leadership*, and the first two chapters were dedicated to Bobby's father, noting that Shakespeare's *Henry V* had influenced his life and work and what Coles described as RFK's moral heroism. Coles had won a Pulitzer Prize for a series of books called Children of Crises, a profile that fit the Kennedy scion. But Bobby reportedly once revealed that Coles had actually confided in him that "psychiatrists are full of shit."

In researching Rose Kennedy's 1974 bestselling autobiography, *Times to Remember*, her ghostwriter, *Life* magazine's Robert Coughlan, had noted in his personal papers that she once told him, "Bobby has gone to a psychiatrist who has helped him tremendously who is also a friend and admirer of Bobby's father. And he is tremendously interested. And I think the boy's been straightened out now. He's back in school."

But the matriarch was wrong, whether she was deceived, or was covering up for her grandson, or was just adding to the myth.

Coles had become a kind of house shrink to the Kennedy clan's third generation. He had worked with Bobby's troubled older brother, Joe, and was consulted when their cousin Christopher Kennedy Lawford had, like Bobby, become involved with heroin. He also had a role, along with several Kennedy family members, in getting Bobby and Joe's younger brother David into rehab after he suffered a serious infection from a drug dealer's stab wound while attempting to score heroin in a Boston suburb's crime-riddled black neighborhood.

Richard E. Burke, who was a top aide to Bobby's uncle Ted Kennedy, recalled that Ethel Kennedy "seemed to be at the end of her rope" with Bobby and David. Burke said he expressed his concerns to the senator, who told him he had "clearly seen the problems coming for a long time," and knew that Bobby and David, who was doing drugs at another boarding school, "needed fatherly guidance," and he was aware that Lem Billings "had tried to fill the bill. But that wasn't working."

Burke claimed that Ted Kennedy had attended school functions, but no one at Pomfret remembered him ever visiting Bobby. Dealing with Bobby's problems and the rest of RFK's brood "was too much for any man, even a Kennedy," Burke asserted.

While Geissinger thought of Bobby as a loner, he also was aware that whatever friendships Bobby had made at Pomfret were with some of the blacks who "thought Bobby was their champion in a way" because of the Kennedys' history in civil rights. They recalled that when Dr. Martin Luther King was assassinated on April 4, 1968, it was Bobby's father who had chosen to break the horrific news to a predominantly black crowd at a planned campaign rally in Indianapolis when he was on the final swing of his ill-fated presidential run.

At one point he had told the shocked gathering, "For those of you who are black—considering the evidence evidently is that there were white people who were responsible—you can be filled with bitterness, and with hatred, and a desire for revenge. . . . For those of you who are black and are tempted to be filled with hatred and mistrust of the injustice of such an act, against all white people, I would only say that I can also feel in my own heart the same kind of feeling. I had a member of my family killed, but he was killed by a white man."

RFK called for a peaceful response to the killing in Memphis by a white racist named James Earl Ray. The King murder, however, inflamed America's blacks, and violent riots broke out in a number of major cities.

While some members of the Afro-Latin Society might have viewed Bobby as their champion, as Geissinger avowed, they were never the chosen people in Bobby's tiny social circle at Pomfret who were among the privileged few invited to visit Hickory Hill and/or Hyannis Port to party and get stoned; those few were white boys from well-to-do families. His black school chums would not have fitted in. Many of the African Americans at Pomfret were from the projects and broken families and were recruited from a New York City program called ABC—"A Better Chance"; Pomfret was among some two dozen upscale boarding schools that participated in the program.

ONE OF THE WHITE BOYS who palled around with Bobby and accompanied him once to the Kennedy compound and also to a Boston rock concert was a skinny, long-haired kid with an interesting background. Jacques Bailhé, known in school as "Zip," had moved with his family to Thailand in his early teens, spoke Thai fluently, and had been ordained as a novice priest by the supreme patriarch of Thailand. Bailhé had a different take on Bobby's seemingly close link to members of the Afro-Latin Society. "It was more than just that they sought him out," he maintained decades later. "My feeling was that he had charmed and used his intelligence to befriend them and then gained their trust and confidence."

Bailhé, who went on to produce, write, and direct documentaries, commercials, and motion picture special effects, said that Bobby had been interested in the "black experience" and how the black students felt about going to a "mostly white, not especially exclusive" private boarding school in Connecticut that was "not the kind of school that a black inner-city kid was familiar with."

Bobby's adviser Geissinger said that most, if not all, of the black students had become "kind of a problem" because they had wanted to segregate themselves on the floor of one dorm—the one Bobby had later chosen for himself—and "they wanted special privileges."

When a survey on race relations was conducted at the practically all-white boarding school, just 41 percent of those who responded supported the nonviolent philosophy of Martin Luther King, but 53 percent divided their vote among a trio of notorious black militants—Stokely Carmichael, the deceased Malcolm X, and Eldridge Cleaver.

Aside from the racial unrest, the bigger problem, one with which Bobby was intimately involved, was drugs. "Pomfret became known as the school to send your kids to if you want them to do drugs," Geissinger wryly stated. That reputation was sparked because Jay Milnor, a rarity among headmasters of private boarding schools at the time, had become outspoken about the growing drug problem, while others remained silent and covered up the issue. But Milnor's honesty had backfired. "Pomfret," noted Geissinger, "was suddenly a sinking ship. The school suddenly wasn't having a lot of kids apply, because of the drug reputation. Pomfret almost closed, and I soon got out of there."

One of the igniting incidents had occurred shortly before Bobby arrived, when Milnor threatened to expel a small number of students for smoking marijuana. When the rest of the student body learned of the headmaster's plans, they protested against what they believed was unfair discipline, and at a meeting some fifty students made it known that they also partook of the evil weed and declared that they, too, should be expelled. When the furor had subsided, the original offender was given the boot, but all the others who had sided with him were permitted to stay, but were interrogated about their drug use. The school just couldn't afford to lose all of their tuition had they been expelled. Milnor later was quoted as saying that dealing with the drug issue at Pomfret was like "trying to shut down a geyser by stepping on it, only to have three more pop up."

WHILE HIS CLASSMATE JACQUES BAILHÉ found Bobby to be bright and fun, he also perceived his Kennedy arrogance.

Because Bailhé had a car on campus, Bobby invited him to go to Boston to attend a rock concert. When they reached the little town of Putnam, Connecticut, near Pomfret, Bobby mentioned that he had to cash a personal check. It was from his mother, who was still sending him spending money but had no other known contact with him.

The young woman teller looked suspicious when Bobby presented the personal check for cashing. Looking more like stoned hippie bank robbers than clean-cut prep school boys, both he and Bailhé had dirty-looking shoulder-length hair; Bobby was wearing ragged jeans and a tattered corduroy jacket, and Bailhé had on a gold-embroidered Iranian floor-length leather coat.

"We were looking disheveled and probably smelled like a latrine," he recalled.

"When she saw the Kennedy name on the check," recounted Bailhé, "she asked Bobby for his identification, and he says, 'Like what?' She says, 'Well, your driver's license,' and he says, 'I don't have one,' and she said, 'Well, I have to have some form of ID,' and he said, 'Well, I have nothing. I go to school at Pomfret.'" Bailhé did his best to vouch for him. "I told her, 'He really is Robert Kennedy Jr., he's a good guy, please cash his check.'"

By this point the teller seemed frightened and intimidated. The bank manager, suspiciously watching the scene and possibly ready to call the police, sauntered over and asked Bobby and Bailhé to accompany him to his desk. "He says, 'I have no doubt you are who you say you are, but I can't cash a check without some kind of identification.' Bobby's sitting there and basically saying, I'm Robert Kennedy Jr., cash this check, give me the money, how dare you question me. Bobby just did not have any fear, about the law or authority. I always feared getting arrested, and the idea of getting arrested was preposterous to him. His view was, no one's going to arrest me, you think some cop's going to arrest me? And he thought that way because he was a Kennedy. He just figured that didn't happen to them.

"At the bank, I said to Bobby, 'Don't you have *anything* with your name on it?' And he says, 'Oh, yeah, wait,' and he grabs his coat collar and leans forward and shows it to the guy and it's his Pomfret School laundry tag, and it says 'Robert Kennedy Jr.,' and the guy burst into laughter and said, 'Okay, fine, I'll cash the check.'"

That was Bailhé's typical experience with the Kennedy namesake, that he was completely unassuming, just another guy. "But when necessary he would whip out his charm and flex his Kennedy muscle a little bit. Bobby knew how to use that extremely well and with great sensitivity, and I'm sure he's used it through the years."

Bobby used the Kennedy arrogance, and none of the Kennedy charm, when he and his girlfriend, Kim Kelley, were accosted not long after by a Hyannis Port policeman as they sat in a car eating ice cream cones.

According to Bobby's account, the officer began questioning him; Bobby didn't like his attitude, and literally spit a mouthful of ice cream in the cop's face, and was duly ordered out of the car, handcuffed, and taken into custody. He learned at that moment that Kennedys do, in fact, get arrested. He was charged with sauntering and loitering, and, according to one account, he called the officer a liar several times at his court appearance.

He appeared in court the next day, pleaded no contest, and was ordered to pay fifty dollars in costs. Some years later he called the incident "the most regrettable in my life." But he was only twenty-one then, and there would be more regrettable and more serious incidents to come.

Many years later, that arrest still bothered Bobby, who claimed it hadn't happened the way the cop said it did.

"He said something smart to my girlfriend and I probably said something smart-ass and he slapped the ice cream out of my hand, handcuffed me immediately, put me on the ground and then called a cruiser," Bobby complained to *The Washington Post* in August 1978. "When I got to the police station, he said I was drunk. I wasn't. They sent me off. The desk sergeant probably said, 'He's not drunk and that's Bobby Kennedy.' See, the guy didn't know it was me. I really felt terrible because that is just what some people want to think about the Kennedys."

Baihle recalled that Bobby's arrest was widely talked about at Pomfret, and that everyone thought it was so characteristic of him that when the cop stopped to question him he said, " 'Do you know who I am?' We all thought it was hysterically funny. Bobby definitely had a dark side."

Bobby's arrogance, Bailhé observed, was part and parcel of how he perceived the "entire Kennedy family history. He acted in the way a red-blooded Kennedy behaved, from his grandfather the patriarch, Joe, on down the line."

For example, years after Pomfret, Bailhé had gotten to know Bobby's cousin Maria Shriver in California because his kids and her kids attended the same high school. "Maria was just as arrogant as Bobby ever was," he asserted. "She had that same I-don't-pay-attention-to-the-laws gene. In the middle of Beverly Hills she'd pull up to a store that had absolutely no parking, park her car, and go shopping. And it wouldn't bother her if a cop wrote a ticket. She'd complain, 'Oh, for heaven's sake!' And this was while her husband was governor."

ONE DAY IN LATE WINTER 1971, Harold "Skip" Hine, then a senior at Pomfret, was racing down the stairs to get to class when Bobby—"long hair, very thin, dressed like he was going to a Janis Joplin concert"—suddenly stopped him in his tracks and said he'd heard that Hine was going to the upcoming Vietnam antiwar protest march in Washington, D.C. When Hine said he was, out of the blue Bobby invited him to stay overnight at his home in nearby Virginia, the fabled Hickory Hill.

It was all very odd, Hine thought at the time, because he didn't know Bobby and, in fact, wasn't even aware for a long time that a Kennedy was a student at Pomfret. "To this day, I literally can't believe that he knew my name," he said many years later.

Hine also thought it was "sort of sad" because Bobby seemed to be reaching out to make friends, instead of people befriending him. "He didn't want the spotlight. He tried to stay under the radar. I found him to be somewhat shy. The black kids very much embraced him. But some other people kept their distance. People were overcompensating by giving him space and not intruding. In retrospect, it may have been isolating him even more so than he wanted to be. He did confide in me that it was very lonely at Pomfret because either people avoided him or they didn't know what to say to him. But if you went into town for a pizza someone would always ask, 'Do you go to school with Bobby Kennedy?' So there were rumblings out there."

Hine did take advantage of Bobby's gracious invitation and stayed the night at Hickory Hill, and at breakfast watched as his mother, Ethel, "needled" Bobby—"Bobby, get the hair out of your face . . . Bobby, speak up . . . Bobby, what time are you going back to school?" Mrs. Kennedy was "asking him these things in front of the whole table, asking mom things that any mom or father who was a pain in the ass would ask, and Bobby just sat there eating his eggs. Whether there was deeper stuff going on, I never saw it."

It was clear to Hine, who went on to become a photographer, that Bobby had no intention, at least back then, of following in the political footsteps of his father and uncles, whose photographs adorned the walls of Hickory Hill but about whom he never once talked. "The photos on the walls," observed Hine, were "a rogue's gallery of history." When Hine asked him whether he'd ever throw his hat in the political arena like his forebears, his response was a resounding "Hell, no!"

Hine had heard the reports about Bobby's bad behavior, such as sneaking off campus to go to Boston, and doing drugs, and wondered, "Was Bobby being Bobby Kennedy, or was Bobby being 'boys being boys' in those turbulent times. I never knew. It's very hard to separate the two, or to blame one on the other."

ACADEMICALLY, BOBBY'S TEACHERS CONSIDERED him to be bright—he had five courses—but they also saw that he was lazy and uninterested in his work. One of his instructors, Steve Danenberg, had joined the Pomfret faculty in the fall of 1970 at the same time that Bobby, a forced troubled washout at Millbrook, had arrived to begin his junior year. Danenberg's first teaching assignment had been in JFK's Peace Corps, and he had come to Pomfret after a stint in the blackboard jungle schools of New York City's tough Bedford-Stuyvesant district.

In 1966, when Bobby's father was New York's junior U.S. Senator, he had toured predominately black Bed-Stuy, as it is known, and was shocked by the urban blight and horrific living conditions. Later that same year, RFK, along with Mayor John Lindsay and Senator Jacob Javitts, announced the establishment of the Bedford-Stuyvesant Restoration Corporation to rehabilitate the area. Danenberg, teaching in Bed-Stuy at the time, was one of many who considered RFK a hero.

Years later, Danenberg recalled that late-sixties era and noted, "The Kennedys did a huge thing in Bedford-Stuyvesant and, of course, Bobby's father was one of the few white people who could walk into those areas and get support. Bobby's father was probably the most important person in how my political views developed. My view always was that if that man had not been assassinated and had been president the whole country and the world would be totally different and ten million times better than where we are right now. I believe that now [in 2013] and I believed that then."

So Danenberg was initially excited to learn that one of his pupils in Latin American history, a seminar-like course held in the teacher's living room, was the namesake of his slain political hero.

But he soon came to the realization that Robert Kennedy Jr. was not what he would have expected based on his father. "Bobby," he recalled, "was exceedingly bright, but he didn't participate a whole lot. He was aloof, and he wasn't engaged in anything that I could see. He was kind of drawn into himself when he was in my classroom. Basically, he was just there, but it was not the kind of engagement you'd see from a student who wasn't having issues."

Danenberg was aware that Robert Coles had been called in to counsel the very troubled Bobby, and he found that interesting because he had been reading some of Coles's books on dealing with problem children. He had also been made aware that Bobby's relationship with his mother was "pretty weak—the implication was that her relationship with her son wasn't focused."

Bobby's involvement with drugs was the other major issue that concerned the faculty and the administration.

"It was pretty widely known as the school year progressed that he was using drugs, and it became a widespread concern," Danenberg stated.

"And it was known that it wasn't just marijuana, but harder drugs. But the school assumed that Coles was dealing with Bobby's problems, including the drug issue."

AROUND CHRISTMAS 1970, NEAR the end of the first half of Bobby's turbulent junior year, Pomfret's embattled headmaster, Jay Milnor, announced that he was taking a mini-sabbatical to visit with his family in Europe. When he left in mid-April, he turned over control to Per-Jan Ranhoff, the assistant headmaster, originally from Oslo, and Bob Sloat, his administrative assistant. "Per-Jan acted in my absence, having full authority, and I trusted him completely, and I didn't stay in touch at all with the school while I was away," said Milnor. "But I was aware, clearly, when I left that Bobby Kennedy Jr.'s tenure was bumpy."

One of Milnor's veteran teachers, and one much beloved by his students although he had a reputation for being somewhat tough, was Hagop Merjian, who on Bobby's arrival at Pomfret was teaching a class dealing in issues of social justice and minority involvement by having his class read the literature of minorities—but "not the kind of shit by the likes of H. Rap Brown [one of Bobby's favorites] but American blacks like Ralph Ellison's *Invisible Man*, good stuff. I would never read H. Rap Brown, oh, my God, no!"

Bobby was in Merjian's class, a roundtable discussion situation, and his teacher thought of him as an "extremely bright child, exceptional intellectually," but he immediately saw him as a problem child who tried to withdraw physically from the group, who always came late to class and disheveled, whose eyes appeared bleary, who looked, as Merjian clearly and bluntly recalled years later, "like he went through shit all night long, which he did. It was so obvious—it was more than obvious. It was embarrassingly obvious" that he was doing drugs.

Merjian had arrived at Pomfret in 1961, shortly after JFK took office, and would remain there for four decades until his retirement in 2001 when George W. Bush was president. When he first came to the school it consisted of, he said, "One hundred and forty white boys, most with blond hair and blue eyes, and no blacks and no Jews—*none*. But agitators like me had changed Pomfret by the time young Mr. Kennedy got there. Without Jay Milnor I would never have been allowed to do that. He was progressive, ahead of his time. I was with him when Obama became president and he wept [with joy]."

But Milnor's open-door policy toward minority students eventually backfired. The graduating class in 1975 was 27 percent minority, and, according to Merjian, that statistic would get Milnor fired. "The trustees considered that he had gone overboard," Merjian asserted. "There was a trustee who said, 'You know what the problem is at Pomfret—too many black faces,' and when he said that the school was less than ten percent black."

Merjian, who worked under six headmasters during his long Pomfret tenure, had even greater respect for Milnor because of the way he handled the dire drug problem. "Jay kicked out large numbers of kids. He brought in therapists. He faced it because it was monstrous at that time," Merjian noted. "Fifty percent of our kids were doing weed, at the least. It was a huge problem in America, but in a private school like Pomfret where kids had money there were exotic drugs of all kinds."

If anyone was using or holding them, it was Robert Kennedy Jr., Merjian shrewdly suspected after keeping a sharp eye on him. Thus, Bobby became Merjian's target for expulsion in the early spring of 1971 when Jay Milnor was off vacationing in Europe and his second in command, Per-Jan Ranhoff, was running the show.

Merjian's suspicions had intensified when a number of concerned students whom he respected for their opinion came forward and ratted that Bobby was doing, as he put it, "Really bad, shit drugs—heavy shit. Oh, no," Merjian emphasized, "Bobby wasn't just a pothead. No, I wished he was only a pothead. But I think he was using heroin, and I think he was mixing heavy shit with alcohol, and the other students were saying, 'Mr. Merjian, he passes out at night. You can't even talk to him. He's gone. He's stoned.' His classmates were worried that he was going to kill himself, that we were going to find him dead."

Merjian was saddened by what he was witnessing and hearing. He theorized that the Kennedy namesake was drowning his emotions in drugs because of his father's assassination and all the other issues he faced as a scion of America's royal family in the aftermath of Camelot. "Bobby was a bright, wonderful kid, but just think of the load that was on his

shoulders emotionally—oh my God!" he strenuously asserted in retirement in his mid-seventies in 2013. "Everybody knew who he was. Everybody would talk about him. The whole world knew about his father, his
uncle, his family, and, Jesus Christ, what with the drugs, Bobby was lucky
to have lived."

Merjian spoke to a few of his colleagues and it was decided that, while
it might not enhance or help Pomfret's already tarnished reputation because of drugs and racial issues, the best course of action was to "get
Bobby the hell out before Pomfret went down the tubes because we
found a dead Kennedy."

Merjian voted to have Bobby expelled, and three or four other faculty members who had had Bobby in class or had other dealings with
him at Pomfret seconded the idea.

It was late in April or early in May 1971 that "kind of a cabal" of teachers led by Merjian met with the acting headmaster, Ranhoff.

"All of us in that cabal were using language like 'He's going to kill
himself in our dorm,' which would make any headmaster sit up straight."
After they presented their evidence, they formally proposed that Bobby
be sacked.

"We couched it," said Merjian, "in terms of what was best for Bobby:
Was it best that he stay and risk the possibility of injuring himself seri-
ously or completely, or was it best for him, as nasty as it was, to ask a
Kennedy to leave, to have him leave."

Ranhoff wholeheartedly agreed with Merjian, and immediately made
Lem Billings and Bobby's psychiatrist, Coles, aware of the decision. Merjian believed that Coles "must have had knowledge the kid was struggling with drugs. He must have known the agonies the kid was going
through. That kid didn't want to be here. I'm sure he felt he was incar-
cerated."

The official reason that Bobby was asked to leave Pomfret before the
end of his first year there was only ever revealed to his mother and Billings. In 1984 a well-reported, unauthorized book about the clan—*The
Kennedys: An American Drama*—was published, written by the young
journalists Peter Collier and David Horowitz, who had co-authored a
well-received biography of the Rockefeller dynasty.

Long-haired, hip, and intellectual, they had ingratiated themselves with Bobby when he was in his mid-twenties, and he openly boasted to them about his varied exploits and troubled life as a teenager, and also introduced the writers to some of his wayward brothers, cousins, and friends to tell their stories of drugs and other problems, all of which were reported chapter and verse in titillating detail in a section appropriately entitled "The Lost Boys."

The problem was that some of Bobby's claims were pie in the sky, and simply often self-serving. Regarding his seven or eight drug-addled, troubled months at Pomfret, covered in two densely reported paragraphs by Collier and Horowitz, there was no mention of his drug use there. But Bobby's claim that he had insisted on living in an all-black dorm at Pomfret, when no such dorm ever existed, was reported. "We never had an all-black dorm," maintained Robert Sloat, who had been Jay Milnor's administrative assistant during Bobby's matriculation. It was just a floor in a dorm that the black students had inhabited.

Bobby had also asserted to Collier and Horowitz that his teenage girl-friend Kim Kelley had visited him at the school, that he had hidden her in his room at night, and that during the day he had set her up in the school's basement replete with a hot plate for cooking, so Bobby wouldn't have to get dressed for meals in the dining hall. The authors' brief documentation of his Pomfret time ended with Bobby being expelled, leaving readers to think the reason was the girl.

Perhaps in Bobby's mind, the Kelley tale underscored the rebel, macho Kennedy persona he was promoting to the writers. According to Collier and Horowitz's source notes, Pam Kelley, Kim's sister, backed up Bobby's account, even adding that she occasionally had hitchhiked to Pomfret with her sister.

But Hagop Merjian, along with other retired Pomfret administrators and teachers, had no memory or evidence of such incidents involving Bobby and a girl, and maintained that such a thing had no part in Bobby's expulsion. "As far as I know," maintained Merjian, "it had nothing to do with sexuality with a girl. If she was here, no one knew it. If she was, he was clever enough to sneak her in and sneak her out. But drugs was the reason we wanted him out."

Bobby's classmates realized he was suddenly gone, as if he had never been there. Some claimed they had no idea why he had left—the school made no announcement—but others, such as Lindsey Cole Miesner, who later was a Pomfret trustee, said, "We all knew he was expelled for drugs, and the fact that he was doing more serious drugs, more major drugs than marijuana. Everybody was doing pot; in fact, half the school was. But I never knew anything about him bringing a girl on campus, or that being a reason why he was asked to leave."

When the headmaster, Jay Milnor, returned from his sabbatical in mid-July, he was told what had transpired with Bobby.

"What I felt," he recalled thinking, "was great relief."

Many years after Bobby had left Pomfret and moved on with his turbulent life, the wife of the longtime head of the school's trustees approached Hagop Merjian at an alumni weekend and told him that she had met Mr. Kennedy and he had instructed her to offer him his regards.

"I'll never forget it," Merjian said. "It's close to verbatim, but not verbatim. Bobby said, 'Tell Mr. Merjian he was the only motherfucker who knew what he was doing at that school.' I don't think he ever knew it was I who helped to get him expelled because he was doing bad drugs."

BOBBY RETURNED HOME TO Hickory Hill, where his mother was preparing for the May 1972 annual charity pet show thrown by the Robert F. Kennedy Memorial Foundation. The place was a madhouse, according to Ted Kennedy's top senatorial aide, Richard Burke, who had been enlisted to help prepare the homestead for the event. He recalled that the younger of the Kennedy children were "in various states of undress, running amok. Ethel scurried about, screaming orders at the top of her lungs. The kids were either playing or fighting and screamed constantly."

Hickory Hill, he concluded, was "definitely a place to visit at your own risk."

Regarding Bobby, Burke observed that Ethel seemed to be exhausted. One day Burke ran into RFK's namesake at the house wearing only his jockey shorts and looking dazed and glassy-eyed, the signs of being stoned. Outside in the garden, Burke was using a hoe to clear some weeds when he heard Bobby's brother David screaming at him to stop what he was doing, to not clear the weeds, but to rather put a fence around them.

Just then Ethel's secretary approached Burke and said, "Oh, they stopped you, huh?"

When he asked what the weeds were, she told him marijuana. "They grow it all the time. And smoke it."

Burke was surprised, not so much about the smoking—he'd done his share in college—but the growing, because "it was illegal, and even if Ethel's kids were out of control, this was a very public home for the Kennedys, with press and dignitaries coming in and out all the time, but if they didn't see the problem, I certainly wasn't going to raise it."

ROBERT KENNEDY JR. WASN'T THE first member of the clan to have the dishonor of having his (or her) face and name smeared across the cover of the premier supermarket tabloid of the time, *The National Enquirer*, then billing itself as having the "Largest Circulation of Any Weekly Paper in America." But he was among the youngest of the third generation to become checkout-line tabloid fodder.

A few months after Bobby was asked to leave Pomfret—the second boarding school from which he was expelled in less than three years, mainly for using drugs—"enquiring minds" who had paid twenty cents a copy at the cash register to read about UFOs and celebrity misdeeds beheld the blaring headline "RFK Jr. Leaves Home, Says He Will Marry."

The *Enquirer* noted that the Pomfret School had confirmed that Bobby had been a student there, that he had left in May, and "if he had successfully completed his courses last spring he would now be a senior."

The seventeen-year-old Kennedy scion's future wife, the story claimed, was his girlfriend, sixteen-year-old Kim Kelley, who was with him when he threw the ice cream in the Hyannis Port cop's face—her Bonnie to his Clyde.

According to the tabloid, Bobby had "dropped out of school"—there was no mention, presumably for legal reasons, that he was actually booted for drugs—"no longer lives with his family, and he plans to marry." Ms. Kelley was described as a "blond high-school sophomore." Her mother, Peg Kelley, wife of bartender Frank Kelley, was quoted extensively.

She described Bobby as being "very, very independent," and revealed that his mother, Ethel, had told him "he must live by the rules of her house or else he would have to leave home until he sees things the way the family sees them. So Bobby stays away."

She said she felt Bobby was "sensitive." But she also knew "he's all boy. . . . We love Bobby. He may not be brilliant in school but which Kennedys were? He's a smart kid just the same."

At the Kelley home, near the Kennedy compound, Bobby kept a change of clothes, she claimed, and "often spends the night in a spare bedroom off the kitchen."

The tabloid, which paid "big bucks" for stories—checkbook journalism was a way of life in the Lantana, Florida, newsroom—went on to quote an anonymous neighbor of the Kennedys, who made Bobby sound like some sort of a derelict, asserting that he had "been sleeping wherever someone would take him for the night. Bobby buzzes into my house to listen to records. He's a quiet kid, but he lives a weird life. He might be sitting on the post office steps at 6 a.m. with friends and you might see him there at midnight." There, however, was no mention of young Bobby's current drug usage.

The *Enquirer* story with its titillating tale of Kennedy young love was picked up by the wire services and distributed to the mainstream press. The story, replete with photos of shaggy-haired, skinny Bobby in an oversize sports jacket and wearing a necktie, and Kim, looking a bit chubby and scruffy, along with a photo of the Kelleys' modest family home, quoted Kim's father as saying he had telephoned Ethel Kennedy twice in 1971, telling her she needed to do something about her son's behavior. He related how Bobby had climbed into his daughter's bedroom window in the middle of the night, and another time he had been "on the verge of having Bobby locked up, but I don't want to discuss that. He is very welcome at my home now. He asks my permission when he wants to stay."

Kelley said he took on some fatherly responsibility with Bobby, since no one in the Kennedy family seemed to be doing anything to help him. "I felt he needed some guidance," Kelley told the tabloid. "I asked him what he wanted to do with his life and about school. He quit school last May. Bobby told me, 'I should go back to school. But I don't know if I will.'"

During the course of reporting the story, an *Enquirer* reporter claimed to have picked up Bobby and Kim, who were hitchhiking in Hyannis on their way to Hyannis Port. When the reporter asked Bobby whether he intended to return to school, "Bobby answered, 'No.' Then he glanced back at Kim and said, 'We're getting married.'" Asked what they would live on, Bobby replied, "I've got a job." But the story noted that Bobby had a "reputation" for mischief and he began joking that he was going to get a job "in the garbage department."

Kim's father said his daughter idolized Bobby and that Bobby had told him that he wanted to marry her. But Frank Kelley felt they were "too young even though they are all wrapped up in each other. She thinks there's nobody else like him in the world."

He said he was aware that there were people who considered Bobby "trash," with which he disagreed.

"Bobby's far from it," the father of his daughter's lover declared. "He's very quiet. He's a sincere kid. Bobby's got a long life to live. . . . He's a kid—one who has had more heartbreak than anybody should have to stand."

THIRTEEN

Palfrey Street

Even with all of its drug, racial, and feminist issues, the Pomfret School was like a Franciscan monastery compared with Bobby's next stop on his precarious way to a high school diploma.

Experimental and alternative in the extreme, Palfrey Street School, located on Palfrey Street in the mostly blue-collar Boston suburb of Watertown, was founded just seven years before Bobby first set foot on the small, neighborhood school grounds "wearing dirty, faded jeans, smelling like patchouli oil, and accompanied by two men in suits," recalled his classmate John Cuetara, then a senior in the Class of '72.

Even though Bobby hadn't finished his junior year at Pomfret before he was asked to leave, he was given credit for the turbulent partial school year he had spent there, and entered Palfrey as a full-fledged senior.

The school was the brainchild of Ned Ryerson, a liberal, hippie-like educator in his late forties who was an heir in the wealthy Ryerson dynasty of Chicago; his great-grandfather Joseph T. Ryerson had founded Inland Steel, and Ned's father, Edward L. Ryerson Jr., had been the company's chairman and a popular community leader in the Windy City.

Ned had money on both sides. His first wife, whom he married in

1941 and with whom he started Palfrey, was Alice Judson Ryerson Hayes, a blue blood who was the granddaughter of Howard Van Doren Shaw, a noted Chicago architect, and his poet wife, Frances Shaw. Alice's mother was Sylvia Shaw Judson, a distinguished sculptor who had the honor of having one of her statues in the Rose Garden at the White House, while the Art Institute of Chicago featured her collection. Among the schools Alice attended were Milton Academy, where RFK had gone, and Harvard, home to a lineup of Kennedys.

By the mid-seventies, the Ryersons' marriage—they had four children—was on the rocks, and they were divorced, and a few years later she remarried; her second husband was the professor emeritus in English at the University of Chicago. Around the time of her divorce she established the Ragdale Foundation, an artists' community located in Lake Forest, Illinois, on the grounds of her family's summer estate.

A few years after his divorce, Ned Ryerson began going blind and, according to the scuttlebutt, became a "big medical marijuana person because of that," said Royce Augustine Hoyle III, who was teaching college preparatory English and ninth-grade English at Palfrey when Bobby began classes there. Along with some sort of prescription goggles he wore at school, the weed must have helped Ryerson. Despite losing his eyesight, he took fencing lessons, sailed using an audio compass, and went mountain climbing. Like his ex-wife, he also remarried.

But long before Ryerson got turned on to marijuana for medicinal purposes, it was a recreational staple for most of the Palfrey student body and even some of the faculty. Bobby Kennedy was a perfect fit and in his element, at least where recreational drugs were concerned.

Shortly after Ryerson founded Palfrey, its alternative style of teaching had caught the attention of the local newsmedia, including *The Harvard Crimson*, with a little help from Ryerson's wife, who was an alumna.

In the 1967 profile of the school, the *Crimson* reported that a sixteen-year-old Exeter graduate was teaching phys ed and math; students were admitted with D and E averages; no test scores were ever used to select new students; IQ scores were tossed aside; pressure and competition were discouraged; there was little division between faculty and students; courses were arranged without regard to grade levels; and Ryerson was quoted as boasting, "We have kids who dropped out of high school," and he emphasized that he was wary of the "preciousness and snobbishness" of private school education.

In essence, any student whose parents could afford the tuition of around fifteen hundred dollars when the school first opened—considered quite high at the time—was admitted; others were given partial or full scholarships.

When Bobby arrived for the fall term in September 1971, little had changed except for the cost of tuition, which had risen.

ETHEL SKAKEL KENNEDY HAD DISTANCED herself even more from Bobby after he'd been booted from Pomfret and because of the difficult issues with Kim Kelley—from the ice-cream-in-the cop's-face episode to the embarrassing *National Enquirer* story. So all arrangements for his admission to Palfrey were handled by Lem Billings.

Of all the private schools in New England, Palfrey was virtually unknown. Billings had heard about it from another parent, a close Kennedy family confidant, whose son had gone there. Adam Yarmolinsky had been a trusted adviser to Bobby's father and his uncles JFK and Ted Kennedy. When Yarmolinsky died of leukemia at seventy-seven in 2000, the Massachusetts senator said, "All of us who had the good fortune to know him admired the brilliance of his mind and dedication to improving the quality of life for all Americans."

Yarmolinsky's son, Toby, had graduated from Palfrey about a year before Bobby arrived, but Yarmolinsky said in 2013 that he didn't know the Kennedy scion.

Billings thought the permissive world of Palfrey would be good for his troubled teenage charge, and believed "if there was too much structure Bobby would blow up," according to the woman with whom he would board during his senior year. Moreover, Billings felt certain that Palfrey offered the "only possibility that Bobby might finish high school."

UNLIKE MILLBROOK AND POMFRET, Palfrey was a day school, so Bobby required housing and meals and daily oversight. Enter Joanne "Joey" Brode, a mother of three who would have him as a paying lodger in her family's sprawling yellow 1865 farmhouse, still a fixer-upper, in neighboring Cambridge during his time at Palfrey. When Bobby arrived, Brode was teaching French and then sixth grade in area public schools. But she became a virtual surrogate mother to him because, as she asserted years later, "Ethel didn't even call Bobby on his birthday. She never was here."

Billings had found the Brode family through a mutual friend, Samuel Hutchison Beer, a highly respected Harvard University political scientist who, during JFK's presidency, was head of Americans for Democratic Action, an organization committed to liberal politics. Beer lived in the Brodes' neighborhood and he and Joey Brode's husband, John, a mathematician who had once taught at Harvard, were active together in local politics.

In the late summer of 1971, Beer called Brode and asked him whether he would be willing to talk to his friend Billings about the possibility of having Bobby stay in their home while he was going to the Palfrey Street School. The Brodes, who had had young people as roomers in the past, were amenable, and a bit starstruck at the same time. Longtime liberal democrats, they were becoming a small part of Kennedy family history by having RFK's namesake in their home for a school year.

Agewise, Joey Brode could have been more a big sister to Bobby than the mistress of the house because she was just eleven years older than he; she had gotten married at nineteen. They would develop a close bond during his stay. He had arrived at her welcoming and warm home with Billings in early September for a meet and greet, but Bobby wanted to chat with her privately and had asked Billings to wait outside.

Brode's first reaction was that Bobby looked like "a bird with a broken wing. He was trembling and skinny and looked really like a sad, lonely kid who'd been through hell, and my heart just went out to him," she recalled. "I used the term 'a bird with a broken wing,' but more explicitly and less metaphorically, he just needed to be viewed as a human being, as a person without the endless context of the Kennedy family. He had a frightened, fragile, vulnerable quality, but I didn't really see him as nihilistic."

Brode had done some research on the impact of losing a parent on a boy like Bobby, and she came to the conclusion that she would have a "case history" living with her. "Bobby was at the most vulnerable age from an identity-formation perspective. I kind of made sure that every-body in the family, that every friend who came to visit simply viewed him as a person, not a Kennedy."

And during the school year he stayed with the Brodes there was very little discussion about his politically powerful and privileged family.

"I never ever asked Bobby, and he didn't really talk about his parents much at all," she said. "As far as I can remember, I don't believe he ever actually spent any time talking about his father. I felt he was always on edge."

On just one memorable occasion, however, chatter focused on his emotionally and physically distant mother, whom Bobby described to Joey Brode as "controlling," maintaining that she was on top of him for everything and anything he did. One evening in the Brodes' kitchen, Joey brought up the subject of her husband John's relationship with his own mother, who Joey told Bobby was a wonderful lady, but irrational. "And he looked at me with his piercing eyes and said, 'I can identify with that. My mother's totally irrational and totally controlling,' but that's the only conversation about her that we ever had that I can remember."

Knowing about Bobby's turbulent history and dangerous recreational pursuits, she had rules for him to follow if he was to live in her home.

"I told Bobby, 'I have three really important rules,'" recalled Brode. "'First of all, no drugs—there can be no drugs in this house. Secondly, you always must call if you're going to be late for dinner, because dinners are a big deal around here, and the third thing—I don't really care if you want to have a girl sleep here, but I want it to be the same person all the time because I want my kids to grow up understanding that love is good with one person.'"

It was a curious set of regulations, especially for a troubled boy like Bobby who, despite Lem Billings's belief that he needed more freedom or would blow up, actually required tighter controls, even though he was about to turn eighteen in January, just four months from the date he took up residence.

Joey Brode's rules were curious because, in her very liberal home, sex was permitted for Bobby, but only if it was monogamous. Not many households in America, even back in the early Swinging Seventies, were so openly permissive with their teenagers.

And Joey Brode's strict no-drugs rule had a caveat as well, as it turned out—smoking marijuana in the house was A-okay with her "because that wasn't a drug in my mind, and still isn't," she said in a 2013 interview. "I didn't mind it because I did it in the sixties. I would not have been shocked and appalled if Bobby smoked, but it wasn't my favorite thing with him given everything I knew [about his drug use]. Pot didn't freak me out at all."

She remembered that Bobby toked up in his room, often smoking with Billings when he was visiting, which was frequently. (With Bobby as his drug guru through the years of their curious relationship, Billings would quickly graduate from marijuana. Following Bobby's lead, Billings, decades older and with heart problems, tripped on LSD, did angel dust, and shot speed, cocaine, and eventually heroin, all to show he was as youthful and hip as the young Kennedy he adored.)

For Bobby, the Brode household must have seemed like nirvana—sex with his girlfriend was okay, smoking pot was okay . . . he just had to be at the table in time for dinner.

LEM BILLINGS, BRODE IMMEDIATELY had gathered, was obsessively devoted to Bobby, loyal to him, and extremely dedicated to the Kennedy family. It was Billings who was basically "in *loco parentis*," she noted; it was he, not Ethel, who handled all of Bobby's expenses—his $2,400 tuition at Palfrey, his rent at the Brodes', which Joey said was a couple of hundred dollars a month, mainly to cover Bobby's food bill.

"Lem was the one I contacted if anything happened with Bobby," said Brode, such as the time one of the rent checks bounced. "He would come over fairly frequently for dinner whenever he was in town. He played with Bobby, if you will, more than a father probably would, was just devoted to him, and there was really honest affection between them. They had a joking, warm relationship and, at least from my perspective, it was very positive."

The Brodes were aware that Billings was gay, but it wasn't an issue with them that he and young Bobby had such a close and intimate relationship, mainly because the Brodes themselves had close homosexual friends. A number were in the political world—"men who later became rather well-known politicians in the state of Massachusetts," she boasted, "like Barney Frank and Gerry Studds."

A Harvard graduate and a leading Democrat, Frank, like Billings, was closeted for many years, even, unlike Billings, dating women. But Frank came out publicly in 1987 when the media began examining his personal life; Billings never did. At that time, a reputed bisexual Republican congressman from Connecticut had died, and Frank was quoted in *The Washington Post* stating, "There was an unfortunate debate about 'Was he, or wasn't he? Didn't he, or did he?' I said to myself, I don't want that to happen to me." He retired from Congress in 2013 and was succeeded by Bobby's nephew Joseph P. Kennedy III, son of Bobby's brother Joe.

The first openly gay member of Congress, Studds was censured in 1983 by the House of Representatives for having a sexual relationship with a seventeen-year-old male congressional page, an affair that Studds claimed was "consensual." The page scandal rocked Washington and Studds was stripped of a powerful subcommittee chairmanship. He left Congress in 1997, and married his longtime lover in 2004, shortly after same-sex marriage became legal in Massachusetts. He died in 2006.

"Because I had plenty of gay friends, and I think there is a kind of gaydar, I sensed Lem was gay, but he was pretty buttoned down, and communicated himself as being Ivy League preppy," Joey Brode asserted. "He had a kind of gentleness and sensitivity that was not kind of the way the typical straight guy of his age would behave. I never said to anyone, 'Do you think Lem's gay?' It never came into our heads because we didn't care. I didn't dwell on it, and I trusted Lem to really have Bobby's interests at heart."

WHILE KIM KELLEY WAS UNDER the impression that Bobby was her steady, he had quickly developed a close relationship with an exotic-looking, "kind of a hippie, very sexy, very smart," Armenian American Palfrey Street junior, a rebel like him, by the name of Vicki Boyajian, who had become his unwitting accomplice in what became known as the Kennedy Cupola Caper.

Headmaster Ryerson had been asked for permission to permit Bobby, Boyajian, and a friend of Bobby's to go up into the white clapboard

Italianate school's cupola and paint the interior walls. It seemed like an innocent-enough request and demonstrated school spirit, so he gave them his wholehearted approval.

"They thought we were just going to go up there and paint it like purple or yellow or whatever—but no, it was something completely different," said Boyajian. "And that cupola, when we were done with it, was pretty damn freaky. A teacher walked up there and looked at the walls and he was like, 'Shit, are you crazy? Ned's going to freak out when he sees this!' And I even remember saying to the teacher, 'It wasn't me, he did it,' pointing to Bobby's friend. I said I wanted to paint trees and suns and peace signs. And I was like, no, Ned will not freak out, don't worry."

In fact, Ryerson was indeed upset by what he saw on the walls.

"It was," Boyajian revealed, "a dead body with an erection, and all kinds of other things, all these weird things that we painted—a weird mural and a weird person and that erection, and they made us paint over it."

The incident was still being talked about years later when members of several Palfrey classes held a reunion, said their classmate John Cuetara, who had become a psychologist. "They were in the cupola and they were painting gigantic penises."

Boyajian, like so many females over the years who had fallen for Kennedy men, fell for Bobby. Looking back wistfully to her Palfrey Street School romance with him, she acknowledged that they became "a little intimate being together and hanging out" in Bobby's room at the Brodes' home, ten minutes from the school, where she also got to meet his druggie brother, David. "I went to that house many times. We'd hang out, listen to music, smoke pot—a little bit of this, a little bit of that."

While Bobby snuck Boyajian into the Brode home in the afternoons when no one else was around, Bobby's longtime girlfriend, Kim Kelley, had better privileges.

"Bobby would occasionally bring her to the house," Brode said. "She had dinner with us, but I had no real impression of her except that she was pretty and blond and he'd known her for a long time, and they seemed to trust each other. But Bobby never talked to me about her."

• • •

BOBBY'S LOOK AT THE TIME was pure Haight-Ashbury, Washington Square, Lower East Side grunge. He had grown a scraggly beard and his long hair was a mess; he looked, one classmate observed, "as stoned out and hippie as one can imagine." Lathered in patchouli oil to cover the smell of his daily intake of marijuana, he seemed to always be either gazing off into space or gazing at the floor, and rarely if ever made much eye contact with anyone.

"He was definitely stoned most of the time, possibly a little depressed, and certainly rebellious," John Cuetara observed. "Bobby just didn't have a lot of affect, and that's partly because he was always stoned. He seemed kind of nonresponsive. If you said something to him, he'd just say, 'Whatever, man.' He was not really engaging."

Still, sixteen-year-old Vicki Boyajian was entranced. She thought he was handsome, and liked his long hair. "Maybe to me it was intriguing that he was Bobby Kennedy," she acknowledged more than four decades later, after becoming a successful businesswoman. "We certainly all grew up in an era where we adored the Kennedys, and being in Massachusetts it was [adoration] big-time."

When Ryerson and other administrators learned that Bobby was seeing Vicki, however, they became concerned about her welfare. "Ned was very worried about me," she recalled. "He was concerned that I was with Bobby and that Bobby was going to be a bad influence on me. That concern is still very vivid. They were all like, 'Uh-oh, she's hanging out with Kennedy, is she going to get in trouble?' But I said, 'Listen, I'm just fine, don't worry about me. I can take care of myself.'"

Because the Brodes worked during the day, their home became playground central for their Kennedy boarder's recreational pursuits. If he didn't have the Kelley girl or Boyajian over for matinee fun—in true Kennedy womanizing fashion, presumably neither knew about the other—he invited a few male classmates to accompany him from school to the big yellow house to get high.

Because Palfrey didn't have a cafeteria, the school was flexible about what students did for lunch. Some went to a nearby sub shop, others went home. Since Bobby didn't have a car, he invited John Cuetara, who had a beat-up 1961 red Ford Falcon that was so rusted passengers could see the road through the floor, to drive him to the Brode home for lunch along with several other Palfrey classmates who, Cuetara remembered, "liked to do drugs with Bobby." One of them was the long-haired, troubled scion of a family that owned substantial land on Martha's Vineyard, and the other two were rebel types from blue-collar, working-class families.

"I knew I was invited because I had a car and they didn't—I had no illusions—but that was fine," said Cuetara, looking back. "I said to Bobby, 'What's for lunch?' and he said, 'I don't know. It's potluck.' So when we got there, of course, that's all there was—pot. Lunch was just marijuana, which was a great disappointment to me because I was looking forward to a good lunch, not to getting stoned."

Bobby and Cuetara had shared what was described as a "watered-down" anthropology class taught by a radical Black Muslim who went by the name of John X, and for a time the student discussion had centered on a problem the Palfrey Street School was having with nearby homeowners.

They were complaining about rowdy behavior by the students, but mostly about the sweet odor of marijuana that was wafting over the area from the school grounds. The neighbors had personally voiced their concerns to the headmaster about drug issues on the Palfrey campus, and as a result Ryerson *tried* to ban pot smoking. He announced to the student body—there were fewer than a hundred in the entire school—that toking must stop, or Palfrey could lose its state charter, and he firmly instructed the students to report anyone they saw smoking pot on the school grounds.

In John X's class, during the discussion about the issue, Cuetara voiced his view that it was reasonable not to smoke marijuana at school. A debate ensued and Bobby took the opposite stand. "We should be able to do whatever we want," he said. Cuetara responded, "If I caught you smoking marijuana, I'd probably turn you in to Ned," which infuriated Bobby. "Hey," he shouted, pointing a finger at Cuetara. "You are really fucked up!"

Bobby, Cuetara said, "thought you should be able to smoke marijuana and nobody should interfere with that." Interviewed in 2013 as marijuana use was actually being legalized in at least two states, Cuetara wryly remarked, "I guess Bobby Kennedy Jr. was ahead of his time—a true visionary."

ALONG WITH USING, BOBBY WAS also said to have been selectively dealing, and reportedly sold a hefty bag of marijuana to his drug-addled younger brother David, then at Middlesex, a boarding school in nearby Concord. When the pot was stolen, sources claimed that Bobby showed up at his brother's school playing the role of a tough drug dealer and reportedly tracked down the thief, frightening him so that he told all to the administration. David refused to finger his brother, the story goes, but Bobby was identified when a witness pointed to his picture in a magazine. As a result David received a suspension.

Bobby played the macho role to the hilt with his wild behavior, drug use, and braggadocio, which was underscored with new friends he was meeting and bringing into his circle, some of whom would remain loyal to him throughout his life. The glitz and glamour and power of the Kennedys would always be a draw for him, helping him lure in bright and talented people just as his uncles and father had done, and he would use that Kennedy star power to his benefit.

Andrew Karsch, for one, was a strapping all-state prep school quarterback studying at Brandeis when Bobby met him during his year at Palfrey. Immediately, Bobby tried to impress Karsch with his physicality and machismo. Strapping on climbing spurs, the kind he used to rescue his hawks, he scaled a tree to show Karsch his Tarzan–like agility. When he visited Karsch's home, he picked up a thick paperback book and bet Karsch that he could tear it in half, emulating those carnival strong men who wowed crowds by tearing the thick Manhattan Yellow Pages book in half. "We bet and then he started going at it, straining until he was purple in the face. He didn't tear it but the book looked like it had been mangled by a wild animal," Karsch recalled.

After they had bonded, Bobby arranged for Karsch to play a game of football with his older brother, Joe, who often bullied him, and who was going to a Boston-area prep school. Joe, who also played quarterback, had no idea that Karsch had been a top player in high school; Joe's team lost. Bobby had finally put one over on him. Victorious, he left the field feeling all-powerful, mainly because of his new friend's ball-snapping, play-calling talent.

During the Boston winter that Bobby was at Palfrey, Karsch joined him and his brother David in a Hyannis Port Terrors–type pursuit— throwing snowballs at passing cars. One driver whose auto was hit braked to a stop. A bruiser who had played college football, he came toward them, "yelling about our irresponsibility," Karsch recalled. That's when scrawny David Kennedy confronted the man and out of the blue punched him in the face.

"The rest of us were too petrified to run," Karsch remembered. But he observed that David had looked at Bobby, the older brother whom he was always trying to impress, to see if he was proud of what he had done.

Over the years Bobby would surround himself with a circle of talented people who excelled, were loyal to him, and were excited to be in the Kennedy magic circle. One of them was Karsch, who went on to be an Academy Award–nominated producer whose films include *The Prince of Tides, Town & Country,* and *The Emperor's Club.*

Through his friendship with Bobby, Karsch had become part of the world of Kennedy politics, including Ted Kennedy's successful 1976 Senatorial campaign, and in 1980 he served as media director when Kennedy ran for the presidency. "I loved his politics. I grew up with the [Kennedy] family. I just have tremendous respect for the whole family, and I really like them all," he told the alternative *Boston Phoenix* weekly in 2002 when he was promoting one of his films.

Moreover, Karsch had literally become a part of the extended clan— as Bobby's brother-in-law, married to the sister of his second wife, the ill-fated Mary Richardson Kennedy, who committed suicide in 2012. But all of that was far in the future.

THE FACT THAT BOBBY WAS from one of the most famous families in America made little if any impression on most of his Palfrey classmates, many of whom came from working-class backgrounds.

"We weren't enamored," recalled a Palfrey graduate. "We didn't care that there was a Kennedy there. Palfrey people were eccentric, different, so most of us didn't even like him there, to be honest—and he didn't seem to give a shit about any of us. Everybody at Palfrey Street School cared about that place, but Bobby Kennedy clearly didn't—none of it impressed him. Because we were all so full of love, we weren't going to call him an arrogant bastard, but some people did."

Boyajian said that while she found Bobby to be "kind of lost and indifferent," he was never arrogant, at least not to her, but she acknowledged that he certainly could have been to others at Palfrey. As such, she often became his defender. "I would say to people, 'Oh, come on, Bobby Kennedy's not that bad of a person, he's okay, give him a chance.' So some people endured him and accepted him more because he was friends with me, and I was like Miss Palfrey Street School because I loved it so much."

Royce Hoyle, who taught ninth-grade English and college preparatory English when Bobby was there, noted, "It was a very tough time for him, and it had to be tough growing up as RFK's son." Given the nature of Palfrey as an alternative school, Hoyle maintained, "the ethic was to give Bobby plenty of room and not treat him specially."

JOEY BRODE WAS SEEMINGLY unaware of Bobby's potluck lunches at her home, his get-togethers with his schoolmate girlfriend in his room, and the dead-body-and-penis pornographic artwork in the Palfrey Street School cupola. "I didn't know much about his activities in the school at all. I didn't participate in his life there. Lem supervised his education. I was just the landlady, so to speak, at least that was my official role." Still, she felt the ultra-experimental school suited him better than a regimented one "because he was so fragile."

The incident in the cupola—the dead bodies, the phalluses—struck her as curious, but not shocking, so aware was she of his emotional state. Her explanation for the strange act was that Bobby had seen "so much loss, so much death in his family—and his hormones were probably raging, and he was feeling so empty and lost." She also was aware that Bobby was being treated by the Harvard psychiatrist Robert Coles, whose work she had read and admired. "I know Bobby respected and liked him a lot, and he probably was very helpful."

As the school year rolled by, Brode observed that "there truly developed a level of trust" between Bobby and her family. In fact, she had never told anyone outside of her immediate family his last name, and if anybody asked it was always just Bobby. She tried to make his home life as different as possible from the one he had come from at Hickory Hill, where he complained of being controlled and dominated and manipulated by his mother. Brode recalled how, before Bobby arrived, she had often read in the press and magazines upbeat, respectful stories that portrayed Hickory Hill as a happy family place, always so much fun and so loving. "But it really wasn't," she observed years later. "I never bought it, and I never thought it."

She and her husband, however, did have one visit to Bobby's fabled homestead. Because they had cared for Bobby during his year at Palfrey, the Brodes were invited by Lem Billings to attend his sixtieth-birthday celebration in April 1976, America's Bicentennial year. As Brode stated with a chuckle, "Who could resist that invitation?" Despite the close connection she had with Bobby, her first and only meeting with his mother consisted of little more than a brief handshake. Brode never forgot how Ethel treated her. "I was in her home and never even had a conversation with her. She acted like a jerk to me."

Many years later Joey Brode watched the 2012 hagiographic HBO documentary *Ethel*, directed by the matriarch's youngest child, Rory. "Talk about sanitized," she said she thought while watching it. "It was like sugar, but that's okay because somebody has to tell the good side of Ethel."

IN THE SPRING OF 1972, with graduation from high school finally looming, eighteen-year-old Bobby planned to take the SAT college board exam. His goal was acceptance at Harvard, which was virtually guaranteed, SATs or no SATs. So many Kennedys before him had gone there: his grandfather, the clan's patriarch; Bobby's own father; his iconic uncle the president, his other uncle the esteemed senator from Massachusetts. The prestigious Kennedy name practically ruled the institution; looming over Cambridge was the John F. Kennedy School of Government. Even his very troubled brother David would be admitted. If anyone was preordained to get into America's most prestigious Ivy League academy it was Robert F. Kennedy Jr.—despite his addictive drug use, his erratic and often bizarre behavior, his run-ins with law enforcement, and what were said to be mediocre grades and little if any extraordinary extracurricular activities. To Bobby the test must have seemed merely a meaningless exercise. Still, he was jumpy about taking it.

"He was eating breakfast and we were talking and he was nervous and thinking about not even going," Brode recalled. "I said, 'Bobby, you just have to go because you'll have so many more options in your life, so much more flexibility if you can go to college.' He just looked at me and he sort of ate his breakfast and went. I almost felt it was important to him that somebody wanted him to succeed at those boards, but he never told me his score."

Brode, a 1965 graduate of Radcliffe, one of the Seven Sisters schools and Harvard's college for women at the time, said she was "quite sure" that he would get into Harvard whether he scored high or low on the SATs. "If you had as many relatives as he did who went to Harvard," she observed, "they'd let him in. Of course, the Kennedy name helped and he had friends like Robert Coles who supported him."

There came a day when Bobby and his classmates were asked to fill out applications for the college or colleges of their choice. Bobby, of course, chose only one and that was Harvard, which he considered his birthright. It should be noted that when his uncle Jack applied to Harvard on April 23, 1935, he wrote just five brief sentences, stating that he felt Harvard would give him a "better background and a better liberal education" than other schools, and he closed by writing, "Then too, I would like to go to the same college as my father. To be a 'Harvard man' is an enviable distinction, and one that I sincerely hope I shall attain."

But Bobby's Harvard application was far different from his uncle's, at least according to Palfrey classmates who claimed that he simply wrote his name—Robert F. Kennedy Jr.—at the top, sent it in, and got accepted. When Joey Brode heard the story years later, she found that what Bobby had done, if true, was "disgusting. It just reeks of arrogance, but I did not experience Bobby as arrogant."

With the SATs completed and his application pending, the Pomfret School teachers Hagop Merjian and Steve Danenberg, both of whom were involved in recommending Bobby's expulsion for drugs, received requests from Robert Coles for letters of recommendation for his patient's Harvard admittance.

"I knew Coles was a close friend of the Kennedy family, and his request was fascinating because he asked that the letters we were to write be sent directly to Coles's office," Merjian said. "I felt like telling him to stick it up his ass because I had no intention of sending my letter to Bobby's shrink's office to peruse it and redact it and to do other things to it."

Merjian informed Coles that he would send his letter "only to the admissions office at Harvard and if you don't approve of that I won't write anything." Following up, he did send a recommendation letter, which he didn't feel carried any weight because "obviously he was going to get in no matter what because the Kennedys own part of Harvard."

In the letter, Merjian basically wrote that he felt Bobby would have little or no problem doing the work because, he noted, "Harvard back then just wanted to know if the kid was able to do the work. I said he was a bright child, very astute and intellectually keen, but I wasn't going to talk about his drugs because I was hoping, but didn't know, that he had cleaned himself up."

Bobby's cousin Christopher Kennedy Lawford was very aware of the close ties his mother's family, the Kennedys, had with Coles. Lawford, who, following Bobby, also lived with the Brodes for a time, maintained, "It was common knowledge that if he [Coles] wrote you a recommendation you'd get in [to Harvard]." Coles had also written one for Bobby's younger brother David, who one day would die of a heroin overdose, and he also wrote one for Chris Lawford. But Lawford wasn't admitted; his last name wasn't Kennedy.

Whether the Palfrey Street School's founder and headmaster, Ned Ryerson, ever received a request for a Harvard recommendation for Bobby is unknown because the records of the entire school vanished after Palfrey closed in 1991, a year before Ryerson's death.

IN JUNE 1972, BOBBY FINALLY graduated, seven months before turning nineteen. He had spent four troubled years at three different secondary schools, and once had to repeat his sophomore year. For Bobby and those who taught him, it was a difficult time, beginning just literally weeks after his father was gunned down, and continuing during the escalation of his drug use and other behavioral and emotional problems.

Bobby was one of fifteen in his graduating class, which posed for a class photo on the lawn in front of the school, but only his shaggy head was visible. His high school graduation certificate, signed by Ned Ryerson, was as different as the alternative school itself, as was the so-called Palfrey Street School yearbook. The artfully crafted diploma was handwritten by Ryerson, and as one graduate recalled was "full of love, as was the spiral-bound yearbook—full of love and photographs. It's a trip!"

After Bobby graduated and went off to Harvard, his relationship with Vicki Boyajian, who still had another year at Palfrey, abruptly ended. "He probably looked at me as somebody who was fun, who was pretty, who was smart, but that's about it."

However, more than a decade later, Boyajian, who became a successful Boston-area pastry chef and restaurateur, was sitting with a male friend at the bar in a popular restaurant in Cambridge's Harvard Square when she heard a voice from the distant past say "Hi, Vicki." She turned around and it was Bobby Kennedy, whom she hadn't seen since he left Palfrey. She had had no other contact with him. "He said, 'You've been living in Vermont and I hear you've been cooking.' For some reason he knew all this stuff about me, and it went through my head, how the hell does he know all these things? It was true—I'd lived in Vermont. I'd been to India. I'd gone halfway around the world. I thought that because of his powerful family he had powers to find out things about me, and I wondered, why did he even care?"

BECAUSE BOBBY HAD SPOKEN so highly of the Brode family and the home's liberal atmosphere, his cousin Chris Lawford subsequently roomed with them for about a year while he was a student at nearby Tufts University.

"For both of us, they were the warm, nurturing family that neither of us seemed to have had but were looking for," Lawford later observed.

In Hollywood, when Lawford visited his actor father, the two had bonded by getting stoned on marijuana. His apartment was "a treasure chest of illicit substances."

Bobby had also enjoyed his swinging uncle Peter Lawford's company. Idolized by the young Kennedys, Lawford had been a member of the Hollywood "Rat Pack," which included the womanizing, hard-drinking Frank Sinatra, Sammy Davis Jr., Dean Martin, the comedian Joey Bishop, and Warren Beatty's movie star sister Shirley MacLaine, who later wrote about her encounters with UFOs and otherworldly beings.

According to Patricia Seaton Lawford, Lawford's fourth, much-younger wife, whom he had married not long before his death, Bobby had arrived on their apartment doorstep after one of the many times his mother had thrown him out of Hickory Hill. And the good uncle that he was, Lawford shared his pot stash with Bobby and escorted him to his friend Hugh Hefner's Playboy Mansion, where they presumably enjoyed the pleasures of the Bunnies who inhabited the place.

Years later, Patricia Lawford, who remarried after Lawford's death, recalled a shocking scene she claimed happened as she and Bobby chatted in the living room during one of his visits. While Peter Lawford was in the bathroom showering, Bobby leaned close to her and said, "I wish you weren't married to my uncle—I'd fuck you right here on the couch."

Bobby wasn't the only Kennedy who had come on to her. She recalled that in June 1980 Lawford had asked her to call his ex-brother-in-law Ted Kennedy as a favor, and when the senator got on the phone, he said, "I hear you're the one with the big tits. The kids all told me." He then asked her when she planned to come east and campaign for him, and said when she did he'd take her on a ski date. She stopped him cold by telling the powerful U.S. Senator, "I'm *married* to Peter!"

In his later years, Lawford fell on hard times. To bring in income, he had turned to leaking stories about the Kennedys and Hollywood celebrities to *The National Enquirer*, a long-held secret revealed in an unpublished memoir by a veteran of the supermarket tabloid, Tony Brenna. In his book, *Anything for a Headline*, Brenna wrote, "We had a symbiotic relationship that was unique in my career; he needed the cash offered for his cooperation, and my standing at the *Enquirer* soared when I wrote stories based on his insider information. As the former husband of Pat

Kennedy, Peter provided an intimate look at the triumphs and tragedies of the Kennedys' extended clan."

Years later, after Peter's son, Chris Lawford, had gotten sober through many rehab stays, he asserted, "I loved getting high . . . I took anything and everything. . . . Drugs were my Wheaties. My breakfast of champions . . . I used drugs for seventeen years." His primary purpose in life, he revealed in his stark 2006 memoir, *Symptoms of Withdrawal*, was "to be high" every day from the age of thirteen until he reached the age of thirty. And he observed, "I may have been in the second tier in the [Kennedy] family, but as far as the world was concerned I was a Kennedy . . . being a Kennedy meant I could get away with a lot of shit."

Looking back to that time, Joey Brode observed that Chris Lawford "adored Bobby. Bobby was the leader. Bobby was the charismatic one they all wanted to be like."

THE LAST TIME JOEY BRODE saw Bobby was in September 1989 when her husband, out jogging, suddenly collapsed and died at fifty-seven and Bobby came to the house to pay his respects. Bobby had heard about John Brode's death from his brother Joe, then a congressman, in whose office Brode's son was working. After Brode's death, the Cambridge intersection where their home was located was renamed John Brode Square.

Naturally, Joey Brode had followed Bobby's life through the years. She was aware of his first failed marriage, his drug problems that had gotten worse, his second marriage and that wife's suicide, and more.

"He must have had a terrible time forming deep and trusting relationships," Brode observed. "I'm glad he decided not to run for office, and I don't blame him. I'm sure he didn't want the exposure. I think he's a much stronger person than he was when he was in my house, and I have a great deal of respect for what he has been able to do in his life in overcoming many, many serious problems and difficulties. But you face your demons over and over in life."

FOURTEEN

Twisted Roots

B obby Kennedy hardly knew his paternal grandfather, Joseph P. Kennedy. He was just seven when, on December 19, 1961, the once-powerful and domineering old man who was the grand architect of the Kennedy dynasty suffered an inoperable intracranial thrombosis, a massive stroke resulting from a blood clot in the brain's artery.

It had turned him, at seventy-three, into a mute invalid, fully paralyzed on his right side, who would be confined to bed and a wheelchair for the rest of his life. Bobby always remembered after visiting him that his grandfather's arm was "twisted grotesquely," and noted that the patriarch would express both happiness and anger only with his eyes. "The grown-ups were all scared of him and asked each other on entering the house, 'How's his mood,' or told the kids, 'Don't get him cross.'"

While the matriarch, Rose Kennedy, adored Bobby, his siblings, and his many cousins, she was never warm and cuddly. As the patriarch's nurse and family confidante, Rita Dallas, observed, "The countless little hordes of youngsters always put on the brakes and approached her with respect and curiosity. She would correct their grammar, the way they walked, or their lack of tidiness. . . ."

Rose Kennedy's mantra was "Children are meant to inherit the earth and should be fit for it."

Ethel Skakel Kennedy, an acolyte of the matriarch, demanded that Bobby and his siblings show their grandfather the utmost respect, and as a result they stood in awe of him. Before Bobby entered the old man's room his mother always told him, "Everything we have we owe to Grandpa. Everything! So when you go in to see him, remember that everything you have, every toy, every pet, the house we live in, everything we owe to Grandpa," recalled Dallas, who noted that Bobby and his young Kennedy peers "were also aware of their wealth . . . and were also aware that they were a special breed of people."

Young Bobby, with his collection of bugs and snakes and his knowledge about them, impressed Dallas and she considered him "a well-informed amateur botanist." But when she mentioned that his parents must be so proud, he surprised her by revealing that they were unaware of his projects; he hadn't told them what he was doing, because he thought, "They might not feel it was good enough," Dallas revealed.

Her favorite of RFK and Ethel's brood, however, wasn't Bobby, but rather his brother the firstborn son, because she viewed him as "more like his grandfather than any of the others," and had concluded that the "long, lanky, bumbling . . . awkward and ill at ease [Joe] . . . possessed the potential to become the principal figurehead in the Kennedy panorama."

This may have been the reason there was only a single reference to Bobby in Rose Kennedy's massive 1975 memoir about her family, and that was just a two-line letter he, at the age of nine, had sent to her and his stroke-stricken grandfather. Without proper capitalization, he said:

Dear Granpa and Granma,
I will be at the cape in a week. how are you feeling. I have a giant turtle. I will see you soon.
xxxxxxxxxxxxxxxxxxx
Bobby
Robert Francis Kennedy Jr.
April 6, 1963
Rockville, Md.

The fact that the patriarch had actually survived for close to nine years was considered "near miraculous." But to everyone who visited—family and friends—he was a virtual vegetable, or as one of his biographers, David Nasaw, described him, "a twisted, gaunt old skeleton, bound to a wheelchair, unable to make himself understood." However, it appeared that he comprehended things that were said, or that he read, or saw, such as the around-the-clock TV coverage when his sons were murdered in cold blood—JFK in 1963, and RFK in 1968. Both times, there were tears in his eyes.

That was not the case when Chappaquiddick happened in 1969. This time his eyes raged with anger. Rita Dallas recalled that when Ted Kennedy returned to the compound, he immediately went to his father's room looking "drawn, downcast, intimidated." The nurse overheard him, like a bad little boy, telling the patriarch, "I'm in some trouble . . . you're going to hear all sorts of things about me . . . terrible things . . . they're not true. It was an accident. I'm telling you the truth."

According to Dallas, the old man was not interested in seeing or hearing anything "that pointed suspicion at his son."

Ironically, Teddy was the son his father had always thought of as "too much of a playboy," and the son he coddled more than any of his brothers, Joe Jr., JFK, and RFK.

Immediately after Chappaquiddick, the nurse remembered, "Mr. Kennedy failed rapidly . . . a pall hung over the compound . . . it was only a matter of time . . . toward late summer Mr. Kennedy lost his appetite, and I knew he had given up."

With the Chappaquiddick scandal still in the headlines, the Kennedy clan gathered at the compound on November 17, 1969, for yet another tragic ending.

The patriarch had received the Last Rites. He was comatose. His son-in-law Sargent Shriver, Eunice's husband, the ambassador to France, knelt by the dying man's bed and said, "Without you, none of us would be anything." Teddy cried over and over, "Dad, it's me, Teddy . . . can you hear me?"

Bobby's mother, Ethel, was getting over a cold at Hickory Hill when she got word that her father-in-law was dying. When the patriarch breathed his last on November 18, 1969—just four months after Chappaquiddick—Ethel was in the room with him.

At the funeral, Ted read from a tribute to his father that his brother RFK had long ago written for a collection of essays by family and friends: "When we were a little older we realized he wasn't perfect; that he made mistakes, but by the time we realized everyone did. In many, many ways, to us, he is something special."

Years later, in Ted Kennedy's memoir, published immediately after his own death at seventy-seven of brain cancer, the last surviving son wrote that he wondered whether he had shortened his father's life "from the shock I had visited on him with my news of the tragic accident on Chappaquiddick Island. The pain of that burden was almost unbearable."

BOBBY KENNEDY JR. HAD EVEN LESS of a relationship with his maternal grandparents, George and Ann Brannack Skakel, than he had with Joe and Rose Kennedy.

Bobby's maternal grandfather, founder in 1919 of the Chicago-headquartered Great Lakes Coal & Coke (later renamed Great Lakes Carbon Corp.), had made a fortune, some believe even bigger than that amassed by Joe Kennedy. It became one of the largest privately held companies in America.

Skakel, a poor boy with big ideas, the son of an abusive alcoholic, had started out as a lowly railroad freight-rate clerk and then traffic manager, followed by a job as a salesman for a coal distributor. That's where he met Bobby's maternal grandmother, Ann Brannack, who was working there as a secretary. She was a staunch Catholic who came from poor, uneducated roots. George and Ann were married during Thanksgiving week 1917. Bobby's mother, Ethel, was born nine years later, the next to last of Ann Skakel's undisciplined and spoiled brood of four girls and three boys.

Bobby was not quite two years old when his grandparents died together in a plane crash. Even then he wouldn't have spent much time in their company, because his mother had devoted herself to the Kennedy

clan—she had "drunk the Kennedy Kool-Aid," as a friend suggested—
and distanced herself from her own family, mainly to avoid their scandalous behavior (as opposed to the Kennedys' scandalous behavior). The
Skakels were hard-core conservative Republicans and some were trouble-
makers, drunkards, and hell-raisers. RFK despised them all.

When the multimillionaire Skakel's private plane, a converted World
War II bomber, en route to California from Connecticut, exploded in
midair over Oklahoma on October 4, 1955, RFK adamantly refused to
permit Ethel to participate in her family's funeral plans, which were being worked out at her parents' three-story, thirty-room English country
manor house. Called Rambleside, the house, once owned by an heir to
the Simmons mattress fortune, was in the fanciest part of very fancy
Greenwich, Connecticut.

"Ethel's not coming to Greenwich. She will come after you make the
funeral arrangements," RFK informed Ethel's brother George Skakel
Jr., according to Mary Begley, a close Skakel family friend, who overheard the conversation. Begley said all of Ethel's siblings "were furious
with Bobby. They were all saying, 'Ethel should be here. . . . Why does
she put up with him?' I do remember them saying of Bobby, 'It's so
typical of that little Napoleon to not let her come.' But Ethel always de-
ferred to Bobby, a vindictive little soul."

According to Begley, the politically conservative Skakels had come to
view Ethel as more a Kennedy "and they were sad about that. They would
have liked her to have been a little more loyal. As a result, the Skakels
were very cavalier about the Kennedys."

Bobby Jr.'s maternal great-grandfather James Curtis Skakel, who came
from Canada, was a womanizer and falling-down drunk who physically
and verbally abused his wife, Grace Mary Jordan, who came from a well-
to-do Virginia family. They were married in 1885. Skakel was a strict
Protestant and a bigot who hated Catholics and Jews. At the same
time, Grace was a racist—fulminating against Lincoln's freeing of the
slaves, and rabidly supporting the Ku Klux Klan. One of Curt Skakel's
brothers—a great-great-uncle of Bobby's—was William Skakel, a onetime gambling and bawdyhouse operator and generally shady character,
who became a Democratic powerbroker in Chicago.

Curt Skakel's sole legacy was his addiction to alcohol. He was found in a drunken stupor in a ditch in Tyndall, South Dakota, where his family had a small ranch, after an episode of barhopping. He caught pneumonia, and died on January 17, 1917.

Alcoholism and other addictions would be inherited by some of Ethel's siblings, and some of Ethel's brood—most notably Bobby.

Bobby's maternal grandfather had also inherited the drinking gene. In the rare autobiographical chapter in Bobby's environmentalist book *The Riverkeepers*, he made only one mention of his coal baron grandfather, George Skakel, whom he described as a "quiet railroad traffic controller from South Dakota" who "made a fortune." In discussing what great outdoorsmen the Skakel men were, he noted, "My grandfather would disappear for a third of the year on hunting expeditions to places unknown."

Ignored, however, were George Skakel's many drinking expeditions. As World War II was breaking out, and Skakel's Great Lakes Carbon was doing booming business, George and Ann discovered the pleasures of Cuba and began wintering there, "living like royalty" in an immense home with servants in a town near the exotic nightlife of Havana. In Cuba, as his son Rushton Skakel later revealed, "He became a serious alcoholic. Mother was very concerned."

Ernest Hemingway, an alcoholic and depressive, had a home in Cuba at the time, and booze brought the famed novelist and the coal baron together in memorable bouts of drinking. "I can remember my mother and I going to Hemingway's house because he called us and said, 'You've got to pick up your father. He's drunk,'" recalled Rushton, a heavy drinker himself. His brother Jim Skakel, also an alcoholic, often went barhopping in Greenwich with his father, who would have one too many and get into fights. And Jim, who stood six foot two, would have to extricate him.

"I'd have to be a quick negotiator for him," Jim recalled. "After we left the bar, I'd tell Dad, 'Don't get into those things.'"

Ethel rarely ever talked about her family, so, to seek more information, Bobby once approached a Skakel cousin, Robert Curtis Skakel, to ask about his great-grandfather's drinking, and whether there was any truth to the whispered family chatter he had heard. "I told Bobby that some say his great-grandfather died of alcoholism and some say he died of pneumonia. I told him the story of what happened and asked Bobby what he thought. He didn't say anything. He got the picture."

In *The Riverkeepers*, Bobby linked his Skakel family roots to the book's environmental theme by describing the Skakel men as "a clan of unruly Republican outdoorsmen," and suggested that their often extreme hunting and fishing exploits might "provide a genetic antecedent to my predispositions." In the context of the book, the predispositions Bobby seemed to be referring to were his interest in the animal world and the environment, rather than his predisposition to drugs and his generally addictive personality.

Bobby described his mother's brothers, his Skakel uncles—George Jr., James, and Rushton—as he-men, "tall, large-boned, and brawny," who spent their time in the wilderness killing big game and reeling in big fish in lakes and oceans around the world. He called them "crack shots and graceful athletes" who "loved back-country skiing . . . shooting dove . . ." Uncle George, he related, had once jumped out of a helicopter to ride giant musk ox, and kept "live mountain lions at his home." Uncle Rush was once mauled while hunting grizzly, and his uncle Jimmy kept sharks in a home aquarium, and had given Bobby's family in northern Virginia a California sea lion as a Christmas present, a pet that, Bobby proudly wrote, "joined the growing menagerie that I had collected from the countryside around Hickory Hill."

As he had written about his Millbrook School life in *The Riverkeepers*, making his time there sound so idyllic, once again Bobby had painted a hagiographic and idealized portrait of his Skakel relatives that was far from the reality.

FIFTEEN

Wild Uncles

The firstborn of Bobby's uncles was the Skakel patriarch's namesake, George Jr., who most certainly did, as Bobby wrote, enjoy hunting. But in *The Riverkeepers*, Bobby ignored the fact that George's favorite game usually were beautiful babes rather than big bears.

During his tumultuous, ill-fated two-decade marriage to Joan Patricia "Pat" Corroon Skakel, he had a series of affairs, many with the wives of wealthy friends. As his friend Bill Whiteford once observed, "George was totally amoral. There were a lot of husbands who were afraid to come out and say anything against George because he could be very intimidating."

Pat Skakel was so devastated by her husband's blatant philandering that she became an alcoholic. Her drinking intensified when she discovered her husband with one of his mistresses in the guesthouse of their estate in Greenwich. She created drunken scenes. On one occasion she ignored decorum at a polo match when she spotted one of his women on the sideline. Furious, she loudly screamed, "Whore!" at her, shocking the staid Greenwich polo crowd.

On one of his many hunts, this one for wild horses on the Ute Indian reservation in Utah, George had a number of his girlfriends stay for the duration and each night he'd jump from one mistress's tent to another.

At one point he left his wife and took up with Bettan Olwaeus, a gorgeous blond, blue-eyed Wall Street stockbroker from Sweden, who perceived him as "charming, sweet, spontaneous," but who drove her "through heaven and hell the whole time we were together."

Like his father and his brothers and many of the Skakels before and some after him, George was an alcoholic, consuming as much as two bottles of vodka a day, but he never appeared to be tipsy. After seeing the film *Days of Wine and Roses*, a candid look at alcoholism, he became very depressed, recalled Olwaeus. She said he hated the film because it hit too close to home. "I'd never seen him look so sad."

It's surprising that in his book Bobby had glorified his uncle, especially since George Skakel Jr. despised the Kennedys, and one Kennedy in particular: Bobby's own beloved father. He once bluntly referred to RFK as "a chicken-shit little bastard. He thinks he's such a tough guy. I can't figure out what Ethel sees in that little prick."

Long before RFK met his future wife, Ethel, he had met her brother George at boarding school—Portsmouth Priory, operated by strict Benedictine monks, in Rhode Island. Both RFK and Skakel were mediocre students. On a visit home, George told his brothers, Jim and Rushton, that he knew the son of the U.S. Ambassador to Great Britain, and described him as "a real little dick." While George liked Priory and stayed, RFK went to six boarding schools in ten years, twice as many as his namesake.

To underscore George Skakel Jr.'s resentment of the Kennedys, one must look at how he acted during the start of what became known mythically as Camelot.

Ethel had invited George to JFK's inauguration, but RFK wouldn't permit him to stay at Hickory Hill with other guests during the celebrations, fearful he'd cause trouble. In the end, George skipped out of the inauguration altogether, giving his VIP ticket to a stranger he ran into on Pennsylvania Avenue. But he did attend one of the boozy inauguration parties, where RFK spotted him pawing at and necking with a Hollywood guest, the glamorous Kim Novak. He ordered Ethel to break it up. "None of that here!" she told her brother, whom she knew as a womanizing troublemaker. "Find someplace else!" she demanded.

George Terrien, who had been RFK's college roommate and later married Ethel's sister Georgeann, who drank heavily and popped pills, recalled a conversation with RFK when he was Attorney General. In their chat, Bobby's father boasted about his own womanizing and said he felt competitive with his philanderer brother-in-law George Skakel, whom he despised.

"Bobby was sounding very macho and full of himself. Out of the blue he said, 'George would keel over if he knew who I was screwing. So I said, 'You are the biggest bullshitter in the world. You wouldn't have the balls to play around [on Ethel].' And he said, 'Just tell George I've had Marilyn's pussy.' I said, 'What the hell are you talking about? Marilyn who?' And Bobby was laughing, 'You know, the woman Jack used to jack off over, Marilyn Monroe. After he finished with her, she fell for me. I think she's in love with me.' I told Bobby, 'You're full of shit,' and he laughed and that was the end of the conversation. I can't imagine Marilyn getting into bed with that little jerk."

Terrien couldn't wait to get off the phone and tell his other brother-in-law what had just transpired. As Terrien remembered the conversation, "George fell over laughing." He didn't believe any of it. As he told Terrien, Marilyn Monroe "wouldn't fuck him even with my dick."

Partying and hunting were two of Skakel's favorite pastimes. They came together fatally in September 1966.

At forty-four, having been president of Great Lakes Carbon for more than a decade following his parents' fatal plane crash, George Skakel Jr. was en route by small private plane to a ranch he was thinking of buying in an isolated area of Idaho. Also on board were several friends, including Dean Markham, a Great Lakes Carbon executive, and one of RFK's closest pals, dating back to their college days.

The plan was for ten days of elk hunting, along with lots of drinking and lots of women; George had invited a klatch of his girlfriends, who had arrived separately. The plane, also carrying a cargo of liquor and a cache of hunting rifles and ammunition, overshot a short runway and crashed into the walls of Crooked Creek Canyon and disintegrated. All were killed. George Jr. became the third Skakel after his parents to die in a plane crash; the Kennedys would eventually surpass that tragic air fatality toll.

TWO MONTHS AFTER HIS FUNERAL, the family faced still another tragedy when sixteen-year-old Kick Skakel—George and Pat's firstborn of four, Ethel's niece and Bobby's cousin—was involved in a bizarre auto incident that resulted in the death of another child. The Skakel girl had been driving a new convertible, a gift from her father, when the car hit a speed bump and a youngster riding in the backseat fell out.

As one of her Skakel cousins asserted later, "To be around Kick was like being around Uncle George. She was always living dangerously. My mother made it perfectly clear—Kick's a bad influence."

Six months after Kick Skakel's fatal auto imbroglio, eight months after the plane crash that killed her father, Pat Skakel threw a dinner party for her teenage son, Mark, who was recovering from injuries suffered when shards of glass struck him in the face and body after he ignited gunpowder that caused an explosion while fooling around with a friend in Greenwich woods.

It was May 19, 1967, and Pat Skakel had invited a Greenwich police captain, his wife, and her brother-in-law George Terrien for drinks and shish kebab.

During the meal, Pat abruptly got up from the table without saying a word. After about ten minutes everyone grew concerned, wondered what was keeping her, and went looking for her.

She was found near the bathroom on the hallway floor. At the age of thirty-nine, she had choked to death on a piece of meat lodged in her larynx.

Just a month after Pat's funeral, in what was described later as "the worst possible timing to throw a party," according to a family friend, Ethel Kennedy tossed one of the biggest shindigs ever seen in the nation's capital—celebrating her and RFK's seventeenth wedding anniversary.

It would be their last anniversary together.

. . .

JAMES CURTIS "JIMMY" SKAKEL III, the firstborn of the three Skakel brothers, who was extolled by Bobby in *The Riverkeepers*, was named after his alcoholic grandfather, the one found inebriated in a ditch who soon after died of pneumonia complications.

Like so many of the Skakels through the generations, Jimmy, too, was an alcoholic.

As Rushton Skakel once revealed about the brothers, he and Jimmy and George started drinking "as little tots," imbibing the liquor and wine left over in glasses in the Skakel mansion's kitchen after the many parties their parents tossed.

"Alcohol ran through our family," Rushton said. "That's how we grew up."

His sister Georgeann had become an alcoholic by the time she was fifteen; Jimmy when he was a year older.

As the Skakel family friend Mary Begley observed, "Jimmy Skakel's reputation was perfectly horrible. You'd hear people say, 'Oh, can you imagine the Skakels, they have a son [Jimmy] who's an alcoholic at age sixteen.'"

As teenagers, Jim and George became gun nuts, following in the footsteps of the Skakel patriarch, George Sr., who had a collection of rifles with the greatest killing power, courtesy of a standing order he had with Abercrombie & Fitch (in the era before it became a haven for teenage fashion). Jim, along with George, shot at everything—from mailboxes to streetlamps, and sometimes even actual game. A family friend once watched horror-stricken when the two brothers began firing their rifles from a window in the Skakels' Greenwich mansion. Their target was a Grecian marble statue on the sprawling grounds near the family pool.

They were having a contest: The last one to shoot an ear off was a "nigger baby," recalled an eyewitness. The statue was destroyed.

Jim Skakel had an official, albeit secret connection with Jack Kennedy's administration. It happened in the immediate wake of the Bay of Pigs fiasco in April 1961—the failed attempt by the U.S. government to unseat the Communist leader Fidel Castro. Jim had agreed to loan the Central Intelligence Agency his high-speed, 42-foot boat named after his wife. The *Virginia* was used to bring 157 Cubans to Miami. The Chris Craft was then armed with machine-gun mounts and new engines by the CIA, but was never returned to Skakel. After many calls to Langley, Jim gave up. "I figured they were in enough trouble without me going after the damned boat," he later stated.

While his CIA operations had never been publicly revealed until several decades later in my book *The Other Mrs. Kennedy*, his harpooning of a whale in 1962 had gotten major coverage in *Life* magazine. *Life* was planning to publish a special issue headlined "The Sea," and needed a brilliant stunt. To show that "the American male was still cut from the same rugged cloth as his forebears had been," *Life* selected Jim Skakel, who had a powerful decision-making friend at the magazine. Skakel's assignment, along with a photographer, was to go fishing for a giant whale in a 38-foot sailboat off the Azores. Incredibly, he harpooned one, of forty-two tons, which made the December 21, 1962, issue.

It also was during the Kennedy administration, when Jim's brother-in-law RFK was attorney general, that brother and sister—Jim and Ethel—essentially stopped speaking. In an effort to distance themselves from both the Skakels and the Kennedys, Jim and his wife, Virginia, had moved to Los Angeles and into a fabulous home near the exclusive Bel Air Country Club. Ethel rarely visited and when she did she caused problems. Jim usually hid from her when he knew she was in the vicinity. "He just couldn't deal with her," related Virginia.

Most of his animosity had to do with Ethel's allegiance to the Kennedy family and his perception (supported by many others) that she was being disloyal to her own flesh and blood, the Skakels.

A lifelong smoker and drinker, who occasionally suffered from agoraphobia, Virginia Skakel died at sixty-seven on February 24, 1998.

Jim died two months later.

IN *THE RIVERKEEPERS*, BOBBY KENNEDY wrote: "My uncle Rush was mauled, some say deservedly, during a grizzly hunt." He never explained what he meant by "deservedly"—who deserves to be mauled by a vicious bear? But it probably had to do with the fact that among the Skakels, especially his uncle's siblings, Rushton Walter Skakel, known to intimates as "Rucky," was the weak and timid one, the brother who had done a disservice to the family business (and the family members' pocketbooks) with his poor management of Great Lakes Carbon.

Like his Skakel brothers and forebears, Rushton was an alcoholic. He once showed up at a neighbor's home in Greenwich with a glass of bourbon in hand, not a big surprise since most of the Skakels were well-known drinkers. But he did surprise them when he said he had just returned home to his French provincial mansion, in Greenwich—not from a cocktail party, but rather from his Alcoholics Anonymous meeting, where, he boasted, he'd sworn off drinking.

They called him "Rush the lush."

Rushton was the last of the Skakel siblings to marry. In 1955, the same year his parents died in the plane crash, he tied the knot with pretty Anne Reynolds, who had gone to his sister Ethel's alma mater, Manhattanville College of the Sacred Heart, a Catholic, white oasis in New York's black Harlem. It was at Manhattanville that wiry, high-spirited Ethel first met and bonded with pudgy, shy Jean Kennedy, a friendship that led to Ethel's introduction to Jean's brother Robert Francis Kennedy. The rest was history; two of the country's wealthiest and most powerful families would have a merger, one made more in hell than in heaven.

In the mid-1960s, after his brother George's death, Rush took over the family business, Great Lakes Carbon, but he wasn't the hard-driving executive type. He was a milquetoast, spoiled, who liked his liquor, his golf, and his hunting. He didn't "relish the role, nor had the same skill and talent to run the business," as did his father and even his playboy brother, George, according to court documents. Rushton "grew exceedingly unhappy in his role running the family company. Over the years, the company's profits declined and it was eventually sold in the early 1990s."

During the Kennedy administration, some five years after Rushton and Anne got married, tragedy once again struck the Skakel family. Anne was diagnosed with brain cancer. Her illness lasted for about a decade. Her death had a devastating effect on her family, especially her husband.

An amateur tennis title-holder, a Greenwich matron active in the Junior League, she was the mother of seven—six boys and a girl. Like her sister-in-law Ethel, she always seemed to be pregnant. She died at just forty-one in March 1973, leaving the alcoholic and emotionally troubled widower, Rushton, to oversee their brood, a job at which he would miserably fail, just as he had seemingly failed at running Great Lakes Carbon.

Along with his questionable management of the family business—he was board chairman at the time of his wife's passing—he was not the best father. According to a court document, "Anne Skakel was Rushton Skakel's emotional compass," and according to family members, "her death left Rushton Skakel with a deep sense of loss and emptiness in his life."

He drank even more, chased women, spent wildly, began abusing prescription pills, and had to be hospitalized several times for his addictions.

And along with abusing his body, he allegedly began abusing some of his seven teenage children—Julie, Rushton Jr., John, David, Steven, Tommy, and Michael. Rushton's alcoholism, a court document stated, "exacerbated his abusive behavior toward his children."

Among those physically injured was his daughter, Julie, whom he was accused of burning with matches. Her troubled brother Michael, a pot smoker and a drinker who later would be implicated in a heinous murder, often was the target of abuse: his father struck him with a hairbrush just as his sister Ethel had once beaten Bobby. Rushton had once even fired a rifle in Michael's direction during a hunting trip.

Rushton died at the age of seventy-nine the day after New Year's 2003.

According to his attorney, he had the brain disease frontal lobe dementia.

He was buried in Greenwich.

SIXTEEN

Harvard Beckons

With the influence of his name and its inherent power, privilege, and prestige, Bobby Kennedy Jr., almost nineteen, followed in the footsteps of his father and uncles and entered Harvard as a freshman in the fall of 1972.

He was assigned to Hurlbut Hall and paired with a roommate, one Peter Kaplan, a bright, bespectacled eighteen-year-old Jew, a graduate of the New Jersey public school system. The son of a staunch Republican father, a West Point graduate and woman's clothing manufacturer, and a psychotherapist mother, Kaplan had upper-middle-class roots, but none of the Kennedy family power. At Harvard and through the years, he offered much to Bobby in terms of knowledge and insight. And Bobby, bonding with Kaplan for a lifetime, took advantage of it all. At the same time, Kaplan enjoyed the glitz and glitter of the Kennedys.

"I never felt so lucky that my last name began with the letter 'K,'" he said years later, noting that they had been put together—Kennedy and Kaplan—alphabetically at Harvard. "Was I starstruck? Sure, no question. I felt lucky to actually be sleeping—not literally, please—with a real-life Kennedy," he wryly added.

As a close friend observed, "Bobby and Peter both had something to gain from the relationship. Bobby was a charismatic kid and Peter was interested in sort of crossing this border and spending time with this element that was very different from that in which he had grown up. He was dazzled by Bobby's family and by his name."

Unlike Bobby, who, in order to be accepted at America's most prestigious university, was said by former classmates to have simply written his famous name on his Harvard application when he was a senior and a pothead at the Palfrey Street School, Kaplan had worked diligently and creatively to submit a brilliant application. He included a work of fiction about a character in Newark, New Jersey, who survived a nuclear holocaust.

Bobby immediately saw the value in getting close to this smart kid.

Early on, beginning at Harvard, Bobby began to have Kennedyesque visions of greatness, aided and abetted by his loving mentor Lem Billings, who frequently propagandized about Bobby's inherited Kennedy power. Bobby believed Billings's pitch and began to have thoughts of a great political career, following in the footsteps of his father and uncles.

It wasn't just any political office for which Billings was priming Bobby; it was the presidency that he was getting into his head. When a Harvard classmate asked Bobby whether such talk had any reality, whether he seriously thought he could win a presidential election and be the second Kennedy to rule the country, Bobby's pretentious, brief, and to-the-point response was: "I feel that is my destiny."

Because Bobby possessed the Kennedy ability and charisma to gather intellectually superior people around him, he was clearly recruiting Kaplan, possibly as a potential speechwriter, possibly as his Boswell—perhaps as a member of a potential brain trust, his new generation of the best and brightest. He should follow the path laid by his father and his uncle Jack, Billings advised. JFK had his speechwriter and ghostwriter Ted Sorensen, and both JFK and RFK had Arthur M. Schlesinger Jr., who penned JFK's bestselling hagiographic presidential biography *A Thousand Days* and RFK's upbeat portrait, *Robert Kennedy and His Times*. When Schlesinger died at eighty-nine in 2007, *The New York Times* observed that some critics suggested he'd had trouble separating history from sentiment . . . many noted that [*A Thousand Days*] "ignored the president's sexual wanderings."

Bobby had wisely chosen Kaplan to be his sidekick with a bright future. And Kaplan would parlay his talents. He became a prominent New York newspaper and magazine editor and writer, for many years ran the influential weekly *New York Observer*, and later was editorial director of Condé Nast's Fairchild Fashion Group. But, struck with cancer in his prime, he died in 2013.

Like Schlesinger, Kaplan was the loyal type, and unquestionably loyal when it came to the Kennedy clan. And to the Kennedys, loyalty was an important trait for an insider to have.

Moreover, Kaplan had another characteristic that was important to Bobby back in their younger days. When he wanted to get high, Kaplan joined in. Unlike Bobby, though, Kaplan didn't have an addictive personality. While he smoked pot and snorted cocaine with Bobby, he was once sickened when Bobby convinced him to try angel dust, the street name for a dangerous drug. After that hellish experience, a friend recalled, Kaplan was wary about further drug experimentation with his chum.

From the moment they met, Kaplan began to closely observe Bobby and came to the belief that he had a "swashbuckling Douglas Fairbanks" style. That was underscored by his boastful feats of daring, such as the time he leaped from the roof of the six-story Hurlbut Hall to the roof of the Pennypacker dorm building that it adjoined, a gap that Kaplan exaggeratedly estimated to be as much as twelve feet. The dangerous stunt had all come about as a result of a bet Bobby had made with a classmate and friend, Mir Bhutto, son of Ali Bhutto, the president of Pakistan.

"People heard about it and gathered below, a large crowd shading their eyes and looking up as if waiting for Superman," Kaplan recalled. "The distance wasn't that great, but it looked twice as big as it was; if he had missed he'd probably die. Suddenly Bobby just soars across. Everybody down on the ground gasped and shook their heads in disbelief."

THERE WERE TWO STRIKINGLY visible things about the Kennedy-Kaplan Harvard suite. The first was that it always looked as if a tornado had hit it; clothing, books, and all sorts of stuff was scattered everywhere. For bookmarks, record album covers were used, and for ashtrays and roaches, the records themselves, mainly because Bobby was used to having servants clean up after him, and Kaplan had always been a messy pack rat, so as one friend recalled, "It was a mess, a big, big mess."

Beyond the Collyer-brothers-like clutter, Bobby as usual had brought one of his pets along with him to school to keep him company—not a relatively tame falcon, or even a cuddly lion cub as in the past, but rather a poisonous rattlesnake that was the subject of much terror and amusement among the other boys in the dorm. The snake, according to Kaplan, was not defanged—at least that's what Bobby had told him—meaning it could inflict major injury. Bobby allowed it "to wrap itself around a ski pole and fed it by hand," Kaplan recalled. Because of the snake's potential danger, Harvard officials made Bobby find another home for it.

The second strikingly visible thing about the Kennedy–Kaplan suite was that females were attracted there in droves, clearly intrigued by quite a different species of Kennedy snake. The female traffic, it was remembered years later, was constant; from the very first day of classes, Bobby was considered Harvard's "babe magnet" throughout his matriculation.

Unlike in his gawky stoner days at Millbrook, Pomfret, and Palfrey, Bobby, by the time he got to Harvard, had become, as one friend recalled, "a gorgeous animal, an incredibly magnetic young man." Even straight guys thought he was sexy-looking. As the male friend noted, "Bobby wasn't getting laid a lot just because his name was Kennedy. If his name was Joe Blow, he would have gotten laid a lot. There was a steady traffic of girls through Bobby's room. One night I was in Kaplan's room in their suite and the door to Bobby's adjoining room was slightly ajar and Bobby was in there with a girl, and the girl was looking with a kind of eroticized fascination at Bobby's various scars from the various accidents he had had since he was a kid. He was describing how he got each scar in a sort of loving way and she was definitely turned on by it."

Bobby's collegiate lust—and what was a jealous and competitive nature when it came to women—was underscored by an incident that occurred involving his year-younger cousin Christopher Kennedy Lawford.

When Bobby was a Harvard freshman, Lawford was a senior at Middlesex, a fancy boarding school named after the Massachusetts town through which Paul Revere rode during his legendary "The British are coming, the British are coming" trip. One of the girls Bobby was seeing, whom he had gotten to know when he was living with the Brode family, had heard that Lawford was planning to travel across country to look at potential colleges, and she asked and he agreed to have her accompany him.

While he fell for her and she for him, they didn't have intercourse, he wrote years later in his 2005 memoir, *Symptoms of Withdrawal.* They returned to Boston to tell Bobby about the trip and their blossoming romance, with Lawford wondering, "How could Bobby be angry if I didn't actually have sex with his girlfriend?" But he also noted, "I was going up against the one peer I didn't really want to go up against."

Bobby was furious.

"It didn't seem to matter that I hadn't had sex with his girlfriend," stated Lawford. "The fact that a female was leaving him for me really pissed him off. We didn't speak for a year. He told me that [Bobby's brother] Joe had said if it had been him he would have beaten the shit out of me."

The young woman in question, who sought anonymity, told a somewhat different story to Peter Collier and David Horowitz for their 1984 book about the Kennedy dynasty. She said she had told Bobby that Lawford was more proficient at cunnilingus than he was, which apparently infuriated him. Having to "be the best at everything," he demanded another opportunity to perform, after which she told him he was still the king of oral sex, at least with her. Bobby had been practicing the technique since he had started fooling around with girls back in his days at Millbrook, as he had once boasted to his roommate there.

Bobby finally came to a bizarre agreement with Lawford over his lost girlfriend, one of a number in his stable while he was at Harvard.

"Bobby settled for a promise that he would sleep with my wife the day after I got married. A threat he didn't have a prayer or the inclination of carrying out," or so Lawford believed. But, as the future would tell, Bobby's deal with Lawford said something about his mind-set regarding women.

The girl in question soon dumped Lawford and took off for Mexico. "I was left in Boston with no girlfriend and a pissed-off cousin,"

Lawford wrote, and he soon came to the depressing conclusion, "I thought I needed a big dick to run with the folks I had grown up around in Hollywood [his actor father and his circle] and Washington [the Kennedys]."

The gay Lem Billings saw the same kind of sexuality in Bobby that he had known in his longtime friend JFK. But he saw Bobby as "more caring" without all of JFK's electric charm. Although he had no sexual interest in women, Billings lived the heterosexual life vicariously through Bobby, opening his Upper East Side Manhattan apartment to Bobby's stream of women, permitting him to have sex there, including threesomes.

DURING THE LATTER PART of his freshman year, Bobby spent time in Peru as part of a Harvard program that had him studying a mountain Indian tribe. He later boasted that while there he had captured a young condor after being lowered over a treacherous cliff. When the Peruvian media discovered that a Camelot heir was studying there, the press pursued him. He quietly left, disguising himself and traveling under the name Francis Kennedy, an alias he sometimes used.

From Peru, Bobby moved on to Chile, then in its winter skiing season, where he hooked up with Andy Karsch, whom Bobby met when he was at Palfrey Street School. Bobby had also brought along his longtime girlfriend Kim Kelley, but she broke her leg and was shipped back home. Her accident, though, foretold of a more dangerous incident that occurred when Bobby, Karsch, and a new member of Bobby's inner circle, a young New Yorker by the name of Harvey Blake Fleetwood, a travel agent and budding freelance writer, took a day trip on skis. Bobby had met Fleetwood in the luxurious Portillo ski resort, where Bobby and Karsch, who had never before skied, were staying that July in 1973.

Meeting Bobby was a break for Fleetwood's budding journalistic career because what happened to them high in the Chilean Andes resulted in a lengthy feature story by Fleetwood in *The New York Times* with a headline that read in part: "I'm wondering what that soldier would do if he knew he'd nearly killed another Kennedy."

Led by a couple of experienced guides, the young pals decided to take a day and ski some twenty miles from their hotel and up some three thousand feet to see the remote statue *Christ the Redeemer of the Andes*, on the Chile-Argentina border.

As they were on the final slope to their destination shots rang out. Incredibly, out of nowhere, they were receiving machine-gun fire from a crazed border guard.

"Bobby, who is about fifteen feet in front of me, drops to the ground just as two or three shots ricochet off a rock not five feet away," Fleetwood recalled in his article. "As Bobby falls, I think he is hit, and that we are all goners. . . . We are all in a state of semishock, relieved to be alive, yet not quite sure that the gunman won't go berserk and finish us off with a quick burst.

"How many shots did he take? How close were they," Fleetwood asked Bobby. "I really don't know," he responded. "I wasn't looking . . . I shudder to think what was going on inside Bobby's head as he lay curled up, his face shoved in the snow, while these shots zipped over his head."

Safely back at the hotel, Bobby or one of his fellow travelers must have mentioned the frightening border guard incident because the news quickly got out and there were urgent TV reports that RFK's namesake, JFK's nephew, had now been shot and was wounded or killed.

Fleetwood's account was published in the *Times* travel section under a second six-column headline: "Skiing the Andes—and Drawing Fire from the Border Patrol." Fleetwood, who became a lifelong friend of Bobby's, dramatically observed that Bobby had had "his share of brushes with death," noting that he was "nearly trampled by an elephant in Africa" on that safari with Lem Billings years before. Regarding how Bobby reacted in the immediate wake of the frightening border incident, he wrote: "Strangely, he seems calmer than the rest of us right now."

During their first time together in Chile, Fleetwood found Bobby to be "daring . . . He simply took more chances than I and he refused to be beaten."

IN THE SUMMER OF 1974, before Bobby began his junior year at Harvard, Lem Billings proposed that they explore the very isolated and dangerous Apurimac River in southern Peru, an adventure that Billings had convinced Bobby would engrave his name alongside that of his father and his uncle Jack in terms of bravery and daring. Bobby enlisted Fleetwood, seven years his senior, to go along and document the trip, with, of course, emphasis on Bobby.

As with Kaplan, Bobby viewed Fleetwood as another potential Boswell, another potential Arthur Schlesinger.

Bobby and Fleetwood were the advance party to the eerie Apurimac, which claimed hundreds of lives annually. They were followed by Bobby's younger brother David Kennedy; Morris Stroud, a young man who was known by Billings; Bobby's cousin Chris Lawford, who later termed the whole affair "completely disorganized"; and Bobby's long-time pal Doug Spooner. A few years older than Bobby, he had met him when Bobby was at Pomfret, and was thumbing a ride on the Cape. Spooner, who reportedly sometimes hustled at both pool and golf, had picked him up, and the two quickly bonded after Bobby complained that his mother had kicked him out, and Spooner offered him a roof over his head if he wanted to stay with him—a shack that the twenty-year-old reportedly lived in.

By the time they reached an isolated village near the Apurimac River, Bobby had dysentery, but still ate anything and everything, including boiled rat, pulling out the eyes from the dead rodent's head and popping them into his mouth. Billings, who idolized Bobby, did the same. Bobby also could kill a chicken for food in a split second by snapping its neck between two of his fingers, and he had the ability to drink half a bottle of beer, then press his hand quickly down on the bottle's mouth, making the thick glass bottom fall out. He had developed loads of such tricks and savored showing them off.

"Reckless" was the diplomatic way Fleetwood later described Bobby.

In advance of the trip Bobby had picked up some rudimentary Spanish, which gave him what Lawford recalled as "a position of power and kept the rest of us at his mercy."

Fleetwood's mother, a physician, had given the group a supply of drugs because of all the potential injuries and diseases one could pick up in the jungle they would be inhabiting for about ten days. Naturally, Bobby—considered the drug connoisseur of the third Kennedy generation—had put himself in charge of the stash, which included morphine and tincture of opium.

When Lawford and David Kennedy, both drug users, wanted to dig in, Bobby announced, "Not yet, man," claiming they needed the drugs for an emergency. "We didn't buy it," stated Lawford. While the bags containing the drugs were sealed, Lawford soon discovered, "Someone had figured out how to get the cookies without opening the cookie jar. David and I were pissed. . . . This was the first salvo in a new proprietary and more territorial approach to fear and loathing in Camelot."

Bobby was presumably the suspect.

At one point Bobby decided to swim across the dangerous river, going under twice, leaving his party to think he had drowned. Described by Lawford as "Bobby's admirer," Fleetwood, who was keeping a diary of the epic trip, recalled David Kennedy, who had come down with strep throat, observing, "Here you have it, my big brother's own personal heart of darkness."

Billings had a different view.

He saw Bobby as heroic and his feats as comparable to JFK's *PT-109* exploits in the South Pacific during World War II, an exaggeration but one that showed how much he idolized Bobby. Moreover, he had begun calling Bobby "Jack" by mistake, and Billings had instructed Chris Lawford to be to Bobby what RFK had been to JFK. It was all quite bizarre.

After the hellish Apurimac trip, Bobby, along with Billings, Michael Kennedy, Lawford, and a number of other chums, explored in rubber rafts the treacherous Caroni River, which cut across Venezuela from the border with Brazil. Recalling that adventure, Lawford said he had brought his own drugs this time for recreational use, but the bag containing them was stolen at the airport in Caracas, putting a big damper on the trip for him. Riding the frightening river only got worse. As one of Bobby's friends later noted, "I did two stints in Vietnam, I've been shot down four times . . . but I've never seen anything like that."

BOBBY'S ADVENTURES HAD CAUGHT the attention of a dynamic young TV producer by the name of Roger Ailes, who would later become the conservative brain behind the founding of Fox News, dubbed "Faux News" by liberals in the early 2000s because of the network's popular right-wing slant on politics and society. Earlier, as a political consultant, Ailes had made his reputation helping Richard Nixon win the 1968 presidential election that RFK believed would be his before he was assassinated.

Despite their political differences, the Kennedys didn't seem to have a problem collecting a paycheck from, or working for, Ailes's various producing endeavors. Bobby's brother Douglas would work for Fox News, and when Bobby turned twenty-one and was a junior at Harvard he collected a fifteen-hundred-dollar fee for his role as a creative consultant and on-camera narrator for an hour-long, Ailes-produced TV special called *The Last Frontier*. The program featured Bobby traveling through Africa.

Ailes was then consulting for a two-year-old television news service called TVN—Television News, Inc.—funded by Joseph Coors, the conservative beer maker and a member of Ronald Reagan's so-called Kitchen Cabinet, which helped financially support his political career up through the presidency. Bobby also had what was described as a "lucrative contract" to do additional shows in the Last Frontier series, but none were ever made, at least with him, probably because of low ratings.

Ailes, who had heard about Bobby's interest in conservation and wildlife, summoned him to a meeting and a deal was consummated in what the tabloid New York *Daily News* aptly characterized as "a rather unlikely association."

In the special, which aired in the fall of 1975, Bobby, billed as "a star adventurer," was seen by viewers on location in Kenya and appeared in one scene sitting in front of a campfire, chatting about primitive African life, and pondering its upside and downside. "I don't really know whether I could walk out of my hut into three feet of cow manure in the morning," he told viewers, this from the same Kennedy who had hunted rats with his falcon on a mound of fetid cow carcasses while he was at Millbrook.

In September 1975, Bobby began a round of publicity for the program looking much different than he had in his days at Millbrook, Pomfret, and Palfrey. Decked out in an expensive tailored suit, a blue oxford shirt, a tie loosely knotted in Sinatra-ish showbiz fashion, and suede desert boots, he told a newspaper interviewer that he liked the work that Ailes had offered him, but he didn't view TV as a career. "I'm no actor," he said. "If we had to do a second take, I just fell apart. It was fun, though. I knew I didn't have to adapt to this environment [in Africa]. I wasn't stuck somewhere that I couldn't get out of it. It was sort of like Harvard students working in a factory and playing blue-collar workers for a while."

Sitting in Ailes's living room with a reporter who was assigned to write a story about him, he openly nursed a beer and smoked a cigarette, but curtly instructed the photographer not to take a photo of him taking a drag. "Public figures shouldn't smoke," he said. "My father didn't think so, either." It was clear that he already was concerned about his public image because one day he might get into politics, something he would suggest on and off through his life, but has never carried through. Echoing RFK, who by then had been dead for seven years, Bobby noted, "People with advantages in our society can use them to change the system and help large groups of people. The more they have advantages, the more they can help, and the more they should help."

Rarely had Bobby at that point talked for public consumption about his father, but he opened up a bit and observed, "I was luckier than most people who have lost their fathers so young. I had the advantage of being able to read about what he thought and to talk to his friends. It has all influenced me and led me to believe in the same ideals that he stood for. It took me a long time to put the pieces together—the memories, the things people said about him."

SEVENTEEN

Author, Author

Bobby decided to write his Harvard senior thesis on the South and began the project in the fall of 1975 with Peter Kaplan at his side. But earlier that year he briefly got involved in his first political campaign, helping Peter Shapiro, a Harvard graduate and friend of Kaplan's brother, Jimmy, win election as a democrat to the New Jersey General Assembly.

All Bobby, then twenty-one, had to do was show up on the day before the June primary and be photographed with Shapiro as he knocked on potential voters' doors in a blue-collar section of Newark. "The truth is," said Shapiro years later, "I was looking for anything that would give me a boost and Bobby was it. We got a story in the New Jersey edition of the New York *Daily News* on Election Day, with a photo on the front page of Bobby campaigning with me. The publicity value of a Kennedy was all I needed to win." Shapiro won the primary by a narrow margin of 180 votes, and later won the general election.

Bobby's next campaign work would be for his uncle Ted's failed presidential bid in 1980. But his immediate goal was to research and write his thesis in order to graduate. Along with Kaplan, Bobby headed into the Deep South in a Jeep, with Bobby's setter, Hogan, curled up in the back. Bobby's intention, he later explained, was to write "on recent historical and political developments" in the state of Alabama.

He had specifically chosen the "Heart of Dixie" state because of its governor, the charismatic racist George Wallace, who was gunned down and left paralyzed in 1972 while campaigning for the presidency in Maryland's Democratic primary. When Bobby and Kaplan arrived, the wheelchair-bound Wallace was once again involved in readying himself for the 1976 presidential primaries; the Kennedys' very own home base, Boston, had even given Wallace a majority in the Massachusetts Democratic primary. The "good Irish citizens of South Boston," Bobby would later write, were suddenly in Wallace's camp. Those voters were, he observed, "our people . . . at least my family always considered them thus."

Bobby and Kaplan had crossed the Mason-Dixon Line "loaded with our standard Yankee preconceptions"—"small-town ignorance," "burly white sheriffs wielding bullwhips and spitting tobacco, men in sheets burning crosses . . ." In fact, once they arrived in a burg called Hayneville in Lowndes County, Alabama, their preconceptions burst: the local sheriff was black, African Americans were the county's largest voting bloc, and everything seemed just as good—or just as bad—on matters of race as up north in affluent McLean, Virginia, where Bobby had grown up and where there were few black people; the same was true in Kaplan's South Orange, New Jersey, neighborhood.

The two northern boys from Harvard got a warm southern welcome and were invited to stay at the home of a bachelor named John "Sweet Pea" Russell Jr., who had an antebellum home near the Lowndes County courthouse. While they were there, Bobby began hearing fascinating stories—"some good, some bad"—about Frank Johnson, a liberal federal district judge who oversaw a number of prominent civil rights trials, and Bobby soon decided that the jurist would be the subject of his thesis rather than Wallace, who had been a classmate of Johnson's in their youth, and later a foe regarding integration.

Still, Bobby and Kaplan had arranged to have a meeting with Wallace, which became a curious photo op. Taken by one of the governor's aides, it showed the skinny, liberal Harvard boys, one a bespectacled Jew, the

other an Irish-American Catholic, standing on either side of the controversial Southern racist. Kaplan later recalled the meeting. "Wallace received us in his office. He looked pretty awful, sitting behind his desk
in his wheelchair. But it was obvious that he felt a tremendous bond with
Bobby. When he'd been shot, Ethel had gone to see him and invited him
to stay at Hickory Hill. He hadn't done it, but he hadn't forgotten the
offer, either."

In January, Kaplan returned to Harvard, but Bobby stayed on for a
while, mostly messing around. He had gotten himself another dog, a blue-
tick coonhound, as a hunting partner, and he had begun chewing tobacco and dipping snuff, which, he claimed, helped quell his smoking
habit—at least of cigarettes.

Once back at Harvard, Bobby's thesis was accepted.

How much of it he had actually written, however, was up for question.

As someone close to both Bobby and Kaplan observed, "Back then,
Bobby certainly did not think of himself as much of a writer, so Peter
Kaplan was very helpful in getting the thesis finished. He felt he was helping his friend, and I think he felt flattered to be of service, and considered as an intellectual and a writer, which he was. Peter was exploited to
some degree, but it was a two-way street. He was interested in being
friends with Bobby and enjoyed the excitement and the fun and the
glitter of the Kennedy family."

There soon began an effort by a few prominent Kennedy friends on
behalf of Bobby's mother, Ethel, who envisioned Bobby following in
JFK's literary footsteps by having his Harvard thesis put into print by a
mainstream New York publishing house, and becoming a bestseller.

"That's how Jack got started—through writing," Billings, in one of
his many motivational pep talks, had told Bobby.

But there was a dirty little secret concerning JFK's writing, which Billings presumably knew. It was that JFK, the man he adored, hadn't always completely penned the published work that was ascribed to him and
that carried his famous name on the jacket. That was revealed publicly
for the first time in the 2008 memoir of JFK's speechwriter, counselor,
and political strategist Theodore Sorensen.

Kennedy had won a Pulitzer Prize as the sole author of *Profiles in
Courage*, published in 1957. But *The Wall Street Journal*, in reviewing

Sorenson's book, stated that Sorensen "did a first draft of most chapters . . . helped choose the words of many of its sentences," and "indirectly hinted" that he had "written much of the book." Sorensen also disclosed that after JFK won the Pulitzer he had "unexpectedly and generously offered, and I happily accepted, a sum" of money for his clandestine editorial work.

One of JFK's biographers, Nigel Hamilton, in his 1992 book, *JFK: Reckless Youth*, quoted Augustus Soule, a friend of Jack Kennedy's, declaring it was "more than a rumor" that others had written Kennedy's Harvard thesis. "There are those who will tell you," Soule said, "that he never wrote a word of his own thesis, that it was all done by those people over in England when his father was then Ambassador to the Court of St. James's, and his thesis was written for him."

JFK's Harvard paper was entitled "Appeasement at Munich (the Inevitable Result of the Slowness of Conversion of the British Democracy to Change from a Disarmament Policy to a Rearmament Policy)." Despite the complex subject and tongue-twisting title, the future president received the lowest honor grade for his work.

But the longtime Kennedy family friend Arthur Krock of *The New York Times*, known as the "Dean of Washington Newsmen," liked what he read of it, suggested that the title be changed to the more commercial *Why England Slept*, and a literary agent by the name of Gertrude Algase began sending it around to major publishers, with a powerful blurb from the highly respected Krock. However, both Harper Brothers and Harcourt Brace took a pass, thinking it wouldn't sell.

It finally was bought by a small publisher owned by Wilfred Funk, who saw the potential, especially since it now had a foreword by the mighty publisher of *Time* and *Life*, Henry R. Luce, a close Kennedy family friend. The patriarch, Joe Kennedy, had wanted the noted British political thinker and economist Harold Laski to pen the foreword, but he declined. He felt JFK's work was that of "an immature mind," and observed, "If it hadn't been written by the son of a very rich man, he wouldn't have found a publisher."

In an interview with a Boston newspaper, twenty-three-year-old JFK denied that anyone else had had a hand in the writing, calling the book his "brainstorm."

Sales surprisingly took off and *Why England Slept* quickly jumped on to a number of bestseller lists.

According to James Hilty's *Robert Kennedy: Brother Protector*, published by Temple University Press in 1997, five years after Nigel Hamilton's biography, JFK's bestseller had a lot of help from his father. Hilty asserted that the book was "hurriedly assembled" and was "rewritten and edited" by Krock, and "edited further by Harvey Klemmer, Joseph Kennedy's assistant."

Noting that it sold some eighty thousand copies, Hilty further stated that sales were "boosted" by Joe Kennedy's "purchase of a huge number of copies, rumored to be in the thousands."

He quoted the Kennedy patriarch as telling his son, the future president, "You would be surprised how a book that really makes the grade with high-class people stands you in good stead for years to come."

That was essentially what Lem Billings had been preaching to Bobby—that there should be a major push to get his thesis published and become a famous author like his uncle Jack. Billings had said at the time to a doubter, "You don't know Bobby. He's got that incredible ability to bring off the impossible."

As it turned out, Bobby Kennedy Jr.'s people had better luck in 1977 in finding a major publisher for his thesis than had his uncle Jack's people in 1940. Bobby's pages went right to the top of the New York publishing world and were immediately accepted at Putnam by its recently hired publisher, a hotshot by the name of Phyllis Grann, who jumped on the book because, as she acknowledged in 2014, "It was Kennedy, Kennedy, Kennedy!"

Bobby's thesis had been passed on to Grann by Victor Temkin, head of Putnam's paperback division, Berkley Books, she said. Temkin was a Kennedyphile who had worked in both JFK's and RFK's presidential campaigns.

"I was excited, it was by a Kennedy—who wouldn't be?" recalled Grann, who retired in 2011 after a four-decade-long career in publishing. "The reason the Kennedys were receptive to me was because Art Buchwald and I were such close friends," she said. "I published Art, and pushed his books his whole life."

Bobby's thesis required much editing and rewriting "to make it more like a commercial book," noted Grann, who recalled she enjoyed the process of working closely with the young, good-looking Kennedy. "We had a really good time together. We'd go in to the office on the weekends, he'd bring his current girlfriend [Valerie Duff Pacifico], and his dog, and we worked on the book to make it commercial." Two other editors—Barbara Wyden and John Silbersack—were brought in because the writing and organization needed lots of work. Bobby later even described what they had done as "painstaking and insightful" and noted the "considerable amount of love and work that they put into the making of a final copy."

There was much prepublication excitement for the 288-page book, including notes and an index, scheduled for publication in the summer of 1978. Not long before, there were front-page stories that the book's subject, Judge Johnson, was the choice of both President Carter and the attorney general, Griffin Bell, for the post of FBI director, replacing the controversial Clarence Kelley, who had given up the job. The appointment was perfect timing for the book, giving it major public interest, and Bobby had what he called "two months of elation with the possibility of a big seller on my hands."

But it was not to be. Johnson was diagnosed with an aneurysm just one day after he had been nominated and he immediately withdrew his name—to Bobby and his publisher's chagrin.

Moreover, the reviews were dreadful.

Bobby later said that the most positive had appeared in one of those vanilla magazines stuffed by airlines into the seat pocket. He had discovered it on a flight to Los Angeles and it made the trip a bit easier. However, the reviews in the newspapers he was most hoping would give the book raves—*The New York Times* and *The Boston Globe*—were devastating.

Howell Raines, a Southerner in his first year at the *Times* as the Atlanta bureau chief, and the author of an oral history of the civil rights movement and a novel about Alabama's hill country—in other words, an expert on Bobby's broader subject and terrain—declared that the book "neither adequately defines Judge Johnson's role in modern Southern history nor captures the tangled and compelling story."

Further, he opined that Bobby had offered a "plodding, disjointed analysis that clouds rather than clarifies Judge Johnson's achievements as a jurist. . . . There are oversights, too, that seem inexcusable in a biography, even allowing for the fact that this is a first book that had its beginnings as a senior thesis at Harvard.

"It is puzzling, for instance," he continued, "that Mr. Kennedy, a member of a political family dogged by tragedy, does not mention the suicide of Judge Johnson's son and the erratic behavior of the judge's brother, both of whom are said in other accounts to have suffered terribly from attacks visited on the family as a result of Judge Johnson's stand for racial justice . . . the book's principal failing is one of focus. The judge is quoted too sparingly and is frequently shoved offstage altogether."

Bobby later said that he was in Alabama when Johnson's son killed himself, but avoided writing about it because, "I thought somehow I would be betraying a trust. No one outside can understand that kind of pain. You can't convey that kind of pain, unless you're a superb writer, which I'm not."

Headlined "Heroic Rulings," Raines's critique concluded, "For such a large man, a larger book than this is in order."

Equally tough on Bobby was *The Harvard Law Journal*, which called the book "a grave disappointment. . . . A trial judge's biographer must make maximum use of whatever sources are available to him. Regrettably, Kennedy's book displays a number of shortcomings in this regard," the reviewer declared. "While he cites a few unpublished interviews and speeches by Johnson, Kennedy unaccountably ignores more than a dozen published articles and speeches by Johnson that might have contributed substantially to his discussions of Johnson's views on civil disobedience, school desegregation, [and] penal reform . . ."

The Washington Post wasn't very favorable, either. The paper that broke the Watergate scandal said Bobby's biography was "basically an uncritical collection of loping anecdotes which are engaging at times. However, the book lacks introspection, insight and historical perspective worthy of Johnson and his accomplishments. The thesis itself was rated average by many of those who read it at Harvard," wrote the *Post*'s Myra MacPherson, "but they blame the publisher, not Kennedy, for rushing him into print."

Judge Johnson had survived his aneurism, and lived on until the age of eighty. He died in July 1999. Bobby was among the one hundred mourners who attended his funeral service in Montgomery, Alabama, and he told a reporter for the *Times*—in much more focused words than he had in his much criticized biography—"Judge Johnson, really through his courage and integrity, helped make this country a true constitutional democracy. He is as much an American hero as the leaders of the Revolutionary War and the Civil War."

Phyllis Grann felt the book "didn't deserve" the harsh criticism that it had received, and as for it being an expected bestseller, she said, "It didn't happen, so what!"

At the time, Bobby, interviewed in *People* magazine, did a lot of whining, blaming all of the criticism on the fact that he was a member of the most famous and controversial political dynasty in America—"It was political where I and my family name are concerned," he charged, and he further complained that sales were low because "all the publicity also gave people higher expectations of the book than what it set out to be."

The interview with the celebrity weekly, under the headline "His Name's the Game, Bobby Kennedy Jr. Finds on the TV Talk Show Circuit," was part of Bobby's massive publicity campaign for the book. Even though he was giving lots of interviews and being invited to hawk the book on TV shows ranging from *Today* to *Tomorrow with Tom Snyder*, he was left frustrated.

He told *People*, "When I am introduced as Bob Kennedy who will talk about what it was like growing up as a Kennedy, and the book isn't even mentioned in the introduction, well . . ." He complained that most of the questions were about his mother and his idolized grandmother Rose. But he had quickly learned the talking head art of "steering people back to the book. If I could spend a minute out of an eight- or nine-minute segment talking about the judge, then I liked the show."

Most of the time on the road, he avoided saying anything controversial or intimate. But in one interview with *The Washington Post* he revealed, "I'm against abortion on a moral basis, but I have some reservations about how much we can impose our sort of moral ideas and religious beliefs upon other Americans through the law."

No one in the media had accused him of having help writing the book. But an incident happened in the nation's capital during the promotional tour. Bobby was in a bar knocking down a few when another patron spotted him, clearly was aware of all the national hoopla surrounding the publication by the young Kennedy, and accused him of using a ghost-writer. Bobby and his accuser got into a fight and the next day, "The papers said I beat up on a man who criticized my book," he told a reporter.

Besides the poor reviews and disappointing sales, Bobby, at Billings's urging, had applied for a Rhodes scholarship, thinking the publication of his college thesis would hold him in good stead. But the scholarship committee felt otherwise; he didn't get it.

IF THERE WAS ANYONE who was thrilled with the book's aftermath, it was Bobby's girlfriend Valerie Duff Pacifico. Bobby lauded her "for the time, ability, advice and inspiration which she contributed at every stage of the manuscript." According to Phyllis Grann, "Anything Bobby needed, she did."

After Bobby's teenage romance with Kim Kelley, Pacifico had become the most serious love interest in his life for a time when he was in his early twenties.

After graduating with a degree in elementary education in 1973 from the small Park College in Park City, Missouri, where her mother had studied to be a teacher, Pacifico had become a New York City travel agent. Bobby was said to have first met her when he went to book reservations for a trip; he instantly fell for her Italian American good looks, and she was smitten by his Kennedy charm and pedigree.

They quickly became an item.

It was not surprising that Bobby had fallen for her. Pacifico had been voted "best-looking" by her 1968 graduating class at Curtis High School in the New York City blue-collar borough of Staten Island, where she had grown up, the daughter of two public school teachers. As her close friend Grace Rondinelli-Williams observed years later, "It didn't matter that he was a Kennedy, it seemed that most men were swept off their feet by her. The boys were lining up to be her boyfriend, and that continued through high school, and she never understood it, but, of course, the rest of the girls and guys did."

Considering herself to be Bobby's main love interest, Pacifico became part of his tight circle with Lem Billings.

Not only had Billings promoted and pushed Bobby as a writer, which Billings felt would add to Bobby's fame and help with his political future as it had with JFK, but the gay bachelor who had never been romantically involved with a woman had also started giving Bobby advice on the kind of woman he should choose as a wife. It was a profile that the middle-class Staten Island native Pacifico didn't fit, and she, hoping possibly for marriage with Bobby, clearly felt devastated.

"Lem used to tell Bobby that the main quality he had to look for in a wife was money and that I wasn't rich," she later revealed. "He said it in front of me and when he saw that it hurt my feelings he got very apologetic and said, 'I didn't mean to make you feel bad. I just meant that Bobby's got to think about his future. The Kennedy fortune isn't what it used to be, you know. He'll have to marry somebody with a lot of money if he's going to be president.'"

Billings, according to the Kennedy biographers Peter Collier and David Horowitz in their 1984 book, had gone into exacting detail—even asserting that the woman Bobby should marry be much like his well-bred and sophisticated aunt Jackie, the former First Lady, with whom Billings had a close friendship.

Still, Billings had great faith in Pacifico's female judgment, and when he and Bobby would have what some compared to lovers' quarrels, he'd call Pacifico, thinking of her as his personal Dear Abby who could offer him advice on how to fix things with Bobby. She later disclosed that Billings was often "close to tears" and would ask her whether she believed "Bobby loved him" and was his "best friend." And on one occasion, Pacifico said, according to Collier and Horowitz, she had gotten a call from a depressed Billings asking her whether she thought he had "wasted" his life on the Kennedys, and whether they "appreciated" him. In a snit, he had also once telephoned Bobby's friend Harvey Blake Fleetwood to announce that he was stripping his walls of all of his many lovingly framed Kennedy photographs because he didn't want to look at them anymore, that's how fed up he was with the clan that he idolized.

While Duff Pacifico was thrilled with the adoring acknowledgment

Bobby had written for her in his book, she was later shocked to read what a New York tabloid wrote about their relationship.

After the book was published and the publicity had died down, Bobby attended the London School of Economics. In swinging London, however, he had mostly partied and had fallen for another woman, which is what Pacifico was reading about in a gossip column while standing on a crowded New York City subway platform waiting for her train. Bobby, the item said, had become involved with one Rebecca Fraser, a pretty socialite from a famous British family. Rushing to a phone, upset, unbelieving but also furious, Pacifico made a transatlantic call to Bobby and demanded to know whether there was any truth to what she had read. He instantly denied the report, which was a lie. Pacifico's time with the Kennedy namesake had ended.

As her longtime friend Grace Rondinelli-Williams noted years later, "Duff said she really cared for Bobby and she learned she was no longer the important woman in his life by reading it in the paper."

EIGHTEEN

British Affair

I f Duff Pacifico was both livid and saddened to learn from a tabloid gossip column that she had lost Bobby to another woman, his new love across the pond, twenty-year-old model wannabe Rebecca Fraser, was both enjoying and cringing at Fleet Street's sensational coverage of the Kennedy scion's relationship with her. Virtually every day there were gossip items about them with such blaring headlines as "Bobby Junior Settles Down with Becky," and "Worry for Bohemian Bobby."

For Fraser, exposure of her relationship with Bobby was a double whammy because her own famous family had had more than enough scandal with which to contend. Her mother, the glamorous author Lady Antonia Fraser—once dubbed "the golden lioness of London's literary scene"—had had her own headline-making affair when, in 1975, she left her husband, the Conservative Sir Hugh Fraser, for the married playwright Harold Pinter, whom she later married.

The Kennedys and the Frasers had a long and storied history. Hugh Fraser had become friends with Jack Kennedy when he was in his early twenties and his father was the U.S. Ambassador to Great Britain in the late 1930s, and the Kennedy family was living in London.

In 1975 seventeen-year-old Caroline Kennedy was a guest of the Frasers in their elegant home in London's tony Camden Hill Square while she was enrolled in an eleven-month art studies course at Sotheby's. She was training to work in a gallery, or an auction house, a job her mother then thought might be a good career choice for her.

In late October of that year, just a month away from Caroline's eighteenth birthday and the twelfth anniversary of her father's assassination, she barely escaped injury or death when a bomb exploded under Hugh Fraser's red Jaguar, parked outside his home. Just before the blast, Fraser was about to drive Caroline in the bomb-rigged car to her studies at Sotheby's, but he fortunately stopped at the last minute to make a telephone call.

Some six months after the bombing, in the spring of 1977, Rebecca Fraser, who had been working at British *Vogue* as a fashion assistant with hopes of a modeling career, arrived in New York for a holiday and was invited to stay with Caroline's mother in her Fifth Avenue apartment. For a brief time she worked as a hatcheck girl at a trendy restaurant-bar called One Fifth Avenue, which catered to a chic crowd that included a young British fashion editor by the name of Anna Wintour, then working at *Viva*, a sister publication to *Penthouse*.

Mrs. Onassis thought Fraser was gorgeous and began to mentor her for a modeling career in America. She arranged for Fraser to meet the famed fashion photographer Francesco Scavullo, who was knocked out by her look. Jackie also put Fraser together with the powerful model agency head Eileen Ford, who then told *People* magazine that Fraser was "a modern-day Mary Pickford, a delicate, cameo-like creature." The celebrity weekly did a major feature story on Fraser under the headline "Move Over, Margaux! It's Rebecca Fraser Parlaying a Literary Name to Modeling Fame." The Margaux reference was to Margaux Hemingway, Ernest Hemingway's granddaughter, then a popular cover girl, who later died of a drug overdose. *People* described Fraser as a "sulky, silky pre-Raphaelite beauty." Fraser told the magazine, "America's the land of opportunity. It's exciting and where I want to be."

Anna Wintour, at *Viva*, whose father, editor of the London *Evening Standard*, was a friend of Hugh Fraser's, put her on the cover of the magazine's June 1977 issue. Andy Warhol next jumped on the Fraser bandwagon, and made her the "View Girl" in his artsy magazine, *Interview.* It called her "the essence of British Upper Class Soul."

Despite all the attention, Fraser had been in New York without working papers and on a short-stay visitor's visa. Forced to return to London, she told a reporter, "I hope to come back and steal jobs from Americans . . . I just want to make a lot of money. I want to enjoy this nice free age where no one really minds what anyone does anymore."

It was on her return home that she and Bobby were introduced by Caroline, his cousin and her friend, and the two young people began a romance in the fall of 1977. Bobby was knocked out by her erotic look— the frilly white dresses with black cotton stockings that she often wore.

Their relationship triggered a constant stream of Fleet Street tabloid reports, not all positive. There were gossip items, for instance, that Bobby was having health problems. Because of the stern British libel laws, the issue of Bobby's health was believed to be a veiled reference to his possible use of drugs while living in London at a time when heroin was readily available. One news account, under the headline "Worry for Bohemian Bobby," described him as being "very thin" and noted that he had "been ill for some weeks now. The exact nature of his malady is not clear." The writer of the story in the tabloid *Daily Express* had arranged to meet with Bobby for an interview, but Bobby broke the appointment by phone.

"It was very difficult to make any sense of what he was saying," the reporter noted. "He is a charming and serious young man, but his bohemian mode of life must now be a source of worry to his mother Ethel Kennedy." Bobby, he added, "seemed destined for a career in politics. But that does not seem very likely at the moment."

The story also quoted an unnamed "friend" saying, "He has gone through a bad time just lately." It then surfaced that a group of young women, dubbed "Bobbysitters," had, because of his health, been "keeping a vigil" at his Pimlico flat.

Bobby reportedly was living there with Rebecca Fraser while he supposedly was studying for a research degree in, appropriately enough, international relations at the London School of Economics.

Bobby vehemently denied the "love nest" story.

"Jesus," he told a reporter, chewing on a plug of tobacco, a habit he had picked up in Alabama, "I've a girlfriend back in the States. Romance?

Me and Rebecca living together? It's not true." Wearing a beat-up Wind-
breaker and ragged jeans, he declared, "Take it from me, it's all a load of
bullshit. Of course I know Rebecca and her sister—they're great girls.
My uncle, the late President Kennedy, was very close to Rebecca's
father . . . and our families are great friends. But that's all there is to it."
He emphasized his point by spitting a stream of tobacco juice.

When asked the identity of his girlfriend in New York, he refused.
The *Daily Mail* account noted that Bobby seemed concerned at the pros-
pect of his romance with Fraser being reported back home. "Do you
think they'd do that?" he asked anxiously, then answered his own question, "Yes, I suppose they will."

And they did.

That story, dated March 1, 1978, was subsequently picked up in New
York, and from it Duff Pacifico learned that Bobby was cheating on her.

As it turned out, Bobby's matriculation at the London School of
Economics was very brief, less than a month, and was described as "a
halfhearted attempt" at advanced study. His cousin Chris Lawford
viewed Bobby's decision to study at LSE's Strategic Studies Institute as
a way to "cement another brick in his path to becoming the heir apparent." Bobby had gone there on the advice of Lem Billings because both
JFK and his brother Joe Jr. had spent some time there.

Following in Bobby's wake, Lawford also showed up in London,
where he said he had "nothing to do but (1) watch Bobby try to go to
school and (2) attempt to get drugs out of British doctors who were way
more hip to my game than their American counterparts."

According to Peter Collier and David Horowitz, Bobby, while in
London, commuted to the Kennedy ancestral home in Ireland's County
Wexford "to do drugs."

After his time in London, Bobby and Fraser returned together to
the States and he took her to Alabama to introduce her to people he
had met while working on his thesis. There, Bobby had a curious accident. He and Fraser were sitting on a pier when he fell into shallow
water—a few inches at most—and suffered neck and back pains, and was
hospitalized at the Mobile Infirmary in good condition. The next day *The
New York Times* reported that he had dived off the pier. There was no
mention of his companion, Rebecca Fraser.

In London, a follow-up report claimed that Bobby and Fraser had driven nonstop from Massachusetts to Mobile, arriving at three o'clock in the morning, and had been sitting on the pier watching the sunrise when the accident happened. As the *Daily Express* writer observed, "Goodness knows what was going through languid, tobacco-chewing Bobby's mind. For, without testing the depth of the water, he suddenly plunged into the sea."

Soon there were stories that Bobby intended to marry Fraser with the support of her elderly maternal grandfather, Lord Longford, who had earned the nickname "Lord Porn." In 1972 he had published a report denouncing pornography and saying it was bad for an ever-more-permissive society. But his obituary noted that he was a "prurient reactionary and a shameless hypocrite touring the sex clubs that he wanted to close down."

By the summer of 1979, the marriage rumors had reached New York. The *New York Post* ran the first photo of Bobby and Rebecca together in the Big Apple, and claimed that the couple had been living in sin for two years. But a furious Rebecca denounced the rumors. "Our relationship will not lead to the aisle," she declared. "We are not going to get married. It's true we are together but you know as well as I do that though people may spend all their lives in each other's company, they don't necessarily get married."

At the August 1979 RFK Pro-Celebrity Tennis Tournament, Bobby and Fraser were tailed by a reporter and the photographer Ron Gallela, who had made a career and a fortune photographing Bobby's aunt Jackie. Asked about his relationship with Fraser and talk of marriage, Bobby said, "It would serve no purpose to talk about it. I have never spoken about it and don't intend to now." Gallela photographed Bobby and Fraser at the tournament's reception in the Rainbow Room at Rockefeller Center; Bobby looked respectable in a suit and tie, his shirt open at the collar. Rebecca, looking hippie-like in a long gypsy-style dress, was on crutches after a freak accident when workout weights reportedly fell on her foot.

While Ethel Kennedy and Lem Billings didn't think Duff Pacifico was right for Bobby, because she didn't come from money or have an aristocratic background, they and other members of the clan adored Fraser, who had the right profile. When the two young lovers paid visits to the family's compound in Hyannis Port, they were warmly welcomed, and the two reportedly shared a ski lodge during the RFK family's annual Christmas vacation in Aspen. When Bobby's sister Courtney married the network sports executive Jeff Ruhe, Bobby and Fraser were among the celebrants at the Georgetown Club, in Washington.

BY THE SPRING OF 1979, Bobby had begun his law school studies at the University of Virginia, in Charlottesville. In the tiny community of Ivy, not far from the campus, he had rented a nondescript four-room house— two bedrooms, a living room, and a kitchen. And in Alabama, he had bought a big old used car that was thought to have once been a police cruiser. Before long, it was filled with his junk and covered with his dog's hair. As a close pal of Bobby's observed years later, "Bobby back then wasn't one for material things. He never spent a lot of money on clothes, and he wasn't the cleanest guy in the world. He never decorated the house, he was kind of a minimalist."

By then Rebecca Fraser, still seeing Bobby, had taken a job in New York as a researcher for the author Edward Jay Epstein, a Kennedy expert, who had previously written books about the Warren Commission and about JFK's assassin, Lee Harvey Oswald. Epstein had hired her, he recalled, on the recommendation of the London journalist and author Andrew Cockburn. Epstein later credited Fraser for her research work on his book about diamonds, and another about the KGB and the CIA. He recalled many years later that when she came to work for him she was still involved with Bobby and, as he recollected, "she was engaged to him, if I remember. There was a relationship but she never discussed it."

When Epstein threw a going-away party for Fraser on his terrace after she had worked for him for about two years and told him she was returning to London, he said the guests who showed up included Bobby, Caroline Kennedy, and her brother, John Jr.

According to the London gossip columnist William Hickey, a pseudonym, Fraser flew down to Charlottesville from New York on weekends to spend time with Bobby in his "shabby, red brick, distinctly un-

Kennedyish house among the cherry blossoms." He wrote, "Bobby's golden setter Hogan lounges outside while indoors the shy attractive Rebecca wearing a red sweater with jeans rattles the dishes in the kitchen. . . . Most weekends the couple go bare-back riding in the shadow of the mountains. Their friend tells me, 'It's the most unselfish love I've ever seen.' "

According to the close friend who also was studying law at UVA, the house in question was the one Bobby was renting in Ivy.

"Rebecca was living with Bobby in that house," he said. "I had no idea of Rebecca's background and I was surprised to later hear that she was from the British upper crust, and she didn't strike me that way. She was nice and smart and funny and a little ditzy. They got along well, liked each other, but did Bobby philander on her? I'm sure he did."

Around the same time, the New York *Daily News* reported that the couple had asked her estranged parents for permission to marry and they had agreed. In London, another newspaper observed, without elaborating, that if the couple was to wed, "there are various unpleasant habits the young Kennedy will have to be cured of . . ." It was believed to be another veiled reference to Bobby's use of drugs. At the time the report appeared, Rebecca's mother, through her secretary, stated, "I have just spoken to Rebecca in America and she is furious about the stories. She says there is a romance but there is absolutely no truth in the wedding plans. Rebecca and Bobby have never talked about setting a day."

By the fall of 1981, twenty-four-year-old Rebecca Fraser had returned permanently to London, her relationship and American adventure with Bobby, one that lasted as long as two or three years—although she claimed it was just one—was finally over. When the end came, there was a report in October 1981, attributed to "Kennedy insiders," that the London golden girl had not exhibited the "proper reticence when the paparazzi started flashing lightbulbs. They say Rebecca actually enjoyed being snapped."

Back in England, Fraser gave up her youthful modeling, got serious, and following in her mother's literary footsteps, penned a well-received biography of Charlotte Brontë, followed by a popular history of Great Britain, and other books. She also married a prominent barrister and became the mother of three daughters.

In 2014, looking back to her time with Bobby, Fraser observed that she was "going through a short-lived phase of the sort of idiotic behavior which young people in their early twenties can do. It made great copy!" She remembered Bobby as "great fun, very witty and amusing and highly intelligent." She acknowledged that at the end of their relationship she had visited him "a few times" in Charlottesville. "Our relationship was petering out. In fact, during that period he was also going out with Emily Black, unbeknownst to me."

Emily, the new woman in Bobby's life, was a law school classmate, and they were falling in love.

Her life would be turned upside down.

NINETEEN

Bloomington Love

Emily Ruth Black had become romantically involved with Bobby during her second year in Charlottesville, 1979–1980, when Bobby was still seeing Rebecca Fraser. But no one saw the Kennedy–Black relationship becoming serious enough to one day involve marriage.

"They just seemed like good friends, and there were always plenty of women around Bobby," said a law school classmate. To that person and others, Emily seemed just one of a number of young ladies who was attracted to Bobby back then—many simply because he was a Kennedy who had inherited the charm and charisma of his male forebears, but with his own curious edginess, which acted like a magnet on some women. Innocent Emily Black from Bloomington, Indiana, was one.

While both Bobby and Black were in the class starting in September 1978, he also spent time in London and New York with Rebecca Fraser, and then on his uncle Ted's failed presidential run. So, as a friend observed many years later, "It was hard to tell where Emily stood with Bobby because he was in and out of Charlottesville a lot."

Six-foot-two Bobby had met petite, five-foot-four Black for the first time at Lord Hardwicke's, a Charlottesville bar and pizza place popular with UVA undergraduates and law school students. He had gone there for a night of drinking with a new friend, a Yale graduate who had joined Bobby's class, and roomed with him for a short time in the little house Bobby had rented.

"Bobby and I met Emily the same night," recalled the pal, who would remain lifelong friends with both. "We went to Hardwicke's and had drinks and Emily was sitting there, and Bobby just went over and sat down with her. In terms of women, Charlottesville had a less glamorous crowd, but Emily was attractive and very bright. Because she was kind of quiet, she was a change for Bobby and he liked that. She was different from Rebecca Fraser. Was it love at first sight? I don't know about that, but Bobby and Emily got along, and had fun."

Just as the college-educated Duff Pacifico was much different from Bobby's first serious girlfriend, Cape Cod teenager Kim Kelley, and just as the London socialite Rebecca Fraser was a world apart from Staten Island's Pacifico, Emily Black had come from an entirely different place, too, in terms of demographics.

Hers was the modest Midwest. She was the Hoosier daughter of a schoolteacher mother, Elizabeth, known as Libby, and a lumberyard-manager father—it was a family-owned lumberyard, but Thomas Allen Black was on the less successful side of the family tree—who suddenly died of a heart attack at thirty-four when Emily was just two. In order to support Emily and her two siblings, Sarah and Tom, Mrs. Black returned to Indiana University to earn a master's degree and then taught kindergarten and first grade in Bloomington.

When Libby was remarried, to a man named Robert Pawley, and moved to Cameron, Missouri, Emily, a star student and salutatorian in the Class of 1975 at Bloomington's North High School, moved in with an elderly great-aunt, Helen Duncan, who had a modest home in downtown Bloomington. Emily's teenage brother, Tom, nicknamed Aunt Helen "Turkey Vulture" because he thought she looked like one. Duncan later left her house to him.

Unlike studious and academic Emily, young Tom Black graduated high school and then spent two years in the Navy; he worked most of his life at Bloomington Hospital and was a bachelor. In high school, his friends called him "Old Tom" because, as one recalled, "he was kind of crusty, a little profane, not very subtle, and plainspoken." He had inherited the family's big, old Chrysler 300, named it "Daisy Bell," and he and his friends cruised Hoosier National Forest outside Bloomington and, as one remembered, "drank beer and smoked dope, the usual."

Emily, meanwhile, went on to study at her mother's alma mater, Indiana University, where, in 1978, she earned a Phi Beta Kappa key, majoring in political science.

Until she began law school at the University of Virginia in the graduating class of 1981, she had spent her whole life in and around Bloomington, the increasingly depressed factory and fairly liberal college town where the first Kennedy in recent memory to go through was RFK, campaigning in the Indiana primary for the presidency in 1968.

In the crowd that had turned out to see the popular Kennedy candidate, Emily Black never could have imagined in a million years that one day she would marry his namesake.

To her friends it seemed like a Cinderella story come true; to others she was more like Little Red Riding Hood meeting the Big Bad Wolf.

IN HIGH SCHOOL, EMILY was "quiet, pretty shy—one of the smart kids who was definitely not in the in-crowd, didn't run with the popular kids, wasn't in any of the cliques, didn't have many friends (her closest was the pretty daughter of an Iranian college professor at IU who died when she was young, like Emily's father), and wasn't real open or outgoing," recalled Dan Honeycutt, one of the few boys she dated when she was a senior at Bloomington North High and he was a sophomore studying at the university, a bright math and physics major.

He later taught school for a time after graduating from IU, and had a successful career specializing in inertia navigation and ship stabilization for Sperry Marine.

"I was surprised Emily studied law and became a lawyer," he observed many years later, "because in high school she was not very assertive."

Unlike the quiet, reserved Black girl, Honeycutt, who was a friend of her brother, Tom, in high school, had hair past his shoulders and got along with all the different types—the jocks and the rednecks. But he also dated academic Emily Black.

"We went out. I took her to see *Jesus Christ Superstar*, and like everybody in that era we went there stoned, it was the norm," he said. "Emily smoked dope but wasn't a pothead. I smoked pot with her wherever we were, but she was not hanging out with that clique that was called 'the heads.' She was not one of us—if I can consider myself back then one of 'the heads.'"

After dating her for a time, he concluded that she was "a hard person to get to know, a hard person to get to open up and talk. I tried, but it didn't work for me. But I thought she was cute and sweet."

After graduating from IU, Honeycutt immediately left Bloomington, which he later characterized as "kind of a Mayberry in a bigger city," a reference to the fictional hick town made popular on TV's golden-age *Andy Griffith Show* and *Mayberry R.F.D.* The university town became depressed as companies that offered locals well-paying jobs—manufacturing behemoths such as RCA, GE, and Otis Elevator—either shut down or downsized. "Bloomington," he said, "was hard-hit. The only way I could see surviving was to go to school."

His career took him to Charlottesville, and it was there, after several years of not seeing or hearing from Emily while she was at IU, that she called him out of the blue.

DAN HONEYCUTT WAS WRONG if he thought Emily Black had called him on her arrival in Charlottesville to rekindle whatever it was they'd had back in Bloomington when she was in high school. Because she knew he'd been a professional student for a time, her sole goal in touching base after several years was to pump him for information about the best way to go about getting financial aid packages to cover her tuition and expenses at UVA Law, and he was gracious enough to help.

"She had never talked to me about becoming a lawyer, or going to law school, so I was very surprised when she got here and called me. It was out of left field," he said. "We sat down and looked at the financial aid applications and talked about various things she should check into that she'd probably qualify for. She was old enough to be separated from her parents, so her need was based on any income that she had, and back then the terms for a student loan were great."

Back in Bloomington, Black had worked one summer as a clerk in the law office of Guy Loftman, a onetime bearded, bespectacled—Karl Marx–style eyeglasses—member of the radical Students for a Democratic Society (SDS) who had won the presidency of Indiana University's student body in 1967–68 on a platform of student rights. Working for Loftman, she became friends with him and he played a role in her decision to study law.

Honeycutt and Black had gotten together a few times in Charlottesville, but after that he never heard from or saw her again—that is, until he heard that she was seriously involved with Bobby Kennedy Jr. and was going to become a member of one of America's most famous political dynasties.

When he learned that the petite redhead whom he had occasionally dated and gotten high with on marijuana was involved with Bobby, he recalled thinking, "What the heck? Something seems wrong with this picture. The Kennedys have this reputation of hard-core partying and drowning women, the whole Chappaquiddick thing. It struck me as really strange because when I knew Emily she was real sweet, real quiet, reserved, so that seemed to be an odd matchup from the stereotype I had of the Kennedys. To think she was hooked up with somebody who would do heroin was downright spooky.

"I could not imagine that Emily would marry Kennedy for the money—the words *mercenary* and *Emily Black*, they just didn't go together. I had always viewed her as virginal and naive, so I thought, How did she get mixed up in something like that?"

Relatives back in Indiana wondered the same.

As Janet Black, the widowed wife of one of Emily's deceased father's cousins, observed in early 2013, "There were concerns because everyone knew Emily was a very sweet, innocent person to a certain extent, and everything we had read about Bobby Jr., or about any of the Kennedys, of course, was just a different type of upbringing than what Emily had. Emily was a regular person, and there were so many stories going around about the Kennedys—that they were so privileged and so wild. It was wonderful they fell in love, but we were just concerned because Emily was such a sweet, dear girl, and we just didn't want to see anything ruin that sweetness."

· · ·

BY THE TIME EMILY STARTED seeing Bobby, she had become aware that
he had a problem with drugs, one that would continue for some years.
"Emily and I were well aware of his drug use, and I saw it on a number
of occasions," a close friend noted in October 2014, just weeks after he
had attended Bobby's third wedding at the Kennedy compound in
Hyannis Port. The friend, who never used drugs, said that he had on
occasion accompanied Bobby to Harlem and saw him score heroin. "That
was Bobby from the beginning of when I knew him in law school, but
you take what you get in a friend, and I understood that."

At UVA, he said, "It was pretty common knowledge that Bobby did
drugs. This was the late seventies, early eighties, so it wasn't unusual that
he did drugs, and I don't think people were shocked by it. But Bobby
didn't want it to be publicized. Emily was aware, we all were aware, and
everyone offered to help him whenever they could."

There were times when Bobby tried to go cold turkey, the pal said,
and he and Emily tried to help and support him.

"I spent weekends with him when he was getting off drugs, helping
him with rehab," he disclosed. "It was physically a little difficult. He had
a lot of willpower, but the issue was that he had used drugs so much that
it changed the physiology of his body. As I understood it, extended drug
use suppressed certain glandular activity. He needed other actual drugs
to restart stuff in his system. Our efforts were amateurish to say the least.
He'd stop. He'd go cold turkey. He just thought, 'I can beat this whenever I want,' and he did for a while. But then it started again. You can
have incredible willpower but that doesn't mean you can turn addiction
on and off."

DESPITE HIS DRUG ISSUES, Bobby had taken a break from his law
school studies and from Emily to help out in his uncle Ted's 1980 campaign for the presidency. The Massachusetts senator had long feared
running for the nation's highest office after the assassinations of his brothers, expecting that he would be next to get a fatal bullet. But he felt

that President Carter, hoping to be reelected to a second term, showed "malaise" about the future direction of the nation, and reluctantly decided to throw his hat in the ring. It was a big mistake, and he would fail.

Bobby was assigned to work for his uncle in the South because of his past experience there researching his Harvard thesis. He was given campaign marching orders to get Alabama voters in the Kennedy corner. But it wasn't all work. On the road, he reputedly cheated on Emily.

The young journalists Peter Collier and David Horowitz, who had signed a contract to write a biography of the Kennedys, had convinced Bobby to permit them into his life.

It was, as Bobby later rationalized, a disastrously wrong decision.

Looking back in 2013, Horowitz revealed, "I told Bobby we were going to tell his story from his point of view and give him his voice, which we did, so there was a certain romance to him cooperating with us. But we had our point of view. Bobby said he would talk to me. He was looking for a journalist gun, his own biographer. He was told [by Lem Billings] he could be president one day, and that has an effect. Jack Kennedy surrounded himself with writers who were instrumental in his rise, so that could have been an aspect of Bobby's cooperating. He had a twisted mind."

Noted Collier, "Bobby had a bit of an agenda with us. He wanted to be seen as the sort of real heir to Camelot. The RFK kids were very, very anxious about the fact that John-John, whom they saw as sort of a foreigner, was seen as the heir to Camelot, and they felt that it was their father who had really made Camelot in some sense, that he was really the author of the Kennedy myth and that it was a savage miscarriage of justice that the children of Jackie, which is how they saw John and Caroline, should inherit this mantle, that it was theirs."

With Bobby involved in Ted's campaign in Alabama, Horowitz took advantage of the situation and joined him, and was shocked by the scenes that he witnesssed. On a three-day swing with Bobby through Tuskegee, Birmingham, and Huntsville, recalled Horowitz, "Bobby had a girl in every place. There were women there like moths to the flame. I just know that he was fucking everything in sight even though he was involved with Emily Black, who was just very quiet, just seemed like a nice person.

"By the end of the day, the rest of us were exhausted and Bobby was ill, had the flu or something, and all of us collapsed, but there was a girl waiting for him. I was younger then and I'm a healthy male, but I wouldn't have wanted just to go to bed with a strange woman. What is another fuck going to do for you? It was just insanity, compulsive, nutty with him. Maybe in his mind he was building his heroic myth. He certainly couldn't have been getting a lot of pleasure when he was running an over-one-hundred fever, and really looked ill, and was hoarse. He had one girl who was a campaign worker, so he always had that one. At one campaign event, he just went off to screw her."

There was other bizarre and dangerous behavior that a shocked Horowitz witnessed with Bobby as the central figure.

Late one night driving back from Tuskegee, Bobby and Horowitz were in one of two cars filled with the Kennedy scion's campaign aides, mostly people he had picked up along the way. They were on a two-lane highway going as fast as eighty miles an hour, "And they were passing cigarettes between the cars—just insanity."

On another ride through Alabama, Horowitz recalled that the young driver of Bobby's car was consuming a six- or twelve-pack of beer on a two-lane road "and there was this hill in front of us and we could not see over the hill, couldn't see the traffic coming, and the driver got into the opposing lane. That's the kind of things Bobby did, perfectly illegal and crazy, and he did them because he was used to people keeping silent, because nobody wants to be banished from the Kennedy magic circle and lose access."

Horowitz and Collier made a pledge to Bobby—that they wouldn't make mention of any drug use unless it became public, which it did while they were doing their reporting. It involved Bobby's arrest, stoned on a plane, for heroin possession, "so things happened that opened up what we could talk about in the course of the book," said Horowitz.

From a cousin of Billings, they learned about him doing drugs with Bobby. When Billings discovered that "the cat was out of the bag," he blamed David Kennedy for telling the writers of the drug use. "Billings had a real streak of cruelty and abuse in him," Horowitz said. "Here's the guy who's supposed to be the father figure and he's doing heroin with these kids. Lem was doing heroin with Bobby and shooting delusions up his ass that he would be president one day."

At that point, Bobby sent Peter Kaplan as an emissary to meet with Horowitz to keep the drug stories out of the book, "to cut me off," revealed Horowitz. They met on a park bench in New York City and Kaplan pleaded with Horowitz to "close up everything, and by that time the book was pretty well written. Basically his mission was for us to take everything about Lem Billings and drugs out of the book, which I was not going to do.

"Kaplan said to me, 'Bobby is going to run for Congress from Staten Island [Duff Pacifico's home borough], or some shit like that, and he's going to be president one day.' That's the way they [the Kennedys] got everybody. Peter Kaplan was protecting the heir apparent. Kaplan was an intelligent fellow, but one who actually believed that some guy—Bobby—who would be busted for heroin, and would be on the front pages all over the country, could be president one day. He was out of his mind, but that was the case. He was protecting Bobby's political career—as though he had one.

"Kaplan was just so inebriated, intoxicated by Bobby and the Kennedy name. How in the world could he imagine Bobby Kennedy running for office and winning?"

After getting to know about Bobby's dreams for the future and the way he thought, Collier, looking back, came to the realization that "he thought that we would do what all the kept biographers of Kennedys do, which is suppress possibly damaging information and act as part of the party, part of the fantasy world with them. Bobby was shrewd in that he had picked up what the motifs were. Aside from walking on the wild side, one of the motifs was sensitivity to the role literature plays in the building of a career and a life.

"He had large existential hungers," continued Collier. "He was feeling those hungers in the way that kids do—but it was beyond that because he was a Kennedy and what kind of hungers do you feel as a Kennedy kid? It's not to be quarterback for Notre Dame, not to be the head of the Chicago Mercantile Association. He wanted to climb Mount Kennedy. And what Bobby never realized was the incredible discipline it took for Jack to get to the top, for RFK to get to where he got—*great* discipline. He saw the indulgence, but didn't see the discipline. He didn't want to see it because it conveys a daunting message."

Horowitz had had a number of interviews with David Kennedy, and, as later reported in Collier and Horowitz's book, David claimed that it was Bobby who got him involved with drugs.

According to Collier, the Kennedys had begun spreading rumors after the book was published that the writers had done drugs with them, "just to contaminate the book, to exonerate themselves for having cooperated. There was more than one effort to do that, even trying to hold us responsible for David's death."

BECAUSE OF TED KENNEDY'S failing presidential campaign, Bobby returned to UVA to finish law school and continue his relationship with Emily Black.

While Bobby was away, Emily had dated others whom she liked. But when he returned, she decided she liked him the best. As she later told *People*, "We were in love, wanted kids and were ready to limit our lives to each other." Still, they had very different personalities. Emily had a calm way about her, while Bobby was, as he himself acknowledged at the time, "hyperactive. I have a tendency to stay out too late and drink too much beer." Bobby described Emily as "perfect," and she thought of him as a lovable "kind of a slob." His drug use was kept secret.

Emily's closest friend in law school was Alexandra Cury, a University of Pennsylvania graduate with whom she bonded in her first year and roomed with in her second and third years. They shared a three-bedroom rental house in Charlottesville, and remained lifelong friends.

There had been talk that the reputed skirt-chaser Bobby had pursued Cury, but in the summer of 2014, the veteran defense attorney called those rumors "false, loose chatter" and asserted, "we never had a romantic or sexual relationship." She acknowledged that she had become friends with Bobby "through Emily" and still had "very fond memories of Bobby and our times together." Cury would be a bridesmaid at the Black–Kennedy nuptials.

A woman Bobby had gone out with at the same time he was involved with Emily was Tess Dempsey, according to her mother, Connie Dempsey, who owned a prominent Charlottesville equestrian complex called Foxfield Stables, where Bobby kept horses—and a falcon—during his time at UVA Law.

"Tess and Bobby dated a lot," claimed Dempsey. "Bobby was a playboy."

Like Joey Brode, who became a surrogate mother of sorts to the troubled Kennedy when he boarded with her in Cambridge while finishing his senior year at Palfrey Street School, Connie Dempsey had, she asserted, taken on the same role in Charlottesville.

"Bobby considered me his mother—his Charlottesville mother—and he even told Ethel that he considered me his mother," recalled Dempsey many years later. "Bobby practically lived at our house, we spent a lot of time together, he had dinner with us, and he was a *real* moocher," she said affectionately. "But that wasn't a surprise because the Kennedys were all known for being moochers. Bobby always paid his bills—but he didn't pay enthusiastically," she recalled. "He'd pay by writing a check, and then he'd purposefully drop it somewhere, go off, and then somebody would have to hunt him down."

Bobby's tightfistedness was underscored when he got into a legal battle with Jody Ann Jacobson, in the fifty-fifty ownership of a horse with a good Irish name, Killarney. A twenty-four-year-old graduate student at UVA, Jacobson filed suit against Bobby and won an injunction against him from taking full possession of their jointly owned five-year-old bay gelding.

The tug-of-war over the horse, for which each had paid $1,250, was sparked when Jacobson requested to buy out Bobby's half interest, per an agreement they had. Jacobson's attorney said at the time that Bobby had threatened to "take the horse to New York." He told *The Washington Post* that she "can't get Bobby to agree on a price. Even after these disputes arose, he continued to refer to the horse exclusively as his horse." Years later, no one could recall which of the parties kept Killarney.

Bobby's interest in riding had been triggered by his mother, who had three consuming passions—the Kennedys, Catholicism, and horses.

When she was a kid growing up in the Skakels' estate in Greenwich, the walls of her bedroom were a montage of photos of her on horseback. As a student at Greenwich Academy she owned not one but two horses, Smoky Joe and Beau Mischief. One of her pals, Billy Steinkraus, a member of the U.S. Olympic riding team, recalled, "She took to riding the way she took to touch football with the Kennedys." The first show horse she ever rode had been owned by Janet Lee Bouvier, years before Ethel had ever met her daughter, Ethel's sister-in-law Jacqueline.

Ethel rode everywhere, even through the front door of the Skakel mansion and "galloping like hell" out the back door, shocking a friend who was an eyewitness to the event. When she was in college and scheduled to appear in a major horse show in Madison Square Garden, she was running late and took a shortcut across Central Park, risking arrest. The year before RFK was assassinated, Ethel Kennedy took several horses that she deemed had been mistreated, and was charged with rustling, a hanging offense in Virginia, but she won the case.

At times, Ethel came down from Hickory Hill to ride with Dempsey and her crowd. "She was," Dempsey said, "a better rider than her son, one of the best."

For a time, Bobby had been a tenant on the farm owned by Jody Jacobson's family, according to Dempsey. He had also spent a lot of time in a home bought as an investment property by his law school classmate Sheldon Whitehouse, who was part of Bobby's small circle at UVA.

Like Bobby, Whitehouse was the namesake of a prominent political father, Charles Sheldon Whitehouse, who had served in the Central Intelligence Agency, operating in Europe and the Far East, and later was the U.S. Ambassador to Laos and Thailand near the end of the Vietnam War. In the 1980s, he served as an assistant secretary of defense.

Whenever Bobby placed a telephone call to Connie Dempsey, he always prefaced his conversation by saying, "Hello, Connie, this is your favorite law student." But her half-joking, half-serious response always was "You know that isn't true, Bobby. My favorite law student is Sheldon!"

Of the two, she had chosen the one who would be the most successful, at least politically. He later was elected U.S. Senator from Rhode Island with Bobby's support.

• • •

THERE WERE A NUMBER of things about Bobby that rubbed Connie Dempsey the wrong way.

He had built an outdoor cage on Dempsey's property to house his falcon, but he also chose to feed it disgusting roadkill that he stored in Dempsey's home refrigerator. "We tried to encourage him to buy chickens for this purpose," she said, "but we weren't too successful."

While he had taught the Dempseys and others in his UVA circle how to handle his bird, he had upset the horse-loving Dempsey when he began riding with the falcon on his arm, which "upset the horse and made it crazy."

Another issue for Dempsey was how Bobby treated his setter, Hogan, whom, she noted, he "took places and dropped off, leaving it, so people would have trouble finding it, and expecting a reward for its return. He was not," she concluded, "a very good dog owner."

Bobby often brought Emily Black to Dempsey's stable to ride. But as a wife and mother of four, Dempsey didn't see a lot of romance between them. "I thought it was mostly just a friendship thing, and mostly involved riding together. She was a pleasant person, quiet, meek, not confrontational. She married him, but all the girls were trying to marry him."

Bobby and Black were part of a law school crowd who rode and played together. On property that belonged to a law professor, in an area known as Liberty Hill, there was a pond. There, Bobby and Black and some of his male classmates were known to skinny-dip, and Bobby had a trick he liked to play on the guys.

"After they jumped in the water, Bobby would take their clothes and toss them up in a tree," said Dempsey, who had never forgotten the scene. "Bobby thought it was funny as hell to see the naked guys climbing the tree, trying to capture their clothing to put on so they could ride down the highway to my stable."

Dempsey had come to the conclusion that Bobby was more interested in partying than studying, and believed that he "must have had a lot of help graduating because he wasn't the best student. He just didn't do his best."

As an example, one of the classes the future lawyer was required to take involved participating in a mock trial. He along with Sheldon White-house acted as the defense for a student playing the role of a man accused of burglary or a similar crime. But two very sharp, very savvy female students in Bobby's class were the prosecutors. After all the testimony was given, the rest of the class, acting as the jury, voted to convict. Bobby and Whitehouse had lost, a foreshadowing of Kennedy's brief career in criminal law as a prosecutor.

TWENTY

Emotional Changes

Bobby was faced with both love and sorrow in the nine months between asking Emily Black to be his wife and the loss of the one person he truly loved.

In August 1980, he joyfully announced to Emily's mother that he had asked her daughter to marry him. But in May 1981, his mentor and father figure, Lem Billings—who had for years shared his dreams, ambitions, and drugs—suddenly died. The two passages, marriage and death, would have a great emotional impact on Bobby going forward.

Emily's mother naturally was thrilled that her daughter was to become a Kennedy wife but kept the news to herself. Well, almost. She had actually tipped off the ladies in her bridge club that her daughter was going to marry RFK's namesake. "The *real* Bobby Kennedy?" they demanded to know, thinking this was all just a fairy-tale dream of hers.

Bobby had already attempted to bond with his future brother-in-law, the low-level Bloomington Hospital employee Tom Black, by sending him, in early 1980, an odd gift—a pair of boxing shoes. Black was starstruck by his sister's boyfriend and had boasted about the prize gift to a pal, Tom Richardson, who had trouble believing that the small-town,

quiet, bookish Emily, which is how he remembered her, could have become involved with a member of one of the most politically powerful and
privileged families in American history.

"We thought he was full of it," Richardson said. "We thought he was
daydreaming."

By the time the engagement became public—leaked presumably by
one of the Kennedys to a New York gossip column—Emily's proud
mother, Libby Pawley, was boasting to everyone and anyone who would
listen about her future son-in-law and what a "really nice boy" he was. She
told them that he was a Harvard graduate, that he had attended the prestigious London School of Economics, that he had even had a book published, and had been interviewed by *People* magazine, which she often
flipped through at the hairdresser. Moreover, she confided to friends,
there was talk that one day he might even be president, and she envisioned her daughter as his First Lady.

Emily, her mother felt, had hit the jackpot.

It was clear from how excited she had sounded that the retired
kindergarten and first-grade teacher knew very little about what her
daughter was actually getting into—that Bobby had a reputation as a
druggie and a womanizer, and that the Kennedy clan wasn't always held
in the highest esteem. But to her mom, Emily was a real-life Cinderella
marrying the royal family's prince—or, as the local Bloomington newspaper asked in a headline when the engagement became public in October 1981, was "Emily Our Own Lady Di?" As it would turn out, that
was a prescient question because, like Princess Diana's troubled marriage
to Prince Charles, Emily's union with Bobby Kennedy Jr. would be
tumultuous and end badly.

At the time the engagement became publicly known, Emily's mother
still had not had the pleasure of meeting Bobby's mother, and may not
have known that the famous widow was considered a harridan by a number of intimates and employees, and perhaps not much liked at times
even by her own son. The future mothers-in-law had planned a weekend get-together, but Ethel canceled because she was getting yet another
honorarium—a medallion from Congress in honor of RFK, one of many
honors she had collected since his death. Their meeting was put off until
close to the time of the wedding.

After the engagement of her daughter became public—and big news—Emily's mother told a local Bloomington columnist, Greg Dawson, that she'd been "hearing" about Bobby for a "long time" from her daughter, and had concluded that he was "a very down-to-earth kind of boy—man, excuse me. Every time I saw him he was in blue jeans. He might put on a blue jeans jacket to go to dinner, but that's about it. He's quiet, and very funny. I don't believe Emily would go for anyone pretentious at all. She and her friends all like him . . . Emily thinks he's *wonderful*."

The mother of the bride-to-be, who had grown up in very modest circumstances, marveled at the idea of being part of the Kennedy clan. "When I was a teenager," she once told an observer, "we took *Life* magazine and they always had pictures of the Kennedys in England, and I always thought they were fascinating." And now, with her daughter's marriage, and getting to meet the clan, she sighed, "I'm going to try to be myself and not get *too* excited."

Mrs. Artie Klein—the sister of Emily's long-deceased biological father—felt her niece would make Bobby the perfect mate because she was "just a super young girl, and she's beautiful, and a top-flight student." Moreover, according to the Bedford, Missouri, woman—Bedford was the "limestone capital of the world" and the town where Emily was born— "she's always been rather quiet, not timid, just quiet, and she loves to be around people and is very sociable, but just doesn't have a lot to say."

To the Kennedys, Emily possessed the perfect profile for an outsider marrying into the clan: a young woman who would keep her mouth shut and not blab the family secrets.

With the engagement, there was talk that the wedding would be the usual monstrously large Kennedy-style royal affair—think an army of paparazzi camped outside, with choppers overhead—and held in midtown Manhattan at St. Patrick's Cathedral, where Bobby had mourned at his father's casket.

In preparation for her betrothal, Emily, of the Protestant persuasion, had even begun taking instruction to become Catholic at the behest of Bobby and his devout and pious mother. Wryly, Bobby said at the time, "My mother tells me that means I'll go to heaven."

. . .

IT WAS DURING THAT HAPPY time leading up to Bobby's wedding that tragedy struck, placing a dark cloud over him. Lem Billings—the homosexual Svengali who had guided and literally tried to control and to direct every aspect of Bobby's life from the time he was fourteen—suddenly died. As Bobby would later say, "I won't get over Lem's death any more than I'll get over my father's."

Billings had never approved of Emily, just as he'd had negative feelings about Bobby's relationship with Duff Pacifico because she wasn't wealthy and from high society. Despite Emily Black's intelligence and low-key, likable persona, Billings thought of her as little more than a cute Hoosier hayseed. Nevertheless, he was set to be Bobby's best man at the wedding.

On May 27, 1981, feeling chipper, Billings had accompanied Bobby's brother Michael and his new bride, Vicki Gifford Kennedy, to see a British science fiction film at a Manhattan theater. Seemingly stoned, which he usually was in those days, he was rowdy and talkative. Michael later told Billings's biographer, David Pitts, "It was hilarious," because Billings was loudly saying things like "What the hell is going on?" After the movie, according to Michael, "We went back to his apartment and talked. It was a good night."

Another member of Bobby's inner circle, the ubiquitous Harvey Blake Fleetwood, was also at Billings's house, and they all were expecting Bobby to join them from Charlottesville. But he canceled at the last minute.

Fleetwood later claimed that Billings was "very upset about that. He and Bobby had been fighting over the phone about going to Haiti that summer. The real subject was the thousand other things they couldn't talk about, things having to do with the death of the Kennedy dream.

"That night," Fleetwood told Peter Collier and David Horowitz, "Lem got very drunk. He said to me, 'You've got to take care of Bobby.' I said that he shouldn't worry about Bobby because Bobby had a million friends. 'No, you're one of the only ones who cares.' I said all this talk didn't mean much because he'd be there to look after Bobby the way he always had. He shook his head and started to cry. 'No. I made a terrible mistake. I took drugs with him. I made a terrible mistake. I let him down.'"

Sometime during the night of May 28, sixty-five-year-old Billings apparently suffered a heart attack and died in his sleep, practically on the day of the sixty-fourth anniversary of the birth of the man he had loved before Bobby—John F. Kennedy. Billings's body was discovered in the morning by Peter Kaplan, who had spent the night in the fanciful beaux-arts home.

Despite the autopsy report stating that he had suffered a fatal heart attack, Bobby's mother later questioned whether Billings had actually died of a drug overdose. Over the years, Ethel Kennedy had become less enamored of Billings, to whom she had entrusted the care and welfare of her teenage Bobby when he had just lost his father. She had heard rumblings of Billings's drug use and certainly of her son's, which would only get worse and more scandalous for the family.

Through the years Ethel had been witness to some of the odd behavior that existed between Bobby and the gay man whom she had assigned to be her son's surrogate father. On one occasion, with Ethel and a few of her young ones present, Bobby and Billings, in matching terry-cloth robes, sat together at the Hickory Hill breakfast table, downing straight shots at eight-thirty in the morning, and were visibly inebriated. They were planning to fly out together that day and Billings had telephoned for a cab. When the driver arrived, recalled Ethel's then-secretary, Noelle Fell, Billings argued with him for showing up too early, and complained about the cost of the up-front fare. Returning to the table, he fumed, "That fucking son of a bitch wanted to get paid for just fucking coming." As Fell recalled, Bobby exploded in laughter, at which point Billings jumped up from the table and yelled in his high-pitched, effeminate voice, "Ethel, why is this house so fucking hot?" At that moment his robe accidentally opened, and the towel around his waist fell to the floor, exposing his genitalia. The Kennedy cook, carrying in a hot pot of coffee, screamed and nearly fainted from the sight.

THERE WAS A MEMORIAL SERVICE for Billings at an Episcopal church near his home. The funeral was held in the polluted, dreary Rust Belt city of his birthplace, Pittsburgh, Pennsylvania, and he was buried in the Billings family plot near his beloved mother, Romaine.

Billings had once told Bobby that when he died he wanted the pall-bearers to be members of his youthful—and, for the most part, druggie—circle of Kennedys and their friends, and his wish was Bobby's command. He and the others carried the casket and held it throughout the service.

"I'm sure he's already organizing everything in heaven so it will be completely ready for us—with just the right Early American furniture, the right curtains, the right rugs, the right paintings, and everything ready for a big, big party," Bobby told the solemn gathering in his heartfelt and rather candid eulogy. "Yesterday was Jack's birthday. Jack's best friend was Lem, and he would want me to remind everyone of that today. I am sure the good Lord knows that heaven is Jesus and Lem and Jack and Bobby loving one another."

A champagne toast was held in the cemetery, and someone remembered that Billings had once predicted, "After I go, there'll be no more Kennedys."

WHEN WORD OF THE Kennedy–Black engagement became known to the world, Emily's mother revealed that after the marriage the newly-weds would move into the Billings home, which Bobby had inherited. What she didn't know was that the overdecorated bachelor pad had also become a sex-and-drug party house for her future son-in-law, Billings, and some in their circle.

The Billings house was near the Guggenheim Museum on Manhattan's Upper East Side, and was itself like a museum, filled with all things Kennedy, including sketches of JFK and RFK, one inscribed by Ethel Kennedy that read, "For Lem—Jack's best friend."

Along with the Kennedy stuff was priceless art, including Chagalls, pieces of rare sculpture, antique furniture, and all sorts of esoteric collections. "It was," a friend recalled years later, "the epitome of gay kitsch, but classy gay kitsch—a campy kind of place the newspaper Style section might feature." At one time, Billings even kept one of Bobby's frightening-looking boa constrictors in a hall closet.

In a privately published and distributed oral history tribute to Billings, organized after his death in part by Bobby, he called him "the most fun person I had ever met in my life. Lem's house was more than a fun house; it was a museum, a library, a classroom. . . . Whenever I felt lonely, or sad, or left out, I would call Lem and laugh."

Peter Kaplan once observed that being friends with Billings, and accepting all that he demanded and gave, "was like having a wonderful map of life. And it made an awful lot of things better when you shared the same boundaries. You both always knew what you were looking at and talking about. That was Lem's geography."

Another longtime Kennedy family friend, David Michaelis, who wrote a 1983 book about a series of esoteric friendships, noted that Billings and the young Kennedy crowd "often had the spirit of a collegiate fraternity where anything might happen."

But back then all were hiding, or trying to hide, the dark side of the relationship—the many drugs that Billings was using, mostly with Bobby and at Bobby's urging, in order to look young and remain part of the fraternity. Those drugs, from beginners' pot to advanced heroin, might have played a part in his early demise.

EXACTLY HOW INTIMATE THE RELATIONSHIP between the heterosexual Bobby and homosexual Billings had been, and whether it ever involved sex, will probably never be known. It was known that they did drugs together, and that after the death of Billings, a biographer claimed that Billings had performed oral sex on Jack Kennedy at some point during their many years of close friendship.

In his 2007 book, *Jack and Lem: John F. Kennedy and Lem Billings— The Untold Story of an Extraordinary Friendship*, David Pitts dealt only marginally with Billings's long relationship with Bobby, who had declined Pitts's requests for an interview. In characterizing the bond between Bobby and Billings as "very close" in 2013, Pitts observed, "It's a big speculation with reference to any possible sexual abuse. Lem was a gay man and he had a fourteen-year-old, good-looking kid with him, and there had been rumors [of sexual activity] because of that. But I had no evidence one way or the other." He noted, however, that the use of drugs and alcohol, which he was aware that Bobby and Billings had shared, had the effect of "lowered inhibitions." Under such circumstances, Pitts believed, anything could happen.

In researching his book, Pitts said, he had asked Bobby's close cousin Christopher Kennedy Lawford whether he was aware that Billings was gay, since there had been a "rivalry between Lawford and Bobby for Lem's affection . . . and Lawford said something on the lines of, 'No, I didn't know, just that I knew he was kind of flamboyant, which we definitely thought when we were kids. We just didn't put two and two together.'"

In his 2005 memoir, *Symptoms of Withdrawal*, Lawford made no mention of Billings's sexuality, but noted that from the time of RFK's assassination he and Bobby "had found a place where we could exercise our independence" at Billings's home.

Lawford said he came to view Billings as his "surrogate father," and saw Billings as Bobby's "father," and that they "spent most of our time together" at Billings's place.

"Lem saw our need and rushed to fill the void," Lawford asserted. "Lem adopted our generations. He cared about us and treated us like the sons he never had . . . Bobby was lucky to have an adult who was fully devoted to him. I spent years competing for Lem's attention and affection.

"When Lem was angry at Bobby," Lawford continued, "I became his favorite and the extra bedroom in Lem's Eighty-eighth Street apartment became 'Chris and Bobby's room.' But when they made up it was back to being 'Bobby's room.' I never really had a chance . . . Lem's attachment and anointing of Bobby defined him as the second coming . . ."

Billings had died while Peter Collier and David Horowitz were still working on their 1984 book about the Kennedys, with Bobby's somewhat reluctant cooperation concerning his generation. But he and others in his circle had turned against the writers when they revealed Billings's drug use.

Horowitz, asked in 2013 whether he believed there had been any sexual activity between Billings and Bobby as there reportedly had been between Billings and JFK, said, "I suspect that that went on with Bobby as well. Bobby made remarks about him and Billings that I kept out of the book. I did have an indication, but it was kind of off-limits. We just didn't do that."

Collier said that when he and Horowitz were working on their book they couldn't state that Billings was gay, because he was still alive and closeted, and there was fear that he might sue if they revealed his sexual preference in print.

But Collier said that Bobby's aunt Jackie was aware of Billings's sexual preference and had her own fears about him.

"Jackie had kind of gone to Lem and said, you gotta control this [his homosexual urges]. She did that under the guise of his own welfare, that he wouldn't get caught in some public bathroom," said Collier. "It was clear to us that Billings was in love with Bobby. But who knows if anything [of a sexual nature] went on. That was a time before we insisted on knowing the details of people's sexual curriculum vitae. There was no smoking penis from what we were able to find. But anything could have happened, particularly if your whole modus operandi was to see rules as being there to be broken."

TWENTY-ONE

Hate Mail

When word got out that Bobby and Emily Black were to be married, a New York tabloid reporter reached out to the future groom, who said that he and his intended hadn't yet picked a church, but he was confident that the wedding would be held on a Sunday, and in New York City, because "I love St. Patrick's Cathedral."

At that point, Bobby, who still had seven months remaining before law school graduation, was considering joining either a "Park Avenue law firm," he was boasting, or taking one of what he indicated were several offers from "law enforcement agencies." FBI? CIA? NYPD? The U.S. Justice Department, which his father had headed during Camelot? Bobby never said. But with his past record, at least in those days, any law enforcement job, even for a Kennedy namesake, seemed improbable.

However, none of it would pan out: not fabled St. Patrick's, and not a fancy Park Avenue law firm. Not even Sunday-in-Manhattan nuptials. And he would even run into trouble when it came time to pass the New York bar exam.

By early 1982, Bobby's plans for that big, splashy, expensive Big Apple wedding at the famed cathedral on Fifth Avenue had been dashed by his beloved, who made it known that their wedding would be held in Bloomington, and nowhere but her hometown.

"That's where I'm from," she declared. "That's where I was brought up."

She would have it no other way.

Rather than St. Patrick's, the ceremony was now scheduled to take place in Bloomington's First Christian Church, a pretty house of worship where Emily had been baptized twenty-four years earlier, and it was decided that her brother, Tom, would give her away.

He was truly excited to become a minor player in the mythic political dynasty's cast of characters, and was proud that his sister had risen above her middle-class, Middle America roots, had excelled as a student, had earned a law degree, and now would be famous by marrying a Kennedy, and become a part of history. He boasted that his sister "always was a sharp student" who could "do my math when I was in the third grade and she was in the first," and he noted, as others had, that "she's pretty quiet but can be talkative if she has something to say." He firmly believed that Emily was "looking forward more to being married than to getting married."

But he got into hot water with his future brother-in-law's mother when he revealed that the real reason for the location change from celebrated St. Pat's to relatively obscure First Christian in the middle of Indiana was financial. As it turned out, Emily's mother, who could only dream about the kind of wealth the Kennedys possessed, was the one actually footing the bill, and New York City costs for a big Kennedy extravaganza weren't anything she could afford. Ethel Kennedy was said to have been livid that Tom Black had disclosed the money issue, and he was told in no uncertain terms to keep his mouth shut about any and all wedding plans if reporters called him.

By 2013, many years after his sister and Bobby had been divorced, he still was fearful of talking about their wedding and the financial terms for it, believing that he was still subject to the wrath of the Kennedys. "They were mad at me and told me not to say anything anymore," he said. "So I can't talk to you." He then hung up.

However, at the time, the Kennedys put their own inimitable spin on why the venue had changed. An aide to Ted Kennedy, one Eric Sklar, was quoted as telling the local Bloomington press, "Robert Jr. and Emily wanted to keep it a quiet affair and that's one reason they decided to bring the show to Indiana. The couple chose Bloomington after first considering St. Patrick's Cathedral in the heart of New York City, which is not a quiet place." There was no mention, of course, of the cost factor.

"I'd heard kind of a little different twist to why my church was chosen," recalled the Reverend Terry Ewing, who was chosen by Emily's mother to co-officiate the wedding service at First Christian, where he was the thirty-four-year-old associate minister. "The Kennedys thought about St. Patrick's, but Emily wanted to assert herself as new in the Kennedy clan, and her way of doing that was to have the wedding where she was from. That was my interpretation. I heard that from her mother. As I remember it, she said something like, 'Emily wanted to do it her way.'"

The minimum expense for Emily's mother was for the use of the facilities at Ewing's church, a total of $170, which also covered the organist, with half required up front.

A bigger expense involved the bridal gown. Arrangements had been made with Neiman-Marcus in Washington, D.C. It was a classic "candlelight," custom designed by Phyllis of the House of Bianchi. Phyllis Ann Bianchi had run one of the country's major manufacturers of bridal gowns before it went under because of financial problems, reportedly leaving orders unfullfilled. Because Phyllis was a Catholic who had started her business in the Kennedys' hometown of Boston and was a lifelong native of Massachusetts, Mrs. Pawley was said to have gotten a break on the price through Kennedy intercession.

Emily's complex gown had a high Regina neckline with an illusion yoke and dimple-topped long fitted sleeves, as described by Bianchi. It had a corselet bodice with a dropped waist that worked into the all-over Lyon lace "with a touch of point d'esprit" over a fuller skirt, and a traditional court train that "will glow in reflection of the scalloped and clustered pearls and sequins." The latter accentuated the "floral interest" of the lace—all of it complemented by a "long illusion veil cascading from a circle of handmade satin and lace rosebuds."

In other words, it was quite a production. If all went as planned, the future Mrs. Robert F. Kennedy Jr. was going to be the most beautiful bride Bloomington had seen in quite a long time.

Because it was a Kennedy wedding, reporters and photographers from around the world descended on the town—three paparazzi from France alone, all there mainly in hopes of getting the best-known Kennedys on film—the matriarch Rose, the former first lady Jackie, her celebrated children, John and Caroline. But the press was disappointed. From New York, the photographer John Roca and a friend drove nonstop to Bloomington in hopes of snagging some big-money shots. "We drove out because we thought it would be a big gala Kennedy affair—that John Jr. would be there, that Caroline would be there. Needless to say, none of them were there. It was not what we expected."

Because the groom's mother was one of the wealthy and notorious Skakels of Greenwich, Connecticut, their local *Chronicle* newspaper sent one of its reporters, Jessica Walters, to cover the festivities. She told the local press assigned to the media circus–end of the story that Kennedy watchers back east had been "shocked"—*shocked*—at who Bobby was marrying because everyone had just assumed that his intended would be his old girlfriend, the kicky British socialite Rebecca Fraser.

Bobby's usually reticent future wife was a bit more forthcoming back then, but not by much, mainly because she had never in her life had to deal with aggressive reporters. She told one journalist from Indianapolis that she thought her marriage was being overblown by all the news folk. "I don't think this is all that newsworthy," she said. "I don't know how I'm going to keep it low key—avoid talking to reporters, I guess," she said, answering her own question, and then quickly added in her sweet Midwestern manner, "I'm really not trying to be rude."

The final plans to hold the wedding in Bloomington, where Bobby may have visited just once during his courtship of Emily, had been made between her and her mother. Still living in Charlottesville with Bobby, Emily diplomatically noted that her groom didn't mind the change of venue from New York to Bloomington. "He's excited about it."

Only the day of the wedding was still undecided. If bride and groom could blame the timing on any one event, it might be the crucifixion and resurrection of Jesus Christ and that whole biblical story wrapped around Easter Sunday.

Reverend Ewing was in his church office and took Emily's mother's first call, requesting that her daughter's wedding be held on Easter Saturday, April 10. Clearly recalling that moment decades later, Ewing told her, "Easter is the highest holy day and it is a big weekend and there's no way we can do a wedding, and she says, 'Well, we can pay more.' I said that really doesn't have anything to do with it. We just don't have the ability to do that."

He gave Libby Pawley, whose name he didn't instantly connect with the Kennedy affair that was already making headlines, a few optional dates, concluded the call, and hung up.

The young reverend wasn't your typical man of the cloth. He had been a member of a number of rock bands, and experienced all that went with that, and he had written a column about rock 'n' roll for Bloomington's underground paper, and as such considered himself "sort of the rock 'n' roll minister." What had popped into his head as he got off the phone with the future bride's mother, suddenly realizing that he might just have turned away Bloomington's wedding of the century, was the 1968 Rolling Stones song "Sympathy for the Devil," which has the verse, "I shouted out 'Who killed the Kennedys,' when after all it was you and me."

As he was mulling the irony, Libby Pawley called back and said she'd take one of the wedding dates Ewing had offered: Saturday, April 3.

"I just thought, 'Oh, my gosh, here I used to be involved in playing that song about who killed the Kennedys, and here I'm going to be involved in the wedding of one of the sons of those two Kennedys.'"

For Bloomington, a Kennedy wedding in its midst was the biggest thing to happen since the coming-of-age movie *Breaking Away*, about four fictional Bloomington teenagers, that was filmed there in the late 1970s—much of it on the campus of Indiana University, when Emily Black was in her senior year there. Bloomington's other big event, long before the movie and the Kennedy nuptials, was when the church where Bobby and Emily were to be married had caught fire and had to be rebuilt early in the twentieth century. According to the legend, the blaze had been accidentally set by two local boys playing in the bell tower: one of them, Howard Hoagland "Hoagy" Carmichael, later composed such musical greats as "Stardust" and "Georgia on My Mind," and starred in such films as *To Have and Have Not*, with Humphrey Bogart and Lauren Bacall. They were pretty much the big stories in Bloomington before the early eighties, when the next big thing, the Kennedy wedding, was scheduled.

A few weeks before, Bobby came to town with his local fiancée to get the marriage license, and they did it as surreptitiously as they could, at her behest; if it was up to Bobby he would have savored reporters trailing and documenting their every move. On their arrival at the Monroe County Courthouse, the lights were dimmed in the marriage license office, and the event was handled in such a low-key way that one of the clerks working in the office didn't even recognize Bobby's Kennedy face. Another clerk, Glenn Holmes, had typed "Robert F. Kennedy Jr." on the application but didn't realize who he was until Bobby named his mother, Ethel Kennedy, who was internationally known as RFK's glorified, sainted widow, even by the local Bloomington bureaucrat.

"They looked like any other couple coming in to get a marriage license, except they brought a friend with a camera to capture the moment," recalled Holmes. "They kept looking for a sign that says 'marriage licenses' to put up for the picture, but we didn't have one. Then they sneaked out."

Emily's mother had told Reverend Ewing that much of the actual marriage ceremony was going to be arranged back east by the "Kennedy family's priest," Father Gerald Creedon—Ethel's close friend—and that Creedon would eventually touch base with Ewing and lay out the agenda. Ewing would now co-officiate the ceremony—playing second fiddle, so to speak, to the Kennedys' priest. From behind the scenes, Bobby's controlling mother once again appeared to be pulling the strings.

In a letter to Emily's mother, Ewing told her that it was "customary that the minister of the bride is the presiding minister [but] if Emily and Robert would like the priest to be presiding minister that would be fine, I just need to know. . . . It is not difficult at all to have a wedding ceremony with a Protestant minister and a Catholic priest. It can be very meaningful."

If anyone was tuned in to Kennedy clan secrets it was Father Creedon, who had charmed the Kennedys for years, especially Ethel, with his Irish brogue and the Celtic tunes he played on his mandolin. Similar to her own brood of eleven, Creedon, who used the name Gerald instead of his given name, Gerard, had come from a family of fourteen siblings, in Inchigeelagh, County Cork, Ireland.

The year RFK was murdered, Creedon was ordained a priest for the Diocese of Richmond, in Virginia. And one of the parishes to which he was assigned was St. Luke's in McLean, Ethel's church, where she came for daily Mass. It was close to Hickory Hill, and she and Creedon became confidants, as did Creedon with her senator brother-in-law, Ted, who came to the church only on Sundays, according to the priest.

"He paid attention in a way that surprised me," Creedon once said, "and took an interest in the Gospel and applied it to what was going on in his world."

The senator and the priest had a long friendship, but Creedon's relationship with Bobby's mother was even closer.

Before her son David's body had gone completely cold after his 1984 drug overdose in Palm Beach, she was confiding in Creedon, who later disclosed her bravery in the face of adversity. "She showed remarkable inner strength and confidence," he recalled. "She seemed more concerned with other members of the family and how they were taking the loss. Ethel's faith is remarkable and very real, not a cold faith. 'Why me?' has never been in Ethel's vocabulary."

Unlike her sister-in-law Jackie, who, it was claimed in a 2014 book, had, not surprisingly, a post-traumatic stress disorder–like reaction after witnessing JFK's assassination, Ethel had gotten through her assassination trauma with the help of her Catholicism and counsel from the likes of Father Creedon.

As Christopher Kennedy Lawford observed, "My aunt Ethel's brand of Catholicism was more desperate and explosive. She attended Mass every day with a vengeance. The kids were dragged along on Sunday and occasionally during the week if she thought someone's behavior needed an extra dose of God."

Creedon was a natural to be overseeing the Kennedy–Black nuptials, which would be at least the fifth wedding of one of Ethel's kids that he would be involved in officiating or co-officiating. In the past he had conducted the marriage services for Bobby's brothers Joe and Michael, and their sisters Courtney and Kerry. Kerry had married Andrew Cuomo, the eldest son of the governor of New York, Mario Cuomo; it was a wedding billed as the merger of two great political dynasties. As it turned out, all five of the Creedon-officiated marriages would end in divorce.

In order for Reverend Ewing to co-officiate the Kennedy–Black marriage rites, and for a priest to perform the ceremony in a Protestant church, he had to get a special dispensation from the archbishop of Indiana, which the Kennedy side handled.

As Ewing recalled years later, "There really wasn't much for me to do until we approached the wedding day except handle the many calls from reporters from all over the world." There was, however, a dark side to the planned wedding after word of it became public: hate mail that Ewing began receiving, but addressed to Emily, some of it aimed at the Kennedys' Catholicism, others anti-Semitic in nature, such as a tract headed "The Deliberate Execution and Murder of Jesus Christ by the Jews."

There was one important thing Ewing needed to check off his to-do list prior to the ceremony, and that was to have his first face-to-face with the couple to discuss what marriage was all about, and to learn how they felt about it. Father Creedon, the Kennedys' religious consigliere, sat in on the premarital consultation. "I told Bobby and Emily that the components of marriage involved good communication, being open with one another, addressing concerns they might have about one another," Ewing recalled. "And they were very cordial and very receptive. They kind of nodded their heads, and were agreeable."

Still, he was more impressed with the future Mrs. Robert Kennedy Jr. than with the famous groom.

"I thought, what an interesting person she would be in the Kennedy family because she was an impressive young woman—forthright, clear, hospitable—and I thought, wowee, she'll do something impressive with her life. To me, she evoked Jackie. She had a *presence*."

TWENTY-TWO

Wedding Bells

Most of the week before his wedding, Bobby was in the extreme party town of Key West, Florida, sowing his wild oats as a bachelor. A Bloomington attorney had seen an item in the *Key West Citizen* reporting Bobby's whereabouts, and that he had been hitting the nightspots there.

Bobby was staying with, and partying with, one Peppo Vanini, unknown in Bloomington but well-known in Manhattan, where he was co-owner of the popular disco Xenon, whose main competition was Studio 54. The enormous club was located in what was then raunchy Times Square, and had had its grand opening in the late spring of 1978; soon after, Bobby, his brothers Michael and David, and their cousin John Kennedy Jr. had become regulars.

The club featured a deafening sound system and had a spaceship that descended from the ceiling; the place was the essence of full-blown Manhattan late-seventies/early-eighties debauched nightlife chic: marijuana permeated the air, white powder was snorted through dollar bills, men danced with men, transvestites flaunted themselves, and the odd sex act took place in the darkened "playpen" section on the mezzanine level, and even on the crowded, sweaty dance floor.

In that crazy, druggy scene, the young Kennedys rubbed shoulders with other boldface names: Andy Warhol, Mick Jagger, Cher, and Robin Williams. Michael Kennedy was often spotted there, "hanging out with, and playing with" the Australian model-actress Rachel Ward, according to one of the many photographers who staked out the place for celebrity shenanigans in its heyday. One report had it that Ward, then twenty-one, had become David Kennedy's girlfriend for some five months, had often hung out at the penthouse that he rented on Manhattan's Upper East Side, and was frequently on his arm at Xenon. "We smoked joints now and then," she once told *People* for a story headlined "Friends and Family Rally Around David, the Bright and Troubled Kennedy Rebel." The gorgeous Ward was quoted as saying, "He ate like a pig and didn't take very good care of himself, but he was crazy, with a wonderful sense of humor, and he was always very merry."

David had once gotten into a fight at Xenon with Andy Warhol's colleague Fred Hughes. Warhol later noted in his diary that David had told the police after being picked up for buying heroin in Harlem, "I'm David Kennedy, please don't tell my family. I just want to go to Hyannis."

Bobby loved Xenon and had taken his then girlfriend, Rebecca Fraser, there a number of times, but no one remembered Emily ever being there with him prior to a prewedding celebration. Rob Littell, a close pal of John Jr.'s, who wrote a book about their relationship, recalled that the slain president's namesake "loved the energy at Xenon, and enjoyed being the center of attention."

Bobby's bachelor-fling host, Peppo Vanini, was a jet-setter, a onetime restaurateur in Europe, and the first of the four husbands of the British beauty and actress Victoria Tennant (her second was Steve Martin). Despite his past marriage, rumor had it that Vanini was gay or bisexual, and in that druggy Xenon scene anything was possible. Before becoming a partner in Xenon with the former rock promoter Howard Stein, son of a murdered New York loan shark, Vanini ran the King's Club at the Palace Hotel in St. Moritz, and was once described as having the face of a "wonderful old roué," and the style of a "rich playboy uncle."

The Kennedy cousins, Bobby and John, were treated like princes by the Italian-Swiss Vanini, who thought of them as the "closest thing to royals in America," and he was one to know, reportedly having palled around with the likes of the wild young royals from Monaco, Princess Grace's kids. Stein had once observed that Vanini "made overtures to induce them [Bobby and John] into our world."

Bobby was older than John and had been around a bit more than him, and Stein considered JFK's namesake "less a disco baby. He didn't leverage his name the way kids of the famous do in my world. He had star quality, so every time he was there, he got his picture in the papers."

While he had no children of his own, Vanini had practically adopted the two young Kennedys who had lost their fathers to assassins. Unlike Bobby, who had the gay Lem Billings as his companion and overseer who was willing to do whatever Bobby wanted, John had his very domineering mother to carefully watch over him. Still, Vanini called himself the cousins' "disco daddy." His business partner Stein described himself as Bobby and John's "disco uncle."

As one Xenon regular observed years later, "Peppo looked out for Bobby and John to make sure their partying didn't get them or the club in trouble, because photographers and gossip column sources, and even undercover cops, were always around."

The photographer John Roca, then shooting for the New York *Daily News*, recalled that either Bobby or a member of his entourage, which included other young Kennedys and their pals, had "asked us that any photos we shot of Bobby and John at Xenon were to be cleared by Peppo. We said, 'Sure, yeah, right,' but we definitely didn't do it."

The future lawyer Bobby was fascinated with the criminal background of Stein's father, Ruby, who had had his head chopped off by rival gangsters and his body thrown into New York's Jamaica Bay. Stein once told a writer for *New York* magazine that Bobby had a burning interest in hearing the late mobster's story. He recalled that one night at Xenon, Bobby moved close to Stein's ear and whispered, "Tell me about your dad." Stein had a feeling that Bobby might have been a gangster groupie. "You say to them, 'That man's in the mob,' and they light up. It turns them on to think about me that way," Stein said. He felt it gave him "a credit, a certain depth" about his roots, even though he despised his father and was embarrassed by the criminal life he had led.

After a battle with kidney cancer, Stein died in 2007 at sixty-two. Vanini had had Parkinson's for several years, and died in 2012. As a friend noted at the time, "New York, London, Paris, Milan, and St. Moritz will never be quite the same."

As he felt with the death of his "surrogate father" Lem Billings, Bobby was said to have been truly saddened when he heard that Peppo, his "disco daddy," had passed.

BY THE THURSDAY NIGHT BEFORE the Saturday-evening nuptials, Bobby was back in New York City with his pals, who threw a bachelor party for him at Howard Stein's home. "The liquor flowed all night long," one of the guests had never forgotten.

The party continued at Trax, an uptown rock club, where Emily and her chums made an appearance. As usual, Peter Kaplan was at Bobby's side, and, gazing at Emily, acting as the couple's spokesman-of-the-moment, he offered his opinion about the bride-to-be. "She is lovely. She is beautiful, a very intelligent young woman, really serious and quiet, a fantastic student and very Midwestern," he told a gossip column reporter. "There's no doubt that she's from Indiana." As many as two hundred reportedly showed up for the private party, followed by more celebrating at Xenon, where friends of the couple wore baseball caps inscribed "Bobby and Emily—April 3, 1982."

By four A.M. it was over. Emily flew to Bloomington and Bobby, apparently partied out, took a later U.S. Air flight. At LaGuardia Airport, apparently still wired from day after day of celebrating, he had gotten into a tussle with a placard-toting member of the Fusion Energy Party and tore up one of his signs. The organization, headed by the libertarian Lyndon LaRouche, promoted nuclear power, which Bobby, becoming more interested in environmental issues, was vehemently against. The demonstrator claimed that he had been cornered and heckled, but there were no arrests.

At least one blond, blue-eyed, preppy-looking female reporter for a supermarket tabloid had been tailing the celebrants and later reported, "As soon as Bobby's plane took off, the stewardesses were busy pouring liquor. And after the plane landed [in Indianapolis], the one-hour bus ride from the airport [to Bloomington] was like a mobile party on wheels."

On Friday afternoon the wedding party finally arrived at the Indiana Memorial Union on the university's campus in Bloomington, delivered by double-decker IU bus. There in jeans and a white blouse was the fresh-faced bride, who had seemingly recovered from the night before, and a tense-looking groom, followed by the Catholic priest Father Creedon. Peter Kaplan, who replaced the deceased Lem Billings as Bobby's best man, was there, as was Bobby's adventure chronicler Harvey Blake Fleetwood, the two usual sidekicks.

Also leaving the bus were Bobby's cousins Chris Lawford and Stephen Smith Jr., along with Bobby's brothers David and Michael and a slew of others. Many of them were wearing five-and-dime-store fake big noses, mustaches, and eyeglasses in order to hide their identities, or just to be cute. Others wore "Black Is Beautiful" buttons in honor of the bride's maiden name; the slogan was a spin-off of a popular one dating from the '60s Black Consciousness movement.

A short time later, a limousine pulled up and the mother of the groom stepped out, smiling and waving to the photographers and reporters, and with two of her young ones, Doug and Rory, in tow. Ethel Kennedy's personal secretary, a harried young woman named Danielle Paris, one of many who had worked for the difficult matriarch, refused to give up any details of the wedding schedule when surrounded by reporters. "I still want to have my job on Monday," she said. She had been making some of the advance arrangements for her boss, including the complex plans for a big Friday-night wedding-rehearsal dinner.

The sole representatives of the older Kennedy generation who came to Bloomington for the wedding were Bobby's aunt Eunice Kennedy Shriver and his uncle Ted, who happened to be attending meetings in Indianapolis, where he blamed the Reagan administration's economic policies for creating "nothing but despair." The press and Bloomington natives were disappointed when Rose, Jackie, Caroline, and John Jr. were no-shows.

For early April, the day before and the day of the wedding, Bloomington was bitterly cold and windy; there was even an unverified report that a tornado had touched down in a nearby county, destroying a house trailer and a barn, and power lines and tree branches had fallen over a wide area. If the weather on the eve of Bobby's marriage was any barometer, it would be a stormy union. And it was.

Within minutes of their arrival, the Kennedy men did what they usually do at important gatherings of the clan—they got up a game of touch football. It was led by Lawford, but without the groom. Also joining were Bobby's brothers Michael, Max, and David, his cousin Stevie Smith, and his pals Kaplan, Fleetwood, and the Yale-educated lawyer Chris Bartle, who years later cofounded a boutique bottled water company with Bobby.

While the third generation and chums played touch, the rotund Ted Kennedy went to the weight room in the university gym and, clad in an IU T-shirt and matching gray gym shorts, did sit-ups and leg lifts and pumped a ten-pound weight. Kennedy groupies followed his every move, and one cute MBA coed who had been ogling the Kennedy contingent closely later remarked, "They're American royalty. Some seemed to be bending over backward to be nice and some were really demanding and arrogant."

ON THE EVE OF THE WEDDING, a rehearsal was held in First Christian, a scene that Reverend Ewing has never forgotten because of the high-powered Kennedy vibe. Like everyone else, he was starstruck by the famous clan.

"Those folks came into the sanctuary, and it was just like a psychic tidal wave of confidence. You could feel this rush," he recalled decades later. "They were all these potent individuals, the Kennedy icons, the Shrivers—fifteen groomsmen and twenty-five bridesmaids. I was sorry that Arnold [Schwarzenegger] and Maria [Shriver] weren't there. They were on the guest list, but I guess he was shooting a movie someplace. We had to seat all the bridesmaids in the first two rows because we didn't have enough room for that many people to stand up," continued Ewing, who, in particular, had noticed that "the groomsmen were all so agreeable and cordial."

It wasn't until the next day, Saturday, the day of the wedding, that he found out why the atmosphere at the rehearsal and throughout the celebratory weekend was so mellow.

"And that's because they were all high on cocaine and booze," revealed Ewing, a secret he had held closely for decades. "They weren't unruly or rowdy or obnoxious or anything—they were just *very* high. I found that out just because I started to find evidence, and some of them just told me. We were hanging around waiting for things to happen and they were just talking, and I said, 'I really appreciate it that you guys are so helpful,' and one of them said, 'Oh, well, it's pretty easy when you're as high as we all are.'"

IN THE WEEKS LEADING UP to the wedding, Ethel Kennedy had assigned her secretary, Danielle Paris, to make arrangements for a feast to be held at Bloomington's upscale Publick House Restaurant, following the Friday-night rehearsal. The owner, Rudolf Fisher, naturally was thrilled to have the royal family as his customer, especially at a time when business was down because of the recession, which had hit the town like everywhere else in the country.

When he got the famous Kennedys' business, he thought, "I'm used to cooking for celebrities, so I'm not really nervous about it at all." The chef, however, hadn't researched the client well enough to know that when it came to paying her bills, Bobby's mother was often delinquent, despite her wealth. Fisher would learn the hard way.

Bill C. Brown, who owned the building where the restaurant was located, recalled years later that at the dinner a "couple of the Kennedys got a little drunk." That was evident when dueling swords that were part of the restaurant's decor were removed from the wall and a gaggle of inebriated members of the clan "went out in the parking lot and started sword fighting," said Brown.

Alcohol flowed during dinner. Served that night were twenty-eight bottles of Moët & Chandon and nine bottles of Chandon Brut champagne, twenty-eight bottles of Grand-Puy Ducasse, and thirty-six bottles of Moreau Blanc wine, in addition to fifty-one separate drinks, ninety-three call drinks, thirty-eight after-dinner drinks, and sixty-two beers.

"I never saw so many glasses in front of each place setting for different drinks. It was just something else," recalled the minister, Terry Ewing. "We had drinks constantly. We started off with Irish whiskey, then moved to this and that, and red and white. It was fabulous. I can't believe we were able to walk away. I sat next to Ethel, who was patting my leg and kissing me on the cheek."

Aside from the bubbly, the wine, and the hard stuff, the celebrants feasted on a variety of hors d'oeuvres that included sweet shrimp in curry mayonnaise served in a petit pastry shell garni; coronets of fresh smoked salmon with creamed cheese and seasoned butter stuffing served on a soda cracker; Strassberger liver pâté with truffels on buttered crisp fresh toast rounds; steak tartare à la russe with imported caviar on crisp toast rounds; fresh cantaloupe and honeydew fingers wrapped in prosciutto, and eggs Lucullus, egg halfs stuffed with spinach, crabmeat, and egg yolk. For the main courses there was Chateaubriand, fresh filet of sole, fresh asparagus, purée of carrots in pastry shells, and chateau potatoes. And there was a special dessert in honor of the bride— "Strawberries Emily," which consisted of strawberries sprinkled with brown sugar and topped with whipped cream and served in champagne glasses.

Ethel Kennedy certainly knew how to live the high life, even during a national recession.

Following the meal, there were more than two dozen toasts, and following each the Kennedys yelled, "Well said!" And there were a slew of congratulatory telegrams from close family friends such as Ethel's pal the humorist Art Buchwald.

Drinking and toasting was a big thing at Kennedy affairs, noted Chris Lawford. "Giving a funny, smart, or passionate toast was pretty much a prerequisite for any sort of base-level credibility in the public speaking and charisma department."

Bobby, Ted Kennedy noted, "Went for humor, which was often off-color, and if that didn't work, tried to inspire."

At the rehearsal dinner, Bobby's brother Joe got up and toasted their late father and uncle Jack, and observed, "We are the fortunate ones. We are the people who are called to help others."

Ewing recalled that the "most poignant toast" had been made by the youngest sibling of the groom, Rory, who also toasted her father, whom she had never known, having been born six months after he was assassinated.

All had gone off according to plan: The beautifully set tables—replete with round Irish linen tablecloths in Ethel Kennedy's favorite color, pink, which she had loaned the restaurant for the dinner—were in place where she had wanted them, based on seating plans she had approved; the rich and expensive gourmet meal was a mouthwatering success, and everyone who wanted to got smashed on all the alcohol that was served. (According to Fisher, though, the wines Ethel Kennedy had ordered were "not very expensive.")

It was agreed that immediately following the feast, the secretary, Danielle Paris, would meet with Fisher and pay the balance of $7,189.20 on the entire bill of $8,939.80. And the mother of the groom made a special effort to thank Fisher for a job well done.

But there was what seemed at the time to Fisher to be a minor change of plan. Paris said it was getting late and she'd handle the settling of the bill the next morning, the wedding Saturday, at the restaurant. Fisher was fine with that.

AS THE KENNEDYS WERE CELEBRATING at the rehearsal dinner, a group of Southern good ol' boys, attending a convention of auctioneers, were staying in the IU student union, where many of the wedding guests were being put up. By luck, they had a suite next to Bobby's and had overheard that he was RFK's son and was about to get hitched. Something, they concluded, had to be done to help the boy celebrate on his last night as a bachelor. When he arrived back in his room, the hard-partying auctioneers from Georgia and Tennessee were there to greet him with a raunchy singing telegram—and a very special offering.

She was a Bloomington belly dancer by the name of Nadirah who had been hired by the conventioneers and offered up to Bobby as their wedding gift. The local columnist Greg Dawson, who was tailing the groom for a story, recalled that Bobby was thrilled. "He said a few words to the dancer in Arabic and she responded in kind," Dawson noted. "Then Bobby joined in the belly dancing" while an unidentified friend who was with him did some push-ups and back flips.

Not to be outdone, Bobby had a trick of his own. Stretching out, he placed his feet on a chair, his ass on a small table, and his head on another chair. Then, magically, he slid the table out from under him, with only his head and feet supported by the two chairs, and held it over his head. The auctioneers hooted and hollered at the impressive feat as Bobby got up, jumped on the bed, and led his new friends in a loud rendition of "Dixie."

Whether the belly dancer had any further interaction with the Kennedy namesake on the eve of his marriage was never revealed because, well, what happens in Bloomington stays in Bloomington.

THE BANNER HEADLINE IN the Bloomington *Herald-Telephone* blared: "April Love . . . Robert Kennedy Jr. and Emily Black Wed." *The Indianapolis Star* shouted: "Bloomington Agog over Wedding." *People* rhapsodized, "Back Home Again in Indiana, Emily Black Picks Up a Freighted Name: Mrs. Robert F. Kennedy Jr." And the *National Enquirer* barked: "Bobby Kennedy Jr.'s Weird, Wild and Wacky Wedding."

Despite forty-mile-an-hour wind gusts and a bitter temperature in the mid-forties, some thousand bundled-up Bloomingtonians lined the streets around First Christian Church to get a look at what they perceived to be America's royal family. One woman said she was there to see "Kennedys, money, and beautiful gowns." Another carried a sign, "Kennedy for President in '84."

Looking back years later and recalling that scene, Terry Ewing, the minister, said, "If Jackie and company had been there, it would have been an absolute circus." Instead of coming, she had sent a wedding gift: antique Chinese plates.

The wind was so strong that when the bride stepped out of the limousine in front of the church—she was actually late getting there—her long veil curled around her feet and her recently done hair was suddenly a tangled mess. Members of her party rushed to her aide so that she could make a dignified entrance into the church. In her party was her maid of honor and law school roommate, Alexandra Cury; the matron of honor was Emily's married sister, Sarah Hochberg, who sold real estate in Chicago; and the bridesmaids included Bobby's sisters, Kerry, Rory, Courtney, and Kathleen.

Bobby's attendants, in tuxes—one of whom was spotted walking up the church steps swigging beer from a bottle, the empty of which he put down before walking inside—included the usual suspects: his six brothers, and his best friend and best man, Peter Kaplan. A couple of years later, Bobby would serve as Kaplan's best man when he got married. Like Bobby's marriage, Kaplan's would end in divorce, followed by a second marriage. Bobby would have three, a record for Kennedy men.

Also with Bobby were his cousins Stevie Smith, Chris Lawford, and Bobby Shriver, who as a teenager had been arrested with Bobby for marijuana possession. And there were longtime friends, among them Bobby's law school pal Sheldon Whitehouse, who years later became a U.S. Senator; a college friend, Doug Spooner, whom Chris Lawford described as being like "Zelig—if there was a Kennedy or a Kennedy event, he was there"; the freelance writer and travel agent Harvey Blake Fleetwood; Bobby's Harvard classmate Eric Breindel, arrested at twenty-seven while making a heroin buy from a Washington, D.C., undercover cop, and dead at forty-two, rumored as a result of AIDS; Chris Bartle; David Michaelis; and Tim Haydock, a young physician who was joint best man along with Kaplan.

Three of his celebrants were photographed leaving the service looking stoned, and a photograph of them appeared with the *National Enquirer*'s story about the wedding. Security around the church was tight; cops were closely watching the crowd and plainclothes marksmen were sighted on surrounding roofs. "There were armed men on the streets all around the church," recalled Reverend Ewing. "I understand that the Kennedy family had hired its own security people. When I walked into the church with my wife and daughter these two guys came running down the aisle toward me with their hands in their coats—'Who are you? Who are you?' I go, Whoa, whoa, I'm the minister."

Bloomington didn't want to become another Dallas or Los Angeles.

Some of the security was arranged by the local attorney Guy Loftman, Emily's friend and former boss. Several days after the wedding he sent a letter to Chief James Kennedy of the Indiana University Police Department, thanking him for his "seasoned judgement which prevented delicate situations from becoming problems," but he didn't elaborate on what kind of "delicate situations" had occurred, or been avoided. He also noted the "discretion" of the chief's force, and the "cooperation" with the "Bloomington forces."

Some 275 guests were on the list to view the exchange of vows. There were prominent Kennedy acolytes such as the powerful syndicated columnist Joseph Alsop; Richard and Doris Kearns Goodwin, he a key adviser to JFK and RFK, she the noted historian; the American Football League founder Don Klosterman, who had once been romantically linked to Ethel Kennedy; a top Justice Department aide to RFK, John Seigenthaler, who later served as editor, publisher, and chairman of *The Tennessean*; JFK and RFK's Boswell, the biographer Arthur Schlesinger; the Academy Award–winning Hollywood producer Sam Spiegel; Xenon's co-owner Giuseppe "Peppo" Vanini and his business partner Howard Stein; the American Film Institute founder George Stevens, who annually produced the Kennedy Center Honors; JFK's press aide Sue Vogelsinger, who was with the president aboard Air Force One when it landed in Dallas on November 23, 1963; and a slew of others.

Probably unknown to the VIPs was the surprising inclusion on the guest list of Bobby's former girlfriend Duff Pacifico.

There was still another low-key guest on the list—a chubby-cheeked, bearded, bespectacled man by the name of Don Juhl. While he wasn't a Schlesinger or a Seigenthaler, he was, next to the bride, probably one of the most important figures in Bobby's life (and that of his brother David) at the time and later. For Juhl was an addiction counselor from California.

His presence on the guest list underscored a dark fact of which the bride was aware when she tied the knot: that her groom and her new brother-in-law had drug problems that had existed since their teens, and had been covered up for the most part by the Kennedy family and Bobby and David's close friends, many of whom were at the wedding. Juhl reportedly had received $100,000 for his drug rehab work with David, money that was paid out of his trust fund, a form of tough love instigated by David's uncle Ted, and David was furious. "All he wanted was his family's love and he couldn't get it," said Nancie Alexander, a pal of David's. And David would later assert, "I am what I am because I come from a whole line of alcoholics. Just look at how many of us are fucked up. My brother Bobby's a junkie."

As a member of Bobby's circle observed many years later after

David's fatal overdose, "Bobby was seriously an addictive personality—drugs, and sex, too, an addictive personality with both those things that was an unfortunate heritage that had come down from Grandpa Joe, and likely from the Skakels, too. So when he married Emily, she struck me as being too nice, too quiet and calm to be married to Bobby Kennedy—and I think that ultimately proved to be true."

Before the ceremony began, Bobby's uncle Ted caught everyone's attention when he walked down the aisle to the front of the church on the bride's side, kneeled and crossed himself, and sat down in a pew and prayed. The next day, Sunday, when the church was back to normal and the Kennedy invasion had left town, a woman and her two daughters sat in the same pew where Teddy had been and tore out the page from the registry that the famed senator had signed.

Unlike many young couples in that era who drafted their own matrimonial vows, Bobby and Emily didn't, even though "Father Creedon and I both gave them that opportunity," said Ewing, who also noted that "there wasn't anything particularly Catholic in the ceremony that I was a part of." That was because a Catholic ritual had been held in the university's Beck Chapel prior to the service in Ewing's big church downtown.

Creedon offered a blessing and Ewing a welcoming prayer, and each read from the Scriptures. Holding hands, Bobby and Emily faced each other and promised, "I will be true to you for all my days."

In his homily, Creedon said, "When Jesus walked into a church, a building, and things were not right, when people were huckstering and selling what would not satisfy, he turned the tables over. He acted against the unacceptable. Bobby has that same religious impulse driving him to change things. Emily shares that concern. Her gentleness does not hide a strength of character that is as strong as those trees that populate Bloomington."

After the vows had been taken and the bride was given two rings—blessed by Creedon—Ewing thanked the bride's and groom's mothers for giving him the opportunity to be a part of their union and wished them well. In the church's choir balcony the music for the ceremony was played by a group of IU graduate students known as the Rosewood String Trio, but there was no organ music, as requested by the bride, who also rejected the playing of the traditional wedding march.

"I never heard anything from any of them again," said Ewing.

Following the wedding ceremony there was a reception at the University Club, where Bobby and Emily cut a six-tiered white cake, with half a dozen bartenders handling the deluge of drink orders. And a five-piece combo from Chicago formerly known as Fast Eddie supplied the music.

Afterward, the happy newlyweds left for their honeymoon. Many in their circle were mystified as to where they had gone. Bobby had mentioned two spots—sunny Puerto Rico and drab Deadwood, South Dakota. The small town with the ominous name did have a poignant and very secret meaning. Deadwood was the home of the Kennedy family friend, hotel owner, and former Catholic priest Bill Walsh, who had been counseling Bobby regarding his drug issues.

For Reverend Ewing the highly publicized Kennedy–Black union had changed his professional life.

"The fallout was truly unusual," he observed in 2013. "I became the most known, unknown minister in the state of Indiana. All of a sudden everybody wanted me to do their stuff. I was doing all these big-deal weddings. The richest man in the county—strip mining, highway building—asked me to do his daughter's wedding, the fanciest wedding I had ever done." It was, he said, even bigger than the Kennedy affair, which, he noted, "was not the most fanciest by any means."

It was a decade later when Ewing learned about Bobby and Emily's divorce.

"By that time I knew about Bobby's drug and alcohol abuse," he said. "When I married them I knew he was doing cocaine, so when I heard the marriage was ending I thought, 'Well, I'm not surprised because that's what happens if one member of a couple goes down a destructive road that they can't get back from, and it's not a surprise that the marriage suffers.'

"I told them when we had our marriage counseling session before the wedding that anytime they wanted to talk to get hold of me. Obviously, they didn't do that. So, when I heard they divorced, I found myself thinking, 'Boy, Bobby, you screwed up!'"

• • •

THERE WAS AN IMMEDIATE dark footnote to Bobby Kennedy and Emily Black's wedding.

The Publick House owner, Rudy Fisher, who arranged the big rehearsal dinner celebration at his restaurant, couldn't get paid. Attempts by Fisher to reach Ethel Kennedy, who had a reputation for stiffing vendors, or her secretary, had failed.

On April 20, he sent a registered letter to Hickory Hill, 1147 Chain Bridge Road, McLean, Virginia 22101. In his respectful "Dear Mrs. Kennedy" missive, he wrote, "We are a small business and our terms are net seven days . . . I am sure you understand the pressure of business in these trying times and we need the cash flow to pay our suppliers. Again, I want to express our appreciation for having the pleasure of serving you and your family."

When he got no response, he threatened to call the Johnny Carson show and go on TV to "tell the world what a bunch of cheapskates the Kennedys were," he told a friend.

Fisher claimed he had been told by a member of the clan, "It should have been a privilege to serve the Kennedys, and you shouldn't be charging for the dinner at all."

On September 1, 1982, Bloomington's *Herald-Telephone* ran a front-page banner headline: "Honeymoon's Over, Publick House Suing Ethel Kennedy for $7,189 Rehearsal Dinner Bill."

The embarrassing lawsuit clearly worked because by mid-September RFK's widow paid the five-month-old bill, with interest. The excuse for the lateness came from one of the Kennedy spokespersons, claiming a secretary had misplaced the bill.

The Publick House eventually went out of business, having filed for bankruptcy.

TWENTY-THREE

Bar Flop

New York, New York, it's a helluva town, goes the song lyric. But life for Bobby Kennedy Jr. and Emily Ruth Black Kennedy in the big city didn't start out like that of the happy-go-lucky stars Gene Kelly and Ann Miller in the hit MGM musical *On the Town,* even though the newly minted groom rhapsodized that he and his bride felt Manhattan was their kind of town. And Bobby had close ties there. The Big Apple of the Empire State was where his politically ambitious father had carpetbagged his way in as U.S. Senator, his stepping-stone, he believed, to the presidency.

By the summer of 1982, the newlyweds had moved into the elegant quarters that Lem Billings had willed to Bobby. But he had to dip into his trust fund to purchase all of the Kennedy tchotchkes and memorabilia that had adorned the place. Curiously, Billings had left none of them to the boy he loved.

The first major obstacle that Bobby faced was the bar exam that he was required to pass. He had been hired to work as an assistant district attorney in one of the nation's most prestigious prosecutor's offices, that of the Manhattan district attorney.

Not surprisingly, he had gotten the $20,000-a-year post through powerful family connections. His boss was the legendary Manhattan DA Robert M. Morgenthau, who happened to be a boyhood friend of Bobby's uncle the president. During Camelot, JFK had appointed Morgenthau to serve as U.S. attorney for the Southern District of New York. The day JFK was killed in Dallas, Morgenthau happened to be at Hickory Hill having lunch with RFK when FBI director J. Edgar Hoover called with the assassination news.

Thus, Bobby was as predestined to work for Morgenthau as he had been predestined to be admitted to Harvard—because of his family name and platinum connections.

Bobby wasn't the only famous namesake brought on by Morgenthau at the same time. The other was Cyrus Vance Jr., whose father was Secretary of State during the Carter administration. Bobby and Vance were among fifty-five assistant district attorneys hired in 1982.

To avoid any hint of favoritism, the Democrat Morgenthau told reporters that Bobby and Vance "were treated like everybody else when they were interviewed, and they will be treated like everyone else when they come here."

With Morgenthau's encouragement, Bobby had chosen to specialize in criminal prosecution. But he wouldn't last very long in the job.

Meanwhile, Emily was hired as a $21,000-a-year public defender, working with the poor and indigent who faced criminal charges. As Bobby blithely boasted at the time regarding their dual legal careers, "She's interested in keeping people out of jail and I'm interested in putting them in."

Emily was one of more than two dozen recently graduated lawyers who had joined the staff of the New York Legal Aid Society, and she and her hubby with the famous name were thought to be the city's first couple representing both sides in criminal matters. In some quarters, as *The New York Times* pointed out, they were compared to Katharine Hepburn and Spencer Tracy in the film *Adam's Rib*, about a husband and wife who played opposing lawyers in court, which never actually happened with the Kennedy couple; the opposition would happen much later when they had their divorce face-off.

As a member of Morgenthau's staff, Bobby wasn't permitted to argue a case in court until he actually passed the bar exam, a grueling test that many good lawyers fail. And just days before Bobby and Emily's first Christmas together as a married couple, he got the bad news.

It had become public when *The New York Law Journal* published the list of those who had taken the exam in July and had passed. Only one Kennedy name was on it: Emily's. Bobby and Emily had been among 5,618 who had taken the twelve-hour test, and 4,028 had passed, 69.2 percent. Of the new assistant DAs in Morgenthau's office, Bobby was among six who had failed. When word of Bobby's failure reached the press, he and Morgenthau refused to comment. Bobby was eligible to take the exam again in February 1983. Until then—and until he passed—he essentially was being carried by Morgenthau.

Bobby's failure received little if any press attention, unlike the media circus that occurred regarding his cousin, John Kennedy Jr., some eight years later when he flunked the bar exam not once, but twice in seven months. Each time he failed he faced blaring tabloid headlines: "The Hunk Flunks" was typical. Years later, a well-placed source who had been a confidant of the president's namesake attributed his failure to, in part, the use of cocaine.

In May 1990, *People* published a lengthy story about JFK Jr.'s second failure under the headline "Trials of a Rising Son," and hinted at the cocaine problem. An unnamed lawyer who had taken a bar-review course with Kennedy the previous summer recalled how wired he had seemed—a sign of being high on coke. "What really struck me was his restlessness," the corporate lawyer stated. "He couldn't sit still for more than ten minutes at a time."

After his second embarrassing failure, JFK Jr. bravely told reporters, "I am very disappointed again. I am clearly not a legal genius."

Kennedy was more than disappointed by his continued failure—he was actually deeply depressed and it "drove him to drink," recalled his friend and roommate Rob Littell. He said that Kennedy had holed up in a motel and "slowly drank a bottle of Scotch over the course of the week-end, alone and listening to self-help tapes." He subsequently went into therapy. He also sought the services of a tutor, and eventually passed the exam in the summer of 1990; he also took and passed the Connecticut state bar exam. But he still was using cocaine, a friend maintained in 2013, fourteen years after JFK Jr.'s tragic death.

IN THAT PERIOD WHEN BOBBY learned he had failed the bar exam there was much bad karma for him and Emily.

On a chilly night just before Thanksgiving 1982, Emily was walking home at eleven P.M. to 5 East Eighty-eighth Street, across from Central Park, when three teenagers accosted her on the corner and grabbed her pocketbook. According to initial reports, a passing cabdriver saw the purse snatch, nabbed the three boys, who were in their mid-teens, recovered the purse, which had $120 in cash in it—she had just left a Citibank ATM—and held them until New York's Finest arrived. But the cops were shocked when Emily indicated she didn't want to press charges. They reportedly pleaded with her, but she was adamant. At the local precinct, the cops took the boys' names and addresses and let them go.

Because she was a Kennedy wife, the purse snatch, a common crime in the city that never sleeps, received much press. The *Daily News* headline blared, "3 Mugged a Kennedy . . . and Went Free." *The New York Times* announced, "3 Snatch the Purse of Emily Kennedy on Upper East Side." The *New York Post* trumpeted "Kennedy Wife Lets Muggers Go Free."

One report had it that Bobby tried to convince her to do "the right thing" and pursue the case but she was adamant, just as she had been when she nixed St. Patrick's in favor of First Christian. Another news account said that two hours after the incident, Bobby had convinced Emily to call the police precinct and tell them what had happened, but she was still against pressing charges. As a Legal Aid attorney, her philosophy was to *not* send people to jail.

She and Bobby had been invited to the annual Kennedy clan Thanksgiving gathering at the family compound in Hyannis Port, but didn't go because Bobby supposedly had come down with an intestinal bug. While home, he convinced her to, as one headline soon blared, "Charge Teen Thugs."

She also revealed that she had actually chased and caught one of the young hoodlums, and that the cabbie and several others had grabbed his two henchmen, one of whom had a prior arrest for street robbery. She denied saying she wouldn't press charges.

"When they were taken to the police station, they seemed really scared," she told a reporter. "I was in a hurry to get home to my husband and I told police I would let them know about pressing charges. I was so relieved that I had my money. I told Bob, and in the conversation I said I was thinking about not pressing charges, and he said that I should. After I calmed down, I said that I believe these things have to be prosecuted— even though they don't seem like criminals, a person does have to press charges. It was the night before Thanksgiving so the whole idea was let the parents have their children for the holiday while the decision about charges was being made."

BOBBY HAD BEEN PLAYING the rebel since his teen years and had begun portraying himself as a radical of sorts in his twenties when it came to environmental issues, underscored by the tiff he got into on the eve of his wedding with a nuclear energy advocate. He and Emily had later even attended an antinuclear rally in Hollywood.

But it was actually Emily, never considered radical or rebellious, who hit the pavement on a picket line. That October of 1982, she joined more than five hundred of her fellow Legal Aid lawyers in a citywide strike that virtually crippled New York's court system, all of it mainly over the firing of one of the lawyers, and the expiration the previous July of a union contract.

The *Times*, in a commentary, called the strike "calamitous" for thousands of defendants, and asserted that constitutional rights were "eroding" every day the strike continued. The Gray Lady demanded a quick settlement, and the city's mayor, Ed Koch, denounced the strike, calling it "unethical."

Thus, the Kennedy couple's first married year in New York had been a difficult one, and along with everything else—Bobby's bar exam failure, Emily's mugging, and the strike—his beloved setter, Hogan, had gotten lost in the mean streets of Manhattan when a friend of the couple's took him for a walk but forgot to put him on a leash.

The Kennedys pleaded with the public to call the ASPCA if they spotted him.

There was one good piece of news, though. Before the strike started, Emily had won her first case, getting an acquittal for a twenty-year-old Brooklyn man who had been arrested for selling five dollars' worth of marijuana to a narc. She was said to have convinced the jury that it was a case of mistaken identity.

But life for Bobby would only get worse, despite his wonderful bride, his prestigious new job, and the couple's plans to have children. In New York, with his much-publicized job, his failure to pass the bar, and increased media scrutiny, he felt intense pressure to prove himself; after all, he was the self-styled leader of his Kennedy generation. As he said around the time of his wedding, "If you want to compete with the best people, you go to New York. You can't bring out the best in yourself unless you do that."

But the city offered temptations he had difficulty resisting, most of them involving the availability of hard drugs. He often was invited to get high by Kennedy acolytes and hangers-on in the social scene, where heroin had become chic and plentiful.

From years back, he knew where to score: Harlem. It was now just three miles north of where he and Emily were living in high style. Just as he had befriended the radical blacks when he was at Pomfret School before he was asked to leave because of drug use and bad behavior, he was said to have developed similar relationships in New York's ghetto in order to score. He sometimes visited a boarded-up slum building that was a shooting gallery where he was the only white, let alone the only scion of a world-famous family.

At Morgenthau's office, colleagues suspected he came to work high at times, and seemed incoherent. Every so often he requested time off, staying with loyalists tasked with helping him get clean. But it rarely worked out.

"He was so fucked up," said a source. "It was tragic. We feared it had to end badly."

His wife was at a loss as to what to do or how to help, and with no one to whom to turn. "Emily was going through hell," a close associate asserted years later, looking back to that horrific time. "She felt isolated.

On the staircase at Hickory Hill, Ethel and RFK pose with their growing family; Bobby is in the second row at the left. With nine children, Ethel had tied matriarch Rose's childbirth record when this photo was taken, but she would have two more, the last born after RFK's assassination.

Sisters-in-law Jackie and Ethel (with Jean Kennedy Smith in the middle), shown here at the White House in 1961, had a chilly relationship. Through the years the First Lady kept John Jr. and Caroline away from Hickory Hill, fearing Ethel's wild sons—Bobby especially—could be a bad influence.

Presidential photographer Cecil Staughton's August 1961 picture of the Kennedy clan at the fabled Hyannis Port compound. Young Bobby is seated directly in front of his father. To the right, JFK. Holding the toy rifle is first daughter Caroline.

Bobby, seven, visited his uncle, the commander-in-chief, on March 11, 1961, to show him his pet salamander, Shadrach. Bobby had a virtual zoo at Hickory Hill.

At the White House, the President gently poked his nephew's pet salamander. They gave it a new home in the White House fountain.

Two days before presidential hopeful RFK was gunned down, he was greeted by cheering supporters in Los Angeles. When Bobby Jr. saw his mortally wounded father, he later recalled, "his head was bandaged and his eyes were black. His face was bruised…. In the morning, my brother Joe told us, 'He's gone.' We all cried."

The two cousins shared the tragic loss of their fathers to assassins, Bobby at fourteen, John at three. In the nineties, John, editor of *George* magazine, shockingly called Bobby's then-scandal-riddled brothers, Michael and Joe, "poster boys for bad behavior." But in his will, John Jr., who died in a plane crash, left Bobby $250,000.

Kirk LeMoyne "Lem" Billings and JFK in 1962. While pregnant with her eleventh child, widowed Ethel turned over responsibility for the teenaged Bobby to the homosexual Lem Billings, who would transfer his love for JFK to Bobby, becoming his surrogate father. Billings often stayed at the White House.

Billings with JFK and the First Lady holding John Jr. at the Kennedy family residence, Wexford, in Atoka, Virginia, about a month before Dallas. There were published reports after Billings died of a heart attack in May 1981 that he had performed oral sex on JFK, and one Kennedy biographer claimed that Jackie had warned Billings to control his homosexual urges. He did drugs with Bobby.

Ethel Kennedy enrolled Bobby at the Millbrook School, a boarding school. Bobby's teachers and classmates recalled that she only visited him there once, leaving his care to Lem Billings. At Millbrook, Bobby actively began using drugs.

One of Bobby's close Millbrook friends was the artistic Michael Parkinson, who came from a socially prominent New York family. Parkinson drew this dorm room portrait of Bobby. The two had gotten into trouble with drugs in Colombia. Years later, Parkinson was found dead under suspicious circumstances in his bathtub.

From the popular TV talk-show host Jack Paar, Bobby received a lion cub he named Mtoto Mbaya (meaning "Bad Boy" in Swahili), to be housed in Millbrook's Trevor Zoo, sparking controversy among Bobby's classmates, and nipping one of the teachers.

Ethel Kennedy's only demand of Millbrook's headmaster was that troubled Bobby—pale, thin as a rail, and "wired like a radio on scan"—play football. For one season, he became a scrawny wide receiver on lowly Third Football, described as "undersized and generally decimated." Bobby's number 81 in the back row.

Because he was a Kennedy, Bobby easily got into Harvard. There, he bonded with Peter Kaplan, who was said to have helped write his senior thesis on a Southern judge. In Alabama, the bosom buddies met with the state's segregationist former governor George Wallace.

Bobby fell for Emily Ruth Black, first of his three wives, at a beer-and-pizza student hangout while the two were attending the University of Virginia law school. A Phi Beta Kappa, she was from an Indiana family of modest means.

Emily Black became Mrs. Robert Kennedy Jr. on April 3, 1982, in a big wedding at Bloomington, Indiana's First Christian Church, attended by family and friends. Lem Billings, who believed Bobby could one day become president, advised him to marry a woman like Jackie.

The day of the Kennedy–Black nuptials was cold and windy with a reported possible tornado in the area. If the weather was any barometer, it would be a stormy union, and it was, involving Bobby's use of drugs. They divorced after having two children, a boy, RFK III, and a daughter, Kick.

Bobby with his namesake in the mid-1990s. By the time RFK III was in his twenties, he was involved in the film business rather than in a political career. His sister Kick became an actress.

Conservationist Robert Boyle is considered Bobby's mentor in the environmental movement and took him in to his Hudson River Fisherman's Association (later renamed Riverkeepers) in early 1984 as part of court-ordered community service for his heroin possession arrest. Bobby would later do battle with Boyle.

A grim-looking Ethel Kennedy and Bobby circa 1990 as his marriage to Emily Black was on the rocks. She was said to have become aware of his womanizing. A close source asserted, "Whatever relationships Bobby had, he had, and people were aware of it. Emily definitely knew."

Shortly after securing a quickie Dominican Republic divorce, Bobby, forty, married six-months-pregnant, thirty-four-year-old attractive architect Mary Richardson, a close friend of his sister Kerry's. They were wed by a judge on April 15, 1994, aboard a boat on the Hudson River.

Trapping and banding birds circa 1995, Boyle in cap with Bobby and his new wife, Mary Richardson, holding an unidentified child. On the far right with beard is Bobby's friend, bird expert Thomas J.V. Cullen III, who later faced criminal charges involving birds. Bobby was his character witness.

Bobby and Mary with their four children from their marriage, and the two from his first, on March 10, 2002, at the world premiere of *Ice Age*, at Radio City Music Hall.

Mary Richardson Kennedy's smile belies her long-troubled marriage to Bobby. Here, at the Riverkeepers Fishermen's Ball in Manhattan, she shows off her handsome son Conor, who later had brief tabloid notoriety as Taylor Swift's boyfriend.

Three years before troubled, depressed fifty-two-year-old Mary Kennedy hanged herself in May 2012, she is pictured with Bobby and their daughter Kyra, fourteen, at the Robert F. Kennedy Center for Justice and Human Rights' "Ripple of Hope Awards."

Staunch Catholic Bobby's third marriage was to longtime girlfriend Cheryl Hines of TV's *Curb Your Enthusiasm*. The two were wed on a drizzly Saturday in August 2014 at the Kennedy compound. Here, Bobby and Hines celebrate her star on the Hollywood Walk of Fame.

Even when they were together at UVA Law, she knew that Bobby had this problem, but she was in love and naively thought it was a phase, or something he could handle. He couldn't and she was devastated. But she hung in."

According to Peter Collier and David Horowitz, "All the time he was working as an assistant district attorney he was making the forays he'd always made into Harlem." In an effort to disguise his identity, they reported, he wore a Navy watch cap pulled low, looking like some street person. Luckily, narcotics cops staking out the area didn't arrest him.

A close Harvard friend of Bobby's, twenty-seven-year-old Eric Breindel, wasn't so lucky. The recently hired Senate Intelligence Committee staff aide was arrested in mid-May 1983 when he and a friend, a thirty-two-year-old former Justice Department lawyer, Winston Prude—described in a *Spy* magazine account of the arrest as a "fellow Kennedy hanger-on"—tried to score five bags of heroin for $150 from undercover narcotics officers at a Holiday Inn in a black section near the U.S. Capitol in Washington. Both had been on Bobby and Emily's wedding guest list a year earlier.

Breindel had recently received a top security clearance to work in the office of Senator Daniel Patrick Moynihan of New York, who had been an assistant secretary of labor for policy during JFK's administration. Like Bobby, Breindel had graduated from Harvard, but magna cum laude, and had been editorial chairman of the *Crimson*. He had also done work, like Bobby, at the London School of Economics. At the time of Breindel's death at forty-two in 1998, officially from Hodgkin's disease, but rumored to have been from AIDS related to dirty needles, he was a senior vice president of Rupert Murdoch's News Corporation, and an influential neoconservative. Bobby was among those who mourned at his funeral.

Prude had once gone on one of Bobby's exotic South American expeditions and had brought a supply of recreational drugs that had gotten rain-soaked, but he was said to have lapped the mix up as if it were a soggy stew and had become ill. Some years later he also died of a heroin overdose.

When Breindel was arrested, Bobby feared that his own name might surface during the investigation—and reportedly it did. He then tried again to kick his own drug habit, but was unsuccessful. Moreover, his behavior had become odd. The Coast Guard spotted him adrift in a 16-foot Boston Whaler off Hyannis without proper registration papers, a life jacket, or distress signals. When the authorities contacted his mother, she acknowledged that the boat belonged to Bobby's brother Douglas, and Ethel Kennedy reluctantly admitted that she had never bothered to get the boat registered. As a result Bobby was cited.

With the scare triggered by Breindel's arrest, Bobby took a leave from his ADA job, and he and Emily traveled to Deadwood, in South Dakota, to spend time with his ex-priest friend, Bill Walsh, to try to get clean of drugs. Walsh later told a reporter for *People*, "Late at night, he'd come down and have a few beers at the bar and throw darts."

Back in New York, Bobby again took the bar exam, and then he and Emily took off for a Jamaican vacation.

Bobby didn't fare as well as Emily after he passed the bar and tried his first case as a prosecutor, in *People of the State of New York v. Leonard Walker*, charged in the assault of a garment district co-worker. Bobby's courtroom adversary in the three-day Criminal Court trial was actually a colleague of Emily's, another Legal Aid Society defense lawyer, David Stern, also in his first trial. Bobby lost. The judge, Jack Rosenberg, offered a defeated-looking Bobby a ride home and gave him a piece of advice. "I told him not to let it disturb him."

Collier and Horowitz had noted that after Lem Billings's death, Bobby "had lost the emotional support that had helped him 'maintain'—that underpinning of fantasy which had been his hope and strength. Now it was rumored in Morgenthau's office that he was 'nodding out' in court and that his cases were suffering."

In conversations about the future of their fabled clan, Bobby's drug-addicted brother, David, had once said, "America needs a rest from the Kennedys and vice versa." Bobby called it "junkie talk" and David responded, "You're a junkie too. You just haven't admitted it yet."

TWENTY-FOUR

Shooting Up

The last places at which twenty-nine-year-old Bobby Kennedy Jr. needed to be partying were the Manhattan nightspots Rockabout and JP's, both known for a wild scene, strong drinks, and gourmet drugs.

One night in early September 1983, Bobby was at Rockabout, a frenetic punk-chic hangout, to celebrate his cousin William "Willie" Kennedy Smith's twenty-third birthday. Bobby was close to Smith, who would have his own serious, headline-making troubles in the 1990s—charged with rape in Palm Beach while barhopping with his uncle Ted, but later acquitted in a circus-like trial. Smith was the son of Jean Kennedy Smith, who had introduced her college classmate Ethel Skakel to RFK.

The next night, Bobby was at JP's for a bachelor party for the video production company executive Peter McKelvy, who was soon to marry Christopher Kennedy Lawford's twenty-seven-year-old sister, Sydney, one of the four children of Bobby's alcoholic aunt, Patricia Kennedy Lawford. But when the wedding was held later in September at the Kennedy compound, Bobby wouldn't be there. By then, his drug addiction had finally caught up with him and had become public.

JP's—the initials were those of its owner, Jimmy Pullis—was reputed to always have a supply of cocaine available for VIP friends and customers, such as the *Saturday Night Live* star John Belushi, a regular, who would later die of a heroin overdose. Downstairs at JP's was what was described as a "secret room" where a "fair amount of cocaine [was] ingested," according to one of the scions of another troubled dynasty, the family that had founded Johnson & Johnson, of Band-Aid fame. In my 2013 book, *Crazy Rich*, the heir described himself as a JP's regular. "I'd go in around closing time and play backgammon and snort coke with the bartender. It was that kind of place."

The night Bobby was at JP's he had been drinking heavily, and then began getting high. He appeared over the edge.

The reason he couldn't attend his cousin Sydney Lawford's wedding not long after was because, on the evening of September 11, 1983, a few days after his Manhattan partying binge, Bobby Kennedy Jr. had hit bottom.

Fourteen years later, in *The Riverkeepers*, Bobby, in a few rare and candid autobiographical paragraphs, asserted that the "biggest battle" in his life "was with addiction to drugs." He claimed, "I was functional while using and able to put down drugs for long periods of time, months and even years, but I always went back."

In his tight circle of loyal friends he had become known as a "binger" who had the ability to go on and off drugs—it could be cocaine, then alcohol, prescription pills, or heroin. His drug history went way back to his teen boarding-school days after his father's death. And he was always too embarrassed or too ashamed to seek professional help—fearful that if he did he would be publicly humiliated and revealed as an addict, scandalizing his family even more and blacken his father's name.

Still, he boasted in his book that he possessed "strong willpower in every other area of my life" but that it had "fueled my denial."

Incredibly, he also threw blame on what he called "an aggressive and nosy press" for keeping him from attending twelve-step programs "where I might otherwise have found recovery."

Because of the many Kennedy scandals through the decades, Bobby had come to resent the press—the messenger—rather than question his family's faults that sparked the scandals.

His view of the press was that it was "sick," as he once declared.

"They don't explain important issues. They appeal to the prurient interests at the reptilian core of our brains—the craving for sex and celebrity gossip," he said in an interview. "So they give us Laci Peterson and Kobe Bryant and Michael Jackson, Brad and Angelina, Tom and Katie. We're the best-entertained and the least-informed people on earth."

Many close to the Kennedys believed that the cause of Bobby's drug addiction, beginning when he was around fourteen, was the violent death of his father—that getting lost in drugs was Bobby's way to cope, that drugs were a tourniquet for the perceived emotional wound caused by Sirhan Sirhan's fatal bullets. But it wasn't so, at least in Bobby's perception. For his addiction, he mainly blamed the youth revolution of the late sixties that paralleled his father's death. He believed his habit was possibly a political statement. And he believed his addiction might have been in his DNA—inherited from the Kennedy clan and the Skakel dynasty.

"I was part of a generational revolution that looked at drugs almost as a political statement—a rebellion against the preceding generation, which had opposed the civil rights movement and promoted Vietnam. At that time I don't think any of us were aware of how damaging drugs could be."

He expressed that view to Oprah in 2007, when he agreed to be interviewed by her, and she actually did a decent job of interrogating him.

In pressing him on why he became a drug user, she said she thought that "every addiction is a cover for an emotional wound." But Bobby said he couldn't agree with her assumption. "I don't know whether addiction is principally genetic, a result of emotional injury, or a combination of both," he responded. "But all that matters is what I do today.

"Insight doesn't cure the addict any more than insight cures diabetes," he continued. "You may understand perfectly well how diabetes works, but if you don't take your insulin, you're dead. The same is true with addiction. It doesn't matter what got you there, it's how you conduct yourself today, day to day."

When Bobby was a kid, he claimed he always had "iron willpower" to control his appetites and, even at nine, he "gave up candy for Lent," and he maintained that he didn't take a bit of chocolate or any other sweets until he got into Harvard.

If so, he was one of the rare tokers who never got the "munchies," because he was smoking pot long before he got into college.

In his chat with Oprah, he maintained he had "earnestly tried to stop" using drugs, but "I couldn't," which he felt was "the most demoralizing part of addiction. I couldn't keep contracts with myself."

While it was later revealed that he had a sex addiction, he told Oprah, "I've been sober for twenty-three years, and I'm one of the lucky ones. I've never had a single urge [for drugs] since. Once I completed a twelve-step program, the obsession I lived with for fourteen years just lifted.

"I would describe it as miraculous."

One thing that helped, he asserted, was his religion—"I say the Rosary every day."

He kept the prayer beads in his pocket.

When he was a child growing up in Hickory Hill, he professed to have accepted a "very religious moral code," one that he maintained "forbade dishonesty, and illegal activities in general," he wrote in *The Riverkeepers.* But his use of drugs had caused him "to devote less energy to pursuing the principles" that he had been taught. "The addiction," he claimed, "increasingly challenged my capacity to live up to my values and the dictates of my conscience."

Again, there was no mention of his sex addiction—also revealed in his own words in his personal diary, which he never thought would become public.

WHILE *THE RIVERKEEPERS* HAS SOME three hundred pages, mostly about his environmental work, Bobby wrote off in just several dozen words what had happened on Republic Airlines Flight 967 en route, on a Sunday evening, from Minneapolis to Rapid City, South Dakota, where he hoped, once again, to quietly get help for his serious drug addiction. Just seventeen months after he had taken the vows of holy matrimony, Bobby had suffered a conceivably fatal overdose, high on heroin at twenty thousand feet.

One of the other forty-five passengers aboard the Convair turboprop had been dozing when he heard a cry for help coming from the toilet. He looked over, saw the door ajar, and that someone desperately needed assistance. Pasty-faced, sweating, eyes rolling around, seated precariously on the toilet, boots off, icy feet clad in white socks, speaking incoherently, the unidentified young man was clearly very, very ill.

It had taken a good five minutes to convince him, attired in scruffy jeans and a work shirt, to leave the restroom and lie down in the closest passenger seats.

One of the passengers, later identified as William Waeckerle, a school administrator, had first heard the young man's cries, and later told *People* for a cover story headlined "Two Worlds of a Kennedy" that the man was "white as a sheet, cold as an ice cube. There was a loss of muscle control. The eyes were wide open and fully dilated. His pulse was weak. I couldn't get it from his wrist, so I took it from his neck. It was thirty and weak, which concerned me."

By the time the plane landed in Rapid City, an ambulance and two police cars were waiting on the tarmac. Paramedics checked his blood pressure and pulse, which had normalized, and Bobby was permitted to leave the plane on his own power.

Miraculously, he had defied something more serious.

At one point one of the stewardesses had asked Waeckerle to get some identification from the young man. Bobby lied.

"He told me his name was Bobby Francis," Waeckerle later recalled. "He spelled it out for me."

Under police questioning in the airport, however, he was forced to give his true identity. Jaws literally dropped.

Detained for several hours, he spent some of the time idly reading a history book that he had with him, acting as if nothing out of the ordinary had occurred. Some people had been waiting at the airport for his arrival and when they learned what had happened telephone calls were made. Before long a Rapid City lawyer, a onetime Bostonian by the name of John Fitzgerald, arrived at the airport to confer with Bobby. His luggage was confiscated and held by the police while they sought a search warrant that would take a couple of days to be issued.

Meanwhile, Bobby was released and went off with a pretty young woman driving a classic Ford Thunderbird. He was said to have spent the night at the Deadwood home of Bill Walsh, who acknowledged that Bobby was on his way to South Dakota to get help for his addiction.

Back in New York, Emily Black Kennedy was devastated when she heard what had happened. Even before their marriage she had tried to help Bobby kick his addiction. She had kept his problem as private as possible. Now his arrest had made the front pages of newspapers around the country. "On a number of levels," said a close friend years later, "Emily didn't want Bobby's drug addiction to be public. A lot of press people followed her around, and she tried to keep a low profile as much as she could. She persevered. She was always a quiet person, but she just withdrew a little bit more."

Several days after his overdose, Bobby was admitted to a Summit, New Jersey, hospital that had been known for drug and alcohol rehab and psychiatric treatment since the early years of the twentieth century; in the 1980s it was one of the places for celebrities with addiction problems to dry out. Assisting him with travel and admissions was the drug counselor Don Juhl, who had been on the guest list at Bobby's wedding, and who had tried to treat David Kennedy's drug addiction.

From his uncle Ted's Senate office, a brief statement for the press and for the public was released in Bobby's name: "I have admitted myself to the hospital for the treatment of a drug problem. With the best medical help I can find I am determined to beat this problem. I deeply regret the pain which this situation will bring to my family and to so many Americans who admire my parents and the Kennedy family. I am grateful for the support of my wife, Emily, the other members of my family, and my friends during this very difficult time."

Years later in a short paragraph in *The Riverkeepers* he mentioned his arrest and noted that it had "generated tremendous publicity and, ironically, neutralized my fear of scandal, allowing me to get help."

During his stay in rehab, there were a number of medical issues that had to be addressed, according to a confidant. "He was given medication that helped to reestablish whatever his body required. At one point, he had to take interferon, a harsh drug but that was medically necessary." (Interferon was sometimes used to treat the hepatitis C virus caused by intravenous drug use.)

Bobby remained hospitalized for some five months, into early 1984. It was the kind of financially astronomical stay only a family as wealthy as the Kennedys could afford. Others of far lesser means who were caught using and possessing heroin more often than not wound up in junkie hellholes like Rikers Island, or eventually were found dead because no treatment was available.

Five days after he was discovered high in the plane's restroom, he was charged with possession of a small amount of heroin—183 milligrams, about a fifth of a gram—that was found in his carry-on bag, according to the state's attorney in Rapid City. Because Bobby already was in treatment in the Garden State, and his lawyer had pledged that he would attend any court appearances, he was granted a personal recognizance bond. In South Dakota, even the smallest amount of heroin in a person's possession was then considered a felony. In Bobby's case, it was punishable by a prison sentence of as long as two years and a fine of two thousand dollars.

In mid-March 1984, two months after turning thirty, Bobby was out of rehab and had begun his two years of court-enforced probation. He had been ordered by Judge Marshall F. Young of the Seventh Circuit in Rapid City to undergo drug testing, to continue treatment, to become a member of Narcotics Anonymous, and to start fifteen hundred hours of community service, all the while remaining in New York. Violation meant two years in prison. Because of his drug issues, he had left the DA's office after just a year.

Emily Ruth Black Kennedy "was a saint," observed a person who knew her, "because she took Bobby back after all the hell he put her through. People who knew her like me thought she was crazy because we didn't believe he could change. You know, once a junkie, always a junkie, even if the drug was something else, like alcohol or sex. But Emily hung in there."

Moreover, by the time he was on probation he had gotten her pregnant, and on September 2, 1984, she delivered a seven-pound, eleven-ounce boy, named Robert "Bobby" Francis Kennedy III after his recovering drug addict father and his fabled slain presidential candidate grandfather.

In April 1988, ten days after Bobby and Emily's sixth wedding anniversary, she gave birth to their second child—Kathleen "Kick" Alexandra Kennedy. Her first name was in honor of both Bobby's sister Kathleen

Kennedy Townsend and the aunt Bobby never knew, Kathleen "Kick" Agnes Kennedy, his father's sister who was killed in a 1948 plane crash. The middle name, Alexandra, was in honor of Bobby's mother's niece from her Skakel side, who had been born severely handicapped in 1952, a birth that reminded the Skakels and the Kennedys of the retarded Kennedy sister, Rosemary, born to Bobby's grandmother Rose.

Neither of Bobby and Emily's children would follow in the Kennedy family traditions of politics and public service; RFK III saw himself as a filmmaker, and Kick would be an actress.

TWENTY-FIVE

Community Service

Since Bobby Kennedy Jr. was required to perform hundreds of hours of community service and stay within the confines of New York State as part of the sentence on his heroin possession charge, he found a volunteer job in January 1984—the same month that he turned thirty—with an environmental organization that was involved in cleaning up the polluted Hudson River.

The internship launched his career as an outspoken environmentalist and environmental lawyer—eventually considered the most powerful in the nation—all woven into the turbulent fabric of his Kennedy world.

Just three months after he began that new chapter of his life, there was yet more tragedy in his family involving the futility and horror of drug addiction. On April 24, 1984, during the Easter holidays, and after a week of heavy drinking and cocaine use—a marathon bender—his brother David Anthony Kennedy died of an overdose.

His death came a few months before his twenty-ninth birthday, and just a few days after getting out of a month of yet another try at kicking his addiction through rehab.

"It was hideous," said Bobby years later, asserting, "He was my best friend."

Ethel Kennedy learned of her son's tragic end when she called the Brazilian Court Hotel in Palm Beach, where David was staying in a $292-a-night suite. Across the hall, his brother Douglas, then seventeen, was installed with a prep school friend, and the three had shared meals in the hotel dining room. Many of the Kennedys were at the family's fabled oceanfront Palm Beach mansion, gathered to celebrate the holiday and to visit with the ninety-four-year-old ailing matriarch, Rose.

But troubled David had walled himself off from his family and they from him, embarrassed by his behavior and drug issues.

His mother had called the hotel to see whether he had left to catch a flight to Boston. When the room clerk got no answer on the house phone, she went to his room and found him dead.

"I had an ominous feeling," Ethel Kennedy said later.

Her fourth-born, her third son after Joe and then Bobby, had died from using too much high-grade cocaine along with the painkiller Demerol and the tranquilizer Mellaril.

His body was shipped to Hickory Hill, where family members and all of his siblings and friends had gathered for an old fashion Kennedy-style wake, an event at which the clan was expert.

The tale of another scandalous Kennedy tragedy had made news around the world. *The New York Times*, in a lengthy story headlined "A Troubled Kennedy Makes Last Trip Home," observed that since his father's death his "anguished life" had been dominated "by drugs, alcohol and the seeming inability to handle the pressure of being a member of the most closely watched family in America."

After David died, a young woman named Mary Richardson, who later became Bobby's second wife, telephoned her friend Andy Warhol and told him that the only thing David had on the wall of his apartment "was the napkin drawing I gave him," wrote Warhol in his diary. "I don't remember if I drew a cock or just hearts." Curiously, Warhol noted that David was the RFK son that "everyone thought might be gay. Blond and pretty and fey and not like a dog—he didn't have those [Kennedy] teeth."

David Kennedy was buried next to his grandfather, the Kennedy clan patriarch, in the family plot in Holyhood Cemetery, in Brookline, Massachusetts.

He was the first of Ethel Kennedy's brood to predecease her, and the first, but not the last, of his generation—Bobby's generation—to die tragically.

After the funeral, and many years later, a friend recalled Bobby telling him as he watched his brother's casket being lowered into the ground, "There but for the grace of God go I. That could have been me."

IN HIS NEW LIFE, clean from drugs, Bobby was assigned to perform his community service under the auspices of the prominent *Sports Illustrated* writer Robert Boyle, the activist founder of the Hudson River Fishermen's Association—later to be known as Riverkeeper—who believed in science and the law, and was convinced that the environment would never be safe if it was left up to governments.

In *The Riverkeepers*, Bobby asserted that he had fallen in love with the Hudson after he read Boyle's classic, *The Hudson River: A Natural and Unnatural History*. In affectionate detail, Bobby recalled fishing with Boyle, scuba diving with him and his friends, and hiking in the woods. "It was a way," he wrote, "of getting my bearings, of adapting to a new home by systematically developing the same sort of familiarity with my surroundings and its indigenous plants and animals as I'd had with the Virginia and Cape Cod homes of my youth . . . I learned to think of the Hudson Valley as my home, my place."

He even harkened back to his school days in the Hudson Valley when he was at Millbrook—the first boarding school from which he had been expelled for drugs and bad behavior—stating that he had always loved the area.

He also noted he had fallen "easily into life in Mount Kisco," a quaint, upscale commuter village some forty miles north of New York City, and not far from the Hudson. There, with his low-key wife, Emily, and their two children, he bought a Kennedyesque estate and threw big parties and social events—shades of Hickory Hill in Westchester County. The area was home to many celebrities, among them Martha Stewart, Chevy

Chase, Ralph Lauren, and, for a time in neighboring Bedford, the co-founder of Alcoholics Anonymous. The Kennedy scion was yet another.

It had all sounded so idyllic.

But Robert Boyle, who had taken Bobby in to his Hudson River Fishermen's Association, didn't have such positive memories of the recovering drug addict. At eighty-six in 2014, but still outspoken and vigorous, the environmental activist surprisingly declared, "I think he's a despicable person. I have no interest in Mr. Kennedy. I started the organization and he went to work for us. The National Resources Defense Council [another environmental group] parked him with us when he had to do public service for his drug problem. It wasn't my idea."

Still, Boyle took a fatherly and sympathetic approach at first. He recalled telling Bobby, "You know, you can put your past behind you and find a new life. A lot of people go through addiction. But the Hudson River is your salvation, if you will, from the horrible life you have led. You can seek a new life through the river, and through ecology."

Bobby listened and learned.

Looking back, Boyle noted, "I'm regarded by some as his mentor. God forbid that I sat on that egg and let it hatch."

For a time, however, everything was copacetic between them. Occasionally, early in their working relationship, Boyle had dinner at the Kennedys', and got to meet Emily, whom he found to be "very quiet," the consensus of most everyone who got to know her. Still later he got to meet Bobby's second wife, Mary Richardson Kennedy, and found her to be "seemingly admiring of Bobby, and very close to him. I didn't see any disruption." However, he also began hearing chatter about Bobby fooling around with other women. "I heard things, but I paid no attention to it. I never thought of it in terms of problems for the organization."

In *The Riverkeepers*, Bobby said one of his first projects was helping in "transforming" a group of farmhouses into a "scientific field station for the study and protection of the Hudson River" to be used by Boyle's organization.

But, according to Boyle, "All he did was to move furniture and hang pictures during the initial time, that was the sole thing of it."

As time passed, Boyle began to see a change in Bobby, who was there at first mainly to fulfill his community service, and who had acted "very morose and surly for the first year or so. He'd just sit in a chair and sulk. When we'd go out to lunch he'd be rude to the waitress."

But when that attitude passed, he had become more and more dominant and assertive, said Boyle.

In late May 1985, about a year after joining Boyle's organization, thirty-one-year-old Bobby had finally been admitted to the New York State bar after a review by the Committee on Character and Fitness of the Appelate Division of the New York State Supreme Court. His probation had ended a year early, in March 1985. The committee's interviewer told *The New York Times*, for a story headlined, "A Quiet Victory for Robert F. Kennedy Jr.," that Bobby had "impressed me as a person of considerable integrity, a person who is intellectually acute and unusually modest. I unreservedly approved him."

Regarding Bobby's drug addiction, he stated, "He has decisively overcome that problem."

After years of drifting and drugs, Bobby, in his early thirties, had finally begun to see a glorious future for himself in the environmental field, one that was growing in popularity and influence. After all, he always had liked birds and bugs and little animals. He saw himself as a natural with nature, and it didn't hurt that he had the platinum Kennedy moniker, an eventual advanced degree in environmental law, and a background of power and privilege.

"He actually took over the organization," asserted Boyle. "He put his clique or claque on the board of directors. The people he had come in were just fans of his"—a mix of boldface society and Hollywood names, from the heiress Ann Hearst to the actress Lorraine Bracco and the actor Alec Baldwin, among others. "It was the whole cult of his celebrity name. I remember one time at the Kennedys' seeing guys who must have been in their seventies jumping up and down like bobbysoxers seeing Frank Sinatra, but to see Kennedy, and they were yelling, 'Bobby! Bobby!' It was crazy."

Once it became clear that Bobby was going to rule the organization that Boyle had founded, and eventually "did take control," Boyle turned in his resignation.

"I resigned because I wouldn't even want to be close to him. He's an appalling man. He's a despicable person, period."

THE DISPUTE WITH BOBBY, one of several that led to Boyle's resignation in June 2000—one that shocked the environmental community—was ignited when Bobby, without Boyle's authorization, hired a man by the name of William Wegner in the position of "staff scientist."

In hiring Wegner, Bobby had described him as an "environmental activist" and a "devoted conservationist."

But Boyle knew differently.

Wegner, a master falconer like Bobby and with a master's degree in biology, had spent almost a decade smuggling cockatoo eggs, hatching the beautiful and costly birds, and selling them for as much as $12,500 each. In 1994 he and five co-conspirators were indicted. Moreover, Wegner had pleaded guilty to conspiracy to violate a few wildlife protection laws. He had also pleaded to tax fraud and was found to have obstructed justice by lying at a trial of one of those in the smuggling ring with him. One of them was his girlfriend, who had been identified as the "animal keeper" at Hugh Hefner's Playboy Mansion.

Boyle was aware that Wegner had gone to prison for his crimes. He had served a little over three years of a five-year sentence and had been fined ten thousand dollars.

But, according to Boyle, Bobby had mentioned none of these details when he made the unilateral decision to hire Wegner.

When Boyle learned about the hiring from the Riverkeeper's acting executive director, he demanded to see Wegner's résumé. As he suspected, "There was not a thing about prison on it. None of that was in the résumé. It simply said he had been a sanitary technician at a Federal Bureau of Prisons facility in California—without saying he was an inmate."

Wegner had been released from prison in August 1999 and hired by Bobby shortly thereafter. Bobby would later defend the hire by asserting it was no different than his being brought into the Riverkeeper with a record for his heroin possession arrest. But there was a difference: Wegner had been involved in an environmental crime.

. . .

BOYLE HAD FIRST LEARNED about Wegner's smuggling operation some years earlier from another associate of Bobby's, one Thomas J. V. Cullen III, who, according to court records, was "New York's acknowledged expert on birds of prey and an internationally known and respected falconer."

According to Boyle, Bobby got his master falconer's license under the mentorship of Tom Cullen. "Bobby boasted about it, and so did Cullen. Cullen once told me he'd walk through hell for Bobby. Tom Cullen was a brilliant falconer, a brilliant man with birds, and was a pal of Wegner's."

And like Wegner, Cullen had his own problems with the law.

But before he got into trouble regarding the illegal importation of rare birds, he had been hired by the City of New York at $53,951 a year to lure bald eagles back to a Manhattan park. He was quite a colorful character, who had once described himself as looking like a Cooper's hawk because of his reddish blond hair, his beard, and the shape of his nose. At one point, he had rented out some of his birds to chase seagulls from Kennedy International Airport, and pigeons from Bryant Park in midtown Manhattan, where office workers often came to eat lunch on the benches and were bothered by the scruffy birds.

Like Bobby, Cullen's interest in falcons had started when he was a child. In Cullen's case, he claimed he had been watching the popular late-fifties TV program *Walt Disney's Wonderful World of Color* and was bowled over by an episode called "Rusty and the Falcon."

As *The New York Times* noted in a story about Cullen in 2005, "He had hunted with luminaries like Robert F. Kennedy Jr. and worked briefly with the naturalists who established an urban eagle program in Washington, D.C."

Cullen, the grandson of a onetime Orange County, New York, Democratic leader, had once appeared on the CBS TV program *The Early Show* with Betsy, a bald eagle. The bird had been leased just for the program. But not long after, according to *The New York Times,* Cullen contacted the bird's owner to inform him it had died, and a subsequent autopsy determined the cause was dehydration. Cullen later claimed that he had been giving it water, but it had died because of a then current heat wave in the Northeast. However, the pathologist claimed the bird had not received proper care.

In another case in New Jersey, when an eaglet was found near death, Cullen reportedly told the fish and game investigator, "I don't like eagles. They have an attitude."

The Riverkeeper president and founder Bob Boyle had first gotten to know Cullen in the mid-1980s when he spent two months profiling him for a major story for *Sports Illustrated*. "Cullen had the largest collection of birds of prey in the U.S. and maybe the world," Boyle said. "His home in Goshen, New York, looked like it was out of Charles Addams with all these birds of prey tethered on the lawn. I had a *Life* photographer working with me and he took fantastic pictures of fantastic birds—one bird could take down a Doberman pinscher."

Boyle's *Sports Illustrated* piece had been laid out for a whopping eighteen pages in *SI*'s big Superbowl issue. But then he got a call from the story's fact-checker. There was a problem, she told Boyle.

"She said she had learned that he was arrested in Western Australia for using a hatchet while up in a tree to extract cockatoo eggs in a nature preserve," he said.

While interviewing Cullen, Boyle said he had routinely asked him whether he had ever had gotten into any trouble, and Cullen said he hadn't; Boyle had taken him at his word.

But after the researcher turned up problems, Boyle went to the managing editor and told him, " 'The son of a bitch lied to me.' We killed the story. Shortly after that the U.S. Fish and Wildlife seized all of Cullen's birds. What I found was some in the falconry circles like Wegner and Cullen just do what they want to do."

In October 2004, Cullen was charged with filing false statements to the Wildlife Service relating to birds of prey known as black sparrow hawks, and in January 2005, he was charged with importing the birds in violation of the Wild Bird Act, and also charged with importing into the United States a number of Saker falcons in violation of the act. He went to trial in 2005.

Cullen was convicted, but acquitted on one charge regarding the importation of the Saker falcons. In early 2006, he was sentenced to four months in prison, three years supervised release, a thousand-dollar fine, and a special assessment of two hundred dollars. He appealed to the U.S. Court of Appeals in February 2006, but his conviction was affirmed.

After hearing testimony about Cullen's environmental misdeeds, the trial court was surprised when the chief character witness for the defendant turned out to be America's number one defender of the environment, Robert F. Kennedy Jr.

To see Bobby on the witness stand, however, didn't come as much of a surprise to Wayne A. Hall, a veteran reporter who had covered the Cullen trial. An ardent bird-watcher, Hall personally knew both the defendant and his character witness. "Bobby and Cullen had known each other quite a long time, so that's why Bobby thought he could speak in Cullen's defense," said Hall. "Bobby and Cullen had very close ties. Bobby was somebody who had worked with Cullen in falconry. They were friends and fellow falconers."

A reporter for the *Times Herald-Record*, a daily that covered the northwest suburbs of New York City, Hall had personally known Bobby since the 1980s when they "became rather friendly" as fellow birders, and the journalist had also gotten to know Cullen while writing articles about hawks.

In the past, Hall had wondered why, aside from their mutual interest in falcons, Bobby would have the convicted environmentalist as a friend. And he had concluded that like a lot of the wealthy preppies he had attended school with at Manhattan's elite Trinity School and later at Columbia College who liked to slum, Bobby would "want to hang out with the rough-and-tumble kind. I suppose it was a little thrilling, or kind of daring. He may have felt that, yes, this guy Cullen's a criminal, but at the same time he's helping out a little bit with the environment, so maybe I can straighten him out. There is that with Bobby—he's a bit of a crusader—living dangerously but also with a mission. He's a rebel, and that's been his scene throughout his life. He's a rebel but with a cause."

Hall continued: "One of the things that's key to knowing him is that he really does like to be with people who are not in the Kennedy clan because he's able to be more of himself in a way. He gravitates to people like that, and that serves a need of his. Cullen was one of them, and he's another bold spirit."

Bobby, who had been mentored by Cullen as a licensed falconer, had quietly started marketing his falconer art and experience in an eBay auction scheduled during the fall 2014 falconry season that was to benefit the Waterkeeper Alliance. The website had even included a YouTube video, and a photograph of the Kennedy heir holding one of his birds.

According to the auction listing:

The winner and a guest will spend a weekend afternoon with Robert F. Kennedy Jr., master falconer and president of Waterkeeper Alliance, learning the basics of an 8,000-year-old sport at the hands of a true expert! Afternoon of falconry will take place in New York State and include lunch.

TWENTY-SIX

Environmental War

When Bob Boyle learned that Bobby, without having the authority, had hired Tom Cullen's friend, the recently-released-from-prison cockatoo smuggler William Wegner, as a staff scientist, he was furious. By then, Bobby had the title of Riverkeeper's chief prosecuting attorney. Moreover, he had founded Pace University's Environmental Litigation Clinic, which often sued New York City over water pollution issues. Bobby had been building an impressive résumé for himself, and establishing a power base.

When Boyle demanded that Bobby fire Wegner, Bobby refused.

Even more upsetting for Boyle was the fact that he already had arranged for a small group of distinguished scientists to be a part of the Riverkeeper organization.

In early December 1999, shortly after he learned of Wegner's hiring, Boyle sent a letter to the board members "with a sense of sadness, even with reluctance" regarding the hiring of Wegner, and Bobby's behavior in general, which included "disparaging and insulting remarks that he had made to me . . . and undoubtedly others." He wrote that Bobby's "barrage of unfounded, unwarranted criticism" had taken away from "the time and effort that should be spent on the river now facing the threat of reindustrialization. It created division within the board."

Boyle further stated in the letter that for more than a year "Bobby's language and behavior has been so uncooperative, so uncollegial, so ill-mannered, so destructive and, frankly, so off-the-wall that this month . . . he hired, to use his words, an 'environmental activist' and a 'devoted conservationist' to work as a scientist on the watershed for Riverkeeper . . . by reputation Wegner is no stranger to me . . ."

Boyle went on to tell the board about Wegner's and Cullen's checkered history.

Boyle wasn't the only critic who derided Bobby for his behavior. In a story about the Kennedy–Boyle dispute, *The New York Times* quoted George Rodenhausen, legal counsel to Putnam County, New York, who had been involved with Bobby during a watershed negotiation, as asserting, "I think he separates himself from good science at times in order to aggressively pursue an issue and win." A former Putnam County legislator, James Gordon, who was a colleague of Rodenhausen, remarked that Bobby "had a nasty tendency to deride or insult anybody he thought was not on his side."

A board of directors' meeting regarding the retention of Wegner—what Boyle called the "showdown" meeting—was set for June 2000. In preparation, he had sent another letter to the members replete with a stack of documents about the Wegner case.

But Boyle saw that Bobby was in control.

"He was leading the rallying cry. They wanted to shout me down at the meeting. Someone said, 'Secret ballot!' I said we'd never had a secret ballot. Bobby had a lawyer come in and say that any director who voted against hiring Wegner could be sued by Wegner. That was complete bullshit, according to an outside opinion I had from a law firm. I told the board, 'Would you hire a child molester to run a nursery school?' "

But Bobby won.

The vote was thirteen in favor of retaining Wegner, eight against. Boyle, the organization's founder and Bobby's mentor, immediately quit, as did the eight board members who had voted against Wegner's retention.

"I got out of Riverkeeper. They asked me back twice, at least twice, maybe three times, but I wouldn't go near them because Kennedy's there. They are all dominated by him. It's whatever Bobby wants."

Asked whether he thought Bobby's support of Wegner was simply a power play, or whether there was a quid pro quo involved, or something more diabolical, Boyle claimed he didn't know the answer.

"I'm not God and cannot look into Bobby Kennedy's soul or his mind," he said. "How much Bobby was involved with them, I have no idea. But I think of Bobby, Wegner, and Cullen as birds of a feather. They hang together."

Bobby's support of Wegner and the confrontation with Boyle that ensued had weighed for years on a number of people in the movement. It came up again in April 2007, for instance, when Bobby gave a speech before a crowd of some one thousand at the Lied Center for Performing Arts in Lincoln, Nebraska. He was there to blast the Bush administration, declaring, "Most insidiously, they have put polluters in charge of virtually all the agencies that are supposed to protect the rest of us from pollution." He also attacked the media, which he maintained was controlled by corporations, beginning with the repeal in the late 1980s of the Federal Communications Commission's regulation known as the Fairness Doctrine. "You couldn't have Fox News under the Fairness Doctrine," he declared.

For his speech, Bobby was billed as the superhero who had cleaned up the Hudson River. But during a question-and-answer session, Pete Silverstein, who had served as a member of Bob Boyle's Hudson River Fishermen's Association, brought up the Wegner imbroglio and asked Bobby why he had hired him. His quick response was, "William Wegner was a brilliant scientist who did something wrong," but later, Bobby claimed, did valuable work.

The event was covered by the *Lawrence Journal-World*, and after the speech the paper's reporter asked Silverstein to elaborate.

He declared: "Bobby Kennedy hiring Bill Wegner as an environmental scientist as a Riverkeeper . . . was just like Dick Cheney contracting with Halliburton for the reconstruction of Iraq. It was the same kind of cronyism."

Despite the controversy, Wagner was still in good standing as a staff scientist in March 2015.

. . .

BESIDES THE WEGNER ISSUE, there was another situation that had an-
gered Boyle. It involved a proposal by Bobby to start a bottled water
company to be a part of Riverkeeper. Boyle was opposed, telling Bobby,
"We're in the business of protecting public water supplies, not marketing boutique water."

While Boyle was against the idea, he was still willing to consider
it. Noting that he was an environmentalist and not a businessman, he
instructed Bobby to send a detailed written proposal to the five members on the Riverkeeper board who were highly respected businesspeople
and could make a more educated judgment regarding the viability of the
idea, or lack thereof.

"I said to Bobby, 'I want the proposal in black and white and in very
specific terms and I want you to send it to them and them alone,'" Boyle
recalled. "What he did was to send it out to *all* of the board members,
not to just those five, and he told them, 'Bob Boyle told me to send this
to you.' And Bobby did it quickly by express mail before I could find
out."

When he did learn of the wide distribution of the proposal, Boyle
was livid.

"I called him on that. Then he apologized, but when I spoke to him
the next day he denied that he had ever apologized. He didn't follow what
I said should have been done."

In the confrontation, Boyle asked Bobby why he had disobeyed him
and Bobby's response, according to Boyle, was "I was pissed off."

Boyle told him that if he ever did that sort of thing again, "'You are
gone.' He said, 'Am I fired now?' I said, 'No, not right now.'"

"I came to not trust him," continued Boyle in 2014. "I don't say that
about many people that I've met in the environmental movement, but I
absolutely did not, and do not trust him. He shoots from the hip. Anything that comes into Bobby's fevered mind becomes a fact, lunacy can
enter into it, and it becomes complete denial. Black is white, no it isn't,
or it is. Whatever comes into his mind becomes the truth."

Still, Bobby played nice in public.

Boyle recalled attending a library function in the Hudson Valley where

Bobby lauded him for his Hudson River book and his environmental work, declaring, "If I had to be on a desert island with anyone but my wife it would be Bob Boyle."

In the audience, Boyle, who had served in the Marines and had a salty way of speaking, whispered to the person next to him, "And I'd have a big cork up my ass."

BOBBY NEVER DROPPED THE BOUTIQUE bottled water idea and in 1999 he, along with his longtime friend from law school Chris Bartle and John Hoving, another friend who had been an executive at Tiffany & Company, founded Keeper Springs natural spring water.

According to Bobby, he had approached Bartle in 1998 and asked him what they could do to "raise money and awareness for the work the Hudson Riverkeeper and waterkeepers all over the country are doing," and out of the conversation came Keeper Springs, which they said was inspired by Paul Newman's food company, Newman's Own. According to the founders, the company was chartered to give 100 percent of the profits to the Waterkeeper Alliance.

Still, the business came under attack by environmentalists. "Kennedy's idea of selling bottled water and donating all profits after expenses to environmental causes is contradictory on the face of it," declared the environmentalist and writer Anthony Henry Smith in a 2012 essay entitled "Bottled Greenwash." He went on to assert, "Bottled water does more damage to the biotic and physical environment than the so-called profits could possibly mitigate."

In an interview around 2007 with an organization called Bolder Giving, Bartle, a lawyer, revealed that early on "we lost money, but we adjusted our business model and gradually built a customer base." He claimed he put in as much as 20 percent of his "work time running this business, for no salary," and that he'd "come close to throwing in the towel several times."

Bobby said he had helped the company "where I can, and my name sometimes opens doors."

His last name, according to Boyle, is the main reason Bobby became so prominent, powerful, and successful in the environmental field. "In fact, he doesn't even have to proclaim his last name," the Riverkeeper founder asserted. "The media does it because his name is Kennedy. The reason for his success is Kennedy, Kennedy, Kennedy."

The power of the Kennedy name as it related to RFK's namesake was underscored when Bobby was asked to give a talk about the Chesapeake Bay. Apparently knowing little or nothing about the subject, he called Boyle while on his way to the speaking engagement and asked him for anything and everything he knew about the waterway so he could use it in his presentation.

Later, in conversation with Boyle and another respected environmentalist, Bobby made mention of the speech, and the environmentalist asked him whether he had gotten a fee. When Bobby responded that he had received a cool five thousand dollars for an hour of his time (with information he had gotten at the last minute from Boyle), the environmentalist was astounded, and said that maybe he should be doing the same.

Bobby's quick response was "But you don't have the right last name."

IN 2007, *NEW YORK* MAGAZINE published a not-so-positive profile of America's best-known environmentalist, under the headline "American Jeremiad: A Harrowing Ride Up the Proverbial Creek and into the Beating, Bleeding Heart of RFK Jr." The story was done in the wake of Bobby's book attacking President Bush and the Republicans regarding the environment.

When Bobby joined Boyle's organization, the magazine noted, it was a "legendary down-in-the-muck association of scientists, sportsmen and commercial fishers." But when Bobby got his hand in, it "would morph into the less-mess-on-the-Topsiders groups like the Riverkeepers," which provided the title of the 1997 book by Bobby and his co-author and environmentalist colleague, John Cronin.

According to them, New York's Hudson Valley "would emerge as the central battleground of the American environmental movement, and the Hudson River emerge as the Mount Vernon of environmental law."

Not long after Bobby joined Boyle's group he met Cronin, who recently had taken the job as Hudson Riverkeeper at Bob Boyle's urging.

The job, at fifty dollars a week, authorized the thirty-nine-year-old Cronin to "track down polluters, stay on top of government agencies, be a presence on the river."

The New York Times soon ran a story headlined, "New Riverkeeper to Patrol Hudson."

And *People* even did a story in July 1990: "Polluters, Beware! River-keeper John Cronin Patrols the Hudson and Pursues Those Who Foul Its Waters." The celebrity weekly pointed out, "Cronin's effectiveness—and his rugged good looks—have made him a reluctant environmental star. Camera crews follow him . . . he is the subject of a recently published children's book . . . and Warner Brothers plans to make a movie based on his life."

It quoted Bobby as saying of his close associate, "John is the paradigm of the vigorous, sophisticated, aggressive Hudson River environmentalist. The reason we have been able to save the river is that we've used public relations, politics, and the court."

There was just one brief mention of Bob Boyle, who had, with his organization, made both Cronin and Bobby environmental stars.

They were being called the dynamic duo, and the two seemed to make a perfect match.

Bobby thought of Cronin, as he wrote in their book, as "eloquent, thoughtful, and utterly committed," with "an extraordinary talent for politics." And Cronin considered Bobby, according to their book, "a natural-born advocate with a brilliant mind for complex scientific and technical matters . . . one of the nation's preeminent environmental attorneys and the voice of a generation of lawyers who believe that the pioneering days of environmental law are not yet over."

Bobby and Cronin's book made no mention of the in-fighting that had gone on with Boyle, and instead, diplomatically, noted that Boyle was "one of the central figures" in the environmental movement as founder of the Fishermen's Association and chairman of the Hudson River-keeper. "Boyle," they wrote, "championed a brand of environmentalism that put people first and that recognized that the value of nature is its ability to enrich humanity."

In his 2014 interview, Boyle, still sour about his relationship with the

Kennedy heir, guessed that Bobby's environmentalism "had to be part of an act."

But Bobby claimed he had always been an environmentalist of sorts "from the time I was very little." He boasted that when he was ten, he had actually written a book about pollution, and noted, "A certain uncle of mine got me an interview with Stewart Udall, the Secretary of the Interior. I brought a tape recorder and asked him a lot of questions."

He also maintained, "I've always respected Bob Boyle. I always will. We fished together for stripers and black bass. His book did make me fall in love with the river. One of the things that did, anyway."

BOBBY HAD NEVER DISCUSSED with Boyle that he and John Cronin had planned to write a book called *The Riverkeepers*. He learned about the secret project only by chance during a phone call with Cronin, who had called him desperately seeking a five-thousand-dollar infusion of cash "to pay the staff in the morning."

Boyle recalls being confounded by the request for money. "I said, 'Wait a minute.' I said, 'What happened to the hundred thousand we set aside for the initial endowment?' And he said, 'We spent it.' I said, 'You spent the fucking money, what's going on?'

"We talked and I told him he'd get the money in the morning, but that I wanted to go into the financial situation with him."

Boyle has never forgotten what happened next.

"I asked him what else was new and he said, 'Bobby and I are going to be doing a book.' I said, 'Oh, really, what about?' He said the Riverkeepers. They hadn't said anything to me about it, and I immediately thought, if it's intellectual property it's mine. So I said, 'Who's going to publish it,' and he said Scribner."

Boyle, who had been a top magazine writer, journalist, and author for years and was well versed in the publishing game, asked whether they had gotten any kind of advance. He recalled Cronin hemming and hawing before he said, "Four hundred thousand."

Boyle was stunned—*stunned.*

"I said, '*Four hundred thousand fucking dollars!*' You're telling this to me now for the first time and at the end of this conversation when you're asking me for five thousand dollars to make the payroll, and you guys are getting four hundred thousand dollars for a fucking book!"

A week or two later, he went to a meeting of the Riverkeeper board of directors, brought up the planned Kennedy–Cronin book, and recommended that something be done about it. But one of the directors whose judgment Boyle respected said, "Let's let it pass. Let's not go to war over this." Boyle reluctantly agreed, "which was a mistake on my part," he still believed years later. "I should have canned Cronin right then and there."

LIKE BOBBY'S JUDGE FRANK JOHNSON biography, which was panned by *The New York Times*, *The Riverkeepers* also received a negative review from the Gray Lady despite the glowing foreword in the paperback edition by Vice President Al Gore, who called the book "[T]he kind of personal account America needs to hear more often." (While the Gore blurb was used on the cover as a selling point, Bobby later turned on Gore and accused him of "bailing out" on the environment in the 2000 presidential election.)

The *Times* review took exception to Bobby's "out-of-place personal notes," and it pointed to "some embarrassing moments," such as when he wrote that "his love of nature" was inspired, in part, by his Costa Rican nanny reading to him "heavily accented versions" of Brer Rabbit and Uncle Remus.

The reviewer, James Gorman, then the *Times* deputy science editor, stated that parts of Bobby's story were "difficult to read with a straight face," and pointed out that he had made some erroneous assertions, such as claiming that DDT had eradicated certain birds north of the Mason-Dixon Line. Gorman charged that that was untrue—certain birds had been damaged, but not eradicated, he pointed out. "This is not a trivial mistake," he noted. "The environment is Kennedy's claimed field of expertise, after all, and the DDT disaster is a famous one."

Gorman also took exception to Bobby's boastfulness regarding his other writing endeavors, which included penning op-ed pieces for the *Times*, and his powerful media connections, calling his mentioning of them "tedious." "No doubt gaining press coverage is an important tactic," the critic wrote, "but it is treated as an achievement in itself, and of course the heroes, again, are the authors."

To promote the book, Bobby even made a big-time appearance on *The Late Show with David Letterman.*

As one of the New York tabloids noted, "He's going where no Kennedy has gone before."

WHILE NO ONE ELSE IN BOBBY'S family was ever known to have become involved with the Hudson Riverkeeper, there were instances of familial favoritism that ignited criticism within the environmentalist community.

Dan Bacher, a member of the Klamath Riverkeeper organization, headquartered in Humboldt County, California, was furious, for instance, when he learned in 2010 that the Hudson Riverkeeper planned to honor Arnold Schwarzenegger, husband of Bobby's cousin Maria Shriver, for his "environmental advocacy."

The award was to be presented to Schwarzenegger at the Hudson Riverkeeper's annual Fishermen's Ball on Bobby's beloved Hudson River at Pier 60 in Manhattan.

Bacher, a journalist and an environmentalist, called Schwarzenegger "the worst governor for fish and the environment in California history."

Honoring the then-governor and *Terminator* star "is as absurd as Henry Kissinger receiving the Nobel Peace Prize," Bacher said in a blog. "In fact, it's akin to giving Pol Pot an award for his human rights record! I am livid over this move by the Hudson Riverkeeper to honor a guy that makes former California governors Gray Davis and Pete Wilson look like veritable John Muirs in comparison."

Bacher had written a number of articles about what he described as Schwarzenegger's "crimes against fish and the environment." He declared that the Riverkeeper "must be condemned" for honoring Schwarzenegger, "who had presided over the unprecedented collapse of Central Valley salmon . . . and other California fish populations."

Writing in the investigative journalism publication *Counterpunch,* Bacher declared, "I suspect that Schwarzenegger may be receiving the award because of his close relationship to Robert F. Kennedy Jr. . . . and other Kennedy family members through his marriage to Maria Shriver. However, honoring Schwarzenegger, when he is the worst enemy of fishery restoration in California, provides 'green cover' for the governor's attack on Central Valley salmon and the Delta ecosystem."

Bacher quoted Schwarzenegger as telling the Fox News star Sean Hannity, "We gotta stop putting the interest of the salmon and smelt above the interests of people."

He called Schwarzenegger the "Fish Terminator," and said that if Bobby's organization "has any integrity" it should withdraw the invitation and honor, and "apologize" to fishermen everywhere.

The event went on as planned.

As a Riverkeeper member asserted, "Nobody kicks Bobby Kennedy Jr. around or tells him what to do. It's the other way around."

TWENTY-SEVEN

Quickie Divorce

While Bobby Kennedy Jr. may have fallen in love with the Hudson River, he had fallen out of love with his wife, Emily. Above and beyond Bobby's hellish drug problem, Emily had her own issue: transforming her Indiana-born-and-bred natural style into being the model, exuberant Kennedy wife like her mother-in-law, the rah-rah Ethel.

"Emily," as a close family source maintained, "was more Jackie than she was Ethel."

The Ethel–Jackie relationship, or lack thereof, had surfaced even before they became sisters-in-law. When the young Kennedys got together on Saturday afternoons in Georgetown to play touch football, Jackie would sit bored and glum on the sidelines while Ethel tangled with the guys. "Ethel made jokes that Jackie wouldn't play because she was afraid to smear her makeup," one of the other women later recalled. "I remember Ethel, who rarely wore lipstick, shaking her head in wonderment, saying, 'Jackie thinks she's a queen. I can't figure out what Jack sees in her.'"

That's sort of the way the Kennedys—and Bobby—felt about Emily toward the end of their marriage, according to family sources. While Emily wasn't competing with a difficult sister-in-law, she felt overwhelmed by the whole boisterous Kennedy gang, and it only got worse as the years passed.

A close friend recalled seeing Emily at Kennedy family events and noted how she tried to become invisible. "She was the shy, retiring type who didn't want to jump in and play sports, didn't want to become competitive with all of them. In that respect she had a fish-out-of-water quality about her because she also was nice and genuine. Emily wasn't really into being a Kennedy, but she loved Bobby and their home and their kids."

Once Bobby went through rehab and got clean of drugs, was regularly attending Alcoholic Anonymous meetings, and was working with Hudson Riverkeeper, things got better for a time. Having RFK III and Kick had helped because Bobby, from a family of eleven, and Emily, with just two siblings, wanted lots of kids.

"The problem was Bobby was a difficult guy to be married to in general," said a close confidant. "He was always on the go, always doing things, always had people around him, and he always had people who wanted something from him, and people who were offering him stuff. He was always out—summers at the Cape, traveling out in the wilderness. He was always taking off. When he was on drugs he was wired, and when he was off drugs he was wired."

When Bobby wasn't on the go, he had turned their home in Mount Kisco into a veritable party house like the mansion in which he had been raised, Hickory Hill. And life at Hickory Hill had been modeled by Bobby's mother on the Skakel estate where she had grown up in Greenwich, where there were endless rounds of business parties, socializing, carousing, and lots of drinking.

"There was always an open house on weekends in Mount Kisco," said a friend of Bobby and Emily's. "On any given weekend you never knew who was going to be out at that house. It was always a gathering point for fun, for interesting people, for pain-in-the-ass people, every kind of people. But it just wasn't easy for Emily. Bobby was much more social than Emily.

"Before the divorce and even before the separation they began to drift apart. These guys realized they weren't ideally suited for each other. It became clear over time that their marriage wasn't going to work out and they were just figuring how best to end it."

Still, Bobby publicly made their lives together seem perfect. As he once boasted to *People*, "Emily and I go out every Wednesday night. No matter what, we have a date. Then we spend two nights a week at home with the kids. On Tuesday night I baby-sit and she goes out. On Monday night I go out and she baby-sits." He said he awakened every morning at sunrise, fed his animals, ran three miles, and then helped Emily get the kids ready for school, painting himself as the perfect husband and father.

By 1990, the eighth year of their troubled marriage, when RFK III was six and Kick was two, Emily decided to return to her career as a lawyer, at least on a part-time basis. She and her longtime friend and roommate from law school, Alexandra Cury, shared an office in Tribeca, in downtown Manhattan, but Emily worked mostly from home. Her off-and-on practice would continue for about five years, until after she and Bobby split.

More serious than the parties at their home in Mount Kisco was "Bobby's womanizing, and Emily knew what was going on," a close source revealed years later. "Whatever relationships Bobby had, he had, and people were aware of it. Emily definitely knew. I don't want to sugarcoat it, but there wasn't a lot of fighting about it, there wasn't a lot of acrimonious finger-pointing."

WHEN HIS NAMESAKE, RFK III, was eight, and his daughter Kick was four in 1992, Bobby separated from Emily, who had been a loyal, loving Kennedy wife, who had helped see him through his addiction, and who had and would remain tight-lipped about the hellishness—and the good times—of their union.

As a friend observed, "Emily's always been very protective of Bobby. She has always handled that stuff with grace and class. She'd always say to me, 'Go easy on him.' Emily was never bitter about the separation or divorce, and she didn't fight it. It was a relief for both of them."

Bobby had taken up with a glamorous, stylish brunette, Mary Richardson, a longtime friend of his sister Kerry's, whom he had known from the time she was fourteen. But it wasn't until 1993, when he ran into Mary at an art gallery, that they began a relationship. On a trip to Ireland in the summer of 1993, Bobby proposed to her, and they began planning their wedding, which would take place nine months later, after she was pregnant.

In a sworn affidavit filed in New York Supreme Court some years later involving his plans to divorce her for another woman, Bobby acknowledged that he "fell deeply in love with Mary in 1993. At the time I was in the process of finalizing a separation agreement with my first wife (of 11 years), Emily Black, with whom I had been estranged for over a year."

However, when Bobby proposed to Mary in the Emerald Isle he led her and others close to her to believe that he already was divorced from Emily, according to a source familiar with the situation. It's believed that Mary learned the truth from Bobby around the time that she became pregnant.

Bobby's anxiety level had presumably skyrocketed with his marital issues. That was underscored when he accidentally nearly crippled a woman.

The incident happened about 6:30 P.M. on May 9, 1992, when Bobby, driving Emily's minivan, ran over New York attorney Mary Wallace Anderson's foot as she was trying to get into the vehicle in a parking lot in Garrison, New York, where his Riverkeeper organization was holding its annual Shad Festival. Anderson was there at the invitation of one of her closest friends, Jane Fleetwood, wife of Bobby's longtime pal Harvey Blake Fleetwood. Also in the car was Bobby's son RFK III.

According to a lawsuit Anderson's lawyer, David Gould, filed on September 9, 1993, seeking one million dollars, she claimed to have suffered "serious and severe injuries" to her foot—the painful severing of a nerve that required hospitalization—caused by Bobby's "carelessness and recklessness and negligence . . ."

Looking back on the case some years later, Gould said, "It was a run-of-the-mill-type accident. There was a bunch of people in the car, and she was getting in. He somehow got the feeling everybody was in and somebody yelled, 'Don't go,' but he didn't hear and he backed up and the wheel went over her foot. It really impacted her life. He dropped her off at the hospital the same day.

"It was a simple, open-and-shut accident and there was no real fight over damages that there usually is, but it sort of went the other way. It was very strange. It got very, very contentious. His own lawyer was telling me, 'Don't let him affect you. We should get this case resolved.'"

Bobby's attorney, Joel P. Iannuzzi, assigned by Bobby's insurer, Traveller's, recalled that Bobby had been confrontational, controversial, and had an attitude. "There was definitely a touch of arrogance about the way he spoke and acted."

"What started off lovely, didn't end up lovely. I thought this was going to be a simple case, but it got a lot more involved because Kennedy didn't say what we all thought he was going to say," said Mary Anderson's attorney. "The guy's a real fuck—he just had this attitude of shove it up your ass. He couldn't believe that somebody would ever bring a case against him because he's a Kennedy. It's his entitlement."

In his deposition, according to another well-placed source, Bobby claimed that he was not negligent. When Anderson read Bobby's deposition, she was said to have been shocked, and couldn't believe how he had twisted the facts.

"It got to be very contentious," Anderson's lawyer said, complaining that it should have been a simple case. "Their doctor found the same thing our doctor found. We weren't arguing over damages. She had a really bad nerve injury. But Kennedy was trying to intimidate me by accusing me of mistreating his son during the deposition. It was pure bullshit. He was saying things to me that I could not believe—things like 'You're trapping me, aren't you? You're trying to trap me.' I've been up against the nastiest people in my career, but there were some things regarding him that I just was so upset about. My take on him was negative, negative, negative."

Because a settlement couldn't be reached, a trial date was set for around the time *The Riverkeepers* was due to be published. The cable network Court TV, which covered high-profile cases, had its cameras and reporter ready. But, as Gould noted, "There was no way in hell Kennedy was going to let this go to trial."

At the last minute, a settlement was reached. "Bobby had no input," said Iannuzzi. "The carrier decides whether or not to settle, when to settle, and how much to settle for. It was just a meeting of the minds with the carrier on the number. Bobby definitely wanted the case to settle and not spend days in court, and she probably didn't want to go through it, either."

As Gould stated, "It should have been settled in a week."

ON THURSDAY, MARCH 24, 1994—just days before Bobby and Emily's twelfth wedding anniversary—he flew out of New York City and into the city of Santo Domingo in the Dominican Republic for a nine A.M. hearing to obtain a quickie divorce.

The law there permitted foreigners who arrived by the thousands annually to end marriages in just a few hours. It also was a place where divorce records were difficult to find—a way to keep nosy investigators and journalists from snooping—and were merely handwritten entries in a civil registry office book. Moreover, the records weren't in alphabetical order and usually required the services of a local lawyer who knew his or her way around in order to find the discreet information.

But Bobby's hope of keeping the divorce a secret from the world was dashed when the local daily *El Listín* reported it, and the story was picked by the Associated Press and given wide coverage; in Emily's hometown the local paper's headline a few days later blared "Bloomington Marriage of '80s, Black-Kennedy, Ends in Divorce."

At the moment his divorce was ratified in the Caribbean nation, his girlfriend back at home, Mary Richardson, was six months pregnant with Bobby's baby.

When Bobby and Emily initially separated, a close friend maintained, Richardson wasn't the primary reason. "Bobby left Emily for a new life, and Mary was a part of that, but it wasn't like a quid pro quo; it wasn't like he was replacing Emily with Mary. It wasn't like Bobby suddenly came to Emily and said, 'I'm in love with Mary now.' But Mary was always around. She was pretty close to everyone in the Kennedy family, she was Kerry Kennedy's best friend, and spent a lot of time with them. I know she liked being a part of the Kennedys, she liked the social acceptance, and she liked to be a part of something bigger and more interesting. She liked the patina of the Kennedys, and she was into that more than Emily *ever* was."

In Bobby's settlement with Emily she got very little but the basics from her multimillionaire husband, an heir to the billion-dollar Kennedy fortune.

The woman who went through hell and back with him was said to have received half of the value of their Mount Kisco home, and was permitted to stay there until she remarried and moved to Washington, D.C.—about a year after the divorce. Emily also received an undisclosed amount of alimony that was surrendered when she remarried, and child support that was adjusted down with her new marriage. She also got joint custody.

Under the agreement, the couple's children, RFK III and Kick, spent two weekends each month with Bobby and his second wife, Mary Richardson, and most of every summer at the Kennedy compound on the Cape. There was one other demand made of Emily: As part of the custody agreement, she was not permitted to move beyond a fifty-mile radius of Mount Kisco, a condition that was removed when the child support amount was adjusted downward following her second marriage.

Forty-year-old Bobby had become one of the first members of the Kennedy clan to be divorced since his uncle Ted, who was fifty when he filed for divorce just before Christmas 1982 from his forty-eight-year-old wife, Joan. In the senator's case, an "irretrievable breakdown" in their marriage was cited as the official reason. In Bobby's case, he was granted what was known in the Dominican Republic as a "mutual consent divorce." It meant he didn't have to prove a cause for ending his union with Emily, he just needed her mutual agreement, which she was said to have gladly given; she wanted out of the marriage as much as he did.

Unlike Bobby, who had surreptitiously flown to the Dominican Republic to get a divorce in secret, Ted and Joan Kennedy ended their union openly in Barnstable, Massachusetts, during a half-hour session in the court clerk's office, and with a reporter actually taking notes nearby. Under state law, their divorce became final a year later; with pregnant Mary Richardson waiting for him to make her an honest woman, Bobby's divorce was instantaneous.

It had been Ted Kennedy who had recommended that Bobby finalize his divorce in the Dominican Republic because the Kennedy family had a close friend in residence there who could be available if needed, and possibly ease the way if necessary. That friend was present at the start of Bobby's marriage and nearby when the divorce papers were signed: He was Father Gerry Creedon, who had co-officiated at Bobby and Emily's gala nuptials in Bloomington. From 1991 to 1995, Creedon had been a colleague of Bishop José Grullón of the Diocese of San Juan de la Maguana in the Dominican Republic. Known as the Banica Mission, it was in partnership with Creedon's Northern Virginia diocese, encompassing Hickory Hill.

The Rev. Terry Ewing, who had co-officiated with Creedon at the Kennedy–Black wedding, recalled years later that he had heard that Bobby had sought an annulment so he could be married in the Catholic Church the next time around; gossip about the marriage being annulled was rife in the press and among people who knew Bobby and Emily.

"It was really sad to hear that," said Ewing, "because at that point Bobby and Emily had two children, and under Catholic doctrine when marriages are annulled the marriage doesn't exist anymore so the children don't exist. When a marriage is annulled those people are erased."

In 2013, however, Creedon said he was unaware that Bobby had been granted an annulment, "but it's possible. I participated in the premarriage preparation, but I was not involved in the divorce," and he claimed he didn't even know that Bobby had obtained his divorce in the Dominican Republic, where Creedon was stationed at the time. Explaining that his relationship with the Kennedy family "is quite confidential," he added, "I'm always disappointed when a marriage doesn't work out."

Along with being Ethel Kennedy's spiritual leader, Father Creedon had become part of Ethel and Ted Kennedy's social circles, and was a regular at special Kennedy family events, holidays, and parties. Just a week before the "Lion of the Senate" died from a brain tumor in August 2009, Creedon "had the pleasure," he said, of celebrating Mass with him, and during those last days when he was visiting the dying Kennedy, Creedon had stayed at Hickory Hill with Ethel.

TWENTY-EIGHT

Another Bride

Bobby Kennedy Jr.'s beloved Hudson River was the setting for his second marriage, to his new beloved, Mary Richardson, a New York architectural designer who had been a Kennedy family disciple—"groupie," some who knew her called her—from the time she was a teenager.

Just twenty-one days after securing his quickie Dominican Republic divorce, and almost a year after proposing marriage, forty-year-old Bobby wed his thirty-four-year-old girlfriend, who was six months pregnant. The ceremony took place aboard the Hudson Riverkeeper's research vessel, the *Shannon*, on Income Tax day, Friday, April 15, 1994.

Like Bobby, his new bride came from a sprawling Catholic family—she had six siblings—so there was a Roman Catholic Mass followed by the marriage ceremony officiated by a New York State Supreme Court judge, Donald N. Silverman. The jurist wasn't selected at random. Bobby had campaigned for Silverman's judgeship in the past, and the two had affiliation at Pace University Law School.

When he got home to Westchester after the ceremony, Silverman told his wife the Kennedy ceremony, which he thought would be a big, glittery affair, was "bare bones on a barge," she recalled years later after her husband had died. Just a handful witnessed Bobby's second betrothal, including his two children from his marriage to Emily—nine-year-old RFK III and six-year-old Kick. Afterward there was a picnic lunch on board with some friends and family members.

IT WAS ALMOST AS IF Bobby's bride had been born a Kennedy. She'd practically become a member of the family in her mid-teens, a couple of years after her father, a professor at the Stevens Institute of Technology, in Hoboken, New Jersey, died of colon cancer. Mary, whose mother was a public-school English teacher, was a student at Putney, an ultraliberal coed boarding school in Vermont, where she became friends with Bobby's sister Kerry, the seventh of RFK and Ethel Kennedy's eleven.

Bobby once claimed to *The New York Times* that Mary, after her father's death, had run away from home for six months, joining a puppet theater group. It was a bizarre thing to say, since Mary was only twelve when Professor Richardson died. In fact, her only connection to puppetry was as a child, when she and some of her siblings worked summers at the Bread and Puppets theater group in Vermont. It was a mystery to some of those who knew Mary as to why Bobby made up the story.

After Mary and Kerry bonded, Mary spent practically every weekend and vacation with the RFK branch of the Kennedy family, and the two women remained lifelong friends.

After graduating from Putney, where Mary was "the smartest student," according to Kerry, both girls went to Brown University, where they roomed together, and where Mary got straight A's. Later she was a top student at the Rhode Island School of Design. The two continued to room together until they were thirty, when Kerry married a scion of the powerful Cuomo political dynasty—four years before Bobby wed Mary.

"We were inseparable," Kerry recalled. "[W]e shared friendships, a closet, a cash card. People couldn't tell our voices apart."

When Bobby's brother Joe started his heating-oil-for-the-poor business, Citizens Energy, in Boston, Mary, who was then just seventeen, designed the company's first annual report, along with the firm's logo. When Joe ran for Congress the first time, Mary was active in his campaign. As part of her volunteer work, she solicited restaurants to donate fancy foods for the Election Day celebration. She also volunteered to help the RFK Center for Justice and Human Rights—and all of this was years before she even had a single romantic thought about Bobby, who was usually off chasing other women.

Glamorous, sophisticated, creatively talented, and single, Mary had become part of the pop artist Andy Warhol's hip downtown scene, which included such Kennedys as Bobby and his cousin John Jr. Mary worked for a time for Warhol, and when Ted Kennedy was running for the presidency in 1980 she conceived a way to raise funds for him—Artists for Kennedy. She got the likes of Robert Rauschenberg, Roy Lichtenstein, and Julian Schnabel to donate along with "everyone else who walked through the doors of the Factory," Warhol's downtown headquarters.

"At twenty, she raised millions," Kerry said.

In Warhol's gossipy diary, edited and published posthumously in 1989—all 839 pages of it—there were about a dozen mentions of Mary, as well as men in whom she had shown a romantic interest, none of them a Kennedy.

One was John Stockwell Samuels IV, a good-looking Harvard student who also modeled and was a platinum member of Warhol's circle. He had posed in *Interview* magazine and was commissioned to model by Armani. Moreover, he had run around with the Nicaraguan beauty Bianca Jagger, Mick's wife, and was part of the young Kennedy circle. But the Richardson girl had eyes for him.

Warhol had noted in his diary that he and some other swells including Bianca Jagger were all supposed to meet at a fancy Manhattan restaurant for a late dinner. "Mary Richardson had called," Warhol wrote, "and I guess was hinting that she wanted me to invite John Samuels, but I didn't get the hint. . . . It was confusing, everyone was playing different games."

In the summer of 1980, Mary, along with Kerry and Bobby's brother Michael's future wife, Vicki Gifford, daughter of the NFL star Frank Gifford, were together in Monte Carlo, where Warhol had a showing and where the girls—and the artist—ogled Sylvester Stallone, who, according to Warhol, was "all in white, and he looked really beautiful." The next day Warhol wanted to introduce Mary and Kerry to Grace Kelly's son, Prince Albert, but he wasn't interested.

Back in New York, Mary had become friends with Warhol's business manager, Fred Hughes, and along with the artist they attended a glitzy party at Manhattan's chic Le Club, where there was a celebration in honor of Michael Kennedy and Vicki Gifford's upcoming wedding. The paparazzi were out in force because a gaggle of Kennedys were in attendance—Jean Kennedy Smith, Eunice Kennedy Shriver, JFK Jr. and his sister, Caroline. Only Jackie and Ted were missing, Warhol noted, adding in his diary that Bobby "gave the best speech, he'll probably be better than Teddy, he'll probably be the one [meaning President] . . . Kerry wrote some songs and they all sang them. Mary kissed all the boys, she knew them all."

Afterward, Mary, Kerry, Fred Hughes, and Warhol "and a bunch of boys" took a limo to a party being thrown by Calvin Klein and Elton John.

At a Christmas party in 1980, Fred Hughes had brought Mary and one of Bobby's cousins. Warhol wrote in his diary, "I was taking pictures of this handsome kid I thought was a model and then I was embarrassed because it turned out to be John-John Kennedy." While Mary knew and liked JFK Jr., she never dated him.

In the summer of 1981, Mary, according to Warhol, was looking for work—modeling work, apparently—and Warhol had arranged for her to have a meeting with his friend the designer who went by the name of Halston, Roy Halston Frowick. He had made his name and fame as the "premier fashion designer of all America," according to *Newsweek*, when he conceived the famous pillbox hat for Bobby's aunt Jacqueline that she wore at his uncle's inauguration. Instead of showing up for the meeting, however, Mary had lunch with another popular designer, Bill Blass. Warhol was miffed, writing that Blass "was going to pay her $500 an hour to model, and so she was thrilled about that and wasn't even going to see Halston, after I'd gone to all the trouble of getting her the appointment."

In the spring of 1982, Warhol ran into Mary and she told him that she was going to marry a close friend of John Samuels's, one Carlos Mavroleon, who had been Samuels's roommate at Harvard.

Mavroleon was the son of a wealthy Greek shipping tycoon, Manuel Basil "Bluey" Mavroleon, who had settled in England and whose wealth was on a par with that of Aristotle Onassis. One of Bluey's four wives was a granddaughter of Somerset Maugham; Carlos's mother was a Mexican socialite, and his brother, Nicholas Mark "Nicky" Mavroleon, had been one of the three husbands of the Nicaraguan-American actress Barbara Carrera, best known for playing a seductive "Bond Girl" in the 007 movies.

If Bobby's aunt Jackie could marry a Greek shipping mogul, the gorgeous and confident Mary Richardson figured so could she—or at least the mogul's son. While Mary never compared herself to Mrs. Onassis, she did fall in love with Mavroleon. But it wasn't his wealth that had attracted her; she truly loved him. Mavroleon was close to the Richardson family, and Mary and Mavroleon had what a friend described as a "deep and passionate" relationship, "a real and strong intimacy." They had, in fact, talked marriage, but the seriousness of that talk was anybody's guess.

Warhol was surprised by Mary's claim of intending to marry Carlos, who had been educated at Eton, Princeton, and Harvard, and was as close to the Kennedys, especially Bobby, as he was to the Richardsons. Mainly, Warhol was surprised because he had detected in Carlos a minor speech impediment that Warhol had linked stereotypically to effeminate homosexuals. "It'd be funny," he remarked, "if he was a straight person with a lisp, but I don't know."

Mavroleon wasn't gay, and Mary Richardson actually did have an intense relationship with him in the early 1980s—when he was working on Wall Street and doing a lot of cocaine and any other drug he could procure. His brother recalled that when Carlos was "having a good time, he just wanted to get high." In many ways he was a fast-moving, smooth operator like the character played by Leo DiCaprio in *The Wolf of Wall Street*, even down to the slicked-back hair and two-thousand-dollar suits, but very bright and sophisticated.

Besides dating Bobby Kennedy's future second wife, Mavroleon also was involved briefly with a blond Barbie-doll-like secretary by the name of Fawn Hall. She had made headlines in the early '80s when she became embroiled in the infamous Iran–Contra scandal while working for Lt. Col. Oliver North at the National Security Council in Washington. Later, when she was married to the former manager of the Doors and living in the Hollywood Hills, she reportedly became addicted to crack cocaine and had to go into rehab after an overdose.

While Hall survived her addiction, Carlos Mavroleon didn't. The forty-year-old heir to a fortune of more than $100 million was found dead in August 1998 of a heroin overdose in a dumpy fifteen-dollar-a-night hotel room in the town of Peshawar near the Afghan border. His brother remarked in the wake of the tragedy that Carlos did drugs like some people took a drink.

When word filtered back about his sudden death, Ethel Kennedy, who had much experience with sons on drugs, was said to have called the Clinton White House to get details of what had happened to Mavroleon, whom she adored.

Mavroleon had been, as the *Observer* newspaper in London later reported on his life and death, "a war correspondent, a Wall Street broker, a lover of glamorous women from glamorous political dynasties (the Kennedys) and from less glamorous ones. . . . With his money and connections, he was soon mixing with the best of America's East Coast society. He was a favored guest of the Kennedy clan."

SEVENTEEN MONTHS AFTER BOBBY tied the knot for the second time, so did his first wife, Emily. It was a real-life fairy-tale romance.

The new man was another Robert—Robert Damuth, handsome and bright, her senior by five years, who had from the age of thirteen grown up in Bloomington, one of three children. In a curious way he and Emily had always had a connection, because when the Damuth family moved from Minneapolis to Bloomington, they actually had a house on the same block where his future wife was living, but he didn't get to know Emily then, and wouldn't for some years.

Fast-forward to Thanksgiving 1980, when Emily and Bobby came up from their classes at UVA Law—he to spend the holiday with the Kennedys at Hickory Hill in Virginia, and Emily to see a friend from Bloomington, Mary Johnson, who had come down to Washington from New York, where she was pursuing an acting and singing career. At the time Damuth, a bachelor, was living in the nation's capital and working as an economic consultant.

Rather than have turkey dinner at the Kennedys', Emily and Johnson accepted Damuth's invitation to celebrate Thanksgiving with him. It was then that Damuth met Emily for the first time. For him, it was love at first sight; not so much for her: she was tied up with Bobby, whom she would marry seventeen months later.

A couple of years after he had met Emily, Damuth fell for a younger woman, and they lived together for eight years before being married for three.

But whenever he was in New York, he and Emily, for whom he had been pining ever since he first laid eyes on her over turkey and pumpkin pie, would meet; he sensed a connection, and apparently so did she.

A few months after Bobby divorced Emily, Damuth's marriage also ended. Not long after, he called his and Emily's friend Mary Johnson, who was then a singer at a small club in Manhattan's trendy SoHo district, told her that he was single again, and indicated that he would like to get together with Emily.

Realizing that there might still be a match for her two recently divorced friends, Johnson invited Damuth to hear her sing at her club, and made sure that Emily also was there that night. Johnson had known for a long time that Emily was miserable living with Bobby, but had felt uncomfortable going behind her back and telling Damuth.

Over drinks that night at the club, sparks flew and each of them revealed that they had always been jealous of the other's marriage, thinking they were leading wonderful lives, which they weren't, and that maybe they now should finally be together.

The next day was RFK III's tenth birthday, and Emily invited Damuth to the home in Mount Kisco where Bobby now lived with his new wife, Mary. Emily had also invited a number of her friends to the celebration, had passed the word that Damuth was a serious contender for marriage, and asked them to give her their opinion of him.

And that weekend in Manhattan they decided they had always been meant to be together.

The Hollywood ending happened on September 23, 1995, when Emily Black—she had dropped the Kennedy name—married Robert Damuth in a quiet ceremony in their home in Washington.

The newlyweds would share RFK III and Kick with Bobby and his new wife, but that would not always be a pleasant situation.

TWENTY-NINE

Sibling Scandals

Bobby's divorce and remarriage to pregnant Mary Richardson had escaped the usual media frenzy. But marital and other scandals engulfed the Kennedys in the decade of the 1990s, igniting banner headlines, and with Bobby usually somehow involved. All of it placed a dark and devastating cloud over America's most controversial family.

Among the most horrific of those contretemps involved Michael LeMoyne Kennedy—his middle name was in honor of Lem Billings—the sixth of Ethel and RFK's mostly unruly mob of eleven.

Bobby had always found his brother, whom he believed was their mother's "favorite," quite a card. As he once put it, "I doubt that I ever went ten minutes with Michael without laughing."

As an example, when the joker was fifteen, around 1973, he touched off what could have become a serious international incident by spinning a bizarre long-distance tale from Argentina, where he had gone with a cousin, one of Jean Kennedy Smith's kids, Steve Smith Jr., for a rich kids' summer vacation of skiing. At the time, Argentina was a dangerous place for such famous and wealthy young scions to be hanging out, because the country was experiencing a rash of high-profile kidnappings.

Soon after the boys arrived, an urgent telegram addressed to Michael's mother arrived at Hickory Hill in Virginia—a frightening missive that sent Ethel Kennedy into a state of panic.

It read: "*We are holding Michael and Stevie captive, will accept no ransom.*"

Ethel had naturally taken the telegram seriously. Before she actually read the name of the sender, she instantly telephoned the State Department, and a red alert was sounded: an airborne commando force immediately was readied to be deployed to Buenos Aires to rescue the boys.

The urgent mission, however, was hastily aborted when the Kennedy widow called back her contact at State and read him the telegram's signature, which she presumably hadn't taken the time to read, such was her initial fright.

It was signed, "*Ten love-hungry Argentine Women.*"

The telegram underscored two things about Michael Kennedy, even as a teen: his reckless ways and his obsession with the ladies.

Michael, it was clear, liked to live on the edge.

That was demonstrated following reports that he'd become sexually involved as a married father of three in his thirties with his family's teenage babysitter, Marisa Verrochi.

As Bobby would later ironically describe Michael, he was "a pied piper" to "every child he ever met."

VICKI GIFFORD, DAUGHTER OF THE famed football star and TV sports personality Frank Gifford, had never seriously dated anyone before Michael. When he was twenty-four, he asked Vicki, a year younger, for her hand in marriage. They had first met when he was boarding at St. Paul's in Massachusetts, and Vicki was staying one summer at Hickory Hill as a guest of Ethel Kennedy, who was playing Cupid.

The Giffords and the Kennedys went way back. In the 1970s, when RFK's widow was going out with a number of boldface, powerful men in politics and media—but swearing to friends she'd never remarry—she frequently was seen with the good-looking Frank Gifford, who was ending the first of his marriages.

As Gifford later stated, "It was Ethel who brought my daughter Vicki into the Kennedys' orbit."

Ethel had used her influence with her brother-in-law Ted, the senator, to get sixteen-year-old Vicki a summer internship in his Washington office, and had asked the girl to stay with her at Hickory Hill for the duration. Michael's future wife also got into the *Congressional Record*, courtesy of the senator, who quoted from a high school paper she had written on the inequity of women's education.

The Kennedy–Gifford wedding was held on March 14, 1981, at the Roman Catholic Park Avenue Church of St. Ignatius Loyola, and the bridesmaids wore actual nightgowns that had been custom-made in Switzerland at seventy-five dollars each. The reception was on the roof of the St. Regis Hotel, where Andy Warhol was asked by Bobby to trade ties—and, even more curious, pants—with him; Bobby would later usually wear the tie to most every wedding he ever attended.

Frank Gifford thought his new son-in-law, Michael, had a "spooky resemblance" to RFK. Gifford also believed that one day Michael had the goods to be elected president, and envisioned his daughter Vicki as the nation's First Lady.

But all of that was before Gifford had come to know his son-in-law as a booze-guzzling, cocaine-snorting sex addict who was cheating on his beloved daughter.

ONE OF THE FIRST TO witness the relationship between Michael Kennedy and his family's babysitter was his cousin Michael Skakel, one of Ethel Kennedy's nephews. Kennedy had arrived at Skakel's weekend ski chalet in Windham, New York, with his three children, Kyle Francis, Michael LeMoyne Jr., and Rory.

In Vicki's place was the babysitter, who had been on the job since she was twelve—the gorgeous, blond teenager Marisa, daughter of Paul Verrochi, a wealthy Boston businessman. He sat on the board of then Massachusetts gubernatorial hopeful Joseph Patrick Kennedy II's Citizen's Energy Corporation, and Verrochi was a major Democratic fundraiser who had been considered for an ambassadorship in the Clinton administration.

As Skakel and his wife watched in shock, Michael and Marisa drank heavily and openly sexually played with each other.

"Michael asked her for a back rub and lay on the sofa while she straddled him and rubbed lotion on him," Skakel claimed in the proposal for an unpublished late-nineties tell-all entitled *Dead Man Talking: A Kennedy Cousin Comes Clean*. The proposal had a most provocative subtitle: "The First Account by an Insider of the Avarice, Perversion, and Gangsterism of America's Royal Family."

Michael and Vicki Kennedy's young children were aware of his blatant five-year relationship with the Verrochi girl, Skakel claimed. He recalled being on a rafting trip with Michael and his brood—once again, Vicki was not present—when Michael and Marisa, who had disappeared for a while, returned to the campfire from the woods. When someone asked where'd they'd been, Marisa devilishly asked Michael with a wink, "Yeah, where have *you* been?"

Skakel happened to look over at his cousin's son, Michael LeMoyne Jr. "He was not only not laughing," Skakel noted, "but the depth of pain and confusion in his eyes frightened me. What a burden for a thirteen-year-old kid to have to carry."

As a friend of Marisa's at their exclusive private school said at the time the scandal broke in the press in the spring of 1997, "She used to brag all the time about sleeping with the Kennedy guy. But nobody believed her until the stories came out." Another of the teen's friends told a reporter, "She told people she had been caught in bed with him."

At the time, Michael Kennedy was the campaign manager for what would be the successful 1994 U.S. Senate reelection of his sixty-two-year-old uncle, Ted, who was running against the forty-seven-year-old conservative Mormon Republican businessman Mitt Romney. The senator had a close friendship with, and affection for, Michael. Back in 1977, of all of Ted's nephews and nieces, only the Harvard sophomores Michael and his cousin Caroline Kennedy were invited to accompany him on his first and only trip to China.

ON THE SAME WEEKEND THAT Rose Kennedy died on January 22, 1995, at the very ripe old age of 104, Michael Skakel drove Michael Kennedy

to Father Martin's Ashley, a fancy private Catholic alcohol and drug rehab facility in Havre de Grace, Maryland, for treatment for his "out of
control behavior" as an alcoholic and what Skakel termed as his "many
other infidelities" in addition to the babysitter.

At the matriarch's wake, Joe Kennedy confronted Skakel, demanding to know where he had installed his brother for rehab. When Skakel
described the facility, his cousin began laughing. "Michael doesn't have
a booze problem!" Joe Kennedy declared, according to Skakel. "Michael
has a pee-pee problem! What happened? Did he get caught fucking that
babysitter?"

Michael Kennedy's trip to rehab had followed within hours the shocking discovery by Vicki Gifford Kennedy of her husband in bed with
Marisa Verrochi in one of the Kennedys' spare bedrooms at their home.

Kennedy had blamed his drinking for his illicit affair with the teenage babysitter and family friend, and his wife believed him for the time
being.

When Verrochi turned to Skakel to determine what she should do
about Kennedy, he asked his cousins Bobby and Joe for help. Both adamantly refused, Skakel claimed.

According to Skakel, Bobby's response was, "I don't see how that's
any of your business," and his brother Joe's retort was, "My brother can
fuck anybody he wants."

On his own, Skakel took Verrochi to a therapist, who suggested that
she tell her parents about her illicit and illegal relationship.

Around that time, Michael Kennedy was caught stalker-like on a security camera breaking into the garage where the teenager kept her car. He
left behind a bizarre offering—an "artificial penis" that he had attached
to the windshield.

As Skakel claimed, "He was dangerous."

Michael Kennedy's family—particularly his brothers Bobby and Joe
and their mother, Ethel—faced with the magnitude of the scandalous
situation, closed ranks and began, as Skakel put it, "circling the wagons
to protect the cesspool."

When Michael Kennedy got wind that Skakel was assisting and
advising Marisa Verrochi, and that she was finally telling all to her
parents, he went ballistic. Skakel recalled Kennedy declaring, "Oh, my

God, oh, Jesus, I'm going to go to jail. How could you do this to me, Skakel? Who the fuck do you think you are? You've gone off the fucking reservation! What the fuck do you think you're doing, taking Marisa to a therapist? I had her under control. Now you fucked everything up."

Skakel claimed that Kennedy told him, "What if I got Vicki pregnant? What do you think? If we had another kid on the way, they wouldn't put me in jail, would they? And that would take Vicki's mind off all of this for a while, too."

Kennedy subsequently did a stint in an Arizona rehab center for his sex addiction, and he followed one of the rules set down for him: identify in writing the names of all of the women with whom he had had sexual trysts. (A few years later, Bobby, in a diary, would do something similar.)

When the sordid details of Michael Kennedy's philandering were revealed, Vicki Gifford Kennedy—shocked by the number of women with whom he obsessively had had sex, some of whom she knew—took their children in the spring of 1997 and left him after sixteen years of a troubled marriage.

A statement released to the Associated Press stated: "We have reached this decision amicably. Out of respect for our families, we hope the press and public will understand our wish to decline further comment on this personal matter."

The story of the Kennedy–Verrochi affair broke in *The Boston Globe* shortly thereafter.

Having turned eighteen and become a college freshman, Marisa finally decided to confess all to her parents. Her mother was so devastated that the next day she climbed to the roof of the trendy six-story Boston building where she and her husband had a chic apartment and threatened to jump. According to reports, a spokesman for the family denied that suicide was the motive.

IN EARLY JULY 1997, the recently appointed Republican district attorney of Norfolk County, Massachusetts, Jeffrey Locke, revealed that the Verrochis had decided not to pursue a prosecution of the thirty-nine-year-old Kennedy scion. Sex with someone under the age of sixteen constituted statutory rape in the Bay State, and a conviction could result in a life sentence.

Locke disclosed that Marisa Verrochi, who had recently turned nineteen, had let it be known through her attorney that she wouldn't participate further in the investigation of her former lover Michael Kennedy and would, in fact, invoke her Fifth Amendment right not to testify if called. As a result, the case was dropped.

The usually verbose Bobby, who had remained quiet throughout the scandal, had a few words to say after the district attorney's announcement. "A lot of people's lives have been ruined," he observed. "I feel most about the children. I think it's a tragedy for everyone who is involved."

In June 1997, *The New York Times* published a "Special Report," headlined: "Struggling to Please the Father Who Died." The story noted that "the children of Robert Kennedy and their cousins are lumped together and stained by the stumblings and exploits of a few: by the alcohol and drug abuse, the arrests, the sex scandals."

Bobby's drug issues were highlighted, including his trips to "Harlem to buy heroin." He was quoted as saying, "I had impulses. At the time, it seemed kind of innocent, almost like a political statement . . . then it turned into something else. I hadn't seen it coming." And he added, "All of us are blessed not only with gifts but with profound personal struggles. I went through a long period where I was knowingly living against conscience."

Vanity Fair in August 1997 published a similar story under the headline "Bobby's Kids." The "family values" of RFK's brood were compared to those of "the Mafia." Bobby was portrayed as a daredevil who had conquered his drug addiction.

IN THE AFTERMATH OF THE babysitter sex scandal, the Ethel and RFK branch of the Kennedy dynasty celebrated Michael's freedom in the posh ski resort of Aspen, Colorado, where they had wintered for decades, and where some of them also had gotten into trouble.

One of the Kennedys' favorite games on the slopes of Aspen was

ski-football—tossing footballs or various other objects while on skis—
and they were playing it again on New Year's Eve 1998 on their favorite
snow-covered field, Ajax Mountain. They weren't even using a real football that day but rather were said to have been tossing a bottle filled
with water. Bobby's close friend Harvey Blake Fleetwood was in the
game, and it was Fleetwood who threw the fatal final pass that Michael
caught over his shoulder.

In a split second he had slammed headfirst into a birch tree. He died
of massive head injuries on arrival at Aspen Valley Hospital. He was
thirty-nine.

AT HIS FUNERAL AT THE old wooden Roman Catholic church—Our
Lady of Victory—in Centerville, Massachusetts, Bobby asserted that the
personal issues his brother had faced involving the sex scandal "were
about humanity and passion. His transgressions were the kind that Christ
taught us were the first and easiest to forgive. Those of us who know the
truth know that so much of what Michael suffered over the last year was
unfair, and yet every indignity was endured in dignified silence. . . . He
stayed sober. He refused to run away. . . . And he never stopped having
fun.

"Michael's friends can take comfort that because he did his penance here on earth, he went straight to Heaven and now sits with Father
and David and Lem and Jack and Kick and Joe and Grandma and
Grandpa, almost certainly laughing and waiting to greet the rest of us as
we arrive."

THIRTY

Annulment Tell-all

Bobby's politician brother Joe's own controversial marital issues had surfaced in the midst of his brother Michael's sex scandal. It seemed as if the whole third generation was imploding.

Joe and his wife, Sheila Brewster Rauch Kennedy—a Harvard-educated, Philadelphia Main Line socialite, mother of their twin sons—had been married for some twelve years when Kennedy became romantically involved with Anne Elizabeth "Beth" Kelly, a pretty onetime temp he had hired at Citizens Energy, his Boston company that supplied heating oil to the poor.

When Sheila married Kennedy, she had her own non-Catholic minister standing next to her groom's Roman Catholic priest, and she was the one who filed for divorce. The marriage had been an emotional roller coaster for Sheila. Even though she had a master's degree from the Harvard School of Design, Kennedy often denigrated and bullied her, she claimed, calling her a "nobody."

Joe—Ethel and RFK's first son—had earned a reputation as a bully. As his cousin Christopher Kennedy Lawford eloquently noted, "By the time Joe hit the testosterone-producing years of puberty, he had developed a fairly regular addiction to punching someone over something." Lawford recalled that Bobby often was the brunt of Joe's violence, and had suffered a "lifetime of beatings" from his older brother.

While Kennedy often allegedly berated Sheila, like he had berated and bullied his brothers and cousins years earlier, the woman who would become the second Mrs. Joe Kennedy, Beth Kelly, was different in his eyes. She initially impressed him mainly because "she was someone who could really type and get all the grammar and punctuation right," he once avowed after he hired the twenty-five-year-old temp at Citizens Energy in 1982.

Beth Kelly had risen to the post of director of special projects at the firm, and Kennedy described her as its "heart and soul." When he won his first congressional election in 1986, she went to Washington with him and became his scheduler and personal secretary and, as a friend said, "pretty much" managed his professional and personal life. But Kennedy was vociferous in his contention that they hadn't become romantically involved until after he had formally separated from his wife.

When Joe and Sheila were divorced, she got what was described as a nominal settlement and was so cash-poor that she was said to have had to borrow money from her parents to buy a home for her and the two boys.

Two years after his 1991 no-fault civil divorce, he wanted to marry Beth within the Church and in 1993 petitioned the Vatican to grant an annulment of his first marriage, but it had seemingly stalled.

Sheila was mortified when she learned what he was planning, which, in essence, would make it appear as if they had never tied the knot in what had been a big, splashy society wedding in 1973.

In 1997 she shocked the clan and the world by publishing a controversial and well-received book, *Shattered Faith: A Woman's Struggle to Stop the Catholic Church from Annulling Her Marriage.*

In it she declared the annulment "would have rendered their union nonexistent, and their sons would have been regarded as children of an unsanctified union." The book was reviewed positively in *The New York Times* under the headline "A Woman Scorned." But *The Independent*, a liberal British newspaper, called her a "vindictive, embittered, loose cannon of an ex-wife."

In the book, the devout Protestant declared, "I was appalled. My husband and I had known each other for nine years before we married in a Catholic ceremony . . . I could not understand how anyone could claim that our marriage had never been valid."

If she agreed to Kennedy's request for the annulment, she declared, "I would be lying before God."

After the annulment was granted in secret by the Church, Sheila appealed, and a decade after her book was published the annulment was reversed by the Vatican.

As it turned out, thirty-six-year-old Beth Kelly, a Jersey girl, the daughter of a retired Navy pilot and a mother who had been a Navy nurse, became the second Mrs. Joe Kennedy in July 1993. It was a civil ceremony at which Ethel and Ted Kennedy—and Ted's second wife, Vicki—sang "When Irish Eyes Are Smiling" as Joe and Beth walked down the aisle in Joe's home in Brighton, Massachusetts.

Time, in reporting the Vatican's reversal, wryly noted, "The most controversial 'marriage that never was' in recent U.S. political history is back."

The Washington Post reported that all the "messy publicity" about Michael Kennedy's sex scandal and the tangled affairs of Joe Kennedy's own marriage had "combined to smudge the image of the heir apparent to the Kennedy dynasty."

Joe Kennedy had decided to not seek reelection to Congress, which *The New York Times*, in an editorial, declared "runs counter to the family's combative never-say-die image. . . . [C]harges of improper sexual relations with a teen-age baby sitter against his brother Michael had already forced the Congressman to drop out of the Massachusetts governor's race. . . . Even with Mr. Kennedy out of Washington, there is not likely to be any shortage of Kennedys in public life. Nor will there be an end to the complicated feelings aroused by the family's gripping sense of sacrifice and entitlement."

The most swooned-over Kennedy namesake of Bobby's generation, his cousin John F. Kennedy Jr., used the Editor's Letter in the September 1997 issue of his political and pop culture magazine *George* to upbraid Michael and Joe, calling them "poster boys for bad behavior."

Joe Kennedy was furious when he read his more famous and much better-looking cousin's attack—bellowing, "Ask not what you can do for your cousin, ask what you can do for his magazine," which was a snarky play on JFK's famous January 20, 1961, inauguration speech: "And so, my fellow Americans, ask not what your country can do for you, ask what you can do for your country."

JFK Jr. didn't play gentle.

He wrote, in part:

> *Two members of my family chased an idealized alternative to their life. One left behind an embittered wife, and another, in what looked to be a hedge against mortality, fell in love with youth and surrendered his judgment in the process. Both became poster boys for bad behavior. Perhaps they deserved it. Perhaps they should have known better. To whom much is given, much is expected, right?*

The very public assault, pitting a Kennedy against Kennedys, made headlines around the world. The respected *Guardian* newspaper in London called it a "virulent and puzzling critique, accompanied by an odd picture of a half-naked John Junior with the apple of temptation, and quite unprecedented for a family who have always circled the wagons when under attack."

Long supportive of Kennedy-style liberal politics, *The New York Times* was uncharacteristically harsh in its editorial assessment of what it called Kennedy's "sophomoric essay." It termed his writing "vapid and chatty," and declared that his critique "is not likely to put much glow on his own image as an editorial stylist and thinker." And the *Times* termed the commentary "another sign of the end of the Kennedys as an entitled political class."

In November 2012, one of Joe and Sheila's twin sons, thirty-two-year-old Joe Kennedy III, became the first Kennedy of his generation to win public office as a congressman from Massachusetts. His mother, who had never remarried, stood on the podium beside him, and later told a reporter, "Joe is very different from his father . . . very hardworking . . . very aware of the need for balance in his life."

THIRTY-ONE

Rape Rap

William Kennedy Smith was the son of Jean Kennedy Smith, who had famously introduced her close Catholic school friend Ethel Skakel to her brother RFK. In 1991, thirty-year-old Willie, as he was called, was a popular fourth-year Georgetown University medical student. But his status changed in the predawn hours of Holy Saturday, March 31, 1991—Easter weekend—after a night of nightclub-hopping in Palm Beach with his uncle, the hard-drinking womanizer Ted Kennedy, and Kennedy's son, Patrick, then a twenty-three-year-old Rhode Island state representative.

At glitzy Au Bar—a hangout for the rich, famous, and louche—Smith had picked up an attractive thirty-year-old habitué, a single mom by the name of Patricia Bowman, who would accuse him of raping her. She claimed that she was assaulted by Smith after they spent time on the beach in front of the Kennedy mansion—the fabulous, Addison Mizner–designed oceanfront estate called La Guerida, which meant "Bounty of War." About a month after the alleged assault, Smith was charged with felony sexual battery and misdemeanor battery. The scandal made world-wide headlines and Palm Beach was invaded by hundreds of journalists.

During the ten-day trial a number of Kennedy family members were in the courtroom en masse to show support for the accused rapist. Among them were Ethel Kennedy and two of her past and future scandal-riddled sons, Bobby and Michael. John F. Kennedy Jr. made an appearance under family pressure, and there was much Palm Beach ladies-who-lunch chatter as to whether his famous mother, Jackie, would make a showing to offer her support. The writer Dominick Dunne, who covered the trial, had been invited to a dinner party at the time and recalled a childhood chum of Jackie's telling a society pal that the Kennedy family would never be able to convince the former First Lady to attend. She didn't and neither did her daughter, Caroline.

Nevertheless, all Kennedys who were present were joyous when the judge ruled out sworn testimony by three other women who claimed they also had been assaulted by Smith in the 1980s but hadn't reported the alleged attacks to authorities out of embarrassment and fear of retribution.

In the end, the six jurors, having heard the testimony of Ted Kennedy and others, returned a not guilty verdict after just seventy-seven minutes of deliberation.

"I have an enormous debt to the system and to God, and I have terrific faith in both of them," the acquitted Smith said after the verdict. His mother said, "I feel relieved."

The prosecutor who tried the case had a far different take, "What you heard during the course of this trial was not an act of love, not an act of sex. It was an act of violence."

Once again, despite Willie Smith's earnest words, there was general suspicion of a cover-up and the use of Kennedy power and influence to bring about a quick acquittal. To some it was another Chappaquiddick ending.

Some years later, in his book proposal, Michael Skakel claimed that during the Michael Kennedy babysitter sex scandal, Skakel had had a conversation with Bobby, who allegedly said of his brother Michael, "Oh my God. He's just like Willie." When Skakel asked what he meant, he claimed Bobby responded that Smith "was guilty of rape, that his acquittal was the result of Kennedy power."

• • •

WHILE JOHN KENNEDY JR. didn't mention Willie Smith in his biting 1997 *George* editorial that lambasted Michael and Joe, he allegedly had a shocking story involving the Palm Beach rape case.

In a little-known December 30, 1993, sworn affidavit given to a member of the U.S. Congress and read into the Congressional Record by Ohio Democrat James Traficant, an acquaintance of Kennedy's, James Ridgway de Szigethy, claimed that JFK Jr. had questioned Smith's innocence. De Szigethy had decided to come forward and volunteer the information because Kennedy had refused to make public what he claimed he knew. An account of the blockbuster affidavit appeared in both the New York *Daily News* and the *National Enquirer.*

De Szigethy, who had voluntarily taken and passed a polygraph examination in connection with the affidavit, stated that JFK Jr., then an assistant district attorney in New York City, had told him that " 'they [the Kennedy family] should have done something about Willie years ago when he first started doing this,' meaning get help for him when he first started raping women."

Kennedy made the revelation to de Szigethy two months after Smith was charged in the Palm Beach case.

"John told me," de Szigethy continued in his affidavit, "that when the [Smith] trial took place, he would have to put in an appearance in the courtroom. He told me he did not want to do this and his mother did not want him to, either. I suggested that he not do it since Willie was guilty, but he told me who was pressuring and why. He said just his presence in the courtroom would make an impression on the jury, which is how they're using me."

As part of the effort to have Smith acquitted, Kennedy also was asked to pose for a news photo with his cousin. In his affidavit, de Szigethy stated he was "livid with John" for doing it. "It was obvious to me he was participating in the campaign of character assassination being waged by his family against Patricia Bowman, and that the photograph—which was peddled to papers all over the world—was part of that campaign.

"At first he denied it," continued de Szigethy in the affidavit. "I asked how it came to be that even though they were on a beach in the middle of nowhere a photographer just happened to be there? I told him it was obvious the photograph was a public expression of confidence and trust in his cousin concocted by the same PR people who were characterizing Ms. Bowman in the press as a 'lying, crazy slut.' John then admitted the photograph was 'staged.' "

The photo, which had appeared in a number of newspapers, had been taken four months after Smith was charged.

"I then asked him if this was his new hobby, committing character assassination against innocent people," de Szigethy stated. "He would not answer nor look me in the eye. He was sitting on the couch and I was standing, walking around. I then called him a 'Profile in Coward-ice' [a play on his father's bestselling, Pulitzer Prize–winning 1957 book, *Profiles in Courage*], and suggested he step forward and vindicate Patricia Bowman.

"I remember every word of the next two angry questions I asked him: 'How does it feel to be a character assassin, John? How does it feel to be Patricia Bowman's Oswald?' He did not say, nor do anything in response—he just sat there, his head hung down in shame. Then after a long, awful silence, he said, 'You just don't understand the pressure I'm under!' "

In a letter to Traficant subsequent to having given his sworn affida-vit, de Szigethy claimed that if Kennedy didn't cooperate in making a public show of support for Smith, he faced the release of personal infor-mation about his private life.

In his letter, de Szigethy used the word "blackmail." When he gave his affidavit, de Szigethy never identified the person he claimed Kennedy had told him was "forcing" him to "prejudice the jury" in the Smith trial. "Everyone," de Szegethy wrote to Traficant, "assumed that it was John's uncle, Teddy, who forced him . . . It was not his uncle."

An aide to Traficant at the time, Lisa Hall, described de Szigethy as "one hundred percent credible. He passed a polygraph test with flying colors. Everything he had to say about his conversations with John F. Kennedy Jr. is completely true and accurate."

Presumably against his will, Kennedy did make appearances at the Smith trial, beginning with two days during the important jury selection process. As expected, his presence received intense media coverage, but he denied to reporters that his visit was in any way an attempt to influence the case.

Traficant had his own legal problems. In the early 2000s, after being convicted of bribery, racketeering, and tax evasion for personally using campaign contributions, he was expelled from the House on a vote of 420 to 1, and served seven years in prison. He died in September 2014 when a tractor on his daughter's Ohio farm flipped over on him. He was seventy-three.

JFK Jr. wasn't the only Kennedy cousin to suspect Smith of having sex, forced or not, with the Bowman woman.

Ted Kennedy's son Patrick—who had been bar-hopping with his father and Smith—had told police that Smith had admitted sleeping with the woman.

"How was she? Did you wear protection?" Kennedy said he asked Smith the next morning, according to media reports. "No," Smith answered, "but thank God I pulled out."

THIRTY-TWO

Killer Cousin?

In 1998, Ethel Kennedy's nephew Michael Skakel, who figured in the Michael Kennedy babysitter scandal and was the cousin who Bobby once claimed had helped him stay clean after his heroin arrest, was implicated in a gruesome murder.

It had happened on the night before Halloween, Mischief Night, in Greenwich, Connecticut, Thursday, October 30, 1975. But the case had gone cold until new evidence linking Skakel began surfacing in the late 1990s. Witnesses whose veracity was questionable claimed that on a number of occasions he had admitted killing pretty, blond, fifteen-year-old Martha Elizabeth Moxley, a popular high school sophomore, a neighbor in whom Skakel—with a history of drinking, drugs, and bad behavior—had a romantic and sexual interest.

A teenager at the time of the crime, he was charged as an adult almost a quarter century later. Moxley had been beaten and bludgeoned, her jeans pulled down to her ankles, but there was no evidence of rape. Her body, facedown, was found under a pine tree on the edge of the Moxley property, in the exclusive, gated enclave of Belle Haven, where Skakel's family had a mansion just across the road.

The murder weapon was a golf club, and the attack had been so vicious that it had broken from the intense blows. Two pieces were found near the Moxley girl's body, and a third had mysteriously vanished.

Investigators soon learned that one of Michael Skakel's brothers, Tommy, then seventeen, was the last to be seen with the Moxley girl. Tommy, along with a new tutor, Kenneth Littleton, who had recently been hired by Ethel Kennedy's widowed brother, Rushton Skakel, to handle his out-of-control children, became the immediate prime suspects. But investigators eventually ruled him out.

The case had made national headlines, mainly because of the Skakels' connection to the Kennedy clan, specifically Ethel's marriage to RFK.

On January 20, 2000, at the age of thirty-nine, a quarter century after the murder, Michael Skakel was formally charged.

And following Skakel's 2002 conviction and sentencing to twenty years to life in prison, his cousin Bobby began waging a staunch defense of him, claiming he was innocent. His assertion was underscored by the publication in *The Atlantic Monthly* of a controversial story he had written about the case, criticizing the prosecutors, the witnesses, and some in the media, and naming those he *suspected* of being guilty.

While Bobby became Skakel's prime supporter within the Kennedy family, he painted a curious portrait of the cousin whom he claimed had helped get him sober from drugs in the early 1980s. In a convoluted letter to a judge in the sensational murder case, Bobby noted that Skakel was "a mix between John Candy, John Belushi and Curly from the Three Stooges . . . an assemblage of flaws . . . an alcoholic from a young age" but had become "the most solidly spiritual person I've ever met [who] carries a rosary and prays daily." He claimed that together they had attended "hundreds of Alcoholics Anonymous meetings . . . I love Michael."

In Bobby's eighteen-page, fourteen-thousand-word magazine piece, Skakel's attorney, Michael Sherman, was attacked for being "an overconfident and less than zealous defense lawyer."

Bobby also questioned the credibility of some of the prosecution witnesses, and he was highly critical of Dominick Dunne and Mark Fuhrman, both of whom wrote books about the case. He quoted Dunne, who died in 2009, as once declaring, "The Kennedys are the greatest soap opera in American history," and noted that Skakel "would get caught in the cross-hairs where Dunne's ambitions intersected with his obsessions."

Dunne, who covered the Skakel trial, clearly wasn't a big fan of Bobby's, either. As he wrote in *Vanity Fair,* "For all his passion about the injustice he feels was done to his cousin Michael, he managed to find time from his [Hudson] River duties to make only two brief appearances at the trial. For the second of these, he arrived late . . . calling attention to himself like a B-movie star as he walked to the front row. . . . The man's sense of entitlement is breathtaking."

In criticizing the media for constantly linking the Kennedys to the Skakels, Bobby pointed out—quite accurately—that the Kennedy and Skakel families were never close. (The long-standing feud between the two families is documented in my 1994 book, *The Other Mrs. Kennedy.*) Without elaborating, Bobby accused the staunchly Republican Skakels of "taking steps against my father that my mother considered hurtful," and he noted that the relationship between the two families was "distant for many years."

Bobby's article dealt with some of the more bizarre facets of the Moxley case, including the Skakels' curious obsession with masturbation as either a sin or a pleasure.

Tommy Skakel, for instance, had once revealed to private detectives hired by their father, Rushton, that he and the Moxley girl had, as Bobby put it, "a 'sexual' encounter . . . that lasted twenty minutes, ending in mutual masturbation to orgasm." The session had happened on the grounds of the Skakel home on the night of the murder.

Bobby claimed he was told by some Skakel siblings that their father considered masturbation "equivalent to the slaughter of millions of potential Christians." Bobby also dealt in the *Atlantic* piece with Michael Skakel's incriminating story of masturbating in a tree outside the Moxley home on the night of the murder, a sordid piece of evidence that had had a profound impact on the jury that convicted him. Michael, who Bobby noted had been "high on pot and alcohol" that night, had initially thought that he was peering into Martha's window, presumably hoping to catch her in the buff. Bobby called his cousin's actions at the Moxley house "a half-hearted attempt to masturbate in the tree before becoming embarrassed and climbing down."

In Michael Skakel's dealings with the private detective firm his father had hired to look into the Moxley murder, the investigators had burst out laughing when the masturbation story came up. "That's when Skakel learned," Bobby explained to *Atlantic* readers, "that the window he had looked in [while stoned] was John Moxley's [her brother], not Martha's. . . . It would later become a common assumption that Michael had masturbated in the tree below which Martha's body was discovered. In fact," Bobby wrote, "the two trees are on opposite sides of the Moxley house, three hundred feet apart."

Bobby noted that the Skakel masturbation story had become so widespread that Jay Leno had even joked about it on *The Tonight Show*. "Leno suggested, referring to the Skakel trial, many people would rather be found guilty of murder than be suspected of masturbating in a tree," recounted Bobby.

In the *Atlantic* piece, Bobby stated: "I support [Skakel] not out of misguided family loyalty but because I am certain he is innocent. . . . To anyone who knew him at the time, the notion that he was the murderer is laughable." Bobby maintained that the evidence pointed to two men: Ken Littleton, the young live-in tutor, and Franz Wittine, the Skakels' German gardener, who lived in the Skakel family's basement. But Bobby then acknowledged, "I do not know that Ken Littleton killed Martha Moxley." He added, however, that the "state's case against Littleton was much stronger than any case against Michael Skakel."

About Wittine, Bobby wrote that the gardener "liked young blondes," was physically powerful, "liked to boast of how he had raped and beaten girls as a soldier during World War II," and had made "lascivious advances" to Michael Skakel's sister Julie. Wittine, however, died in 2000, many months before Skakel's conviction.

If Bobby proved anything, it was that his uncle Rushton was not the best judge of character when it came to hiring people to work in his home.

The Letters to the Editor published in the June 2003 issue of *The Atlantic Monthly* were mostly critical of Bobby Kennedy's impassioned defense of his imprisoned cousin.

Michael Skakel's prosecutor, Jonathan Benedict, for one, didn't hold back his angry reaction.

"What Kennedy avers in his lengthy diatribe consists, almost paragraph by paragraph, of distortions, facts taken out of context, half truths, non-truths, and Skakel family post-conviction revisionism." He asserted that Bobby had chosen to "soft-pedal or ignore most of the state's most incriminating evidence . . . not the least from the thirteen separate witnesses to whom Skakel made either incriminating admissions or outright confessions."

The combative and egotistic RFK scion wasn't about to let his detractors have the last word.

In a reply of more than two columns in the *Atlantic*, Bobby maintained in a prickly and preachy manner that his article had been fact-checked and "rigorously verified" by the magazine, and he stated that the prosecutor, Benedict, had failed to "name a single inaccuracy in my article."

He blatantly declared, "[T]he real murderer is still free . . . all of the key evidence was tainted."

A FEW YEARS AFTER HIS ESSAY in the *Atlantic* was published, Bobby took his defense of Skakel to prime-time television.

In 2008, Bobby, who had repeatedly attacked Skakel's lawyer Mickey Sherman for being a "media whore," was the star himself of a *48 Hours* true-crime special on CBS entitled "The Ghosts of Greenwich," which recounted the Moxley case in dramatic fashion—some of it re-created—using spooky music and lots of quick cuts. The frosted-blond, glossy-lipped CBS correspondent Lesley Stahl served as the narrator and interviewer.

Stahl excitedly reported that Bobby had tracked down a possible witness named Tony Bryant who had suggested that two young African American men had been in all-white Belle Haven on the night of the killing, and Bobby had interviewed them. Stahl termed Bobby's sleuthing "a stunning discovery." But none of what he turned up was considered evidence by the prosecutors. Bobby himself had even acknowledged to Stahl, "They never actually said they killed Martha Moxley."

Bobby went on to accuse Skakel's prosecutor, Jonathan Benedict, in his trial closing, of using "out of context" words that Skakel had said on tape to the writer who was helping him put together the proposal for his Kennedy tell-all book. Bobby claimed that an edit of the words made it sound like Skakel was confessing to the murder when, in fact, he was confessing to masturbating in the tree.

Stahl pursued Bobby's assertion and confronted Benedict. His response was that the weight of all of the evidence spoke for itself, and that the jury agreed. But the program aired a titillating portion of the Michael Skakel tape in which he said, "Oh, my God. I hope nobody saw me jerking off."

Bobby's *Atlantic Monthly* defense of his cousin also was brought up by Stahl, and Bobby said for the first time that the reason he had written it was for "Michael's son, Georgie," so he wouldn't spend his life believing that his father was a murderer. A brief old home movie clip was shown of Skakel lovingly holding his baby son.

If anything, the *48 Hours* program starring the famous Kennedy namesake appeared more sympathetic to the Skakel family than to the true victims, the Moxley family, and it offered no new evidence to clear his cousin.

BOBBY WASN'T THE ONLY KENNEDY family member who had fingered someone else other than Michael Skakel for the murder of Martha Moxley. John F. Kennedy Jr. had his own private theory. He was convinced that Michael's brother Tommy, Greenwich law enforcement's first prime suspect in the case, was somehow involved in the murder.

Moreover, he claimed to a friend that his uncle Ted, along with a prominent Kennedy brother-in-law and a close Kennedy family friend, were allegedly involved in paying "hush money" to certain officials to protect Skakel. "John," the friend stated years later, "told me that Tommy Skakel was involved in the Moxley murder, and the family had been paying off people for years to cover up the whole thing. When John said that Tommy was involved, I took it to mean that Tommy did it. But being involved in the murder doesn't actually mean that he was the one who murdered her. It could have been one of Tommy's brothers and that Tommy was involved in it somehow."

According to what JFK Jr. told his friend, "Teddy had been running

the cover-up for years, seeing to it that certain people were paid off."
The alleged conspiracy, according to JFK Jr., had also involved Jean Ken-
nedy Smith's husband, Stephen Smith, who oversaw the Kennedy family
finances and managed campaigns for JFK, RFK, and Ted Kennedy. When
Smith died in 1990 at sixty-two, Ted described him as "the wisest adviser.
There wouldn't have been a Camelot without Steve Smith."

Regarding the alleged plan to protect Skakel, JFK Jr. told his friend,
"Money went from Kennedy accounts via contributions to certain people,
but he didn't go into detail. . . . We had this big fight, and I was yelling at
him," the friend recalled. "I suggested to John that he come forward and
help the parents of the girl who had been murdered and he gave me a lot
of bullshit that there was nothing he could do."

ON WEDNESDAY, OCTOBER 23, 2013, a week before the thirty-eighth
anniversary of the murder in Greenwich, Connecticut, Appellate Court
Judge Thomas A. Bishop, in attacking Skakel's attorney Michael Sherman's defense, or lack thereof, ordered a new trial. Bobby was as joyous
as was his long-incarcerated cousin.

"A first-year law student from any of my classes would have done a
better job than Mickey Sherman," Bobby declared. "His ambition was to
be a television lawyer and he thought this trial was going to be his
ticket to that career. He told a bar association meeting that he intended
to have a lot of fun at that trial. Michael had an airtight alibi and five
witnesses [his siblings mostly]. Anybody who couldn't win that case
should not be admitted to the bar."

Just in time for Thanksgiving 2013—his first turkey dinner in nearly
a dozen years with family and not fellow felons—Michael Skakel was
given his freedom when a different judge at a hearing on November 20
granted him bail.

The bail, amounting to $1.2 million, was put up by the wealthy
Skakels—one of the convict's brothers, John, turned over the required
bank checks. Skakel was released with the proviso that he never leave the
state of Connecticut without permission, that he always wear a GPS
tracking device attached to his ankle, and that he have absolutely no
contact with the Moxley family.

Bobby said it was "pure joy" to see his cousin stride out of Superior Court Judge Gary White's courtroom in Stamford, Connecticut, with a big smile on his bloated, red-blotched face and decked out in an expensive business suit, blue tie, and white shirt—unencumbered for the first time by handcuffs and ankle shackles.

As *The New York Times* observed, Skakel's release from prison was the "latest twist in a case that has fascinated the public and confounded investigators since 1975 . . . offering a potent mix of power, money and sex. It inspired a made-for-televison movie, and became a staple for tabloids and an unending source of interest for true-crime writers . . . the link to one of America's most famous families fueled additional interest in the case."

THIRTY-THREE

Another Catastrophe

The horrific decade of the 1990s, beset by scandals and tragedies involving the third generation of Kennedys, had ended with still another catastrophe, but also a quarter-million-dollar windfall for Bobby.

Around eight-thirty P.M. on Friday, July 16, 1999, thirty-eight-year-old JFK Jr., at the controls of a Piper Saratoga PA32 II HP, and with his wife, Carolyn, and her sister Lauren Bessette belted in as passengers, took off from Essex County Airport in Fairfield, New Jersey, en route to Martha's Vineyard. There, Kennedy planned to drop off his sister-in-law and then fly on to Hyannis Port, where his cousin Bobby's baby sister, Rory, was to be married on Sunday, July 18.

It was not a good night to fly. As another pilot who was at the airport when the Kennedy party arrived noted, "The weather was very marginal—four to five miles visibility, extremely hazy." That pilot, who also had planned a flight to the Vineyard, decided the weather wouldn't cooperate and smartly canceled his trip.

Kennedy was a neophyte in the air. He had logged no more than a reported two hundred hours flying time and had been a licensed pilot for just over a year. Moreover, he was used to piloting a much smaller plane, a Cessna 182, compared to the larger, high-performance Piper Saratoga. And just a month earlier he had broken an ankle and was still recuperating. Despite everything, he was determined to make the trip; the bags were packed and the plans had been made for a joyful weekend with his family at the compound.

But an hour out of New Jersey, over the Atlantic, and not far from the coast of Martha's Vineyard, Kennedy's plane disappeared.

Most of the clan had already gathered and had retired for the night when notification arrived that John's plane was missing. Bobby, for one, was awakened by his sister Kerry at three A.M. and told the horrific news. "I knew then that John was dead," he wrote in his diary that was leaked and became public in 2013. "The water was sixty-eight degrees so some people had hope they might still be alive but I had none."

Earlier in the evening, Bobby and his wife, Mary, had planned to spend some quality time with John and Carolyn, aware of some problems the couple was facing. A week before, Mary had visited them in their chic downtown Manhattan loft and learned from gorgeous thirty-three-year-old Bessette-Kennedy that her husband was "so depressed," as Bobby noted in his diary, regarding in-fighting involving his sister, Caroline. They had been battling over pieces of their mother's furniture that had been left to them along with Mrs. Onassis's spectacular Vineyard country home, Red Gate Farm.

"John," Bobby noted, "confided to me also about how hurt he was by Caroline's actions," which he didn't describe.

A 1996 Sotheby's auction of some of Mrs. Onassis's things —a sale that had been the former First Lady's idea before she died—had raised $34 million. "But when the dust settled," stated JFK Jr.'s close friend Rob Littell, "John and Caroline received less than $100,000 each" after auction fees and taxes owed on the estates. "It was," Littell asserted, "a far cry from the millions they were reported to have received." Littell remembered the moment Kennedy received his check: "After all that," the multimillionaire scion sputtered, "this is what we get, less than a hundred grand."

Another issue John faced that appeared to be depressing him, according to Bobby's diary, was criticism he had received from his uncle Ted for inviting the *Hustler* magazine founder and publisher, Larry Flynt, to be his guest at a prestigious dinner in Washington for celebrities, media stars, and politicians. Bobby wrote in his diary that the senator had sent his nephew a "disappointed letter" and John felt terrible "because his family is so important."

Because of the problems that were facing John and Carolyn, Bobby and Mary had decided to "go see them this weekend and spend a lot of time with them," Bobby wrote in his diary. On the night before Rory Kennedy's wedding rehearsal dinner, the Robert Kennedy Jr.s had made several attempts to visit John and Carolyn at their house in the compound—the last time as late as 11:30 P.M—but they still hadn't arrived. Only the housekeeper and a friend were there, and dinner was still waiting for them.

Three and a half hours later, Bobby learned that their plane was missing, and he knew instinctively that all were dead.

Unknown at the time, but according to Bobby's diary, even before the bodies were recovered, a battle was brewing between the Kennedy and Bessette families over burial plans. Bessette's mother, Ann Freeman, had wanted burial near the family home in Greenwich. Bobby wrote that she "wants them close by and is terrified that the K family might try to spirit them to Brookline."

He was referring to the cemetery, Holyhood, in the Boston suburb where his brother Michael had been buried just eighteen months before the latest Kennedy tragedy, and where his brother David and the Kennedy patriarch and matriarch had been interred. Bobby revealed that a meeting was arranged in New York attended by Caroline Kennedy's husband, Edwin Schlossberg, and Ted Kennedy's wife, Vicki Reggie, to hash out the burial controversy.

And Bobby made a startling disclosure: "All the Bessette family knows that Ed hated Carolyn and did everything in his power to make her life miserable and . . . he bullied, bullied, bullied the shattered grieving mother." At the tense meeting in New York, Bessette's mother was told, according to Bobby's diary entry, that JFK Jr. would be buried in the family plot and "they could do with Carolyn as they pleased."

In the end, however, it was decided that the crash victims would be cremated and buried in the sea that had claimed their lives.

Some three miles from where Kennedy's plane crashed, the USS *Briscoe*, a Navy destroyer, committed their ashes to the ocean as part of a Roman Catholic ceremony witnessed by seventeen mourning relatives of the victims, among them Kennedy's cousins Bobby and Willie Smith and Kennedy's sister, Caroline, along with two Navy chaplains and a Catholic priest. It had been John Kennedy Jr.'s expressed desire, family members claimed, that he be buried at sea.

In his diary, Bobby noted, "When they let go of the ashes, the plume erupted and settled in the water and passed by in the green current like a ghost. We tossed flowers onto the ghosts. Some of the girls tossed letters from a packet they'd assembled from John's and Carolyn's friends. It was a civil violation but the Coast Guard let it go." He wrote that a Navy band had played "mournful music and we all cried like babies." At the funeral reception his uncle Ted "danced his silly Teddy dances and sang loudly and beautifully and made everyone . . . love him."

But Bobby also made pointed references to his late cousin John's brother-in-law, Ed Schlossberg, Caroline's husband. He noted that at the service for the Bessettes in Greenwich he had tried "to get through as a good soldier and making only positive comments and thoughts" about Schlossberg. But Bobby stated that at one point at the church in New York, Schlossberg stopped Bobby from delivering a eulogy. According to Bobby, the one surviving Bessette sister, Lisa, was told by Schlossberg, "Kennedys don't eulogize non-Kennedys," a reference to her dead sister.

Bobby added another reference to Schlossberg. He wrote that the wife of John Jr.'s close cousin Anthony Radziwill, who died of testicular cancer a month after the plane crash, had called to discuss what she characterized as Schlossberg's despotic and arrogant behavior. "She says she wants to start an 'I Hate Ed Club.' There would be many, many members. John & Carolyn would have certainly applied."

JFK Jr. and Schlossberg had once gotten into a heated dispute after Schlossberg had inserted himself, uninvited, into a project for the John F. Kennedy Center for the Performing Arts in Washington. Once dubbed by *Spy* magazine "Mr. Caroline Kennedy" and "Camelot's egghead-in-residence," Schlossberg sought to be involved in making a film about JFK's role in the arts.

When John Jr. heard about it, he was furious, even though in the past he had gotten along with Schlossberg. "It was all he could talk about," Rob Littell recalled. "He went on and on about how Ed should have consulted with him, and questioned whether Ed should be involved in the project anyway . . . he saw Ed's involvement in the tribute as poaching. The two of them sparred for a bit, which resulted in the project's cancellation."

In late July of that very tragic year 1999, the eve of the new millennium, Bobby, a multimillionaire many times over from all of his inheritances and trusts, received a bittersweet surprise. His cousin had unexpectedly named him in his will to the tune of $250,000.

"I cried," he wrote after receiving the gift. "I've lost a good friend."

THIRTY-FOUR

Marital Hell

In the dedication to the 1997 book *The Riverkeepers*, Bobby Kennedy Jr. wrote "with love and respect" to his wife, "Mary Richardson and our children . . . Bobby, Kick, Conor, Kyra and Finbar." (Their fourth and last, Aiden, was born in 2001.)

He offered a more vociferous and loving dedication in his 2004 *Crimes Against Nature: How George W. Bush & His Corporate Pals Are Plundering the Country & Hijacking Our Democracy.* In that book, he declared, "To my wife, Mary Richardson, who encourages me with her love, patience, and faith; inspires me with her energy; and is the best environmentalist in our family."

Seven years later, in a sworn court affidavit in which he made horrific allegations against Mary when he was seeking a divorce from her, he prefaced it by describing her as a "kind, generous person, open and considerate to and curious about all people from royalty to cabdrivers. She was stunningly beautiful, with pitch-perfect taste, electric charm, and a genius for friendship that had won her an army of loyal and loving friends. . . . She was blessed with a profound spirituality . . . I loved the way she blossomed in crowds . . . I adored her grand gestures and her careful attention to tiny details and the elegance and enthusiasm with which she undertook every enterprise . . ."

It all sounded so warm and cuddly, making him appear to be the ultimate loyal and loving husband and dad from a Kennedy clan scandalized so often by womanizers and adulterers.

In 2007, Bobby was interviewed by Oprah Winfrey for a story in her popular *O Magazine*. The article called Bobby "clearly a family man," and asserted that his home was a "priority" in his life. The sprawling house in the New York City suburb of Mount Kisco included in the front hallway a framed letter from the Kennedys' nemesis President Richard Nixon, the article noted, and in the living room one of the chairs had a comfy pillow that read BORN TO FISH. When Oprah interviewed him, Bobby had arranged to be seen just arriving home from taking his son Conor—who later would gain his fifteen minutes of tabloid fame as the publicity-hungry pop singer Taylor Swift's boy toy—to his hockey practice, and the family dog, a dachshund named Cupid, was always scurrying about.

It was home sweet home, Kennedy-style.

Readers who knew little about RFK's namesake must have thought, What a wonderful, loving husband and father.

In the article, Oprah praised Bobby for speaking with "such clarity and conviction about protecting our earth" in his environmental work.

At one point, however, she asked her prominent Kennedy guest, "Your wife's not here with us today. What kind of husband would she call you?"

Bobby hesitated—possibly wondering what Oprah really knew—and then responded, "I think Mary would call me a pretty good husband." But he avoided elaborating, and quickly changed the subject. "Mary remembers you as a great sport, because she once picked you up in Boston to take you to Maria [Shriver]'s wedding. She said you'd just had your hair done. The convertible top wouldn't go up, so she drove you at seventy-six miles an hour with an open roof. She says you were gracious and good-humored about it."

Oprah, delighted, said she remembered that day, but in so doing she let herself be sidetracked by Bobby from talking about his marriage.

Oprah never asked why, for instance, his wife wasn't present for the family-style feature story. Bobby's candid answer might have been that his marriage was in dire jeopardy.

He had, however, smoothly escaped a sticky Oprah interrogation. The fact was that Mary would not have agreed with his assessment that he was a "pretty good husband," given his womanizing. And Mary was his very troubled and cuckolded spouse.

The same year that Oprah interviewed Bobby and asked him about his home life, he had called police on two different occasions claiming that Mary might be suicidal. The incidents had been leaked to a local newspaper, and Mary was publicly humiliated.

In fact, confidantes of Mary allege that she became aware of his womanizing "and was furious." Bobby "had had some big epiphany, and started divulging a lot of personal stuff that she'd never known, a lot of affairs that had happened."

Mary had actually begun to consider holidays as "nuclear events" that horrified her. For instance, according to sources, Bobby had chosen the same week as Mother's Day in 2010 to begin divorce proceedings, and he decided to tell her about his affairs on Father's Day.

Women who apparently felt sorry for Mary's situation also came to her to confess having affairs with Bobby. Some of them were long-term affairs, said one source who claimed knowledge of the situation. "When he was in A.A., he had multiple affairs with people."

His history of womanizing went back many years.

For instance, when Bobby was still married to Emily Black Kennedy in the late 1980s, she had been accompanying him to his Alcoholics Anonymous twelve-step program for couples in recovery in the village of Bedford near their home in Mount Kisco. A member of that group recalled how Bobby had made a "sexual advance" that she termed "a typical Kennedy thing." He had invited himself to her home for a party, and throughout dinner Bobby was "touching" her leg. But that wasn't enough. As the hostess later learned, he had been doing the same thing to her friend who was seated on the other side of him.

That kind of behavior continued, according to a trusted friend of Mary's. "He would be at the dinner table and his hands would go all up their legs or skirts and they just laughed. The Kennedy aura kept them from saying, 'You're an asshole.'"

There was other "inappropriate behavior" on the Kennedy scion's part, such as when, on at least one occasion, he strutted around the family home with a towel wrapped around his waist, then was said to have dropped it, exposing his genitals, and embarrassing Mary and a friend of hers who was present.

At one point, Mary revealed to a friend that Bobby "wanted to bring another woman into the bedroom," and have a ménage à trois, but Mary had adamantly refused, and Bobby was said to have been furious with her for turning him down.

The Mary Kennedy source who mentioned the failed ménage à trois request by Bobby said that during the last six months of Mary's life, she had talked about Bobby's numerous affairs, and that it was an "astronomical number."

But those people making the claims of Bobby Kennedy Jr.'s infidelity weren't the final word. Bobby himself was.

In his own words, in his own handwriting, he appeared to have indicted himself. In a personal diary that was leaked without his knowledge to the *New York Post*, Bobby had listed a number of alleged sexual conquests during just one year while he was married to Mary. In what seemed to be a compulsive compendium of sexual conquests, he characterized his greatest flaw as his "lust demons."

He stated that after his father's assassination, "I struggled to be a grown-up . . . I felt he was watching me from heaven. Every time I was afflicted with sexual thoughts, I felt a failure. I hated myself. I began to lie . . . to make up a character who was the hero and leader that I wished I was."

In July 2001, Bobby had been arrested and sentenced by a federal judge to thirty days in prison on civil disobedience charges of trespassing when he took part in a rowdy demonstration at Camp Garcia on the island of Vieques in Puerto Rico to protest U.S. Navy practice bombing missions, target training, and mock guerrilla combat there. Bobby was elated because after his arrest President Bush announced that military exercises on Vieques would eventually be stopped.

But Bobby also was elated for another, far less obvious and far more secretive reason.

It involved his self-proclaimed "lust demons."

Being behind bars, he felt, had temporarily quelled his compulsion because there were no women there.

That was underscored in an entry in his personal diary that he made while serving his time in a federal detention center: "I'm so content here. I have to say it. There's no women. I'm happy!" he confided. "It's not misogyny. It's the opposite! . . . I love my wife and I tell it to her every day, and I never tire of it and I write her tender letters."

A couple of days after his sentencing, Bobby, in confinement, spoke to Mary by phone and then wrote in his diary that she was "wonderful," and chatting with her was "a joy." He described her as "very strong and cheerful."

At the time of Bobby's arrest, Mary was due with her fourth and last child, who was born while Bobby was serving his sentence, and he first saw his thirteen-day-old, seven-pound, twelve-ounce son when Mary, along with Bobby's sister and her close friend Kerry Kennedy, came to visit. Bobby had actually considered naming the boy Vieques Libre Kennedy in honor of the disputed island. Instead, he was named Aiden Caohman Vieques Kennedy.

In his diary, Bobby wrote, "I'm so proud of my Mary. She has become the woman I fell in love with," but he added the curious line, "through hard work."

Without explanation, he also noted, "She has overcome her fears, enshrined her faith, abandoned self-pity and blame and immersed herself in gratitude and God gave her a baby . . . a beautiful and serene and happy soul. I am so happy. I couldn't be happier or more grateful for the life and the wife God has given me."

Mary Kennedy presumably had no idea that when she received Bobby's "tender" jailhouse letters he would also be documenting in his diary some of the many sordid affairs he allegedly had during 2001, the year he was arrested and the year Mary gave birth to their last child.

After Bobby was released from confinement and returned to New York, he was interviewed on CNN. Naturally, he didn't mention his diary. Instead, he stated, "The only kind of hero in my family was my wife, who stayed at home with our kids and actually had another child while I was away. She was the one who kind of shouldered the burden of my imprisonment."

With his diary entries, Bobby became the first Kennedy male known to have documented his philandering in writing, albeit in a private journal.

His reputed womanizing forebears—the patriarch, Joe; his uncles JFK and Ted; and Bobby's own father—had never done so.

Reading published portions of the diary, one might wonder whether Bobby inherited his uncle Jack's affliction. As the president told power broker Bobby Baker, "You know, I get a migraine if I don't get a strange piece of ass every day," according to Seymour Hersh's *The Dark Side of Camelot*.

The almost four-hundred-page diary had a legend. The number "10" represented women with whom he had had intercourse. Sixteen had fallen into that category. In one day alone, less than two weeks before he and his family celebrated Thanksgiving 2001, he documented that he had had three separate sexual encounters. That same month one woman's name—only first names were written—was noted in the diary twenty-two times, and on thirteen consecutive days, the *Post* reported

One of the women reportedly was the wife of a well-known actor. Others in his stable included a physician and, like Bobby, an environmental activist. When he wasn't sexually involved, he wrote the word "victory," which had to do with the Catholic guilt he felt about his affairs. When he was involved with a woman other than his wife, he claimed he was the one who was seduced—or as he curiously put it in his diary, "mugged." A week before St. Valentine's Day in 2001, for instance, he wrote that he had "narrowly escaped being mugged" by two women that he characterized as a "double team," a sexual situation that he stated was "tempting but I prayed and God gave me the strength to say no."

Bobby wrote that he had a "three-point plan" for ending his compulsive, addictive womanizing, but didn't elaborate. Whatever he had in mind didn't work. A few weeks later, he had jotted more names of women with whom he had had a sexual encounter.

In the spring of 2001, after he had hosted a dinner for the actor Leonardo DiCaprio, Bobby told his diary that on his drive home from Manhattan he had gotten "mugged," called the rationalized seduction a "10"—intercourse—and added, "I've got to do better," presumably meaning controlling his addiction to sex. He apparently did have a method, according to the diary, which called for him to "avoid the company of women. You have not the strength to resist their charms . . . be humble like a monk. Keep your hands to yourself."

In early November 2001—two months after 9/11—he wrote that he felt "great," and went on to note, "So I've been looking for ways to screw it up. I'm like Adam and live on Eden, and I can have everything but the fruit. But the fruit is all I want."

At another point, he boasted: "I have been given everything that I coveted—a beautiful wife and kids and loving family, wealth, education, good health and a job I love yet always on the lookout for something I can't have. I want it all. No matter how much I have—I want more."

IN THE EARLY 2000S, BOBBY was said to have purchased a three-hundred-dollar-a-month family plan for him and Mary and their children at a posh gym and health club with a number of celebrity members not far from the Kennedys' Mount Kisco estate. They were joined at the club by the Cuomos—Bobby's sister Kerry and her then-husband, Andrew, and their children. Mary and Kerry often worked out together, doing cardio.

As Bobby's marriage was going downhill, however, he approached the club's management, according to a longtime member, with a special request. He had them agree to change the rules for him, and him alone, so that he could continue working out there with a trainer he liked but without a full membership. Under the arrangement, he paid for just his weekly workout, considered by observers to be rather extreme.

"Every Tuesday morning," claimed the club member, "he would have his trainer, an Arnold Schwarzenegger wannabe kind of guy, get every forty-five-pound barbell plate in the club and put the maximum amount of weight possible on the leg press machine—eight hundred to a thousand pounds. This was Bobby's idea and he would be straining himself using completely horrible form and risking injury to himself. He was all hung up on the number of pounds he could press. The trainer would indulge him with this exercise program that really didn't make any sense. No matter how much leg power he had, what he was doing was idiotic and risky, and I thought to myself, Who's he trying to impress?"

A fit blonde in her thirties—married and a mother—had been avidly watching Bobby's workout, and one day before he arrived she was spotted using the leg press machine, according to the longtime club member.

Bobby's trainer was said to have politely asked her to move because the machine was reserved. "And Bobby jumps in," said the longtime member, "and says to the woman, 'Oh, no, no, no, feel free to work in with me.' So she exercises with the light weights and then the trainer rolls up with maybe eight hundred pounds of weights, installs them, and Bobby takes his turn, and then the trainer has to unload them for the lady, and they go back and forth like this, and there's this obvious flirtation between Bobby and the woman while the trainer is loading and unloading all those weights."

The consensus among observers was that Bobby and the woman had a more intimate relationship outside the gym—they would, it was alleged, "rendezvous" in the club's parking lot.

While Bobby's deal with the club was to work out alone and just pay for the time he was there, his children, their friends, and others were said to have begun showing up with Bobby on weekends, utilizing the full privileges of the club without paying the required membership fee.

"Finally, Bobby got called out on it," said the club member. "He didn't respond well. He stormed out of the club, yelling, 'Fucking Republicans!'— not knowing the owners were Democrats."

ALONG WITH ALCOHOLICS ANONYMOUS and Narcotics Anonymous for drug addicts, Bobby was said to have once belonged to a group called Sexaholics Anonymous (SA), headquartered in Tennessee, but with fellowship groups around the country. At one point, according to Mary, he had begun holding SA meetings at the Kennedys' Mount Kisco home. But she supposedly ended the practice, fearing it was dangerous having strange men with sexual addiction problems around the house, especially when her children were there.

Bobby's blatant womanizing was well known to his close circle of male friends, the ones who went back all the way to his Harvard and UVA days, so they weren't surprised when Mary, the mother of his four children, became a victim of his Casanova ways.

"Mary understood Bobby's strengths and weaknesses," one of his friends of more than three decades asserted. "Nothing that he did should ever have surprised her, and his womanizing was a part of it. He had even womanized with her when he was still married to Emily, so she knew what he was like."

One of the big shockers for Mary, a confidante maintained, was when she learned that Bobby was having an affair with the TV actress Cheryl Hines, who would become his third wife. It was a shocker because Mary claimed she had introduced Hines to Bobby at a charity event, although Bobby and Hines asserted that their friend the comedian Larry David had brought about the introduction. Still, Mary felt "very betrayed" by what she termed the "Sisterhood," said a confidante. "The Sisterhood was very important to her—women sticking together, women supporting one another."

Hines already was publicly boasting about her relationship with Bobby, which infuriated and humiliated Mary. Online, she saw that Hines had tweeted that she had become friends with one of Mary's pals, the actress Glenn Close, and had bonded with Kerry Kennedy. She boasted on Twitter that she had become pals with Bobby's then-eleven-year-old son, Aiden, talking football with him.

In the wake of Hines's controversial and embarrassing tweets, an Internet commenter observed, "Was Hines so self-absorbed that she did not think her giddy and public celebration would have no effect on the woman left behind?"

THIRTY-FIVE

Toxic Household

By the spring of 2010, Bobby had decided to finally end it with Mary, and he soon took up publicly with Cheryl Hines. It had been building for some time. On Wednesday, May 12, 2010, he filed divorce papers, leaving his wife and the mother of their four children devastated. Mary Richardson Kennedy did not want a divorce, or thought she didn't.

On May 10 and again on May 13, police were summoned to the Kennedy estate for what officers described, in one instance, as a "domestic incident." Bobby had called the cops and claimed Mary was "intoxicated." As a lawyer, he was an expert at those kinds of machinations, and by getting on record with the police, he clearly was establishing a case against Mary, and a paper trail as part of his divorce action. The other call to police involved what was described as a dispute between children. In one incident, Mary complained that Bobby was being abusive to her and their children, and Bobby claimed she was acting "irrational." However, no arrests were made, and no crimes were found to have been committed. There was, a Bedford Police Department official said at the time, "no need for follow-up."

Then, on Saturday, May 15, Mary was charged with drunken driving.

All of this had come crashing down on her the same week she should have happily been celebrating Mother's Day with her family on Sunday, May 9. Just three weeks earlier, on April 15, her sixteenth wedding anniversary had come and gone with little joy for her.

Like Bobby's uncle Ted's first wife, Joan, who had drowned her sorrows in alcohol and had also faced DUI charges because of her husband's philandering, Mary had sadly followed suit. She had started having problems with alcohol in 2005 because of issues with Bobby, at which time she went into Alcoholics Anonymous, but her sponsor was said to have never seen her inebriated. The triggering issues, claimed a source, involved Bobby's allegedly being "brutal, relentless, and mean to Mary." He was said to have told her that he slept with other women because he didn't want to have sex with her.

The DWI charge against Mary had happened as a result of an incident outside St. Patrick's School in Bedford, not far from the Kennedy home. She had driven there to pick up some people from a carnival, but a police officer witnessed her car jump the curb. She was tested, and her blood alcohol level was 0.11 percent—just slightly over the legal limit of 0.08.

The story of her arrest—along with her mug shot, in which she looked bleary-eyed and forlorn—made headlines. She pleaded not guilty, and a local justice ordered her license suspended and had her evaluated for abusing alcohol. In July she pleaded guilty to a lesser charge, but admitted that her driving ability had been impaired. She was fined five hundred dollars, her license was suspended for ninety days, and she was ordered to attend two programs for drivers with drinking problems.

The next month, in mid-August, she was stopped again for driving under the influence and taken into custody. She had been speeding in a 2004 Volvo on one of the parkways in Pleasant Valley, New York, when she was stopped, clocked at eighty-two miles an hour. At the time she reportedly had a conditional license that permitted her to drive under special circumstances. That day she was on her way to the Omega Institute in Rhinebeck, a spiritual, health, and wellness center where one of the cofounders had written a book, *Broken Open: How Difficult Times Can Help Us Grow.*

At the state police barracks in Millbrook, Mary was examined and it was determined she was under the influence of a prescription medication. The charges were eventually dropped.

DESPITE ALL OF HER PROBLEMS, Mary, in 2010, was able to complete an enormous task—overseeing the total three-year renovation of the Kennedys' historic clapboard-with-green-shutters Georgian Colonial at 326 South Bedford Road in Mount Kisco. She had renamed it the "Kennedy Green Estate" because, as an architect, she had redesigned and planned the environmentally friendly and technologically advanced home. The mansion had originally been built in 1920 for the Scribner publishing family as a summer escape from the city, and was planned by the same firm that had designed the New York Public Library and the Frick Museum.

By the time Mary had finished the job, Bobby was already romantically involved with Cheryl Hines. He soon moved to a house at 236 Byram Lake Road, also in Mount Kisco.

The reason for the massive renovation was because the house had become as toxic—literally—as the marriage of the couple inhabiting it.

Mary had discovered that the place had been permeated by a horrific black fungus caused by flooding water. The black mold was dangerous to the family's health. Moreover, it had affected the asthma and allergies that some of her children had. The family moved out and into a rental while the house was being completely renovated. Bobby, the environmental lawyer and activist, was said to have been "very angry" about the renovation and, according to a person familiar with the situation, "did not think that the mold problem was that serious."

Despite her emotional and marital issues, a very healthy-looking Mary appeared in a pilot for a Web series hosted by Bob Vila of TV's *This Old House* program, in which she talked in detail about the home disaster and her redesign.

"We walked into the house and were absolutely in a state of shock," she told Vila. "I found a foot of standing water in the basement and I found mold throughout the house—from the basement through the third floor, through the attic."

Responded Vila: "Mary, you have had a huge job here because part of that job was breaking the news to your family that the house had become a sick house and was beyond repair and couldn't be salvaged, isn't that right?"

She answered in the affirmative.

Like the house, Mary Kennedy's marriage was sick, beyond repair, and could not be salvaged.

The renovation soon became the subject of a coffee table book entitled *Kennedy Green House,* published in April 2010, with a foreword by Bobby.

Robin Wilson, the book's author, who had worked on the renovation with Mary, later claimed that the Kennedys had gotten major discounts on supplies, and had generated some $1.3 million in free products.

The onetime comedian and then-current Democratic senator from Minnesota Al Franken—an ally of Bobby's; he had appeared in a 2006 documentary about Franken—had been asked to lobby a Minnesota company, Marvin Windows and Doors, to donate energy-efficient windows. While Franken, through a spokesman, denied any role, a local distributor of Marvin Windows reportedly gave Bobby a discount of more than $100,000. Wilson was quoted as stating that part of her job was to secure materials and services for "free or as free as possible."

THROUGH BOBBY, MARY HAD become friendly with the TV mogul Larry David's ex-wife, Laurie, a liberal campaign fund-raiser and environmentalist. The two women were said to have spent time together, and the David and Kennedy families had vacationed together. In late 2010, Laurie David's book, *The Family Dinner: Great Ways to Connect with Your Kids, One Meal at a Time,* had been published, and it had a chapter that piqued Mary's interest because it had to do with family dining *after* a divorce. When Laurie David came to New York to promote the book at a SoHo store, Mary was there to greet her.

"Soignée in a navy satin pants suit," as *The New Yorker,* which briefly covered the book signing, noted, Mary purchased two hundred copies to supposedly give away as presents. "Usually, we give people a book my husband has written," she proudly said, "but Laurie beat him to it." The devastated Kennedy wife acted as if everything in her marriage was normal. She went on to cheerfully claim that dinner at the Kennedy house was virtually sacred, as if life at the Kennedys' was pure bliss. "We say grace before and after meals, and we play games at the dinner table," she offered. "We play categories—name ten colors, name ten presidents." She was practically repeating lines her mother-in-law Ethel Kennedy used to feed to the press about life with RFK and her tribe of eleven, most if not all of it spin to make things look better than they were. Mary bragged that her nine-year-old had just finished reading the *Odyssey*, and another planned to be an author. She declared that her resolution for the New Year, 2011, was to "make sure everyone is journaling daily."

She gave no indication that anything was amiss.

In fact, September 2011, a year after the house renovation was completed, and after Bobby had left Mary to move into a nearby home, he filed a sworn affidavit in New York Supreme Court in which he made horrendous allegations against her as a wife and mother. The affidavit was in support of a motion to have her sign a temporary child custody agreement guaranteeing what he claimed would give him fair access to their four children.

In the court papers, and in tough lawyerly fashion, he had thrown in all but video in what some viewed as an effort to smear Mary's name— and many of his allegations were said to be untrue. He had accused her of allegedly physically attacking him, of allegedly being drunk in front of their children, of allegedly preventing him from driving his car, of allegedly verbally abusing him, of allegedly stealing his personal property, of allegedly making uninvited visits to the home to which he had moved, and the home he used in the Kennedy compound in Hyannis Port, of allegedly making disparaging remarks to him and their children, and of allegedly threatening suicide in front of their children.

He even alleged that Mary had suffered from "eating disorders" when she was young, disorders that had "caused her hospitalizations and nearly killed her," all of which was irrelevant to the case he was making against her, and conceivably never proven.

And he alleged that "soon after our marriage" Mary had become "abusive" toward the two children he had had with Emily Black Kennedy, "and [was] particularly hateful toward Kick. . . . [A]fter only three years of marriage, I saw enough evidence of troubling conduct to trigger my first efforts to divorce Mary."

He claimed that young Kick often lost things while traveling between her mother's home in Washington and her trips to visit her father and stepmother, Mary, in New York. When he confronted his then-nine-year-old daughter, he stated she told him, "Daddy, I think Mary is stealing from me." When he told her, "Mary loves you," Kick responded, according to Bobby, "No, Daddy, Mary hates me."

Bobby made the claim that he was in the process of looking for something in his wife's bureau and "found a collection of Kick's lost items concealed beneath a layer of Mary's clothing."

He concluded the sworn affidavit by stating, "For the sake of my children and for my own safety and sanity, I need protection from this court to minimize any contact between Mary and myself by granting the requested injunction for a protective order and requiring Mary to sign a fair child custody agreement."

The affidavit, long kept private in court files, was then somehow leaked to a Kennedy-friendly journalist who wrote a story about it, which had the effect of posthumously sullying Mary's reputation.

Her lawyer called the allegations "trash," its release "beyond the pale," and termed Bobby a "tenacious and devious adversary."

THIRTY-SIX

Fatal Ending

In the months before Mary Kennedy decided to take her life in May 2012, she made a number of alarming comments to a longtime friend. She allegedly said she "feared for her life," claimed that Bobby "repeatedly" told her that she would be "better off dead," and that it would be "so much easier" if she killed herself. Whether her disturbing claims were true or false, no one knew for certain.

She asserted that she had started feeling "gaslighted in the marriage" by Bobby, and that he kept telling her that she was a "borderline personality." Mary claimed that her own therapist didn't believe that she suffered from borderline personality disorder, a form of mental illness, but had some of the illness's traits, which were considered common and difficult to diagnose. By "gaslighted," Mary was referring to the 1944 film *Gaslight*, in which Charles Boyer attempts to make Ingrid Bergman believe she's gone mad. And Mary told a confidante that Bobby "was making her feel like she was crazy."

Moreover, Bobby had gained temporary custody of their children in 2011, which was devastating for their mother. At the same time, Mary claimed to friends she had been banned from visiting the Kennedy compound and had been cut off from the family. All of it had caused her great anxiety. She started drinking and reportedly twice went to an expensive rehab facility in California.

In April 2012, about five weeks before she killed herself, she took a drink after previously having attained sobriety. Concerned, she immediately sought out a sponsor in Alcoholics Anonymous and worked through one of A.A.'s intensive, emotionally demanding twelve steps. The two spent some sixty hours together. But her "rage and resentment" toward Bobby was barely touched upon. Mary had once told a friend that she felt she was "addicted" to him, and was advised to take off her wedding rings in order to "empower herself."

On several weekends at the Kennedy home, Mary and her sponsor spent eight to twelve hours together, during which time they read, word for word, the 576-page "Big Book of Alcoholics Anonymous," the bible of A.A. Mary understood that after she was finished she would be in better emotional shape to handle upcoming child custody hearings that she faced with Bobby and his lawyers; she felt she was being "screwed" regarding custody of the children "because all of these legal people were all Bobby's people," she told a confidante.

Because of her work with her sponsor, Mary was emotionally healthier than she had been in a long time. She had taken up yoga and was going to classes every day, along with religiously attending A.A. meetings. She had begun grooming herself again, and had even gone to a party with a friend who thought she looked terrific.

"There was an extreme lift in her," a pal noted. "She was really peaking. She had turned a corner."

Feeling more confident, Mary was considering going to the California-headquartered Hoffman Institute Foundation, which she was said to have heard about from Bobby's brother Max, who had told her he had gone through the weeklong personal growth retreat and that it had been life-changing for him. The almost-five-thousand-dollar program billed itself as helping clients "identify negative behaviors, moods and ways of thinking that developed unconsciously and were conditioned in childhood."

Mary had also become involved in a craft project. She had done some redecorating and had a number of empty paint cans that she didn't want to throw in the trash, because it wasn't an environmentally friendly thing to do. Instead, she had decided to cover the cans with the remnants of an expensive fabric she had used on some furniture. The fabric-covered cans were to become part of a piece of furniture she had conceived. But when she returned to the design store to get the remnants, they apparently were lost. When Mary left the shop, she said in passing, "If you can't find them, I'll just kill myself." Later, the clerk found it all "so sad and spooky" when Mary actually did commit suicide some weeks later.

Although they were separated, Bobby's alleged womanizing was an ongoing, agonizing concern for Mary. In one instance, she had begun to suspect that he had become involved with a socialite who was an influential board member of his Riverkeeper organization. After the alleged affair was reported in the *New York Post*, Ann Colley claimed that she and Bobby were merely "professional colleagues and dear friends. The accusation that I had a romantic relationship with Bobby Kennedy is false."

Mary Kennedy also claimed to a confidante that Bobby's Sprint Samsung cell phone directory contained the first names and telephone numbers of more than forty women who were from all over the United States, Canada, and even Paris. Moreover, she claimed to have found evidence suggesting that when he traveled he used the alias "Robert Strong."

ON THE EVENING OF MONDAY, May 14, 2012—three days before Mary would take her own life—Bobby's sister Kerry arrived unexpectedly at the Kennedy home in Mount Kisco at a time when Mary was meeting there with someone. It was, Kerry would say, a friendly visit, that they had had a "long talk" about school and summer plans for Mary and Bobby's daughter Kyra, the second of their four children, who was turning seventeen in July, just two months away. According to Kerry, "Mary said Kyra was excited about going to Los Angeles" to visit a friend, and Mary wanted to "be sure Kyra had time" to spend with her "Hyannis Port cousins."

But there was another side to the girlfriend chat. Kerry was said to have been putting intense pressure on Mary that night and in the weeks before to sign Bobby's divorce settlement agreement, described as a "very bitter, harsh, and Draconian proposal," limiting Mary's custody of her children and slashing her financial support.

The guest was "terrified" at the "pressure" that Kerry had been putting on Mary and felt that she should have reported it to someone.

Kerry's visit was so disturbing to Mary that she burst into tears, and probably for the first time in the many years of their friendship, she ordered Kerry to leave her home.

A few weeks before the troubling visit, Kerry had accompanied Mary on road trips to see her sons, eleven-year-old William "Finn" Finbar Kennedy at the Stratton Mountain School, in the ski country of Vermont, and seventeen-year-old John Conor Kennedy at Deerfield Academy in Massachusetts. A friend of Mary's who had heard about the trips said Kerry had "hammered constantly" at Mary to sign Bobby's settlement and told her, "There's not an endless pool of money; you're making everybody broke."

Disheartened by the change in the woman she always trusted unconditionally and considered her best, if not her only friend within the Kennedy clan, Mary had confided to others that Kerry had become "Bobby's mouthpiece," as one remembered. Mary believed that Kerry had turned against her, and that her big brother's interests were more important to Kerry than her close pal from their teen years.

As a confidante asserted, "Mary felt betrayed."

ON TUESDAY, MAY 15, Mary Kennedy, seemingly depressed after Kerry Kennedy's upsetting visit, was still in her pajamas at ten A.M., when she usually was up and about, going off to the gym, doing her yoga, running errands. The Kennedys' longtime housekeeper later told the police that she had "noticed some changes in Mary. I thought something was wrong with her . . . I told Bobby about her, and I told him that she needs help . . . Bobby told me that she doesn't want to help herself."

Earlier on that Tuesday morning, the housekeeper was cleaning at Bobby's nearby home when she answered the phone and it was Mary looking for her estranged husband. Because Bobby didn't pick up, Mary told the housekeeper to let the phone continue to ring until he answered. "The phone," the housekeeper stated, "rang for a lot of times after that, and Bobby never picked up."

But later Bobby would tell police that he had, in fact, taken a call from

Mary that Tuesday morning, and self-servingly claimed, "She told me that she was sorry for everything. . . . She said that I was right about everything and everything was her fault," according to his statement to investigators, a lengthy portion of which was redacted, presumably for privacy reasons.

That morning Mary had also questioned the household help, a married couple, about whether they had told Bobby that she had recently bought a new treadmill, a massage seat, and a cappuccino machine— all part of her newfound positive view of a healthy life. They told her they hadn't and that Bobby had probably seen her credit card statement. Mary, said the housekeeper, "looked mad, and a little upset. I think she thought that we had told Bobby about the purchases," that the couple was spying on her for him.

Credit cards and finances had become important to Mary.

A petition filed in court by her lawyers stated, "Unfortunately, the last months of Ms. Richardson Kennedy's life were full of daily financial challenges, directly attributable to Mr. Kennedy's litigation tactics executed through his family office." Under an arrangement, Mary was to have a twenty-thousand-dollar-a-month expense limit on a credit card to be paid by the Park Agency, the Kennedy family's money handlers in New York. But, according to the petition, the deal was ended in order "to squeeze her and make her panic" regarding child custody and other issues.

Around three in the afternoon on that Tuesday after Kerry Kennedy's visit, Mary came down to the kitchen and took one of the juices that the housekeeper had earlier prepared, said she was "a little tired," and returned to her bedroom.

"That was the last time I saw her or talked to her," the housekeeper told police.

"My husband asked me if we should check on Mary, but I told him no, because I didn't want to disturb her."

By eight-thirty, the house was dark.

ON WEDNESDAY, MAY 16, 2012, around ten in the morning, the housekeeper went to check on Mary, called out for her, but got no response. She checked the bedroom, the bathroom, the office, and the

kitchen, and saw that Mary's car was still in the driveway, but the mistress of the house was nowhere to be found.

Returning to Mary's bedroom, the housekeeper and her husband discovered her eyeglasses, her cell phone, her car keys, and her wallet on the bed.

Also on the bed, in a small tangle, was a short length of rope.

After checking down by the large pond on the Kennedy property, and peering into an open but usually closed garage bay, the household couple, now very concerned as to the mistress's whereabouts, telephoned Bobby, their employer for many years.

"I told him we were worried," she stated.

Bobby came to the house from his place a short distance away and, with the housekeeper's husband, began another futile search. He later told police that he had gotten the call around 12:50 P.M. and that the housekeeper had "sounded very scared . . . I then decided to drive over there, and help her and her husband look for Mary."

In her bedroom, on the bed, he saw her stuff—and the rope.

"I then checked the attic, and she wasn't there," he later told a detective, adding, "Mary and I are near the end of a long process of divorce. We are under court order to sever contact and to stay away from each other's houses. Yesterday [Tuesday] she nevertheless called me repeatedly."

Failing to find Mary anywhere in the house or on the sprawling estate grounds, Bobby drove to the nearby town of Armonk to see if Mary had gone to an A.A. meeting—even though he had seen her car keys on the bed and her car in the driveway. Unless someone had picked her up, there was no way she could have gotten there.

A couple of people who knew Bobby at A.A. were surprised to see him because he hadn't been to a recent meeting. Mary had been telling people that Bobby should have been attending A.A. meetings because, as she claimed, he was popping painkillers and taking a drug called Klonopin that he said was for his voice problem, but is usually prescribed to treat panic or seizure disorders.

Bobby approached two women, one who had been Mary's A.A. sponsor some years earlier, and the woman who was her current sponsor, to find out if they had seen her. Both said they had not, but that she had been at Monday's meeting and had looked "fantastic," had lost weight,

and was doing yoga. The evening of that Monday was when Kerry Kennedy had confronted Mary.

Bobby said he was worried—"I think she's done something to herself"—because Mary could not be found anywhere and he noted that she had been "missing since last night [Tuesday]," and also said he had found a piece of rope on her bed. Mary's sponsor told Bobby that Mary was doing well, that she had "blossomed" and had been in "such a good place recently." Her remarks seemed to anger Bobby, she felt. He further claimed that the previous day, Tuesday, Mary had called him "seventeen times," and had asked him to come back to her. Bobby said his response was, "Mary, I am with somebody," presumably a reference to Cheryl Hines.

Bobby, followed by Mary's sponsor, drove back to the Kennedy home and, for some reason, immediately began searching the wooded area of his property. Meanwhile, Mary's sponsor along with the housekeeping couple began searching the house again, and checking the pond.

Finally, the sponsor decided to inspect the second bay in the old garage whose door was open.

Inside, Mary was discovered hanging with a rope around her neck.

As the housekeeper began screaming and crying, Mary's sponsor began yelling for Bobby and sounding the car horn, telling him to come to the garage. After five minutes or so he responded, and accompanied her to view his wife's body. He began crying and moaning, asked if she had telephoned the police, and when she told him she didn't have her phone with her, he called 911.

At 1:51 P.M., an EMS medic pronounced Mary Richardson Kennedy dead. She was dressed in workout clothing and wearing sandals. Near her on the floor were three metal crates and a metal ladder, apparently used to stand on when she tied the hangman's knot.

Concerned about how to tell his children, Bobby was overheard on his cell phone allegedly telling someone, "Call her fucking family and tell them to get up here and help me with the kids." The person who overheard the call was shocked.

When one of the officers asked Bobby to give a statement, he said he didn't have time and would do so later, which he did. But no significant interview was conducted with him at the scene, even though police were aware of the bitter ongoing divorce action between him and his wife.

THIRTY-SEVEN

Aftermath

On Thursday, May 17, the day after Mary Richardson Kennedy hanged herself, an autopsy was performed by Dr. Kunjlata Ashar, the Westchester County, New York, female medical examiner. She determined that Mary had died of asphyxiation, and found nothing suspicious about her death.

She had strangled herself, her examination showed, with a beige-colored rope nine-sixteenths of an inch in diameter, the knot of which had nine loops. She noted that some of Mary's fingers, which were bruised, were between the rope and her neck, suggesting that she might have tried to abort her suicide, which probably was a natural reaction. There was a brownish-red abrasion on the left side of her neck.

The toxicology report showed no alcohol in her system, but there were levels of three prescription antidepressants, Trazodone, Venlafaxine, and Desmethylvenlafaxine—one of which, Trazodone, carried a warning that it could cause suicidal thoughts. But Mary's psychiatrist subsequently stated that the drugs were Mary's normal dosage.

In the immediate aftermath, her horrified family, the Richardsons, said in a statement, "We deeply regret the death of our beloved Mary, whose radiant and creative spirit will be sorely missed by those who loved her. Our heart goes out to her children who she loved without reservation."

Underscoring what was a longtime breach between the two families, the Kennedys issued a separate statement: "It is with deep sadness that the family of Robert F. Kennedy Jr. mourns the loss of Mary Richardson Kennedy, wife and mother of their four beloved children. Mary inspired our family with her kindness, her love, her gentle soul and generous spirit." The statement went on to add that Mary was a "tremendously gifted architect and a pioneer and relentless advocate of green design who enhanced her cutting edge, energy efficient creations with exquisite taste and style."

The words were a far cry from some of the allegations Bobby had earlier made against Mary in his affidavit that was mysteriously leaked to a journalist after her death and that were picked up in some news reports. "The description of Mary carried by certain news organizations since her passing yesterday," the family later told CNN, "is wholly inconsistent with the sister we knew and the life she, in fact, lived. Countless people have described her as an extraordinary mother, selfless in her desire to help others, and one of the finest people in the world. We know her as all those things, and more."

While Bobby had told people that some of Mary's sisters planned to attend the Kennedy-family-arranged funeral service, not one member of the Richardson family showed up. They privately blamed Bobby for causing her to end her life—aware of his philandering and her claimed emotionally abusive treatment by him.

The Kennedy service was at St. Patrick's Roman Catholic Church, in Bedford, not far from the Kennedy home, on Saturday, May 19. Bobby, in his eulogy, used the opportunity to reject any and all blame, directly or indirectly, for her death. "I know I did everything I could to help her," he maintained. "The day before she died she called me and said, 'You know me better than anyone in the world.' She said, 'I was such a good girl.' I said, 'I know you are and you still are.' She really fought so hard. She had these demons, and she didn't deserve it.'"

In the filled-to-capacity Kennedy church, where Bobby's four children with Mary had their First Communions, celebrities who knew the couple—Larry David, Glenn Close, Chevy Chase, Susan Sarandon, Edward James Olmos, John McEnroe, and André Balazs, but not Cheryl Hines—mourned. Among other Kennedy family members attending the service were Ethel, a veteran of many clan tragedies; and Bobby's cousin Caroline Kennedy Schlossberg, the soon-to-be-named U.S. Ambassador to Japan, who had lost her father, mother, and brother.

"Mary," Bobby told them all, "was the most extraordinary woman I ever met. I had feelings for her I will never have for another human being." But he would later marry Hines, his longtime girlfriend.

In a eulogy written by Kerry Kennedy entitled "Ode to My Best Friend, Mary Richardson Kennedy" that appeared in *The Huffington Post*, Bobby's sister raved about what a wonderful woman Mary had been. She noted that when Bobby married Mary, "I have never seen two people more thoroughly enchanted with one another and more completely in love. They brought out the best in one another, and spoke about each other with wonder and awe. And even at the more difficult times, they were still devoted to one another, compassionate, caring, and concerned."

Of course, there was no mention by Kerry, president of the Robert F. Kennedy Center for Justice and Human Rights, of her brother's philandering or the effect of the bitter divorce, both of which might be said to have contributed to Mary's suicide. Like many of the Kennedys, Kerry was an expert at spin, and like some of the Kennedys, she had been a reputed cheater herself, such as in her much-publicized affair during her troubled marriage to Andrew Cuomo.

At the same time that Kerry was praising Mary as a popular, beautiful, extraordinarily bright student and creative woman, she also emphasized what she claimed was Mary's dark side—fighting back "the demons who were trying to invade the Paradise of her very being," as she put it. She claimed that Mary "suffered from depression" for the "last six years or more," and went on to assert that the depression had existed "for as long as I knew her," stating that it had "reared up in high school, college, and beyond." Buried in Kerry's narrative, in just one brief paragraph, was a mention of what she characterized as her pleasant visit on Monday night, May 14—three days before Mary killed herself.

The Richardsons, meanwhile, held a private memorial service at the stylish Standard Hotel in Manhattan's trendy Meatpacking District on rainy Monday, May 21. That service concluded with the playing of a recording of "Proud Mary," by Ike and Tina Turner.

The Richardson family had battled unsuccessfully in court over which family—they or the Kennedys—controlled Mary's remains. The Kennedys won and she was buried in a plain wooden casket in St. Francis Xavier Cemetery, in Centerville, Massachusetts, where Bobby's aunt Eunice was interred. She was later exhumed by the Kennedys and moved to another grave in the same cemetery, a move that sparked some controversy.

Within a few months of Mary's suicide, Bobby put their home in Mount Kisco on the market for $3.995 million. When he and his first wife, Emily, bought it in 1985, they had paid just $745,000. The home's value had soared, in part, as a result of Mary's "green" renovation.

TWO MONTHS AFTER THE Mary Kennedy tragedy, her "best friend," Kerry Kennedy, was arrested.

On the morning of July 13, 2012, she had mistakenly taken the controversial prescription sleeping pill Ambien instead of her thyroid medication. On her way to the gym in her Lexus SUV, she slammed into a tractor-trailer truck, but continued driving until she was found by a motorist nearby, slumped over the steering wheel but not seriously injured. One theory first offered by her doctors was that she had suffered a "complex partial seizure" as the result of a previous unexplained head injury. But toxicology tests showed that she had ingested the strong sleeping medication.

Just days before she went on trial in late February 2014, the *New York Post*'s columnist Andrea Peyser wrote that Bobby had called her and pleaded with her for compassion when writing about the latest Kennedy scandal. He asserted that his fifty-four-year-old sister—the seventh-born of RFK and Ethel Kennedy's children—deserved to be considered innocent because she had done so many good deeds for humanity throughout her life, Mother Teresa–like.

He boasted that she had been "instrumental in freeing political prisoners and dissidents from around the globe from imprisonment and torture," and made the far-fetched claim, with no supporting evidence, that if she were to be convicted at her trial on the misdemeanor drug driving rap and put in jail, political agitators and gay Africans could wind up being imprisoned, tortured, or even killed.

Ethel Kennedy, two months away from her eighty-sixth birthday, showed up at the White Plains, New York, courthouse confined to a wheelchair and surrounded by concerned family members, friends, and assorted entourage. The matriarch's aged condition generated much sympathetic media and courtroom attention. A veteran of many Kennedy courtroom dramas through the years, Ethel knew well how to play her role.

When Kerry took the stand in her own defense she also played the Kennedy card to the hilt, invoking her murdered father, telling the six-member jury, "Daddy was the attorney general during the civil rights movement, and then a senator . . . he was assassinated while running for president."

Not surprisingly, she was acquitted.

The New York Times pointed out that the not-guilty verdict came with some irony. While the prosecution had, in part, put Kerry Kennedy on trial to show she wasn't being given favored treatment because of her name, "it was her very prominence as a Kennedy that helped her mount a defense that made prosecutors look inept and even heartless."

At the close of the four-and-a-half-day trial, Ethel Kennedy was miraculously out of the wheelchair and jauntily walking arm in arm with her victorious daughter.

SOME SIX MONTHS AFTER Mary Kennedy's tragic end, a joyous Cheryl Hines accompanied a seemingly contented Bobby to Paris to celebrate his eighteen-year-old daughter Kyra's formal debut at the Bal des Débutantes 2013. "It's my first time wearing haute couture, so that's really exciting," boasted Kyra to reporters, "and I'm obsessed by the color [blue]" of her Christian Dior gown. Kyra, who closely resembled her late mother, was among twenty debs chosen exclusively for the ball.

On a drizzly Saturday, August 2, 2014, in the Kennedy compound in Hyannis Port, sixty-year-old Bobby married the forty-eight-year-old divorcée Hines, who became his third wife. A Unitarian Universalist minister officiated.

Not long after the wedding, the newlyweds purchased a $4.995 million gated estate with a recording studio and a two-story treehouse that was advertised as a "Connecticut compound in Malibu," according to *Variety*. Hines had sold her five-bedroom, four-bath gated Cape Cod–style home in the tony Bel-Air section of Los Angeles. She had bought the "bachelorette" pad for $2.350 million after her 2010 divorce. Shortly after marrying Bobby, she put it on the market for $2.995 million. It sold for $3.105 million.

Bobby's sister Rory, the filmmaker, had also bought in Malibu, a foreclosed gem of an estate with an ocean view, for $2.9 million.

Some in the Kennedy circle believed that Bobby was leading part of the third generation in a migration west from the Kennedys' old domains in the East as a way to put behind them the haunting tragedies and scandals of the past.

BEFORE BECOMING A KENNEDY WIFE, Cheryl Ruth Hines had been married for almost eight years to a Hollywood producer and manager, Paul R. Young, who had helped her with her acting career. Hines married Young, reportedly a descendant of the Mormon Church founder and polygamist Brigham Young, on December 30, 2002. Two years later, Hines gave birth to a daughter, who was named Catherine Rose.

Paul Young was a handsome, bright English literature major at Swarthmore College, but with dreams of becoming a movie and TV mogul. When he first moved to Hollywood in the early 1990s he worked as a waiter. His first job in a creative field was as an assistant to the *Variety* editor Peter Bart, a onetime studio executive who had written a book about Mormon culture and also was a Swarthmore alumnus. According to Bart, who profiled Young for *Variety* in 2010, "He didn't know a damn thing about the entertainment business [but] soon Paul was deciding who I should talk to on the phone and who I should ignore."

Bart readily concluded that Paul Young was a "smart hustler."

In the late nineties, Young had gone into partnership with Peter Principato, a Long Island–raised graduate of Adelphi University, where he was vice president of the junior and senior classes. By the age of twenty-four, he was one of the youngest talent agents at William Morris. He and

Young later formed Principato-Young Entertainment, which managed a stable of comedic actors, including Cheryl Hines, and that's when she and Young began their relationship.

It was in late July 2010 that Young filed for divorce from Hines, citing the boilerplate Hollywood reason, "irreconcilable differences," with property rights to be determined.

Unlike Bobby's first wife, Emily, who was a Phi Beta Kappa in college, got a law degree, and served as a Legal Aid attorney in New York City, and unlike his second wife, Mary, who graduated near the top of her Ivy League class and became a talented architectural designer, Cheryl Hines's claim to academic fame was as homecoming queen, elected as a write-in candidate, for her Class of 1983 at Tallahassee's public Leon High School.

The daughter of a building contractor father and a state employee mother, Hines later claimed to her hometown newspaper that she won the title because of the "dork and chorus nerd vote. Those were my people. I was not the prettiest or the most popular girl in school. I never got the big part in [Tallahassee's Young Actors Theater] musicals because I wasn't a very good singer." When the group was casting for a production of *The Sound of Music*, Hines didn't get the Julie Andrews part. She played a nun.

For a time after high school, she attended the University of Central Florida. Then she drove west to Hollywood to pursue an acting career. For a time she waitressed, and then became a personal assistant to Rob Reiner. She studied improv and sketch comedy with the Groundlings before landing her first TV roles, the biggest of which was as the perky wife of the very Jewish and neurotic Larry David character on HBO's black-humor sitcom *Curb Your Enthusiasm*. For her role, she earned a couple of Emmy nominations and a star on the Hollywood Walk of Fame.

But her most successful role was her part in the Kennedy clan drama. "They are a lot like other families," she once said, "except they are the Kennedys."

After she married Bobby, Hines expressed her "excitement" about having the iconic Kennedy name, and boasted about going to the White House with her groom to see her new mother-in-law, Ethel, receive the 2014 Presidential Medal of Freedom. Ethel's daughter Kerry, who

made the announcement, stated that her widowed mother "is so deserv-
ing of this award." The medal, the nation's highest civilian honor, was
being kept in the family; it had been established by JFK in 1963.

In noting the trip to 1600 Pennsylvania Avenue, N.W., Bobby's bride
was quoted in the press as saying that her life with him was "spicier,"
and a lot of laughs. "People in my circle tend to look at people in politics
as being boring," but that wasn't the case, she noted, with her second
husband—even though he *wasn't* in politics.

In his sixth decade, Bobby had begun another domestic life, with his
third wife.

The couple's close pal Larry David had even told Bobby, "Nothing
you ever do will rattle her."

A decades-long friend of Bobby's who was among the three hundred
guests at the Kennedy–Hines wedding was mystified as to why Hines
married Bobby, since his history as a womanizer had become so public
and was entwined in scandal.

As the friend later observed: "Any woman who gets involved with
Bobby does so with her eyes open, or their brains lopped off. Any woman
who thinks they're going to change Bobby is misguided and purposefully ignorant. Women have to understand what they're getting into when
they're with him. You can hate it, you can make excuses for it, you can
do whatever you want to do, it doesn't change the fact that he has a long
history of doing certain things. And if you think, Wow, I'll be different,
then you're fucked."

Of RFK and Ethel Skakel Kennedy's eleven children, Robert Francis Kennedy Jr. did not turn out to be the best or the worst, but rather the most complex, the most controversial, and the most enigmatic. His older sister, Kathleen, and his older brother, Joe, had followed their assassinated father into politics. The baby of the family, Rory, had become a respected documentary filmmaker. At the other extreme, their brother Michael, accused of having a sexual relationship with a teenage girl, had escaped prosecution and probable incarceration but was killed a year later in a bizarre ski accident. Their young brother David, long addicted to drugs, died of a lethal overdose. In that star-crossed, dysfunctional branch of the Kennedy clan alone there was a succession of broken marriages, and abuse of alcohol and other substances. Of all his siblings—and even many of his Kennedy and Skakel relatives—Bobby infamously held the record for the most marriages, three, and probably the longest addiction problem.

Some close to him wondered how he was able to survive at all, let alone make an esteemed professional life for himself. That was underscored by Bobby himself at the funeral for his closest friend, Peter

Kaplan, who died of cancer in November 2013 at the age of fifty-nine. At Kaplan's funeral service, Bobby was heard to say, "This wasn't supposed to happen. You were supposed to be giving *my* eulogy."

As a friend of both men observed later, "Everyone expected Bobby to die first."

Closing in on the seventh decade of his life, having overcome years of drug use beginning when he was just fourteen, having been expelled from two boarding schools, having been arrested for possession of drugs at least twice, having faced a near-fatal heroin overdose, having had two failed marriages and having fathered six children, having suffered the suicide of his estranged second wife, and having ignited scandal because of his drugs and womanizing, Bobby's successful life as the nation's most prominent environmental activist and lawyer was still, miraculously, on track in the second decade of the twenty-first century.

His plan going forward was to focus on the important issue of climate change. He'd already sparked controversy on the hot-button topic by suggesting that those who were skeptics about global warming— mainly those naysayers who didn't agree with him—should be thrown in jail. Bobby denied having put it that way. Still, his timing was on the mark. As it happened, scientists determined that 2014 had been the hottest year on Earth since record-keeping began in 1880.

Nevertheless, with all he had done in the environmental field, and planned to do, he personally faced great disappointment—that he never actually realized the expectations for him as his family's bearer of the torch. If Bobby ever had a blueprint for a political future, it was never fulfilled.

As a close associate of more than three decades noted, "He would have very much liked to have followed in his father's footsteps and been a senator and a public servant. He would have liked to have held political office. He would have liked to debate, and that's one of the things he's good at. But he reconciled himself to that *not* happening, and Bobby's been very disappointed that it never happened."

From the moment he was born, he was deemed destined for political greatness. After all, he possessed his idolized father's name; he was a Kennedy with all the power and privilege that came with it. There was nothing that could go wrong, nothing that could keep him from reaching the pinnacle. That possibility had been drummed into him by his surrogate father, Lem Billings, the homosexual Kennedy clan acolyte who took control of Bobby's life after his father was murdered. It was Billings who convinced Bobby, beginning when he was an undergrad at Harvard, that one day he could be president, and Bobby began to believe that was his destiny.

But so much did go wrong.

Later in life he refused to blame the trauma of his father's assassination, or his Kennedy and Skakel genes, for his addictive personality. Rather, he blamed the era in which he had grown up, the turbulent sixties. However, not everyone who knew Bobby well agreed with his assessment, particularly in regard to the issues of addiction and genes.

As Robert Boyle, the respected environmentalist who had taken Bobby into the Riverkeeper organization after his heroin possession arrest, asserted in early 2015: "He's picked up every flaw that any Kennedy ever had—from his grandfather onward—and concentrated them, whether it's drugs or sex. All of the negative has just drained into him genetically. Just imagine his wife hanging herself. If his wife had emotional troubles, you look after her. You don't shake her off and screw fifty other women or whatever he put in his diary. Quite frankly, I don't think he has a conscience, which means he can never reflect on something that he thought he did wrong. He externalizes all of this, and that's his approach to life."

For years Bobby's name had been considered for one political office or another. So many times he was asked by reporters when—not whether—he was going to throw his hat in the ring, and he always left the option open, titillating the media, teasing political operatives, and giving hope to a public hungry for another Kennedy in high office.

Once, when asked by *The New York Times* why he hadn't gone into politics, he curiously boasted, "I have enough friends and family who are in the House and Senate, so if I want legislation, I have the access."

Still, Bobby had quietly looked into running in 2000 for the vacated seat of Senator Daniel Patrick Moynihan. Bobby was considered an obvious choice for a run. He possessed the historical context; his father had set up residency in New York, was termed a carpetbagger, but won the senatorial election in 1966, setting the stage for his fatal presidential campaign.

Knowing he could be the chosen one, Bobby had met with a couple of savvy New York politicos to get their take on what he should do, and he came away deciding to stay out of the race. His conversations, he said, had been with the newly elected Senator Charles Schumer and the city's public advocate, Mark Green, both of whom, Bobby claimed, had advised him that the job would take up too much of his time and keep him away from his growing family. At the time, Mary Kennedy had had their fourth child—a son, Aiden, who was turning a year old. Bobby now had a brood of six, including RFK III and Kick with his first wife, Emily.

Claiming the demands of the office would keep him from seeing Aiden until he was "4½"—clearly an exaggeration—he denied that his decision had anything to do with the obvious, the many skeletons, known and unknown, in his dark past.

Indeed, Bobby had much to hide, and good reason to fear entering the political arena.

But when asked about his past drug problems by reporters covering his possible senate run, he said he didn't think it would be an issue. "I have thick skin," he declared, and boasted, "If I wanted to run for something, there's always something to run for."

In fact, Bobby had quietly decided in the late 1990s to remain in the environmental field. He had earned a national reputation for helping to build the Waterkeeper Alliance into an international organization. He had successfully sued major polluters. He was credited with cleaning up the Hudson River and making New York City's drinking water safe. And he was known for using radical tactics to accomplish his goals, such as when he was involved in creating a controversial public service message regarding clean drinking water in New York reservoirs. In it, he bizarrely wondered how much of the "Long Island Lolita" Amy Fisher's urine was flowing into a New York City reservoir from the Bedford Hills Correctional Facility where she was confined for shooting her lover's wife. The ad, considered too weird, never ran.

Bobby was considered by friend and foe alike to be "relentless," "not easily put off," "provocative," but *not* a consensus builder.

There had been media talk in 2004 that if John Kerry had won the presidency—which he lost to George W. Bush—the post of head of the Environmental Protection Agency would have gone to Bobby; the two had even discussed it, but nothing came of it.

Then, in 2007, there was chatter that Bobby might run for attorney general of New York State. But that never happened.

Some liberals who supported him politically because of his family name and the Kennedy brand of politics were taken aback when he was quoted as saying: "I wouldn't be a reliably liberal senator. My father was never a liberal. He was a devout Catholic with an open mind . . . I'm not trying to pretend I'm not who I am. I understand the gift I've been given, being in this family. I also know the losses . . ."

Bobby would even pen an admiring afterword for a 2007 reprint of *Conscience of a Conservative*, Barry Goldwater's ghostwritten 1964 screed that was must-reading for right-leaning conservative Republicans.

And Bobby told *New York* magazine in 2007 that he was "more conservative, in the traditional sense" than George Bush, whom he despised, as evidenced by Bobby's third book, *Crimes Against Nature: How George W. Bush & His Corporate Pals Are Plundering the Country & Hijacking Our Democracy*.

When Bobby sat for a 2007 interview with Oprah, she, like so many others in the past, pointedly asked him: "Why haven't you run for office?"

Once again, he said it was because of his family, but with a caveat this time.

"I've got six reasons running around the house," he said. In fact, when he gave that answer, two of those six were already adults. RFK III was twenty-three years old and living his own life, as was his nineteen-year-old daughter, Kick, who was in college in California. Neither was running around the house, as he claimed.

But Bobby continued teasingly, "I would run if there were an office open because I'm so distressed about the kind of country my children will inherit. I've tried to cling to the idea that I could be of public service without compromising my family life. But at this point, I would run."

"For what?" Oprah asked.

For the Senate, or for the New York governor's office, he said. But the problem was, he quickly added, "My friends are in those offices, and I'm not going to run against them."

Asked why he hadn't run for the attorney general's job in New York, he once again used family as the reason: "I have the kind of life where I can take my kids on trips with me. I can involve them in my work. I've always avoided politics because I didn't want to make commitments that would take me away from raising these children. But now America has changed so dramatically that I'm asking myself—what's going to be left of this country? I'm spending time with my kids, but maybe my time would be spent just as well if I tried to save the country."

Oprah asked if he would ever run for the presidency, but he avoided a direct response: "I really just try to live my life one day at a time and do what I'm supposed to on that day. But if opportunities came up for me to run for office, I would probably do it. If that doesn't happen, then I'll happily continue doing what I'm doing. . . . If Hillary left the Senate, I might run for that seat."

When, in 2008, that possibility arose after President Obama chose Hillary Rodham Clinton to be Secretary of State, Bobby said he conferred with his uncle Ted, the senator, who, Bobby claimed at the time, "[A]lways advises me to spend time with my family. He always tells me that it often seems like things won't open up. But yet they do. I hope one day that I'll be able to do public service and government. It might happen one day."

However, in an article about Bobby in *The New York Times*, in which his drug issues were mentioned, Ted Kennedy indicated he had second thoughts about his nephew in politics: "I think, in a very dramatic way, Bobby's surviving, and his determination to get to a state of mind where he can be constructive has been central to him. He has faced some enormous challenges, some enormously serious challenges."

In Kennedy's 532-page memoir, *True Compass*, published posthumously in 2009, he wondered like "a lot of people" whether his nephew JFK Jr., Bobby's cousin, would have ever sought public office had he not died so young. "I think he might have, and that he would have excelled," Kennedy wrote. Many other young Kennedys were mentioned in the senator's book, including a few of Bobby's siblings such as Michael and Rory and Max. But, curiously, not a single word about Bobby was found.

When Barack Obama was elected president, *The Washington Post* and *Politico* ran stories saying that Bobby was among those being considered to head the Environmental Protection Agency (EPA), or be named Secretary of the Interior. "[Bobby] Kennedy would be a shrewd early move for the new presidential team," *Politico* asserted. "Obama advisers said the nomination [for the EPA post] would please both" Hillary

Clinton and Ted Kennedy. "It also would raise the profile of the EPA which would help endear Obama to liberals . . . Kennedy has long championed a cleaner water supply for New York City."

But there were a number of environmentalists who were adamantly against Bobby's nomination if it occurred. One reason was his opposition to installing wind turbines in Nantucket Sound to make cheap electricity; even *The New York Times* had editorialized that "the project should be approved."

The authors of a 2007 book entitled *Cape Wind: Money, Celebrity, Class, Politics and the Battle for Our Energy Future on Nantucket Island* claimed that Ted Kennedy had fought against the clean-energy project because "that's where I sail." And one of the authors, Robert Whitcomb, called Bobby's reaction to the project "so irrational and incoherent, there's not much to say. . . . He's a troubled person," he told the New York *Daily News.* Bobby claimed he got involved to help local fishermen who were against the project. "We're not against the wind farm," he asserted. "We just think there are better places for it." He even wrote an op-ed piece for the *Times* headlined, "An Ill Wind Off Cape Cod."

After *The Washington Post* mentioned Bobby as a potential EPA head, a Sierra Club member observed, "My concern regarding RFK Jr. would be that, while he has a lot of passion about environmental protection, he is more of a 'show horse' than a 'work horse.' The WP should have done their homework before throwing his name out there. Kennedy has never been able to actually get hired by anyone since his heroin conviction, even [California Governor Arnold] Schwarzenegger was unable to get him a job in his administration."

Bobby's onetime Riverkeeper mentor and colleague, Robert Boyle, was also an opponent. As he said in early 2015, "I would have testified in front of Congress and said this man is absolutely unfit to hold office."

The other objection to Bobby's selection for a powerful post in the Obama administration was his claim that there was a link between autism and childhood vaccines.

Writing for *Slate* in August 2005, the investigative journalist and author Arthur Allen, a vaccine proponent, noted that Bobby had been making the rounds of popular radio and TV programs such as *The Daily Show with Jon Stewart* and *Imus in the Morning*, accusing government vaccine scientists of "covering up" a link between thimerosal, a preservative used in vaccines, and a massive increase in childhood autism in America. (The other celebrity spokesperson for the same cause was the onetime *Playboy* Playmate Jenny McCarthy.) Allen also pointed out that in a July 2005 *Rolling Stone* article championing his thimerosal theory, Bobby had made "large and small errors, and distortions."

In 2014 an article about Bobby and the vaccine controversy in *The Washington Post*'s Sunday magazine, written by the former *Audubon* magazine editor Keith Kloor, noted that at first, for his *Rolling Stone* piece, Bobby was "feted like a prizewinning muckraker. . . . Then came the backlash. Critics charged Kennedy with quoting material out of context. *Rolling Stone* had to make corrections. Enough doubts were raised that Salon [which also ran the piece] eventually retracted the story. Unbowed," continued Kloor, "Kennedy stands by the piece and admits to only a few inconsequential errors."

After the *Post* story ran, *Slate*'s science editor, Laura Helmuth, wrote that she thought the story had portrayed Bobby as too "passionate and sympathetic." The *Slate* headline included the line: "He's actually obsessive and dangerous."

The *Slate* piece sparked commenters to denounce Bobby—one called him "too partisan and kind of a nut when it comes to policy," and added, "Throw in Kennedy's 1983 heroin bust, and you've got yourself an uncomfortable nominee."

Another critic called Bobby "an antivaccinationist crank and activist extraordinaire . . . a booster of pseudoscience, a hothead prone to comparing political enemies to Hitler and Mussolini, and a lawyer whose science background appears to be primarily torturing science to fit his agenda more than anything else."

In other words, there were many more against Bobby being nominated than for him getting a top administration post.

Obama must have agreed, because in December 2008, he chose a New Jersey official to head the EPA, Lisa Jackson, who had served as the commissioner of the Department of Environmental Protection, the first African American woman to head the EPA. (Two days after Christmas 2012, she stepped down with critics claiming that Obama was failing in his commitment to climate change and other environmental issues.)

Bobby had been taking other questionable stands. One had to do with the assassination of his uncle the president, which had occurred when Bobby was nine.

On the evening of Friday, January 11, 2013, Bobby and his sister Rory appeared together to discuss the Kennedys with Charlie Rose at the AT&T Performing Arts Center in, of all places, Dallas, Texas, infamously the scene of JFK's murder fifty years earlier. The event was advertised as an "once-in-a-lifetime interview."

The *Dallas Morning News* reported favorably on the appearance, with David Flick writing that Bobby entertained "the audience with stories about growing up in the most famous family in America."

But according to Betsy Lewis, an arts writer for *The Dallas Observer*, "[I]t was a bizarre performance by a bizarre and charming" Bobby, who, Lewis noted, "avoided answering questions about his family." She described him as "animated . . . he leaned into the round oak table with his chin in his hand, covering his mouth. It was like [he] had an automatic on/off switch."

Instead of the folksy Kennedy stories Charlie Rose and the sold-out audience expected to hear, Bobby went on and on about how his father had conducted his own investigation into his brother's murder. Bobby, Lewis observed, "was losing the audience, so he burst out, 'My father believed that the Warren Report was a shoddy piece of craftsmanship.'" The controversial Warren Commission report had concluded that Lee Harvey Oswald was the lone assassin, and had ruled out a conspiracy. In his talk, Bobby also claimed that America was "becoming a national security state," that corporations "want profits" and "we'd be nuts to let them run government," and "Nationalism in Africa! The end of colonialism!" among other rants.

"At this point," Lewis noted, "I don't think anyone knew what the hell he was talking about. It was something about the Kennedy family airlifting President Obama's father out of Kenya to begin a new life in America."

When the clearly exasperated Rose, noted for his calm questioning of famous figures on PBS, tried to get the interview back on track, he asked Bobby, "Why haven't you run for office?" His response: "I have six kids."

According to Betsy Lewis, "He should have answered, 'My 1983 arrest for heroin possession.'"

A POLITICAL CONSULTANT WITH LONG-STANDING close ties to Bobby observed in early 2015: "It's partially accurate that his use of drugs, his marriages, and his womanizing would come up in a campaign—by the media and by the opposition. But his use of heroin would never be an issue. It wouldn't keep him out of any race at any time because it happened when he was young, in the sixties. We looked at his drug use and we talked about it, and determined it was actually a plus because Bobby could say, 'I've gotten myself up and this is what I've done since then.' There were a lot of issues that went into Bobby's decision never to run for office. They were financial, personal, and opportunistic, and he was never going to bare his soul publicly about any of it. But those are things that were taken into consideration in making the decisions he chose about the direction of his life."

Continued the source, who was a confidant of Bobby's for decades: "He's a very complex guy who has had very difficult things thrown at him through his life. He's attracted all kinds of people to him—people picked at him all his life, people have wanted to be around him, people have asked things of him, have taken advantage of him, or tried to give him things like drugs and sex. And he had that essentially from birth because of his name. People think he's a Kennedy who can do whatever he wants, but he can't. He's circumscribed by that name, too. Being a Kennedy isn't a be-all and end-all. It's also a cudgel people use against you. Bobby's handled it extraordinarily well given all the shit that's been thrown at him. He's come out the other end as a remarkable public servant, a good man in a difficult situation."

Through the years many people have had so many opinions about RFK Jr., namesake of his iconic father. His character flaws and his environmental activism have sparked controversy and scandal. But only history will tell what his legacy will be, and define his standing in the Kennedy pantheon. This book hopefully has offered some clues.

ACKNOWLEDGMENTS

The story of Robert F. Kennedy Jr. is based on public and private documents, news accounts, his own writings, and—most important—the many, many people whom I interviewed over a two-year period. There were those who liked and respected him, those who didn't, and I wanted to know why in both cases. Most were honest, candid, and perceptive. Among them were boarding school classmates, college and law school chums, women in his life, political and environmental associates, supporters and detractors. In other words, in order to write a fair and balanced portrait, it was important to probe every aspect of his life.

As it turned out, of the many people I interviewed, Bobby was not one of them. While this book was always meant to be an independent biography—popularly called "unauthorized"—I had also always planned to contact him with questions to get his side of the many issues that surfaced during my research. Prior to my reaching out to him, however, he presumably was well aware that I was writing a book about him; there had been mentions in the media of the work-in-progress, and some people I had called to interview told me that they first wanted to check with him before they committed.

In early December 2014, I sent an e-mail to Christine O'Neill, his assistant at Pace University Law School, and asked her to pass along to Bobby my request for an interview for the book I was completing. She soon responded by e-mail: "As soon as he reviews, I'll get back to you." When I got no response, I e-mailed her once again, asking whether she had passed on my request. Her response was yes and that "Mr. Kennedy is currently traveling. As soon as he reviews, I will get back to you." Another e-mail was sent in late December, but I heard nothing more from her, or from him.

That said, I'd like to offer my gratitude to all those who agreed to be interviewed, and to talk candidly and openly, and on the record. Their names and their words are documented throughout the book. There were those few who asked for anonymity, mainly to avoid losing friendships or access. You know who you are and I thank you for your insights and perception.

Several books were invaluable in my research. Bobby Kennedy's co-authored volume, *The Riverkeepers*, was especially helpful because, in a rare autobiographical chapter, he revealed some interesting things about his early life, his schooling, his past drug use, and his involvement in the environmental movement. Another book that I found especially helpful was Christopher Kennedy Lawford's memoir, *Symptoms of Withdrawal*, which was groundbreakingly candid and insightful for a member of the Kennedy family. What I view as the bible of the Kennedy clan's third generation, and Bobby's role in it, is Peter Collier and David Horowitz's 1984 *The Kennedys: An American Drama*.

Throughout this book, and in my source notes, I cite a number of news and magazine sources used in my research and reporting, such as *The New York Times*, *The Washington Post*, *Time*, *People*, and so on. I want to make special reference to the *New York Post* for its exclusive reporting on certain aspects of Mr. Kennedy's life.

I'd also like to thank the team at St. Martin's Press for guiding the project along, among them my editor, Charles Spicer; his right hand, April Osborn, publisher Sally Richardson, and Michael Cantwell, who reviewed the manuscript with a fine-tooth comb. Many thanks to all.

NOTES

PROLOGUE

2 One of *Time* magazine's: *Time*, May 12, 1997.

3 "I've just met": Peter Collier and David Horowitz, *The Kennedys: An American Drama*. New York: Summit Books, 1984, p. 342.

3 "The loss of": Christopher Kennedy Lawford, *Symptoms of Withdrawal*. New York: William Morrow, 2005, p. 101.

ONE: PAROCHIAL SCHOOLING

5 Monroe married DiMaggio on January 14, 1954. They were divorced 274 days later.

7 "Ethel would say": Author interview with Hennessey-Donovan, sourced in author's book *The Other Mrs. Kennedy*. New York: St. Martin's Press, 1994, p. 169.

7 Animals and birds: John Cronin and Robert F. Kennedy, Jr., *The Riverkeepers*. New York: Touchstone, 1999, p. 19.

9 "I thought the Craigheads": Ibid.

10 His first school: *The Other Mrs. Kennedy*, op. cit., p. 258.

11 As a Catholic childhood: Ibid., p. 56.

11 She once seriously: Ibid., p. 57.

12 "Well, here we are": *The Other Mrs. Kennedy*, op. cit.; *McCall's*, August 1965.

13 "Children are cheaper": *The Other Mrs. Kennedy,* op. cit.; *New York Times*, January 20, 1965.

14 Subsequently, he confided: Author interview with source.

14 "This stunned Dr. Locher": Author interview with Tim Ruane.

15 "Bobby didn't act": Author interview with Maurice Nee.

15 "Our school was on ninety": Author interview with Robert Katzen.

16 "It was a circus out there": Author interview with source.

16 "Napoleonic complex": Author interview with source.

17 "He was an ex–Golden Gloves": Author interview with Nee, op. cit.

17 "alcoholism was rampant": Author interview with Mark Judge.

17 "We had a joke": Author interview with source.

18 "Wrestling in phys ed": Author interview with source.

19 "Bobby and I certainly": Author interview with Jack Sirica.

TWO: DADDY'S DEAD

20 "invoked a level": *Symptoms of Withdrawal*, op. cit., p. 99.

21 "The crowds, the press": Author interview with Jim Skakel, *The Other Mrs. Kennedy*, op. cit., p. 307.

22 "You're talking to young Bobby": Author interview with Bob Galland, *The Other Mrs. Kennedy*, op. cit., p. 309.

22 "Mrs. Kennedy ought": *The Other Mrs. Kennedy*, op. cit., p. 315; *D.C. Examiner*, May 24, 1968.

22 "I plan to remain active": *The Other Mrs. Kennedy*, op. cit., p. 314.

24 "Among us freshmen": Author interview with Ruane, op. cit.

25 "His face looked": Jack Newfield, *Robert Kennedy: A Memoir*. New York: E.P. Dutton, 1969.

25 "Mummy's so tired": Theodore H. White, *The Making of the President*. New York: Atheneum, 1969.

25 "The kids were constantly": Author interview with Galland, *The Other Mrs. Kennedy*, op. cit., p. 323.

26 "I got the impression": *National Enquirer*, October 26, 1976.

27 "It was like Hades": Author interview with Roger Mudd, *The Other Mrs. Kennedy*, op. cit., p. 327.

29 "He was grown up": Author interview with Sirica, op. cit.

THREE: SURROGATE FATHER

31 "Millbrook was known": Author interview with Peter Cole.

33 "It was like a staffing": Author interview with source.

33 "Millbrook at its darkest": Author interview with source.

33 Bobby had spiked: *An American Drama*, op. cit., p. 358.

33 "Just leave home": Ibid., p. 358.

33–34 Suddenly she became angry: Ibid.

34 became a "surrogate father": *The Riverkeepers*, op. cit., p. 88.

34 "From the beginning": Author interview with Martin Boswell McKneally, *The Other Mrs. Kennedy*, op. cit., p. 43.

34 "with his live-in": Ibid., p. 43.

35 "display deep homophobia": Evan Thomas, *Robert Kennedy: His Life*. New York: Touchstone, 2000, p. 65.

35 "rich bitch": Ibid.

35 "To some aides": Ibid, p. 244.

36 "So you're down here": Ibid., p. 263.

36 "absolutely could not": Ibid., p. 346.

38 "You're dying just like Daddy!": *An American Drama*, op. cit., p. 362. Two books have credibly reported on the intimate relationship between JFK and Lem Billings—*Jack and Lem: The Untold Story of an Extraordinary Friendship*, by David Pitts, published by Carroll & Graf, 2007, and *The Kennedys in Hollywood*, by Lawrence J. Quirk, published by Cooper Square Press, 2004. The quotes in these three pages regarding the sexual relationship are mostly from Quirk's book.

41 "Everyone knew Lem was queer": Author interview with George Terrien, *The Other Mrs. Kennedy*, op. cit.

FOUR: "UNREQUITED LOVE"

42 "a radio on scan": Author interview with Scott Riviere.

42 "Where's my husband's book!": Author interview with source.

43 "We never saw": Author interview with James Hejduk.

43 "He seemed a very": Author interview with Mark Bontecou.

44 "this odd character": Author interview with Brian Carroll.

44 "In the months and years": Edward M. Kennedy, *True Compass*. New York: Twelve, 2009, p. 281.

45 "They're going to shoot": Ibid., p. 282.

45 "We had a couple": Author interview with widow.

46 "The Skakels now had": Author interview with McKneally, *The Other Mrs. Kennedy*, op. cit., p. 146.

FIVE: PRACTICALLY NAKED

49 was coming to the school: Author interview with Cole, op. cit.

49 "He would receive": Author interview with Carroll, op. cit.

50 "He gave us": Author interview with Tom Kellogg.

50 "The first actual physical": Author interview with Hejduk, op. cit.

50 "Knowing Jack, he was": Author interview with Cole, op. cit.

52 "They were lurking": Author interview with Nick Forster.

52 "There was a lot of": Author interview with Martin Lynn.

52 "treated with deference": Author interview with Joseph Kisting.

53 "Soon after my father's death": *The Riverkeepers*, op. cit., p. 90.

53 "It was obviously": Author interview with widow.

54 "Drugs were the flavor": Author interview with Bontecou, op. cit.

54 "It was during": Author interview with Hejduk, op. cit.

55 "I graduated and was bound": Author interview with Marc Giattini.

55 "Marc was pretty carefully": Author interview with Cole, op. cit.

57 "Bob always seemed": Author interview with Jamie Fanning.

SIX: "RUMPLED KID"

59 "In the autumn": *The Riverkeepers*, op. cit., p. 88.

60 "Myself and a couple": Author interview with Richard "Rob" Bierregaard.

60 "Bobby's rat scene": Author interview with Sumner Pingree III.

61 "I still to this day": Author interview with Fanning, op. cit.

61 "That's kind of a template": Author interview with Wayne Hall.

61 "morbid interest enjoying": Author interview with Ned Rousmaniere.

62 "the occasional joint": Pingree, op. cit.

62 "It kind of followed": Hejduk, op. cit.

SEVEN: BREAKING BAD

65 "It was a fairly healthy": Forster, op. cit.

66 "We'd have these conversations": Fanning, op. cit.

67 our "pathetic homage": *Symptoms of Withdrawal*, op. cit., p. 97.

67 They threw firecrackers: *An American Drama*, op. cit., p. 382.

68 "Bobby was self-destructive": Fanning, op. cit.

68 "We only felt sick": Ibid.

68 "until all the blood": Kisting, op. cit.

69 "I didn't find him": Kellogg, op. cit.

69 "You could look Bobby": Carroll, op. cit.

69 "I was horrified": Forster, op. cit.

70 "We were really good liars": Fanning, op. cit.

70 "Yeah, yeah, yeah": Ibid.

71 "On the faculty": Cole, op. cit.

EIGHT: MILLBROOK TRIUMVIRATE

73 "I can't say": Fanning, op. cit.

73 "From what I heard": Author interview with Bruce Whitcomb.

74 "Bobby was fairly": Author interview with source.

74 "Bobby and Michael": Author interview with Peter Parkinson.

75 Over the years: Author interviews with Noelle Fell, *The Other Mrs. Kennedy*, op. cit.

75 "When they saw them": Riviere, op. cit.

76 "There was no way": Ibid.

77 "Ethel was still": Ibid.

77 "Watching it is": *New York Times*, October 17, 2012.

78 "I was curious about": Riviere, op. cit.

78 One of the most blatant: *The Other Mrs. Kennedy*, op. cit., pp. 392–393.

79 "Ethel had people": Riviere, op. cit.

80 Lawford didn't much care: *Symptoms of Withdrawal*, op. cit., pp. 91–94.

NINE: FRIENDS DIE

81 "My father felt": Author interview with Mark Rivinus.

84 "They were both": Author interview with Parkinson, op. cit.

84 "Michael was a brilliant": Author interview with source.

85 "Michael loved society": Ibid.

86 "It was a rather rough": Parkinson, op. cit.

87 "The circumstances of": Source, op. cit.

87 "My brother was": Parkinson, op. cit.

TEN: CHAPPAQUIDDICK SUMMER

88 Edgartown's police chief: *The Other Mrs. Kennedy*, op. cit., pp. 374–379, based on numerous news accounts of one of the Kennedy clan's darkest scandals.

90 He'd been caught: Various news accounts, and Kennedy's memoir, *True Compass*, op. cit., pp. 95–96.

90 "She had a lot of anger": Author interview with Terrien, *The Other Mrs. Kennedy*, op. cit., p. 379.

90 "My uncle is": Author interview with source.

91 "But Bobby got up": Whitcomb, op. cit.

91 "I was there": Carroll, op. cit.

91 "to pick up the flag": *The Riverkeepers*, op. cit., p. 88.

92 "We were not allowed": Forster, op. cit.

93 "Bobby preyed": Carroll, op. cit.

93 "I didn't think": Fanning, op. cit.

93 "Bobby had women hanging": Author interview with Christopher West.

93 "At church on Sunday": Fanning, op. cit.

94 "they were fine": Rousmaniere, op. cit.

95 "Lem felt very": Forster, op. cit.

95 "Robin was a kind of": Author interview with Dudley Bahlman.

96 "generalized knowledge among": Cole, op. cit.

97 "Neil asked me": Author interview with Donn Wright.

97 "bending over backwards": Cole, op. cit.

97 "very hush-hush": Hejduk, op. cit.

98 "Having a Kennedy speak": Ibid.

ELEVEN: POT BUST

100 "You've dragged your": *An American Drama*, op. cit., p. 382.

101 "has never been involved": *New York Times*, August 6, 1970.

101 "This is, of course": Ibid.

102 "I'm throwing you out": *An American Drama*, op. cit., p. 382.

102 raided his savings: Ibid., p. 383.

103 "I was riding around with bums": Ibid.

103 "inconvenient family matter": Barbara A. Perry, *Rose Kennedy: The Life and Times of a Political Matriarch*. New York: W. W. Norton & Company, 2013.

TWELVE: POMFRET BLACKS

104 "When Bobby and I": Author interview with Lindsey Miesmer.

104 Beyond those issues: Author interview with Joseph K. Milnor.

105 "There was no school": Miesmer, op. cit.

107 "The kids were all aflutter": Author interview with source.

107 "Everybody was at least": Author interview with John Seibel.

108 "The blacks and whites": Author interview with Milton Butts.

109 "It was clear to me": Miesmer, op. cit.

109 "quite a bit of hostility": Seibel, op. cit.

110 "It was a wonderful time": Author interview with Don Hinman.

110 "saw this body": Ibid.

111 In the compound: *An American Drama*, op. cit., p. 374.

111 "a cute guy": Miesmer, op. cit.

112 "I didn't do much": Author interview with Warren Geissinger.

113 "seemed to be at the end": Richard E. Burke, *The Senator: My Ten Years with Ted Kennedy*. New York: St. Martin's Press, 1992.

113 "thought Bobby was their": Geissinger, op. cit.

114 "It was more than": Author interview with Jacque Bailhe.

115 "kind of a problem": Geissinger, op. cit.

115 When a survey: Brad Pearson, Emerson Stone, executive editor, *The Spirit That Is Pomfret*, Pomfret Alumni Association, 1993, p. 240.

115 "Pomfret became known": Geissinger, op. cit.

116 "We were looking": Bailhé, op. cit.

117 According to Bobby's account: *An American Drama*, op. cit., p. 385.

118 "Bobby definitely had": Bailhé, op. cit.

118 One day in late winter: Author interview with Harold Hine.

120 "The Kennedys did a huge": Author interview with Steve Danenberg.

120 "Bobby was exceedingly bright": Ibid.

121 "Per-Jan acted": Milnor, op. cit.

121 "not the kind of shit": Author interview with Hagop Merjian.

121 "One hundred and forty": Ibid.

122 "Bobby wasn't just a pothead": Ibid.

123 "get Bobby the hell out": Ibid.

124 Regarding his seven or eight: *An American Drama*, op. cit., p. 385.

124 "We never had": Author interview with Robert Sloat.

124 "As far as I know": Merjian, op. cit.

125 "We all knew he was expelled": Miesmer, op. cit.

125 Bobby returned home: *The Senator: My Ten Years with Ted Kennedy*, op. cit., pp. 24–25.

126 "RFK Jr. Leaves Home": *National Enquirer*, October 24, 1971.

THIRTEEN: PALFREY STREET

129 "wearing dirty, faded jeans": Author interview with John Cuetera.

130 "big medical marijuana": Author interview with Royce Augustine Hoyle III.

131 "All of us who had": *New York Times*, January 27, 2000.

131 Yarmolinsky's son: Author interview with Toby Yarmolinsky.

132 "Ethel didn't even call": Author interviews with Joanne "Joey" Brode for this book, and for *The Other Mrs. Kennedy*.

135 "kind of a hippie": Author interview with source.

136 "They thought we": Author interview with Vicki Boyajian.

136 "It was a dead body": Ibid.

136 "a little intimate": Ibid.

136 "Bobby would occasionally": Brode, op. cit.

137 "as stoned out": Author interview with source.

137 "He was definitely": Cuetara, op. cit.

137 "maybe to me": Boyajian, op. cit.

137 "He was concerned": Ibid.

138 "liked to do drugs": Cuetara, op. cit.

138 "We should be able": Ibid.

139 Along with using: *An American Drama*, op. cit., p. 387.

139 Andrew Karsch, for one, was: Ibid., p. 386.

140 "The rest of us": Ibid., p. 387.

140 "We weren't enamored": Author interview with source.

141 "kind of lost and indifferent": Boyajian, op. cit.

141 "it was a very tough time": Hoyle, op. cit.

141 "I didn't know much": Brode, op. cit.

143 "He was eating breakfast": Ibid.

143 Bobby's Harvard application: Author interview with source.

144 "I knew Coles": Merjian, op. cit.

144 "only to the admissions office": Ibid.

144 "It was common knowledge": *Symptoms of Withdrawal*, op. cit., p. 192.

145 "full of love": Author interview with source.

145 "He probably looked": Boyajian, op. cit.

145 "For both of us": *Symptoms of Withdrawal*, op. cit., p. 161.

146 "a treasure chest of": Ibid., p. 181.

146 According to Patricia Seaton: *The Other Mrs. Kennedy*, op. cit., p. 426.

146 "I wish you weren't": *New York Post*, May 27, 2012.

147 "I loved getting high": *Symptoms of Withdrawal*, op. cit., p. 159.

147 "He must have had": Brode, op. cit.

FOURTEEN: TWISTED ROOTS

148 "twisted grotesquely": David Nasaw, *The Patriarch: The Remarkable Life and Turbulent Times of Joseph P. Kennedy*. New York: Penguin Press, 2012, p. 780.

148 "The grownups were": Ibid., p. 781.

148 "The countless little": Rita Dallas and Jeanira Ratcliffe, *The Kennedy Case*. New York: G.P Putnam's Sons, 1973, p. 57.

149 "Children are meant": Ibid.

149 "Everything we have": Ibid., p. 168.

149 "more like his grandfather": Ibid., p. 170.

149 "Dear Granpa": *Times to Remember*, op. cit., p. 435.

150 "a twisted, gaunt": *The Patriarch*, op. cit., p. 782.

150 "drawn, downcast, intimidated": *The Kennedy Case*, op. cit., p. 330.

150 "I'm in some trouble": Ibid.

150 "that pointed suspicion": Ibid., p. 334.

150 "Mr. Kennedy failed": Ibid.

150 "Without you, none": Ibid., p. 337.

151 "from the shock": *True Compass*, op. cit., p. 293.

153 "quiet railroad traffic": *The Riverkeepers*, op. cit., p. 79.

154 "a clan of unruly": Ibid.

154 "provide a genetic": Ibid.

154 "tall, large-boned": Ibid.

154 "loved back-country": Ibid.

154 "live mountain lions": Ibid., p. 80.

154 "joined the growing": Ibid.

FIFTEEN: WILD UNCLES

155 "George was totally": *The Other Mrs. Kennedy*, op. cit., p. 251.

156 "I'd never seen": Ibid., p. 253.

156 "chicken-shit": Ibid., p. 137.

156 "a real little dick": Ibid., p. 44.

157 "None of that here!": Ibid., p. 202.

157 "Bobby was sounding": Ibid., p. 235.

158 "To be around Kick": Ibid., p. 292.

158 "the worst possible timing": Ibid., p. 302.

159 "Alcohol ran through": Ibid., p. 40.

159 "nigger baby": Ibid., p. 69.

160 "I figured they were": Ibid., p. 211.

160 "He just couldn't": Ibid., p. 255.

160 "My uncle Rush was mauled": *The Riverkeepers*, op. cit., p. 80.

161 "Rush the lush": Author interview with source.

SIXTEEN: HARVARD BECKONS

163 "I never felt so lucky": Author interview with Peter Kaplan.

164 "Bobby and Peter both": Author interview with source.

164 "I feel that is": *An American Drama*, op. cit., p. 409.

165 While he smoked pot: Author interview with source.

165 "swashbuckling Douglas Fairbanks": *An American Drama*, op. cit., p. 388.

165 "People heard about it": Ibid.

165 There were two strikingly: Author interview with source.

166 "to wrap itself around": *An American Drama*, op. cit., p. 388.

166 The second strikingly: Author interview with source.

166 "a gorgeous animal": Ibid.

170 "completely disorganized": *Symptoms of Withdrawal*, op. cit., p. 213.

170 including boiled rat: *An American Drama*, op. cit., p. 405.

170 "a position of power": *Symptoms of Withdrawal*, op. cit., p. 213.

171 "Here you have it": *An American Drama*, op. cit., p. 405.

172 "a rather unlikely association": *Daily News*, September 1975.

172 "I don't really know whether": *Newsweek*, September 15, 1975.

173 "I'm no actor": *Daily News*, op. cit.
173 "Public figures shouldn't": Ibid.

SEVENTEEN: AUTHOR, AUTHOR

174 "The truth is": Author interview with Peter Shapiro.
175 "on recent historical": Robert F. Kennedy, Jr., *Judge Frank M. Johnson, Jr.* New York: G.P. Putnam's Sons, p. 27.
175 "good Irish citizens": Ibid., p. 30.
175 "loaded with our standard": Ibid., p. 27.
176 "Wallace received us": *An American Drama*, op. cit., p. 410.
176 "Back then, Bobby": Author interview with source.
176 "That's how Jack got started": *An American Drama*, op. cit., p. 389.
177 "more than a rumor": Nigel Hamilton, *JFK: Reckless Youth.* New York: Random House, 1992, p. 315.
178 "You don't know Bobby": *An American Drama*, op. cit., p. 411.
178 "It was Kennedy, Kennedy, Kennedy!": Author interview with Phyllis Grann.
178 "I was excited": Ibid.
179 "neither adequately defines": *New York Times*, July 30, 1978.
180 "a grave disappointment": *Harvard Law Journal*, 165 (1979).
181 "didn't deserve": Grann, op. cit.
181 "It was political": *People*, op. cit.
182 "The papers said": Ibid.
182 "Anything Bobby needed": Grann, op. cit.
182 "It didn't matter": Author interview with Grace Rondinelli-Williams.
183 "Lem used to tell Bobby": *The Kennedys*, op. cit., p. 409.
183 "close to tears": Ibid., p. 444.
183 In a snit: Ibid., 445.
184 Rushing to a pay phone: Ibid., 426.
184 "Duff said she really": Rondinelli-Williams, op. cit.

EIGHTEEN: BRITISH AFFAIR

185 "Bobby Junior Settles Down": Gossip columnist William Hickey, June 11, 1979.
185 "Worry for Bohemian": *Daily Express*, March 23, 1978.
185 "the golden lioness": *People*, July 18, 1977.
186 "a modern-day": Ibid.
187 "I hope to come back": Ibid.
187 It then surfaced that a group: *Daily Express*, April 3, 1978.
187 "Jesus, I've a girlfriend": *Daily Mail*, March 1, 1978.

189 "Goodness knows what": *Daily Express*, April 19, 1978; *New York Times*, April 16, 1978.

189 "Our relationship will not": *New York Post*, August 29, 1979.

189 "It would serve no": Ibid.

190 In the tiny community: Author interview with source.

190 "Bobby back then": Ibid.

190 Epstein had hired her: Author interview with Edward Jay Epstein.

190 "she was engaged": Ibid.

190 "shabby, red brick": *Daily Express*, May 2, 1979.

191 "Rebecca was living": Author interview with source.

191 Around the same time: *Daily Mail*, June 13, 1979.

191 "there are various unpleasant": *Daily Express*, July 18, 1980.

191 "I have just spoken": *London Evening News*, June 13, 1979.

191 "proper reticence": *New York Post*, October 13, 1981.

192 "going through a short-lived": E-mail to author.

NINETEEN: BLOOMINGTON LOVE

193 "They just seemed like": Author interview with source.

193 "It was hard to tell": Ibid.

194 "Bobby and I met": Ibid.

194 "He was kind of": Author interview with source.

195 "quiet, pretty shy": Author interview with Dan Honeycutt.

196 "kind of a Mayberry": Ibid.

196 "She had never talked": Ibid.

197 "What the heck?": Ibid.

197 "There were concerns": Author interview with Janet Black.

198 "Emily and I were": Author interview with source.

198 "It was pretty common": Ibid.

198 "I spent weekends": Ibid.

198 he felt that President Carter: *True Compass*, op. cit., p. 359.

199 "I told Bobby": Author interview with David Horowitz.

199 "Bobby had a bit": Author interview with Peter Collier.

199 "Bobby had a girl": Horowitz, op. cit.

200 "the cat was out": Ibid.

201 "he thought that we would": Collier, op. cit.

202 "a number of interviews": Horowitz, op. cit.

202 "just to contaminate": Collier, op. cit.

202 "false, loose chatter": E-mail from Alexandra Cury to author.

203 "Tess and Bobby dated": Author interview with Connie Dempsey.

204 "She took to riding": *The Other Mrs. Kennedy*, op. cit., p. 64.

204 "a better rider than her son": Dempsey, op. cit.

204 "Hello, Connie": Ibid.

205 "After they jumped": Ibid.

TWENTY: EMOTIONAL CHANGES

207 "The real Bobby Kennedy?": *People*, April 12, 1982.

207 Bobby had already attempted: Bloomington *Herald-Telephone*, October 13, 1981.

208 "We thought he was": Ibid.

208 "Emily Our Own Lady Di": Ibid.

209 "hearing" about Bobby: Ibid.

209 "When I was a teenager": Ibid.

209 "just a super young": *Herald-Telephone*, op. cit., October 14, 1981.

209 "My mother tells me": *People*, op. cit.

210 Despite Emily Black's: Author interview with source.

210 "It was hilarious": *Jack and Lem*, op. cit., p. 305.

210 "very upset about": *The Kennedys*, op. cit., p. 444.

210 "That night Lem got": Ibid.

212 "I'm sure he's already": Ibid., p. 445.

212 "After I go": Ibid.

212 "For Lem—Jack's best": *Jack and Lem*, op. cit., p. 186.

212 "It was the epitome": Author interview with source.

212 "[T]he most fun": From Billings Oral History in John F. Kennedy Library, in *Jack and Lem*, op. cit.

213 "was like having a wonderful": David Michaelis, *The Best of Friends*. New York: William Morrow, 1983, p. 185.

213 "often had the spirit": *The Best of Friends*, op. cit., p. 183.

213 "very close": Author interview with Pitts.

214 "rivalry between Lawford": Ibid.

214 "had found a place": *Symptoms of Withdrawal*, op. cit., pp. 100–102.

214 "I suspect": Author interview with Horowitz.

215 "Jackie had kind of": Author interview with Collier.

TWENTY-ONE: HATE MAIL

216 "I love St. Patrick's": *Daily News*, October 11, 1981.

216 "Park Avenue law firm": Ibid.

217 "That's where I'm from": *Indianapolis Star*, January 28, 1982.

217 "always was a sharp": Ibid.

217 "They were mad": Author brief chat with Tom Black.

218 "Robert Jr. and Emily": *Herald-Telephone*, April 2, 1982.

218 "I'd heard kind of": Author interview with the Rev. Terry Ewing.

219 "We drove out": Author interview with John Roca.

219 "I don't think": *Indianapolis Star*, op. cit.

219 "He's excited": Ibid.

220 "Easter is the highest": Rev. Ewing, op. cit.

220 "sort of the rock 'n' roll": Ibid.

220 the blaze had been: Ibid.

221 "They looked like any": *Herald-Telephone*, March 17, 1982.

221 In a letter to: Letter dated January 22, 1982, from Rev. Ewing to Mrs. R. W. Pawley, 204 Carol Lane, Cameron, Mo. 64429.

222 "He paid attention": IrishCentral.com, September 23, 2009.

222 "She showed remarkable": *The Other Mrs. Kennedy*, op. cit., p. 409.

222 "My aunt Ethel's": *Symptoms of Withdrawal*, op. cit., p. 129.

223 "There really wasn't much": Rev. Ewing, op. cit.

223 "The Deliberate Execution": The mimeographed hate mail was sent to "Emily Black c/o Pastor," and was from an address in Waukegan, Illinois.

223 "I told Bobby and Emily": Rev. Ewing, op. cit.

TWENTY-TWO: WEDDING BELLS

224 Most of the week: *Herald-Telephone*, April 2, 1982.

225 "hanging out with": Author interview with source.

225 "Friends and Family Rally": *People*, September 24, 1979.

225 "I'm David Kennedy": *The Andy Warhol Diaries*. New York: Warner Books, 1989, p. 238.

225 "loved the energy": Author interview with Robert T. Littell, author of *The Men We Became: My Friendship with John F. Kennedy, Jr.* New York: St. Martin's Press, 2004.

225 "wonderful old roué": *New York*, September 15, 1980.

226 "closest thing to royals": *New York*, March 20, 1989.

226 "made overtures": Ibid.

226 "less a disco baby": Ibid.

226 "disco uncle": Ibid.

226 "Peppo looked out": Author interview with source.

226 "asked us that any": Roca, op. cit.

226 "Tell me about your": *New York*, September 15, 1980.

227 "She is lovely": *New York Times*, October 12, 1981.

229 "They're American royalty": *Herald-Telephone*, op. cit.

229 "Those folks came": Rev. Ewing, op. cit.

230 "And that's because": Ibid.

230 "I'm used to cooking": *Herald-Telephone*, April 1, 1982.

230 "couple of the Kennedys": Author interview with Bill Brown.

230 "I never saw": Rev. Ewing, op. cit.

231 "Giving a funny": *Symptoms of Withdrawal*, op. cit.

233 "If Jackie and company": Rev. Ewing, op. cit.

234 "There were armed": Ibid.

234 "seasoned judgement": Letter dated April 5, 1982, from Ewing files.

235 "All he wanted": *The Other Mrs. Kennedy*, op. cit., p. 464.

236 "Bobby was seriously": Author interview with source.

236 "Father Creedon and I": Rev. Ewing, op. cit.

236 In his homily: *Herald-Telephone*, April 4, 1982.

237 "I never heard anything": Rev. Ewing, op. cit.

237 "The fallout": Ibid.

237 "By that time I knew": Ibid.

237 "I told them": Ibid.

238 "tell the world": Brown, op. cit.

238 "It should have been": Ibid.

TWENTY-THREE: BAR FLOP

240 "treated like everybody": *New York Times*, March 30, 1982.

240 "She's interested in keeping": *New York Post*, April 5, 1982.

241 It had become public: *New York Post*, December 9, 1982.

241 Years later, a well-placed: Author interview with source.

241 "drove him to drink": *The Men We Became: My Friendship with John F. Kennedy, Jr.*, op. cit., pp. 89–90.

243 "When they were taken": *Daily News*, November 27, 1982.

243 The *Times*, in a commentary: *New York Times*, November 10, 1982.

244 "If you want to compete": *People*, April 12, 1982.

244 "He was so fucked up": Author interview with source.

244 "Emily was going through hell": Ibid.

245 "All the time he was": *The Kennedys*, op. cit., p. 451.

246 "I told him not to let": *New York Times*, March 18, 1983.

246 "You're a junkie too": *The Kennedys*, op. cit.

TWENTY-FOUR: SHOOTING UP

248 "secret room": Jerry Oppenheimer, *Crazy Rich: Power, Scandal, and Tragedy Inside the Johnson & Johnson Dynasty*. New York: St. Martin's Press, 2013, pp. 400–401.

248 "biggest battle": *The Riverkeepers*, op. cit., p. 90.

248 "strong willpower": Ibid.

248 "an aggressive and nosy": Ibid.

249 "They don't explain": Repeated in various interviews, in full or in part, including *Real Time with Bill Maher*, October 22, 2004.

250 When he was a child: *The Riverkeepers*, op. cit., p. 90.

251 "white as a sheet": *People*, October 3, 1983.

252 "On a number of levels": Author interview with source.

252 "I have admitted": United Press International, September 16, 1983.

252 "generated tremendous publicity": *The Riverkeepers*, op. cit., p. 90.

252 "He was given medication": Author interview with source.

253 "was a saint": Ibid.

TWENTY-FIVE: COMMUNITY SERVICE

256 "I had an ominous": *The Other Mrs. Kennedy*, op. cit., p. 468.

256 was a napkin drawing": *The Andy Warhol Diaries*, op. cit., pp. 570–571.

257 "There but for": Author interview with source.

257 "It was a way of getting": *The Riverkeepers*, op. cit., p. 92.

257 "easily into life": Ibid.

258 "I think he's a despicable": Author interview with Robert Boyle.

258 "I'm regarded by some": Ibid.

258 "scientific field station": *The Riverkeepers*, op. cit., p. 91.

258 "All he did was": Boyle, op. cit.

259 impressed him "as a person": *New York Times*, June 4, 1985.

259 "He actually took over": Boyle, op. cit.

260 "I resigned because": Ibid.

260 Wegner, a master: *New York Times*, November 5, 2000.

260 "There was not a thing": Boyle, op. cit.

261 "Bobby boasted about it": Ibid.

262 "I don't like eagles": *New York Times*, April 17, 2005.

262 "Cullen had the largest": Boyle, op. cit.

263 "Bobby and Cullen had": Author interview with Wayne Hall.

263 "want to hang out with": Ibid.

TWENTY-SIX: ENVIRONMENTAL WAR

266 "I think he separates": *New York Times*, November 5, 2000.

266 "had a nasty": Ibid.

266 "He was leading": Boyle, op. cit.

266 "I got out": Ibid.

267 "I'm not God": Ibid.

267 "Most insidiously": *Lawrence Journal-World*, April 12, 2007.

267 "William Wegner was": Ibid.

267 "Bobby Kennedy hiring": Ibid.

268 "We're in the business": Boyle, op. cit.

268 "I called him on that": Ibid.

269 "If I had to be": *New York Times*, op. cit.

269 "And I'd have a big": Boyle op. cit.

269 "raise money and awareness": Boldergiving.org.

269 "Kennedy's idea of": *Williamhaston.Blogspot.com.*

269 "where I can": Boldergiving.org, op. cit.

270 "In fact, he doesn't": Boyle op. cit.

270 "But you don't have": Ibid.

270 "would emerge as": *The Riverkeepers*, op. cit., p. 22.

271 "eloquent, thoughtful": Ibid., p. 91.

271 "a natural-born": Ibid., p. 77.

271 "one of the central figures": Ibid., p. 22.

272 "had to be part of an act" Boyle, op. cit.

272 Boyle recalls being: Ibid.

272 "I said, '*Four hundred*' ": Ibid.

273 The *Times* review: *New York Times*, November 16, 1997.

273 "difficult to read": Ibid.

275 "Nobody kicks Bobby": Author interview with source.

TWENTY-SEVEN: QUICKIE DIVORCE

276 "Emily was more Jackie": Author interview with source.

276 "Ethel made jokes": *The Other Mrs. Kennedy*, op. cit., p. 163.

277 "She was the shy": Author interview with source.

277 "The problem was Bobby": Ibid.

277 "There was always an open house": Ibid.

278 "Emily and I go out": *People*, July 22, 1991.

278 By 1990: E-mail to author from Cury.

278 "Bobby's womanizing, and Emily": Author interview with source, op. cit.

278 "Emily's always been": Ibid.

279 In a sworn affidavit: Document dated September 16, 2007.

279 However, when Bobby proposed: Author interview with source.

279 "It was a run-of-the-mill": Author interview with Gould.

280 "There was definitely": Author interview with Iannuzzi.

280 "according to another well-placed source": Author interview with source.

280 "It got to be very": Gould, op. cit.

280 "There was no way": Ibid.

281 "Bloomington Marriage": *Herald-Telephone*, Associated Press, March 27, 1994.

281 "Bobby left Emily for": Author interview with source.

282 In Bobby's settlement: Author interview with source.

282 Under the agreement: Ibid.

283 "It was really sad": Author interview with Rev. Ewing, op. cit.

283 "It's possible": Author interview with Father Creedon.

TWENTY-EIGHT: ANOTHER BRIDE

285 "bare bones on a barge": Author interview with Mrs. Silverman.

285 Bobby once claimed: *New York Times*, May 17, 2012.

285 "We were inseparable": *Huffington Post*, July 13, 2012.

285 When Bobby's brother Joe: *Huffington Post*, May 22, 2012.

286 "everyone else who": Ibid.

287 Back in New York: *The Andy Warhol Diaries*. The references to Mary appear on pages 247, 256, 302, 303, 323, 350, 363, 395, and 435. References to RFK Jr. appear on pages 140, 186, and 323.

287 Mavroleon was the son: *Telegraph*, March 17, 2006.

288 "deep and passionate": Author interview with source.

288 "It'd be funny": *The Andy Warhol Diaries*, op. cit., p. 435.

288 His brother recalled: *The Observer*, August 19, 2000.

288 Besides dating Bobby Kennedy's: Ibid.; *Washington Post*, April 18, 2012.

289 While Hall survived: *Observer*, op. cit.

289 Ethel Kennedy, who had: Ibid.

289 Seventeen months: Author interview with source.

TWENTY-NINE: SIBLING SCANDALS

291 "I doubt that I ever": RFK Jr., eulogy for his brother.

292 "*We are holding*": Ibid.

292 "a pied piper": Ibid.

292 The Giffords and the Kennedys: *The Other Mrs. Kennedy*, op. cit., pp. 405–406.

293 "It was Ethel": Frank Gifford and Harry Waters, *The Whole Ten Yards*. New York: Random House, 1993, p. 262.

293 "spooky resemblance": Ibid.

294 "She used to brag": *People*, May 12, 1997.

295 "Michael doesn't have": Michael Skakel, book proposal. *Dead Man Talking.*

295 "I don't see how": Ibid.

295 "artificial penis": Ibid.

297 "A lot of people's lives": *New York Times*, July 10, 1997.

298 "were about humanity": RFK Jr., eulogy, op. cit.

THIRTY: ANNULMENT TELL-ALL

299 "By the time Joe": *Symptoms of Withdrawal*, op. cit., p. 88.

300 "She was someone who could": *The Other Mrs. Kennedy*, op. cit., p. 486.

300 "heart and soul": Ibid.

300 was so cash-poor: *The Independent*, October 5, 1997.

301 "I was appalled": Sheila Rauch Kennedy, *Shattered Faith*. New York: Pantheon Books, 1997, p. xiii.

301 "I would be lying": Ibid.

301 "When Irish Eyes": *The Other Mrs. Kennedy*, op. cit., p. 487.

301 "The most controversial": *Time*, June 19, 2007.

301 "messy publicity": *Washington Post*, August 29, 1997.

301 "runs counter to": *New York Times*, March 14, 1998.

302 "Ask not what you": *Guardian*, August 17, 1997.

302 "Joe is very different": Daily Mail.com, November 8, 2012.

THIRTY-ONE: RAPE RAP

304 "I have an enormous": *Washington Post*, December 12, 1991.

304 "What you heard": Ibid.

304 "Oh my God": *Dead Man Talking*, op. cit.

305 "In a little-known December 30, 1993, sworn affidavit": Affidavit of James Ridgeway de Szigethy, given to U.S. Representative James Traficant, and read into the Congressional Record vol. 140, no. 12 (Wednesday, February 9, 1999), Hon. James A. Traficant Jr.

307 "How was she?": *Fort Lauderdale Sun-Sentinal*, December 1, 1991.

THIRTY-TWO: KILLER COUSIN

309 "a mix between": *Hartford Courant*, August 28, 2002.

310 "For all his passion": *Vanity Fair*, March 2002.

310 "taking steps": *Atlantic Monthly*, January–February 2003.

310 "a 'sexual' encounter": Ibid.

313 paying "hush money": Author interview with source.

313 "Teddy had been running": Ibid.

314 "the wisest adviser": *Los Angeles Times*, August 21, 1990.

314 "Money went from": Author interview with source, op. cit.

314 "A first-year": *New York Times*, October 23, 2013.

315 "latest twist": *New York Times*, November 21, 2013.

THIRTY-THREE: ANOTHER CATASTROPHE

317 "I knew then that John was dead": RFK Jr. diary notation. Pages from the 2001 diary were leaked to the *New York Post*, November 3, 2013.

317 "But when the dust": *The Men We Became: My Friendship with John F. Kennedy, Jr.,* op. cit., p. 167.

318 "All the Bessette family knows": Diary, op. cit.

319 "Kennedys don't eulogize": Ibid.

320 "It was all he could talk": *The Men We Became: My Friendship with John F. Kennedy, Jr.*, op. cit., p. 169.

320 "I cried. I've lost": Diary, op. cit.

THIRTY-FOUR: MARITAL HELL

321 "kind, generous person": Affidavit, September 16, 2007, op. cit.

323 "and was furious": Author interview with source.

323 "nuclear events": Ibid.

323 "sexual advance": Ibid.

323 "He would be": Ibid.

323 "inappropriate behavior": Ibid.

324 "wanted to bring another": *New York Post*, September 8, 2013. Ibid.

324 In a personal diary that was leaked: Bobby claimed that the diary was not meant for publication but, rather, "served as a tool for self-examination and for dealing with my spiritual struggles at the time."

324 "I struggled to be": Ibid.

325 "I'm so content here": Ibid.

325 "The only kind of hero": CNN, August 3, 2001.

326 Reading published portions: Seymour Hersh, *The Dark Side of Camelot*. New York: Little, Brown, 1997, p. 389.

327 In the early 2000s: Author interviews with sources.

328 "Mary understood Bobby's": Author interview with source.

THIRTY-FIVE: TOXIC HOUSEHOLD

330 On May 10 and again: *Journal News*, July 13, 2010. News accounts of those incidents mostly appeared after RFK Jr. sued for divorce.

331 "brutal, relentless, and mean": Author interview with source.

331 didn't want to have sex: Ibid.

332 "did not think that the mold": Ibid.

333 the book's author, who had worked on: *New York Post*, October 28, 2012.

333 The onetime comedian: Ibid.

333 "Soignée in a navy": *The New Yorker*, January 3, 2011.

334 many of his allegations were said: Author interview with source.

THIRTY-SIX: FATAL ENDING

336 allegedly said she "feared for her life": Author interview with source.

336 "gaslighted in the marriage": Ibid.

337　The two spent: Ibid.

337　"There was an extreme": Ibid.

338　"If you can't find them": Author interview with source.

338　"professional colleagues": *New York Post*, May 25, 2012.

338　Mary Kennedy also claimed: *New York Post*, July 13, 2014.

338　"Mary said Kyra": *Huffington Post*, May 22, 2012.

338　But there was another side: Author interview with source.

339　The guest was: Ibid.

339　"hammered constantly": Ibid.

339　"noticed some changes": Bedford, New York, police department report.

340　"She told me that she": Ibid.

340　"looked mad, and a little": Author interview with source.

340　"Unfortunately, the last": *New York Post*, July 1, 2012.

341　he was popping painkillers: Author interview with source.

342　"Call her fucking family": Ibid.

THIRTY-SEVEN: AFTERMATH

344　"The description of Mary": CNN, May 18, 2012.

346　Just days before: *New York Post*, February 23, 2014.

347　"Daddy was the attorney general": ABC News, February 26, 2014.

347　"it was her very prominence": *New York Times*, February 28, 2014.

347　"It's my first time": *New York Post*, November 30, 2013.

349　"dork and chorus nerd": *Tallahassee Democrat*, August 4, 2014.

349　"They are a lot like": Ibid.

350　"People in my circle": *New York Times*, August 3, 2014.

350　"Nothing you ever do": Ibid.

350　"Any woman who gets": Author interview with source.

EPILOGUE

352　"This wasn't supposed to happen": Author interview with source.

352　"Everyone expected Bobby": Ibid.

352　"He would have very much": Ibid.

353　"He's picked up every flaw": Author interview with Boyle, op. cit.

353　"I have enough friends": *New York Times*, February 13, 1995.

354　"If I wanted to run": *New York Times*, November 24, 1998.

354　Amy Fisher's urine: *New York Times*, op. cit.

355　"I wouldn't be a reliably": *New York*, October 24, 2007.

356　"[A]lways advises me": *New York Times* City Room Blog, December 2, 2008.

356　"I think, in a very dramatic": *New York Times*, June 25, 2006.

356　"a lot of people": *True Compass*, op. cit., p. 478.

356 "Kennedy would be a shrewd": *Politico*, November 5, 2008.

357 "so irrational and incoherent": *Daily News*, May 29, 2007.

357 "My concern regarding": A comment in the *Washington Post* Politics and Policy blog, November 8, 2008.

357 "I would have testified": Author interview with Boyle, op. cit.

358 "an antivaccinationist crank": Comment on the pediatric website Pedsource .com.

360 "It's partially accurate": Author interview with source.

SELECTED BIBLIOGRAPHY

Burke, Richard E. *The Senator: My Ten Years with Ted Kennedy.* New York: St. Martin's Press, 1992.

Collier, Peter, and David Horowitz. *The Kennedys: An American Drama.* New York: Summit Books, 1984.

Cronin, John, and Robert F. Kennedy, Jr. *The Riverkeepers.* New York: Simon & Schuster/Touchstone, 1999.

Dallas, Rita, and Jeanira Ratcliffe. *The Kennedy Case.* New York: G. P. Putnam's Sons, 1973.

Fitzgerald, Rose Kennedy. *Times to Remember.* Garden City, N.Y.: Doubleday, 1974.

Furhman, Mark. *Murder in Greenwich.* New York: HarperPaperbacks, 1998.

Gifford, Frank, and Harry Waters. *The Whole Ten Yards.* New York: Random House, 1993.

Hackett, Pat, ed. *The Andy Warhol Diaries.* New York: Warner Books, 1989.

Hamilton, Nigel. *JFK: Reckless Youth.* New York: Random House, 1992.

Kennedy, Edward M. *True Compass.* New York: Twelve, 2009.

Kennedy, Robert F., Jr. *Judge Frank M. Johnson, Jr.* New York: G. P. Putnam's Sons, 1978.

Kennedy, Sheila Rauch. *Shattered Faith.* New York: Pantheon Books, 1997.

Lawford, Christopher Kennedy. *Symptoms of Withdrawal.* New York: William Morrow, 2005.

Lawford, Patricia Seaton, with Ted Schwartz. *The Peter Lawford Story*. New York: Carroll & Graf, 1988.

Levitt, Leonard. *Conviction: Solving the Moxley Murder*. New York: ReganBooks, 2004.

Littell, Robert T. *The Men We Became: My Friendship with John F. Kennedy, Jr*. New York: St. Martin's Press, 2004.

Michaelis, David. *The Best of Friends*. New York: William Morrow, 1983.

Nasaw, David. *The Patriarch: The Remarkable Life and Turbulent Times of Joseph P. Kennedy*. New York: Penguin Press, 2012.

Newfield, Jack. *Robert Kennedy: A Memoir*. New York: E. P. Dutton, 1969.

Oppenheimer, Jerry. *Crazy Rich: Power, Scandal, and Tragedy Inside the Johnson & Johnson Dynasty*. New York: St. Martin's Press, 2013.

———. *The Other Mrs. Kennedy*. New York: St. Martin's Press, 1994.

Pearson, Brad, and Emerson Stone, executive editor. *The Spirit That Is Pomfret*. Pomfret Alumni Association, 1993.

Perry, Barbara A. *Rose Kennedy: The Life and Times of a Political Matriarch*. New York: W.W. Norton, 2013.

Pitts, David. *Jack and Lem: The Untold Story of an Extraordinary Friendship*. New York: Carroll & Graf, 2007.

Quirk, Lawrence J. *The Kennedys in Hollywood*. New York: Cooper Square Press, 2004.

Rainie, Harrison, and John Quinn. *Growing Up Kennedy*. New York: G. P. Putnam's Sons, 1983.

Spada, James. *Peter Lawford: The Man Who Kept the Secrets*. New York: Bantam Books, 1991.

Summers, Anthony. *Goddess: The Secret Lives of Marilyn Monroe*. New York: Macmillan Publishing, 1985.

Thomas, Evan. *Robert Kennedy: His Life*. New York: Touchstone, 2000.

White, Theodore H. *The Making of the President*. New York: Atheneum, 1969.

INDEX

PHOTO CREDITS

RFK family on staircase at Hickory Hill: Globe Photos

Jackie Kennedy, Jean Kennedy Smith, and Ethel Kennedy: Globe Photos

Kennedy family at Hyannis in group: Cecil Staughton, JFK Presidential Library

RFK Jr. with JFK looking at salamander: Abbie Rowe, JFK Presidential Library

JFK poking RFK Jr.'s salamander: Abbie Rowe, JFK Presidential Library

RFK greeted by supporters before assassination: JFK Presidential Library

RFK Jr. and JFK Jr. standing together: Globe Photos

JFK and Lem Billings at the White House: Robert Knudson, JFK Presidential Library

JFK, Jackie, and Lem Billings on cart: Cecil Staughton, JFK Presidential Library

RFK Jr. in snow at Millbrook School: Millbrook Yearbook

Sketch of RFK Jr. by Michael Parkinson: Courtesy of Andrew R. Humes

RFK Jr. with lion cub: Millbrook Yearbook

RFK Jr. with football team: Millbrook Yearbook

RFK Jr., George Wallace, and Peter Kaplan: Courtesy of source

RFK Jr. and Emily Black with arms folded: Larry Crewell, *Herald-Times*

RFK Jr. with arms around bride Emily: John Roca, *Herald-Times*

RFK Jr. and bride Emily walking: Larry Crewell, *Herald-Times*

RFK Jr. with young Bobby III: Acepixs

Bob Boyle with arms folded: Kathryn Belus Boyle

Bob Boyle, RFK Jr., Mary Richardson Kennedy, and others: Kathryn Belous Boyle

RFK Jr. and mother, Ethel Kennedy: Globe Photos

Mary Kennedy and RFK Jr.: Globe Photos

Mary, RFK Jr., and six children: Acepixs

Mary with son Conor: Globe Photos

Mary, RFK Jr., and daughter Kyra: Adam Nemser

RFK Jr. with wife Cheryl Hines: S. Bukley